The Long Pretense

The Long Pretense

Soviet Treaty Diplomacy
from Lenin to Gorbachev

Arnold Beichman

With a foreword by
William F. Buckley, Jr.

Transaction Publishers
New Brunswick (U.S.A.) and London (U.K.)

Copyright © 1991 by Transaction Publishers, New Brunswick, New Jersey
08903

Library of Congress Catalog Number: 90-10815
ISBN: 0-88738-360-2
Printed in the United States of America

Library of Congress Cataloging-in-Publication Data

Beichman, Arnold.
    The long pretense : Soviet treaty diplomacy from Lenin to Gorbachev /
Arnold Beichman.
    p.   cm.
    ISBN 0-88738-360-2
    1. United States—Foreign relations—Soviet Union—Treaties. 2. Soviet
Union—Foreign relations—United States—Treaties. 3. Soviet Union—
Foreign relations—Treaties. I. Title.
E183.8.S65B45 1990   90-10815
327.73047—dc20   CIP

iv

In Memory of Sidney Hook, 1902-1989

Contents

Foreword, by William F. Buckley, Jr.   ix
Acknowledgments   xiii

Introduction   1
  1. Treadmill Diplomacy: Bewitched, Bothered, and Bewildered   11
  2. What If Nobody Came   25
  3. Would You Believe?   39
  4. What's a Little Ideology Among Friends?   61
  5. 'A Paradox, a Paradox, a Most Ingenious Paradox ...'   91
  6. The Protracted Confrontation: Forever?   121
  7. Optimists, Pessimists, Realissimists   137
  8. When Is a Treaty Not a Treaty? The Lenin Doctrine   163
  9. Of Pitfalls and Booby Traps   181
 10. Brezhnev Doctrine: Is It Yes, No, or Maybe?   205
 11. *"Mis*trust—But Verify"   227
Epilogue   259

Appendix A   269
Appendix B   273
Appendix C   277
References   281

Index   293

Foreword

Five years after the date George Orwell made synonymous with the finality of totalitarianism, the world was astounded by the opening up, and the breaking up, of the Soviet bloc. Even the most hateful of its tyrants, Nicolae Ceausescu, could not hold back the insistent popular clamor for the freedom the victims of communism suddenly felt within their grasp. In Poland, East Germany, Czechoslovakia, Hungary, Romania, Bulgaria, and Russia itself, strange and joyous events took place.

It takes a remarkable crustiness to resist the general euphoria, capped when *Time*, instead of merely selecting its usual Man of the Year, named Mikhail Gorbachev its Man of the Decade. But at least one seasoned and skeptical observer wants to ask a few hard questions. Mr. Gorbachev, meet Mr. Beichman.

Arnold Beichman has been a student of the Soviet Union, and of the world communist enterprise, for half a century. It is safe today that no communist, anywhere, has ever stolen a base on him. The reader will soon discover why.

Like a detective accosting the respectable citizen who is apparently above suspicion, Beichman refuses to settle for appearances. He is willing to grant that Gorbachev's reforms are fine, as far as they go. But how far, really, *do* they go? Do they really touch the essential structure of the Soviet system?

It is his thesis—some will call it gloomy, though he thinks it only realistic—that the Soviet system is incapable of liberalization. And he makes a double appeal: to the historical record, and to the sacred texts (the "patristic writings," as he calls them, with his fine turn of phrase) of Soviet communism. The Soviet record vis-à-vis the West, from Lenin onward, is an unbroken one of contemptuously violated treaties, mendacious propaganda, aggressive subversion. Its holy writ remains Lenin's justifications of these practices.

Whether these practices will continue in the future is still to be determined. Beichman points out (in chapter 7) how as late as May 1989, Soviet Foreign Minister Shevardnadze threatened that the Soviet Union would quit dismantling SS-23 missiles, as required by the INF (intermediate-range nuclear forces missiles) treaty if the United States dared replace its vestigial Lance short-range missiles, which the INF treaty allows. Were the U.S. secretary of state to speculate about revising an arms control treaty by violating its provisions, as Mr. Shevardnadze threatened to do, the anticipated uproar in Congress on both sides of the aisle would inhibit such an act of illegality.

Even now, in this period of spectacular forced contraction, Gorbachev reaffirms his devotion to socialism. Mere rhetoric? For Beichman, there is nothing "mere" about it. He reminds us that the Soviet ruling elite cites its founding documents far more often than American politicians cite ours. Leninism furnishes them with their only claim to legitimacy, their only semblance of a political idiom and tradition. It is the sole basis of the institutions they command. The mere suggestion that the Communist party will retreat in its devotion to Leninism has intensified the crisis in the Soviet Union. We shall have to wait and see whether a system based on the revolutionary ideology of ruin and conquest can survive without any ideology at all.

All this is not to say that nothing has changed in the Soviet Union. Beichman can read the papers. But repression was greatly relaxed after the death of Stalin, which did not prevent the Soviet Union, over the next 30 years, from slaughtering countless Hungarians, Czechs, and Afghans, or from extending Soviet power and influence far beyond the satellite bloc, to Cuba, Vietnam, Angola, Ethiopia, and Nicaragua.

The new freedoms enjoyed by Russians do not include the right to own private property, to form independent labor unions, to engage in the everyday acts of commerce the noncommunist world takes for granted. True, there has been talk about allowing private property, private commercial transactions, and even nongovernmental trade unions. We shall have to see whether the talk will be, or even can be, translated into a definable reality. The Soviet Union has no autonomous judicial system—the sine qua non of the free society. The Soviet secret police, the KGB, still exists to harass the Soviet peoples. The Russian historian and leader of the opposition in the People's Congress of Deputies, Yuri N. Afanasyev, in February 1990 warned, as had Andrei Sakharov before him, that "we are witnessing the creation of authoritarian-totalitarian power headed by the initiator of perestroika." He was referring to the attempt by President Gorbachev to concentrate even greater power than he already has. The new freedoms are, in fact, entirely revocable. They exist by sufferance, not by the sort of institutionalized right that can be enforced against the state itself. What Gorbachev has given his people so far is not an irreversible manumission, but tyranny with a human face. The face may harden again.

Beichman quotes a Finnish diplomat: "All that Gorbachev is doing is trying to reform the system within the system. It simply can't be done." The system is locked into futile motions by what Jean-François Revel has called communism's "genetic code." Gorbachev refuses to surrender communism's essential mechanism—the centralized economy. But the state dictation of economic activity is the most irrational form of tyranny, a general embargo against practical intelligence that can only ensure backwardness and poverty. Beichman notes that *Pravda*'s Japan correspondent had to explain to his Russian readers what a fax machine is, by way of re6
porting that the Japanese own 2.2 million of them.

The opinion leaders of the West have a naive habit of trying to predict Soviet behavior by focussing on the personality of the current leader. The forecasts are always rosy, never more fatuously so than in the case of Yuri Andropov, the KGB director who was hailed as a jazz-loving, Scotch-drinking soul with liberal tendencies. In Gorbachev's case, the optimism seems to have been partly warranted.

But for Beichman, such divinations are irrelevant. He searches for a higher vantage point, overlooking the Soviet system as a historic whole. And he sees no reason to expect fundamental improvement. "So long as the Soviet economy, operating on what is called central planning, is welded to a bureaucracy responsible solely to a single interest group, namely the Soviet Communist Party," he writes, "so long will the Soviet Union remain what it has been for more than seventy years—an economic depression without end, the Sahel of Europe. Even more urgently for Western policy makers to consider is that whatever political changes have been brought about by Glasnost & Co. they are always in danger of a recidivist fate."

Beichman reminds us that the Soviet record of tyranny and deceit is matched by a Western record of glossing over it. At the very peak of Stalin's reign, Franklin Roosevelt's ambassador to Moscow, Joseph Davies, could say: "In my opinion the Russian people, the Soviet government, and the Soviet leaders are moved basically by altruistic concepts. It is their purpose to promote the brotherhood of man and to improve the lot of the common people. They wish to create a society in which men may live as equals, governed by ethical ideals." And even Harry Truman, in 1949, remarked: "I like Stalin.... He is very fond of classical music.... I got the impression Stalin would stand by his agreements and also that he had a Politburo on his hands like the 80th Congress."

Nobody supposes that Gorbachev is another Stalin, although it should be recalled that Stalin also began as a "moderate." All the same, he has yet to renounce Stalin in terms even as robust as those of Nikita Khrushchev in

1956, and he has accused the West of inventing the concept of "Stalinism" for the purpose of discrediting communism. Beichman finds this curious in a man who is being hailed as Stalin's antithesis.

The wonderful news from the Soviet bloc gives one hope that we are witnessing the end of the Soviet empire, but Beichman insists it is not enough—not enough to warrant our lowering our guard, signing new treaties, or assuming the current trend is permanent. The Soviet Union is not yet a democracy. It is not yet even a traditional nation-state whose chief concerns lie within its own borders. It is what it has always been constructed to be: a base for global revolution, the overthrow of "capitalism" in the name of "the working classes." The ideology does not exist only in the heads of the Soviet ruling elite; it is reified in all the forms of Soviet life, funneling vast energies into mischievous channels of action.

If so, Gorbachev's intentions, however good we suppose them to be, may not matter in the long run. With the best will in the world, he may find the Soviet system intractable. To the extent that it does overcome its own economic bafflement, it may resume the aggressive mode natural to it. According to Leninist doctrine, aggression is less its policy than its nature.

Beichman will be accused of pessimism and worse. But he is doing something that is not being done often enough: He is looking at the Soviet order objectively and unsentimentally. He asks not what we, or for that matter Gorbachev, would like it to be, but what, given its history, it is bound to be. His answer is disturbing. But it deserves to be pondered, as it is in this important book.

WILLIAM F. BUCKLEY, JR.

Acknowledgments

A number of people and institutions helped me greatly in preparing this book. First and foremost is the Historical Research Foundation that financed the study. The patience and counsel of its director, William F. Buckley, Jr., who generously contributed the preface, is deeply appreciated.

Second is the Hoover Institution on War, Revolution and Peace, where I have been a stipendiary for the past seven years. The Hoover Institution is a scholar's dream thanks to its longtime former director and presently its counselor, Glenn Campbell, and most recently to its director, John Raisian. Among Hoover colleagues, my thanks go to the late Sidney Hook, Robert Conquest, Martin Anderson, William Van Cleave, Thomas Sowell, Mikhail Bernstam, John Dunlop, Alvin Rabushka, and Angelo Codevilla from whose writings I have benefited greatly as I have from the writings of Richard Pipes, Adam Ulam, and Joseph Whelan. None of the foregoing nor the Hoover Institution bear any responsibility for my conclusions. Mrs. Brent Bozell contributed sound editing to the manuscript, as did Arri Parker. And my gratitude to my sons, Charles and John, and my daughter, Janine, for bringing me into the Computer Age.

I owe much to Arnaud de Borchgrave, editor-in-chief of the *Washington Times*, and Mary Lou Forbes, editor of that paper's Commentary section. Earlier versions of some of the material in the book appeared in the *Washington Times* where I have been a regular columnist. Especial thanks also to Radio Liberty/Radio Free Europe and to the British publication, *Soviet Analyst,* for superb scholarship about Soviet developments.

The Heritage Foundation, thanks to Edward Feulner and Burton Pines, kindly gave me shelter during research activity in Washington, D.C. The Heritage publications on national security were most useful. Conversations over the years with Joseph Churba sharpened the critical senses. My thanks especially to the Hoover library staff as well as to Harvey Mansfield, Stanton Evans, John Windmuller, and Dorothy McCartney. From the conclusions and opinions in this book, all of the foregoing are absolved.

And, above all, to Carroll Aikins Beichman; without her love, patience, and editorial wisdom it couldn't have been done.

ARNOLD BEICHMAN

Naramata, British Columbia
Hoover Institution, Stanford, California

Introduction

The leading theme of this book is that a Marxist-Leninist totalitarian state cannot become a peace-loving, peace-observing, and treaty-complying member of the international community unless it effects—verifiably—four fundamental changes: it

1. dismantles its machinery of repression
2. surrenders its monopoly of the political process
3. yields party control of the economic system
4. abandons its sense of world mission

In other words, relationships with a Marxist-Leninist state will remain unpredictable until such time as it becomes a constitutional state with, for example, the untrammeled right of juridical defense. This paradigm applies, specifically, to the Soviet Union and, of course, to the People's Republic of China. President Gorbachev's epiphany has raised one of the most significant questions since November 1917: Is reformist communism possible? Jean-François Revel ("The Crisis in Western Democracy." *Imprimis* 17[4] [1989], page 20) has written:

> What Gorbachev has had to discover, in brief, is that Communism really *is* effectively irreversible as a political structure, in the sense that the system is admirably conceived and constructed so as to prohibit its own reform. Irreversibility, indeed, may be the only promise Communism has ever kept. To attempt to reform such a system is to attempt to destroy it.

Real, fundamental reform obviously calls for tearing down the system— drastic systemic changes. Can such systemic changes be effected peacefully? Perhaps the more useful question would be: Can the Soviet Union become or

1

is it in the process of becoming a status quo power and, more significantly, is it willing to forego its messianism and thus accept the status quo of noncommunist powers?

As of February 1990, President Gorbachev had recommended to a Communist Party Central Committee plenum what might be regarded as a surrender of the party's monopoly of the political process as prescribed in Article 6 of the Soviet constitution.[1] Whether he would dismantle the machinery of repression exemplified by the KGB, yield party control of the economy, or would abandon the party sense of world mission remained to be seen. Perhaps the "revolution from below" (mass demonstrations in the streets of the Soviet Union) would force him to follow Lenin's dictum: He who says "A" must say "B."

The majority of the world's countries—except revolutionary conspiracies like Libya, North Korea, Syria, or Cuba—could be reasonably described as status quo powers. Some countries—like Argentina, which lays claim to territories belonging to another country—may be seeking, justifiably or not, rectification of borders. They are not, however, imbued with a sense of world mission and destiny that demands overthrow of the existing order, the status quo.

Let us attribute to Mikhail Gorbachev all good intentions. The question still remains: Is reformist communism (or free market communism) a realistic prospect, given the enormous power and tenacity of the Soviet leadership and bureaucracy to resist what even some Soviet influentials consider essential changes in the Soviet structure? And we must keep in mind the destabilizing effect that reformist communism—"revolution from above"—would have on the rest of the Soviet empire and the ethnic minorities—the Balts, Tartars, Ukrainians, Armenians, Azeris, and other Central Asian Muslims—and, of course, the ever restless East European members of the Warsaw Pact, at least five of whom—Czechoslovakia, East Germany Hungary, Poland, and Romania—can no longer be regarded as "captive nations."

---

1   "The Political System" chapter 1, article 6, Soviet Constitution, adopted 1977, reads in part: "The leading and guiding force of Soviet society and the nucleus of its political system, of all state organizations and public organizations, is the Communist Party of the Soviet Union.... The Communist Party, armed with Marxism-Leninism, determines the general perspectives of the development of society and the course of the home and foreign policy of the USSR, directs the great constructive work of the Soviet people, and imparts a planned, systematic and theoretically substantiated character to their struggle for the victory of communism." (*Constitutions of the Countries of the World* [Dobbs Ferry, N.Y.: Oceana Publications, 1989], binder 17, page 21)

Realistically, it is prudent to assume that the present Soviet system cannot reform itself—that it cannot surrender its monopolistic power (which is what communism is all about).[2] As Milovan Djilas has written:

> Communism looks upon itself as fully entitled by the design of history to change and control *not only* man's allegiances and behavior as a political being, but also his teachings, his tastes, his leisure time and, indeed, the whole of his private universe. Communism cannot, therefore, transform itself into a free society. That would be squaring the circle. ("Gorbachev: Djilas, A Long Conversation, Geroge Urban," *Encounter* 18 [1988], pages 2-3)

After Stalin's death in March 1953, the Soviet experience with reformism could not have been reassuring to the Soviet privileged caste, the *nomenklatura,* that sought stability, legitimacy, and security for itself. "Reformist communism" led to uprisings against Soviet power in East Germany, Poland, and Hungary in the 1950s and to the makings of an uncontrolled cultural revolution within the Soviet Union that led to Khrushchev's *Kulturkampf* and eventually to his dismissal as "a hare-brained schemer."

The sight of a million marchers in Beijing's Tiananmen Square in May 1989 and the subsequent massacre of several thousand marchers has unquestionably concentrated the minds not merely of Gorbachev's opponents in the *apparat* but even among Gorbachev's supporters. Is reformist communism possible without vast purges of a probably mutinous *apparat?* The events in Eastern Europe—Poland and Hungary, primarily—and in East Germany do not yet fully answer the question as to whether reformist communism is possible.

Tyranny of Prevailing Opinion

Before proceeding further I would like here to answer some objections to the problems I have begun to discuss and will continue to discuss in subsequent chapters. I know that my views, my analyses of past events, will be greeted with criticism from publicists and scholars, many of whom I respect enormously. It is a case, no doubt, of confronting what John Stuart Mill called "the tyranny of prevailing opinion."

---

2   The same could apply to the People's Republic of China, where the present leadership has emphasized that "no matter what else changes, the party must remain supreme and unchallenged" ("Perestroika Without Glasnost: The Chinese Heresy," *Encounter* April 1988, page 27). In June 1989, Zhao Ziyang, general secretary of the Chinese Communist Party, sided with the prodemocracy demonstrators in Tiananmen Square and was purged.

I find it strange and unsettling that an influential sector of Western opinion has accepted President Gorbachev's virtuous professions at face value. As Françoise Thom has written:

> Imagine for a moment how it would have been if the Germans, still under the Nazi regime, had introduced an adverse criticism of the Holocaust in order to bring about a favorable perestroika in international relations.[3]

While the road to German unification is blockaded by proceed-with-caution signs, little skepticism is evidenced about President Gorbachev's reformist pledges. I can understand a sense of alarm about a united Germany with its unforgivable Nazi past. Why not, then, a similar alarm, certainly as a treaty partner, about Russia with its terrifying Lenin-Stalin-Khrushchev-Brezhnev-Andropov seventy-year past and its long record of broken treaties?

If skepticism about West Germany, a Western democracy, which has no continuity with its short-lived (twelve-year) Nazi past is regarded as prudential, why isn't it prudential to be all the more skeptical about Russia, a tottering totalitarian dictatorship with unrepudiated ties to its bloody Stalinist past? If anxiety about the implications of a unified German democracy is understandable, why isn't anxiety about the implications of a *nuclear-armed* dictatorship in its disintegration even more understandable? If Chancellor Helmut Kohl is an untrustworthy statesman, is President Gorbachev any less so?

To my critics I say I am doing nothing more than any prudent government would do vis-à-vis another government with a record of aggression and treaty violations and driven by an operational code totally at odds with the democratic ethos.

Intelligence agencies of any West European government—if they are doing their job—engage in assessing the risk of the ever-present possibility of a full-scale Soviet attack in Europe. NATO's job is to make similar risk assessments. The Pentagon's Defense Planning Guidance, a basic planning document, is designed to estimate how many days' warning the West would have should the Soviet Union begin to mobilize for such an attack. Monitoring Soviet troop movements via "spy in the sky" satellites would enable Western military planners to assess the risk of a Soviet confrontation. According to the *New York Times* of 26 November 1989 ("Changes in Europe Mean More Warning of Any Soviet Attack," page 6), what was once estimated to be a two-week advance warning has, since Gorbachev's accession and recent developments in Eastern Europe, led Pentagon planners

---

3   Françoise Thom, *Le Moment Gorbachev* (Paris, France: Hachette, 1989), quoted by Charles Janson in "Newspeak and Gorbachev's Reforms," *Soviet Analyst* 18(18) (13 September 1989), page 7.

to estimate that the West would now have a month's or more such advance warning.

It was considered a normal exercise as part of risk assessment to hold a fully-televised "war game" crisis between the United States and the Soviet Union over the ABC network in December 1989. Ted Koppel's scenario didn't consider the possibility of a war risk "crisis" between the United States and Canada, Japan, or San Marino. The only real fully-armed adversary to the West in the world today is the Soviet Union.

The theme of this book is *treaty* risk assessment. As a treaty partner not only of the United States but of other countries as well, the Soviet Union has violated solemn treaty commitments. The recent contretemps over the Krasnoyarsk radar is a glaring example of Soviet lying (finally confirmed by Foreign Secretary Eduard Shevardnadze) in the face of indisputable evidence of ABM treaty violations.[4] Matters may have improved since 1985, but we still have a long way to go before we can lower the Western guard which has kept world peace for almost half a century.

A New Breeze

Gorbachev's accession in March 1985 to the leadership of the Communist Party and, in 1988, of the Soviet government persuaded democratic leaders like Prime Minister Margaret Thatcher, Chancellor Helmut Kohl, former President Ronald Reagan, and now President Bush, as well as informed publics in the democratic world, that a new breeze is blowing in Gorbachev's Russia, a wind which bodes well for world peace.[5]

Disraeli once said that finality is not the language of politics. That is true for democratic societies that by their very nature inhibit the concept of finality. Disraeli's words, however, are inapplicable to a state that claims that because its ideology is ultimate truth it has the right to impose it on the willfully faithless and the inadequately instructed. The Soviet Union makes this claim since its very legitimacy depends on finality—the finality of the laws of history that Marxism-Leninism alone claims to understand. For Soviet leaders, the Soviet state represents the final design for Economic Man. Leonid Brezhnev, Gorbachev's predecessor twice-removed, made that clear in what has come to be known as the Brezhnev Doctrine:[6]

---

4   For a more detailed examination of the Krasnoyarsk radar flap, see chapters 3 and 11.

5   There's little question that of the eight Soviet leaders since the Bolshevik Revolution Mikhail Gorbachev is second only to Josef Stalin as the most influential leader in managing Western public opinion and swaying Western political elites. Gorbachev's agenda has become the West's agenda.

6   See chapter 10, "Brezhnev Doctrine: Is It Yes, No, or Maybe?"

Experience shows that in present conditions the victory of the socialist order in this or that country *can be regarded as final* and the restoration of capitalism can be regarded as excluded only if the Communist Party, as the guiding force of society, firmly carries through a Marxist-Leninist policy in the development of all spheres of public life. (U.S. Senate 1969)

A Risky Business

I am applying my research and analysis to an important sector of international relations. I refer to treaty diplomacy, particularly as practiced between the United States and the Soviet Union; i.e., the negotiation of and compliance with treaties or other bilateral or multilateral instruments ("An Inquiry into the Workings of Arms Control Agreements," *Harvard Law Review* 85[5] [March 1972], page 906 n. 1, 907).[7]

It is my argument that treaty diplomacy with the Soviet Union has been a risky business from the day in 1933 when the United States recognized the Soviet Union. Yet risky or not, to deal—i.e., to negotiate binational instruments—with the Soviet Union is inevitable in a world where democratic opinion intrudes so powerfully into the agenda of foreign policy and the precincts of international negotiation. But to deal effectively with the Soviet Union takes a special but not arcane knowledge, something that normally intelligent people—statesmen, politicians, publicists—on the whole simply refuse to acquire. It is this ignorance of Soviet history and practice that accounts greatly for the breath-taking success of President Gorbachev as a world leader.[8]

---

7   Professor Abram Chayes says that a treaty is "a legal instrument [that] defines a range of prohibited conduct and gives the prohibition the force of law. In so doing it imports a whole set of attitudes and inhibitions associated with law into what, absent the treaty, was a purely prudential decision" ("An Inquiry into the Workings of Arms Control Agreements," *Harvard Law Review* 85[5] [March 1972]). Following Professor Chayes, I am using the words "treaty" and "agreement" interchangeably. There is, of course, a distinction between the two in U.S. law—"treaties" are ratified by the president and the Senate while "agreements" are concluded by the president pursuant to legislation or in the exercise of his inherent powers.

8   One reason for this ignorance is that every outgoing U.S. president takes his correspondence with the secretary of the Communist Party of the Soviet Union with him when he vacates the White House. Richard Pipes, who served for two years on the National Security Council as director of its East European and Soviet Affairs bureau, asked to see copies or originals of the correspondence between U.S. presidents and Soviet leaders going back to President Eisenhower. Pipes wanted in particular to see what happened during the Cuban missile crisis of 1962. "I was told this cannot be gotten because it does not exist in Washington.... So there is no collective memory of this at all" ("Team B: The Reality Behind the Myth," *Commentary* 82 [October 1986], page 60).

Alain Besançon, the French historian and editor, has explained that Soviet diplomacy triumphs are not due to any inferiority of Western diplomats or journalists but rather to "the habits of traditional diplomacy and the habits of traditional journalism." As Besançon writes:

> From the moment Western diplomacy recognized the Soviet regime *de jure*, it conceded the premise that the Soviet Union was a state like any other, a state with which normal, peaceful relations could and should obtain.... With such a state, diplomacy must tirelessly seek to define areas of common interest and locate grounds for political accommodation. By the same logic it is forbidden for others to adopt a global strategy aimed at destabilizing or undoing the Soviet regime—in other words, to adopt a strategy like the one the Soviet regime directs against the West. ("Gorbachev Without Illusions," Commentary 85[4] [April 1988], page 50)

It could be said that former President Reagan was being misrepresented by his one-time chief of staff. Referring to a summit meeting with Gorbachev, Donald Regan described the president's "basic and abiding belief that two men of goodwill could move the world together if they could only speak as one human being to another" (Regan 1989, 346-7).

Unfortunately, the 180-degree turn in U.S. policy toward the Soviet Union during President Reagan's second term leads me to accept Donald Regan's observation as on the mark. Unfortunately, that is, recalling that President Franklin D. Roosevelt, whose ignorance about the ambitions of Marxism-Leninism contributed to the loss to the Soviet empire of large areas of the free world, was the progenitor of the "two men of goodwill" view.

I prefer to believe that Gorbachev doesn't operate on so noble a principle. Rather, I believe he shares Andrei Gromyko's views on negotiations with an opposing superpower. A U.S. diplomat once told Gromyko that he believed that he and the Soviet representative were both sincere in seeking an agreement. Gromyko responded: "You may be sincere but governments are never sincere" (U.S. Senate 1969, 37 n. 4).[9]

To deal effectively with the Soviet Union calls for abandonment of the genuine Western enthusiasm for what has become the Iron Law of International Diplomacy—summit meetings, that unfortunate superpower postwar practice initiated in 1955.[10] Or, since we cannot disenthrall the Western powers from the belief in "jaw-jaw" summitry, at least let us keep the number of such meetings to the barest minimum. My guide in offering

---

9 In 1977, after President Carter canceled production of the B-1 bomber, Senator John Tower asked Academician Aleksandr Shchuykin in Moscow whether the Soviets might be prepared to reciprocate. Shchuykin replied: "Sir, I am neither a pacifist nor a philanthropist" ("Negotiating Arms Reductions," *New York Times* 19 January 1987, page 2).

10 For a positive view on summitry, see President Nixon, chapter 9.

this advice is Sir Harold Nicolson, who took a dim view of personal contact among diplomats and among sovereigns. Sir Harold once wrote:

> Diplomacy is the art of negotiating documents in a ratifiable and therefore dependable form. It is by no means the art of conversation. The affability inseparable from any conversation between Foreign Ministers produces allusiveness, compromises, and high intentions.... Nothing could be more fatal than the habit (the at present fatal and pernicious habit) of personal contact between the statesmen of the world.... [T]here is nothing more damaging to precision in international relations than friendliness between contracting parties. (Thayer 1959, 109; Nicolson 1964, 52-53)[11]

Whether such a position makes sense in the era of instant world communication by satellite television and by "hot line" might be a rewarding speculation. I only offer Sir Harold's admonition as a partial solution to the permanent problem that the United States suffers from in negotiating agreements with the Soviet Union. The permanent problem and the one I will discuss is the noncompliance policy of the Soviet Union with its treaty commitments from day one of the Bolshevik Revolution.

And why this problem? Discussing the consequences of United Nations General Assembly votes on U.S. foreign policy, Raymond Aron explained that "democratic states are more sensitive to the judgments of world opinion and of their friends than are states of the Soviet type, which are always able to justify their actions, however cruel they may be, by a metaphysics of history" (Aron 1966, 558).

It may be, however, that in the Gorbachev era the old Marxist-Leninist "metaphysics of history" system, that from a Kremlin standpoint worked so well for so long, is permanently out of commission. Nevertheless, the coming decades will not see a communism with a human face despite the still unquenchable hopes in the West about treaty diplomacy with the Soviet Union. (Such a willed transformation is impossible, as we saw once again the historic scenario—party-state against civil society—played out in Beijing and on Tiananmen Square on 3, 4, and 5 June 1989).

Instead what we will see will be a Soviet Union seemingly trying to compete on the same nonmilitary terms with the democracies, as the democracies historically have competed with each other. And it should be remembered that there has never been a military war between the

---

11   As far back as the fifteenth century, Philippe de Commynes, adviser to Louis XI of France, observed that "two great princes who wish to establish good personal relations should never meet with each other face-to-face but ought to communicate through good and wise ambassadors" ("An Uncontrolled Arms Control," *Insight* 2 October 1989, page 62).

democracies since the United States, "the first new nation," came into being in 1789.[12]

Our world is now such that superpower negotiations on agreements, particularly on arms control, are almost predestined. Yet we know in advance—and the documentation exists—that the odds are overwhelming that the Soviet Union will do everything it can to bend, to violate, and to threaten violations; to reinterpret and to misinterpret; to circumvent what, at the treaty signing ceremony, seemed to have been unambiguous provisions in the instrument.

In the same way, the United States remains in the United Nations, even though Charter violations by member nations abound—violations often against the U.S. national interest (Adelman[13] 1989, D3); in the same way, we negotiated with Moscow an end to the war in Afghanistan, a war which has not ended; in the same way, the democracies, with the United States in the lead, are bound to negotiate with a nation-state which declared war on them in 1917.[14]

Perhaps the way to look at modern treaty diplomacy in the era of President Gorbachev is from the perspective of Sören Kierkegaard, who disdained rational philosophy and theology. Instead, the Danish theologian proposed in his essay, *Fear and Trembling*, the "act of faith" concept: When faced by complete irrationality, try to maintain one's beliefs despite overpowering evidence to the contrary.

---

12 On this historical phenomenon, see chapter 5.
13 Adelman cites a UN General Assembly voting study which shows that the top fifty recipients of U.S. aid voted with the United States 14 percent of the time and with the Soviet Union—whose foreign aid program is next to nonexistent—97 percent of the time. On UN resolutions about economic development and international regulation, UN members voted with the U.S. position 3 percent of the time and with the Soviet Union 97 percent of the time. Nevertheless, the American ambassador to the UN in a 1989 report to Congress said that "U.S. foreign policy interests were significantly advanced" during the General Assembly session.
14 See Vassilev 1989, 19. A member of the Bulgarian Mission to the UN for eight years until he defected in 1988, Vassilev writes: "In violation of its own rules, the UN has agreed to hire only those nationals of communist countries who have been proposed by their own governments. Furthermore, the nationals of communist countries can be hired only on short-term contracts that cannot be renewed without the consent of the government seconding the individual—who normally is a government official and frequently an intelligence officer. This makes the supposedly independent international civil servants obedient tools in the hands of their governments." Many of these communist "civil servants" use the diplomatic license plates of the UN mission of their country, another violation of UN rules and regulations.

In the chapters that follow I will show what I regard as a studied plan by the Soviet leadership to exploit this "act of faith" concept. The Soviet leadership does what it does so as to strengthen itself in the face of endless economic and political crises and, above all, in the face of the most recent and the most threatening crisis of all: legitimacy of Communist Party rule among the peoples who live under the crumbling system of Marxism-Leninism.[15]

Realistically, there is no way out of the dilemma created by the malpractices of Soviet treaty diplomacy because the making and keeping of agreements among the nation-states is a necessary condition of civilization. Yet ever hoping against hope, we must keep trying. We have to proceed, as Bertrand Russell said somewhere, in a spirit of unyielding despair.

---

15   The "crumbling system" of Marxism was foreseen more than 80 years ago by Werner Sombart, the German economist, who titled a now famous essay "Why is there no socialism in the United States?" His metaphorical answer was: "On the reefs of roast beef and apple pie socialistic Utopias of every sort are sent to their doom" (Bell 1974, 87). The world of socialism and statism seems to have been unhinged by socialism's failure to gain a foothold in the most successful—by every conceivable socio-politico-economic standard—capitalist democracy in the world.

1

Treadmill Diplomacy:
Bewitched, Bothered, and Bewildered

On 7 December 1988, Mikhail Gorbachev took the rostrum at the United Nations to address the General Assembly. He said many things of interest that were duly covered by the media. One short paragraph, however, was overlooked. That paragraph should be of the utmost interest to foreign policy publicists and to students of Soviet treaty diplomacy. It certainly is to me since it involves the theme of this book: the compliance record of the Soviet Union during the past seven decades with treaties signed with what the Soviets like to call "bourgeois" countries.

I cannot say for sure, not having read all of Lenin's voluminous collected works, whether in his speeches or writings the architect of the Bolshevik Revolution ever used a Latin phrase. I am certain, however, that his six successors—Stalin, Malenkov, Khrushchev, Brezhnev, Andropov and Chernenko—never did. With Mikhail Gorbachev, who like Lenin was trained as a lawyer, it is another story.

Gorbachev's Two Attributes

The relevant sentences in Gorbachev's UN speech demonstrate two personal attributes of the Soviet leader. First, as a trained lawyer, Gorbachev knows something about international law. At least, he knows enough to have cited in his UN speech in the original Latin the significant doctrinal apothegm, *pacta sunt servanda* (treaties must be obeyed), the first principle of

11

international law. Second, Mikhail Gorbachev is a statesman of extraordinary audacity, which in his case goes hand in hand with self-righteousness. He might as well have announced that the Sermon on the Mount was his guiding philosophy as to have implied strict adherence of international commitments by the Soviets.[16]

The seventy-two-year history of the Soviet Union is, after all, the history of a political regime that since its first major state-to-state agreement, the Treaty of Brest-Litovsk, has broken more treaties than any other country during the same period. Yet Gorbachev stands before the UN and piously demands that "treaties must be obeyed." He was speaking in the context of the Geneva accords on Afghanistan when he referred to "the political, legal, and moral significance of the Roman maxim, *pacta sunt servanda."* Moral significance, indeed! [17]

International morality being what it is, and journalistic knowledge, especially about Soviet history, being rather limited, there was little concern that at the moment of Gorbachev's UN address the Soviets were in violation of the 1988 Geneva accords on Afghanistan. Nor was Gorbachev ever asked just what the Soviet Union was doing in Afghanistan in the first place—or in the Baltic countries or in Eastern Europe, particularly Poland. Yet Western leaders, no doubt, found some solace in Gorbachev's intoning, *"Pacta sunt servanda."* The Western reception of the Gorbachev sermon was a documented case of Western credence in Soviet rhetoric, another dismal example of successful Soviet rhetoric's creating new delusions in the noncommunist world.

Let me offer another example of successful Soviet manipulation of Western media.

"SOVIET UNION TO HALT PLUTONIUM PRODUCTION" read the front-page headline in the *Washington Post.* The story, as related in the 12

---

16 The same kind of audacity is characteristic of Soviet policy statements. *Kommunist,* the Soviet Communist Party's theoretical journal, wrote in 1987 (no. 1), that the "United Nations declared 1986 the Year of Peace. Regrettably that year was not marked by a noticeable reduction in the dangers of war. As before, shots were fired, blood flowed, and people died in various hot spots around the globe. The guilt was above all that of forces of imperialism." Afghanistan was never mentioned even though it was in the eighth year of Soviet aggression against that country.

17 The exact passage (from Gorbachev 1988, 15) reads as follows: "The Geneva accords [on Afghanistan] whose fundamental and practical significance has been praised throughout the world, provided a possibility for completing the process of settlement even before the end of this year. That did not happen. This unfortunate fact reminds us again of the political legal and moral significance of the Roman maxim: *Pacta sunt servanda*—Treaties must be observed."

April 1989 issue of *The Washington Times* ("Bumper Sticker Arms Control," page E1), described Gorbachev's announcement that the Soviet Union would close down two plutonium reactors by 1990. Gorbachev forgot to mention that eight to ten Soviet plutonium reactors would still be operating; in other words, an empty gesture. The headline implied an end to all plutonium production when all that Gorbachev had announced was the shutdown of two plants.

Even worse, little notice was taken of a historic fact: Namely, that in his 1964 State of the Union address, President Lyndon B. Johnson had announced that the United States was shutting down four plutonium piles. *For twenty-five years the United States has not produced highly enriched uranium for weapons.* The United States has no plutonium reactors now operating, as Dr. Kenneth Adelman (*Washington Times* 12 April 1989, page E1) has pointed out, while the Soviets are still producing plutonium despite Gorbachev's announcement.

Can the Soviets Be Trusted?

If there were a Guinness Book of Records for treaty violations, there is little doubt that the Soviet Union would top the list, with no close second. According to Professors Jan Triska and Robert Slusser (1962, 3), "Soviet treaty violations have been on a scale and of a character for which it would be hard to find an adequate precedent."[18] This statement is even truer today than it was when it was made a quarter of a century ago, even though the Triska-Slusser survey deals only with Soviet treaties concluded between 1917 and 1957.

The cardinal question as formulated by Professors Triska and Slusser is still the main question today: "[C]an the Soviet leaders be trusted to honor the commitments they voluntarily assume in international treaties?" (Ibid.)

Since the Bolshevik Revolution, Western treaty diplomacy has operated on two levels: with democratic or noncommunist countries, and with the Soviet Union. With the former, full compliance with treaty provisions is expected and usually takes place. One reason for anticipating such behavior from noncommunist nations is that there is some kind of shared commitment among them.[19] This does not mean that each and every clause receives the

---

18   I deal with the Brest-Litovsk Treaty in the next chapter. For a wide-ranging, scholarly history of the treaty, see Wheeler-Bennett 1963.

19   As Montesquieu wrote (1977, 4:128-130), "As honor has its laws and rules ... it can be found only in countries in which the constitution is fixed and where [the nations] are governed by settled laws."

same interpretation by both sides. There are disputes—sometimes bitter disputes. The U.S.-Canada trade pact of 1988 has already revealed disagreements on specific items, but these will be arbitrated and resolved without too much difficulty. The Free Market Democracies (FMDs) are not out to destroy their market opposition. They are engaging in a fairly harmless pursuit—to achieve a monetary advantage over the other. Their behavior exemplifies self interest and profit seeking. Peace, however, is endangered when one nation makes "continuous claims on assets and/or behavioral choices of another nation" (Bernstam 1988, 3). In fine, there is a crucial difference between the financial arbitrageur and the political saboteur.

With the Soviet Union, however, it's another matter. The West has for over seven decades developed a special standard for Soviet treaty diplomacy based on what must be transcendental visions about a revolutionary power. The West believes it must make exceptions for the Soviet Union for two reasons: First, because the Soviet Union is a superpower and, if exceptions are not made, they'll create serious mischief; second, because the Soviets have persuaded large sectors of influential people in the FMDs that they deserve special conditions because they represent a certain idealism missing in bourgeois or right-wing regimes.

As a result, we have by and large come to expect noncompliance, in greater or lesser degree, by the Soviet Union concerning its treaty commitments. The Helsinki process which I discuss in chapter 7 is a case in point. To the question, what is to be done about Soviet violations, the Western answer is nothing—ignore them. Say nothing and, above all, keep Soviet treaty transgressions secret. Such was the case in the United States from 1964 until 1984.(see appendix C).

Soviet-American diplomatic relations since 1933, except for a few years after World War II, have been based on what I call the ideology of "treatyism" (see chapter 2 on the initiation of Soviet-American relations). By "treatyism" I mean:

1. The strongly held belief among U.S. policy-making elites that treaties on any and all subjects between the United States and the Soviet Union are inherently a good thing.
2. The conscious and consistent acceptance (i.e., ratification) by one of the negotiating powers, usually the United States, of a treaty or other agreement (like the UN Charter or the Helsinki agreement) or the ratification of multinational documents even though past experience demonstrates that there will be partial compliance or none at all by the other signatory party, usually the Soviet Union.
3. The demands that noncompliance by the Soviet Union is to be ignored, except for occasional ritualistic attacks, because of the character and

influence of American political culture and the enforcement of the widely accepted double standard of international behavior, i.e., one standard for the United States and another for the Soviet Union (Pye 1965, 513; "Culture, Political Culture, and Communist Society," *Political Science Quarterly* 88[2] [June 1973], pages 173-190).

4. The view that any attempt to enforce compliance or to propose sanctions for violations indicates that the would-be enforcer, although operating within his rights, is:

    a. acting in such a way as to endanger world peace by engaging in Cold War propaganda;

    b. since the violation is trivial *sub specie aeternatis*, for the United States to press for some adjudication of acts of noncompliance would be needlessly provocative to the Soviet Union; or

    c. both.

5. The view that a new treaty must be renegotiated when a treaty is violated by the Soviet Union or by one of its allies.

"Treatyism" has been the single dominant characteristic in the diplomacy of the FMDs since the Bolshevik Revolution. "Treatyism" became most visible after World War II, with the emergence of a bipolar nuclear world and U.S.-Soviet summit diplomacy. "Treatyism," a derivative of U.S.-Soviet diplomatic relations, has been and is the invariable variable among U.S. foreign policy-making elites. It is their *déformation professionelle*. Presently, treatyism positively dazzles on the international stage, reflecting the emergence of a Soviet leader whose public diplomacy skills would make the Soviet Union's founding father proud.[20]

Among the sharpest critics of what I call "treatyism" has been Henry Kissinger. His attack on the State Department followed the imposition of martial law in Poland on 13 December 1981 and what he called "the emptiness of the Western reaction" ("Poland's Lessons for Mr. Reagan," *New York Times* 17 January 1982, page E23). He condemned State Department "eagerness" for negotiations with the Soviet Union and for "continued participation in the Madrid Conference on the very Helsinki agreements that

---

20 At the higher official level, treatyism is combined with what William Safire has called "summit-itis," defined as "the détente fever that afflicts American presidents as they approach a superpower summit toward the end of their careers" ("Not a Bad Thing?" *New York Times* 8 June 1987, page 32). His example of "summit-itis" (or "the first step toward a New Yalta") was White House Chief of Staff Howard Baker's proposal of a deal that the United States and the Soviet Union jointly patrol the Persian Gulf during the 1987 crisis.

are violated so utterly in Poland" (Ibid.). He said he was familiar with the counterarguments by the State Department that defended continued dealings with the Soviet Union. He wrote:

> The foreign policy bureaucracy never lacks ingenuity for devising rationales for its preference for talk over action and for its conviction that by the sincerity of our discourse we will moderate the behavior even of the Kremlin.... It cannot be national policy that we multiply high-level contacts during crises caused by the Soviet Union unless we want to give the Soviets an incentive to produce more crises. (Ibid.; "Diplomacy vs. Foreign Policy in the U.S.," *Wall Street Journal* 15 April 1982, Op-Ed page)

Part of Cold War Strategy

The Soviet Union's treaty diplomacy is part of the Cold War strategy created by Lenin on the day after the triumph of his November revolution. The traditions of European treaty diplomacy have been turned to good use by the Kremlin in keeping with one of Lenin's most important strategic doctrines:

> An army which does not train itself to wield all arms, all the means and methods of warfare that the enemy possesses or may possess, behaves in an unwise or even in a criminal manner. But this applies to politics even more than it does to war. In politics it is even harder to forecast what methods of warfare will be applicable and useful under certain future conditions. Unless we master all means of warfare, we may suffer grave and even decisive defeat. (Lenin 1930, 31)

The great advantage of the Soviet Union in its diplomacy is that the West ignores many things: the history of Soviet international behavior, the ideology which informs Soviet diplomacy, and the strategy which has emerged out of that ideology and *modus operandi*. This has resulted in a two-tier diplomacy. Just as the West's diplomatic behavior differentiates between the communist and the noncommunist worlds, so too does Moscow make distinctions in its treaty diplomacy.

Stalin insisted that there was a difference between treaties signed with capitalist countries and those signed with socialist countries because "the basic content of [Soviet-capitalist] international relations is determined by the struggle of the two systems" (Triska & Slusser 1962, 223).

Bertrand Russell's Early View

The distinction between treaties with capitalist and socialist systems had been noted as early as 1920 by Bertrand Russell, an admirer of the Soviet revolution. He wrote at the time:

The communist theory of international affairs is exceedingly simple. The revolution foretold by Marx, which is to abolish capitalism throughout the world, happened to begin in Russia.... In countries where the revolution has not yet broken out, the sole duty of a communist is to hasten its advent. Agreements with capitalist States can only be makeshifts, and can never amount on either side to a sincere peace.... (Russell 1920, 30-31)

Alexander Solzhenitsyn has another view of Soviet treaty diplomacy for the West. As he put it, "Stoppage of information makes international signatures and treaties unreal: within the zone of STUNNED SILENCE any treaty can easily be reinterpreted at will or, more simply, covered up, as if it had never existed" (Solzhenitsyn 1972, 25) (Orwell understood this beautifully).

It would be the height of folly in the absence of hard evidence to the contrary to believe that Mikhail Gorbachev's definition of morality and his view of treaties signed with capitalist countries differ in any particular from those of Marx, Lenin, or Stalin.[21] Lenin's maxim about "one step backward, two steps forward" *(reculer pour mieux sauter)* was part of his operational code, not a great moral truth.

Adelman's Extraordinary Revelation

That the Soviet Union may, indeed, be uncontrollable as a treaty-negotiating partner can be seen in the extraordinary revelation by Kenneth Adelman, former director of the Arms Control and Disarmament Agency. Describing the continued Soviet violations of arms control agreements with the United States, he wrote:

We never really found anything much to do about Soviet cheating. That's the sad truth. Those outside government may well wonder why, year after year, we reported a pattern of Soviet violations and did nothing about it.... That's not how normal folks act when cheated by a merchant, for instance.... We tried—oh! how we tried—to come up with effective countermeasures, but there didn't seem to be

---

21 Lenin's political strategy has a Marxist origin. Marx himself warned against compromises with nonrevolutionary, "bourgeois" elements, because to do so would accord moral legitimacy to the "other side." Compromises meant acknowledging that the "other side" had legitimate claims and therefore it weakened the class struggle doctrine, as Marx pointed out. Where compromises do occur, according to the official *Great Soviet Encyclopedia* (1975, 8:278), they are made "in the interests of peace and peaceful coexistence without, however, retreating from the basic principles of the socialist system or communist ideology."

any.... [Congress] mandated that we stay in arms agreements that the Soviets were violating. ("Where We Succeeded, Where We Failed," *Policy Review* 43 [Winter 1988], page 44)

This is truly reason dethroned—reason dethroned in the executive branch. Soviet treaty misbehavior may be measurable, quantifiable, visible, documentable—whatever. No matter. Soviet treaty misbehavior is certainly predictable because the variables are quite limited in number. No matter. The executive branch is unable or unwilling to pursue such countermeasures as ceasing to negotiate other treaties with the Soviet Union until existing ones are obeyed. And reason is dangerously dethroned in the legislative branch that is not only unconcerned about Soviet noncompliance but is ready to punish the executive branch should it dare adopt countermeasures.

In short, treaty diplomacy with the Soviet Union is only possible if reason, teamed with the laws of probability, is ignored. Today, illusory perceptions dominate: Treatymaking with the Soviet Union is a nonrational enterprise resulting from decades of indoctrination that treaties are a "good" thing.[22] *Non cogito, ergo sum.* Treaty texts are a diplomatic form of that latest literary cant word *deconstruction*; the text and author's intention are not as worthy as the critic's private agenda. The game goes on.

Or, as George Will wrote about the failures of the Helsinki process: "There is no penalty for treating agreements contemptuously; the Americans will come back for more, thereby blurring any indictment of Soviet wrongdoing" (*Newsweek* 1 April 1985, page 90).

Radio Jamming

One of the best examples of how the Soviets flout agreements is their jamming (or, technically, "intentional interference") for decades of Western shortwave broadcasts. Jamming violates the following agreements to which the Soviets are a party:[23]

1.   The 1948 Universal Declaration of Human Rights, Article 19
2.   The 1975 Helsinki Final Act, Basket 3, Article 2
3.   The 1982 International Telecommunications Union (ITU) Convention, Article 35

---

22   See Hook ("The Future of Marxism," *Free Inquiry* Summer 1989, page 8), who defines indoctrination "as a process of teaching through which acceptance of belief is induced by nonrational or irrational means, or both."
23   From a 21 February 1987 letter to the author from Charles Z. Wick, once director of the U.S. Information Agency. Article 48 of the ITU convention was also violated.

Suddenly one day, on 29 November 1988, after years and years of "jamming" violations and ignored protests, the Soviet Union announced it would stop these unlawful practices that it was estimated had cost the Soviet Union between $700 million and $1.2 billion a year ("Why the Jamming Had to Stop," *Soviet Analyst* 18[1] [11 January 1989], page 5). Radio Free Europe/Radio Liberty, Deutsche Welle, and Voice of Israel, longtime targets of Soviet jammers, would no longer be interfered with (Radio Liberty Research Bulletin no. 50 [3515] [RL537/88] [7 December 1988] page 2).[24]

The sinner was shortly awarded the Order of the Fatted Calf for the "reform": specifically, an agreement by the Reagan State Department that the U.S. Government was agreeable to holding a Helsinki human rights session in Moscow in 1991—something like holding a conference on terrorism in Libya. Who would have believed in January 1981 when President Reagan took office that one of his final actions as president would be to approve of a human rights conference in Moscow, epicenter of the Gulag Archipelago?[25]

It is a measure of Gorbachev's success as a great practitioner of the art of public relations that the idea of holding such a conference in the capital of the most powerful (militarily) totalitarian empire in the world and one of the greatest violators of human rights and of agreements to observe them, was greeted perfunctorily. Can anyone imagine a similar quietude about a proposal to hold an international human rights conference in Pretoria?[26]

Successful Soviet Treaty Diplomacy

Soviet treaty diplomacy has been enormously successful, especially since the end of World War II, in that Soviet leaders and spokesmen have gained remarkable access to public opinion in the United States and Western Europe.

---

24 There may have been another reason for the end of jamming. According to a 5 January 1989 *Tass* interview ("Report on the USSR," *Radio Liberty* 13 January 1989, page 33), jamming of Western radio broadcasts may be dangerous to people because it produces high levels of electromagnetic radiation. The interview was with USSR Deputy Minister of Communications Gennadii Kudryavtsev who said that the jamming stations "were usually placed in the center of towns, [and] the electromagnetic radiation in adjacent areas exceeded the safety norms." The minister did not explain the effects on humans of prolonged exposure to high levels of electromagnetic radiation.

25 The event would be within the framework of the thirty-five-nation Conference on Security and Cooperation, a.k.a., eponymously, the "Helsinki Process" because it followed an East-West meeting at Helsinki in 1975. The review conferences meet in different European cities, until now only in West European capitals—Vienna and Madrid—where human rights are real.

26 See chapter 7 for a discussion of the Moscow human rights conference-to-be.

When Dr. Adelman says, as quoted above, "We never really found anything much to do about Soviet cheating.... We tried—oh! how we tried— to come up with effective countermeasures, but there didn't seem to be any ...," he was attesting to the shift in power and influence over U.S. public opinion from the U.S. government to the Soviet Politburo. This shift is due to what I have called the "treatyism" factor in American political culture and diplomatic life.[27] How this shift in power came about may best be explained in a passage from the political theorist, C. J. Friedrich (1950, 12): "The power seeker must find human beings who value the things [he controls] sufficiently to obey his orders in return."

Perhaps a more immediate explanation for this shift in power is that by ignoring Soviet violations, the U.S. government is encouraging further violations, greater noncompliance.

General Issues Have Large Constituencies

Soviet treaty diplomacy deals with generalized issues—war and peace, arms control, nuclear weapons, arms negotiations—that have influential constituencies in the West. At the same time, resolution of these problems involves highly technical and arcane concepts that few people have the patience to examine and analyze. The Soviet Union raises questions that have universal appeal, like war and peace, and it is therefore able to mobilize Western public opinion, from Greenham Common to Washington's Foggy Bottom to the West German Bundestag, behind its negotiating proposals. Most importantly, Western negotiating positions are rarely affected by either history or experience. In fact, the FMD negotiating positions represent, as Samuel Johnson described second marriages, the triumph of hope over experience.

Treatyism, the compulsion to negotiate treaties with a treaty violator at whatever cost, is demonstrated by Donald T. Regan, White House chief of staff. In his memoirs, Regan cites the Gorbachev invitation of 19 September 1986, that President Reagan and the Soviet leader meet as soon as possible. Purpose? To discuss complete elimination of Soviet and U.S. intermediate-range nuclear missiles from Europe without counting the 194 already

---

27 Lionel Trilling (1971, 125) defined culture in modern times as the idea "of a unitary complex of interacting assumptions, modes of thoughts, habits, and styles, which are connected in secret as well as overt ways with the practical arrangements of a society and which, because they are not brought to consciousness, are unopposed in their influence over men's minds."

deployed nuclear-armed French and British missiles. This, says Regan, was a historic breakthrough since hitherto the Soviet Union had always insisted that the West European missiles be included in any agreement. Even so, according to Regan, some of the president's foreign policy advisers had reservations about Gorbachev's proposal for an early summit. Writes Regan:

> It was clearly impossible for Reagan to refuse to meet Gorbachev on an issue involving world peace.... The president had been speaking out vigorously on disarmament ever since [the] Geneva [summit] and to temporize when he had been offered the chance to negotiate could have incalculable consequences in terms of world opinion and the atmosphere in which future talks would take place. (Regan 1989, 380)

Treatyism can on occasion affect U.S. foreign policy vis-à-vis a Soviet ally, as in the case of its relationship with the terrorist Palestine Liberation Organization (PLO). Treatyism can be seen in action in the State Department's sudden reversal in December 1988 of its policy of no negotiation with the PLO. As was written in a *Wall Street Journal* editorial of 16 December 1988 (page A14):

> The State Department's willingness to talk with the PLO leads the United States toward a familiar trap that the Soviet bloc and its proxies set continuously around the globe. Faced with a determined, U.S.-aligned adversary, all these opponents decide to go over the heads of their U.S.-aligned adversaries and communicate directly with the American public.... This tactic has been used in Korea, in southern Africa, in Central America and in the Middle East. It is used because it works. The insurrection on the West Bank, the PLO's "Intifada," has little to do with the Israeli government and everything to do with U.S. opinion.

Another Soviet ally that has benefited from the dispensation about treaty noncompliance is Iraq, which used poison gas in the Iran-Iraq war. Iraq's gas attacks violated the 1925 Geneva protocol banning chemical warfare. No action was taken by the UN to punish the Iraqi for violating the treaty. Indeed, what punishment could be imposed, other than unilateral military action by the United States that in the circumstances in 1988 was inconceivable, *pace* Muammar Qadaffi's warnings that an attack was imminent?

Suggestions were heard that a new chemical warfare treaty (treatyism marches on) ought to be negotiated to ban not merely use but also possession of chemical weapons. Nothing was heard of that principle of international law, *pacta sunt servanda*, cited so sturdily by President Gorbachev in his UN address. As far as the Soviet president was concerned, the writ of *pacta sunt servanda* runs in Afghanistan against the mujaheddin but not against Iraq. In a joint article, Amoretta M. Hoeber and Douglas J. Feith ("Poisoned Gas, Poisoned Treaties," *New York Times* 6 December 1988, page A19) asked:

"But why should we produce new treaties if we can't solve the problem of upholding the integrity of existing treaties?"

Number One Treatyist

Among journalists, the Number One Treatyist is Strobe Talbott, Washington bureau chief of *Time* Magazine and author of *The Master of the Game: Paul Nitze and the Nuclear Peace* (New York, N.Y.: Knopf, 1988). In assessing Talbott's book, Patrick Glynn wrote:[28]

> In morality, [Talbott) is a strict consequentialist. The means is always justified by the end, provided the end is a new arms agreement with the Soviet Union. If you are pushing for new treaties by whatever methods, you are good, noble, reasonable, intelligent (Mr. McFarlane, Mr. Nitze, George Shultz); if you are standing in the way of a new agreement, for whatever reasons, you are foolish (Edward Rowny), evil (Mr. Perle), inexplicably perverse (Henry Kissinger) or some combination of the three. ("'Insider' history ignores fact of Soviet response," *Washington Times* 24 October 1988, page D9)

Referring to the "arms control juggernaut," Glynn warned that, driven by the treatyist component in elite political culture, the United States was heading toward a START treaty that "many, if not most Western experts recognize ... will be destabilizing, probably cannot be verified, poses a major potential for Soviet breakout, and will increase rather than lessen the economic costs of deterrence" (Ibid.).

For the West, treaty negotiation with the Soviet Union is inevitable and exemplifies what can be called "treadmill diplomacy"—there is no way of stopping the treadmill and if there were I am not so sure it ought to be stopped. A good deal of the legitimacy of the Free Market Democracies, where public opinion matters greatly, depends upon a seeming willingness to sit around a table, seemingly to discuss the issue of war and peace. Whenever the Soviet Union calls upon the United States for a treaty-negotiating conference, "treadmill diplomacy" begins.

Our continued and inevitable membership in the United Nations is another example of treadmill diplomacy. This organization (and its ancillary agencies, like UNESCO and the ILO), which has violated the UN Charter

---

28 Patrick Glynn was special assistant to the director of the Arms Control and Disarmament Agency, 1986-87. His assessment was published just before the election of President Bush.

systematically, which probably endangers more than it secures world peace, which regards the United States, South Africa, and Israel as polecats of the international system, is an organization from which the FMDs probably should have seceded long ago.[29] Yet no administration in Washington would dare initiate such withdrawal. No matter how much the UN member kleptocracies and their powerful allies act against the interests of the United States and the other free nations, we pay our dues and assessments, eventually if not now, for the privilege of being pilloried by the beneficiaries of U.S. taxpayer largesse. And, sadly, there is no alternative. The UN has a life of its own like, closer to home, the Department of State.

UN Disgrace

The United Nations disgraced itself for the nth time in the summer of 1989 by its deafening silence on the Massacre of Beijing. The argument was made on behalf of the UN that it could not interfere in the killings and arrests of the demonstrators because such actions would constitute gross interference in the internal affairs of a sovereign country. Such an alibi had failed over the decades to deter the UN from condemning over and over again South Africa and from demanding sanctions because of apartheid, which is no more within the domestic jurisdiction of South Africa than the Beijing slaughter is within the domestic jurisdiction of China. To the UN majority, human rights' violations in Communist countries or African states don't count ("Does the UN Have a Double Standard," *Christian Science Monitor* 2 July 1989, page 18).

Schopenhauer once suggested that mankind is condemned forever to be in bondage to the will-to-live. And the West, because of treatyism, is doubly condemned: condemned to the will-to-negotiate with an adversary for whom negotiations are a form of warfare by other means, and condemned to the will-to-belong to an assembly of nation-states which means the United States and its FMD allies no good. The West, trapped by the fetish of treatyism, views negotiations in the spirit of Leibnitz—that despite all evils, "this is the best of all possible worlds."

The will-to-negotiate goes hand in hand with the will-to-believe. As William James wrote, "faith-tendencies are extremely active psychological forces, constantly outstripping evidence" (James 1968, 737).

---

29 In the many resolutions passed by the UN General Assembly about the invasion of Afghanistan, the Soviet Union was never once mentioned as the aggressor. The euphemism used was "foreign armies." The UN General Assembly, however, does not hesitate to deplore—by name—U.S. "colonialism" in Puerto Rico.

2

What If Nobody Came

This book makes the modest claim of following the advice of Dr. Johnson, who once said that people need to be reminded more than to be informed. The book's thesis may generate many questions for which there may be no satisfying answers.

The thesis: As noted earlier, the Soviet Union has the worst record of treaty compliance of any country in the twentieth century, most markedly since World War II. It violates agreements whenever possible—especially those with the United States, whose policy makers keep coming back for more.

Now the main question. It comes in two parts:

1. If Soviet treaty violations since Lenin took power in 1917 are by now routine and inevitable, why don't we do something about it?
2. Supposing we didn't negotiate any treaties with the Soviet Union—what then?

Why the Pactomania?

Ancillary questions follow: Should we stop negotiating treaties with the Soviet Union altogether? We don't spend much time negotiating with the People's Republic of China or Yugoslavia or Madagascar or scores of other countries, big and small, and we manage to survive.

Why this pactomania directed at the Soviet Union?[30] Soviet policy, one could argue, especially under Gorbachev, seeks to promote division and conflict, especially with the Federal German Republic and in NATO. What better way to do it than by pactomania?

If the Soviets are going to violate treaties, why do they sign them in the first place?

Is treaty diplomacy for the Soviet Union an ideological growth industry intended to seduce the United States into making security-risky commitments?

If treaties are intended to bring stability and peaceful change in a world of nations, can a superpower dedicated to creating instability and violent change fulfill those worthy objectives?

These questions have long interested scholars in the field of international relations. As Professors Triska and Slusser have written:

> Seldom have international contractual and legal relations aroused so much sustained concern throughout the world as have Soviet treaties, agreements and conventions. (Triska & Slusser 1962, vii)

"Conflict Rather Than Integration"

Such concern arises because Soviet foreign policy has frequently proved to be "one of conflict rather than of integration" (Ibid.). Therefore, the authors argue, Soviet international treaties, agreements, and conventions have often been viewed with suspicion and distrust.

After decades of Soviet noncompliance with signed agreements, Western policy makers have become accustomed to this abnormality or idiosyncrasy about which nothing, it seems, can be done. Currently, violations receive almost no attention other than vaporous rhetoric. In fact, U.S. senators or publicists who declaim against Soviet treaty violations are frequently given the dismissive treatment accorded crackpots and other fanatics.[31]

---

30   "Pactomania" may be an inseparable part of the "national character" of American diplomacy. Let us recall the weird Kellogg-Briand Pact signed 27 August 1928 by fifteen nations and that renounced war as an instrument of national policy. Aristide Briand, the French foreign minister, had proposed an agreement renouncing war between the United States and France. Spurred by U.S. peace groups, Secretary of State Frank B. Kellogg proposed a worldwide pact—what may be the first documented instance of what Clare Boothe Luce, in another context, called "globaloney." The French could do nothing but agree to what George Kennan (1966, 21) called "one of the most meaningless and futile of all international agreements."

31   The *New York Times* , like many professional arms controllers, takes a relatively indulgent attitude toward Soviet treaty infractions. See chapter 3.

Soviet treaty violations have become a "given" in international relations. Soviet treaty diplomacy can do what it pleases with little fear of reprisal or even criticism. For example, the 5 August 1988 Associated Press story out of Moscow began:

The Kremlin's No. 2 leader said Friday [5 August 1988] officials who allowed strikes that paralyzed Armenia and the enclave of Nagorno-Karabakh should be punished.

Yegor K. Ligachev also said that any Communist Party members who engaged in strikes should be expelled from the party.

Ligachev's words are but another example of Soviet self-exemption from the normal rules of international behavior and treaty obligations that the West has learned to accept with barely a shrug. His words confirm the long-standing immunity from reprisal, sanction, or penalty that the Soviet Union enjoys whenever it ignores standards of international morality—more significantly, the immunity it enjoys within those very international organizations which are based on moral perceptions and obligations.[32]

Violations of ILO Charter

Ligachev's command, spoken in the name of the Politburo, violates international agreements to which the Soviet Union is a party. I refer to the conventions of the International Labor Organization (ILO), one of whose founding principles guarantees freedom of association, including the right to strike (Convention No. 87).[33]

---

32 The Soviet newspaper *Trud* reported on 3 May 1989 that the Soviet government had decided to grant labor unions the legal right to strike. A proposed new law was to be enacted late in 1989, according to Stepan A. Shalayev, head of the government-controlled unions. Technically, there is no law banning strikes, but the government got around that problem with the excuse that work stoppages violate the constitutional duty of every citizen to work. The proposed legislation, however, makes "no explicit provision for the creation of genuinely free trade unions that might compete for members with the existing unions," says the *New York Times* , as reported in *Time Magazine* of 16 October 1989 ("In the School of Democracy," page 44). "In the past, workers have been arrested, harassed or committed to psychiatric hospitals for trying to form independent trade unions" ("After Rash of Wildcat Moves, Soviets Admit Right to Strike," *New York Times* 4 May 1989, page 1).

33 Other ILO conventions to which the Soviet Union, by virtue of its membership in the ILO, has an obligation include: the right to organize and bargain collectively (Convention No. 98); prohibition of forced or compulsory labor; a minimum age for the employment of children; and acceptable conditions of work with respect

As then Secretary of State Kissinger wrote in 1975 during a United States-ILO crisis that led to the temporary withdrawal of the United States from the UN agency:

> The ILO Conference for some years now has shown an appallingly selective concern in the applications of the ILO's basic conventions on freedom of association and forced labor. It pursues the violation of human rights in some member states. It grants immunity from such citation to others. This seriously undermines the credibility of the ILO's support of freedom of association, which is central to its tripartite structure, and strengthens the proposition that these human rights are not universally applicable, but rather are subject to different interpretations for states with different political systems. (Galenson 1982, 7)

Ligachev Commands

No leader of a democratic party in a democratic country would dare say, as Ligachev did and as the Associated Press reported on 5 August 1988, that society should create an atmosphere in which such strike protests "are not tolerated." Had Ligachev's words of command been uttered by a South African president, they would have aroused storms of protest the world over, especially among those countries and labor organizations that forced South Africa from the ILO because that country was defined as being in violation of the ILO Charter. However bedeviled they are by the South African government, independent black unions and black strikes do exist.

And yet the Soviet Union, which has put its rebellious labor dissidents in psychiatric prisons, and Poland, which tried everything to suppress the phoenix-like Solidarity, and the other Soviet satellites in Eastern Europe, whose abuses of ILO conventions are too numerous to detail—all these remain honored ILO members. What countries are always under attack in the ILO? Chile, Israel, and South Africa—naturally. And shall all be forgiven the Soviet Union because Solidarity has had its temporary triumph, "temporary" because their existence has not yet been written into the unamendable statute of legitimacy? Or forgiven because the Siberian and Ukrainian coal miners were allowed to strike in July 1989 without delegitimizing the government-and party-controlled labor front?

When someone like Ligachev speaks, action follows. Strikers and strike leaders in Armenia in the summer of 1988 faced severe punishment—how

---

to minimum wages, hours of work, and occupational safety and health. For more on this, see Appendix C.

severe we may never know. But the right to strike, long ignored in the Soviet Union, should be the price of membership in the ILO. Here is the Soviet Union brazenly violating the ILO Charter, and no one—not even the ILO—pays any attention. Would not these same charges of ILO charter violations be brought appropriately against Communist China in the light of the Massacre at Beijing in June 1989? Chinese workers, not just students, were openly deprived of their right of free association.[34]

In fact, no one seems to be troubled even by the Soviet lies concerning its violations of freedom of association—workers' rights stipulated in the ILO Charter and expanded in ILO conventions.

Six Soviet Lies

A Soviet spokesman at the ILO in 1977 told six lies in two hundred words in defending Communist Party domination of Soviet trade unions (Galenson 1982, 13; International Labor Organization, *Record of Proceedings* 1977, pages 24-25):

LIE NO. 1: "The guiding role of the Party has not been imposed on the trade unions."

LIE NO. 2: "[T]he tie between the trade unions and the Party was voluntarily created even before the October Revolution of 1917."

LIE NO. 3: "The guiding role of the party was not the result of legislative matters, but had come about on a voluntary basis."

LIE NO. 4: "The guiding role was exercised by only one voice; by the members of the party who at the same time were members of the trade union and acted within the framework of internal democracy of the trade union."

LIE NO. 5: "Their sole means were persuasion."

LIE NO. 6: "The autonomy and the independence of the trade unions were totally preserved, and the party possessed no means of coercion even if in fact its influence was great, as was that of the trade unions within the party."

I have selected the Soviet attitude to the ILO because, as international organizations go, the ILO receives virtually no attention from the world

---

34   The massacre might even be something for the United Nations to worry about in view of the estimated killing of 7,000 people: 6,000 civilians and 1,000 soldiers, almost all of them killed by other soldiers, as was reported in the *London Economist* of 10 June 1989 ("As Armies March," page 19).

media and even government. Compared to arms control bargaining, the ILO obviously is a minor matter. Yet the arena in Geneva is where the Soviet Union engages in daily desecration of the ILO Charter and conventions. Western reaction? Well-practiced shoulder shrugs.

ILO violations are an important example of Soviet international behavior and, far worse, of Western complicity in encouraging that behavior—the "do-nothing" policy of Western governments and independent voluntary organizations, like the AFL-CIO, that sit in the ILO with the law-breaking Soviet Union.

The complicity by the Western democracies in ignoring or indulging Soviet circumvention, let alone outright breaking, of treaty commitments arises from the hope that such appeasement tactics will somehow persuade the Soviet Union eventually to behave according to existing norms of international behavior.

The ILO is a tripartite organization comprising government, labor, and management, the latter two customarily independent of government and its directives. But in socialist dictatorships there is no independent labor or independent management; both labor and management are totally subservient to the Politburo and the Party Central Committee. Yet the Soviet representatives of "labor" and "management" sit in the ILO, morally equivalent to those bona fide representatives in the Western democracies. This abnormal situation is, of course, regarded as normal.

The Received Wisdom

The very raising of the question of Soviet membership in the ILO will be regarded as abnormal since it is far better, goes the received wisdom in the field of international politics, to leave "these things alone." The "hands-off-these-things" policy does not, however, apply to South Africa where, as I have earlier pointed out, there are black trade unions independent of the apartheid government, as well as strikes and collective bargaining.

Perhaps the overriding question is this: Can you cheat an honest man? Or put another way, can you cheat regularly and get away with it consistently without raising the suspicion that there may be a vested interest by the cheated in being cheated? Might not World War II have been averted had Neville Chamberlain or Franklin Roosevelt studied the evidence that neither Hitler nor Stalin nor Mussolini could be trusted? As Saul Bellow once said: "A great deal of intelligence can be invested in ignorance when the need for illusion is great."

One must admit that Soviet gains in arms control agreements have been won not only through their violations and circumventions of bilateral agreements but, according to Senator Wallop and Dr. Angelo Codevilla

(1987, 110), "mostly within the letter of the treaties" as signed by the United States. Which, of course, raises the question: What kind of negotiators do we appoint?

Nonperformance of signed treaties was built into the Bolshevik system from the very beginnings of Soviet treaty diplomacy. Faced with opposition from his followers, who wanted him to reject the Treaty of Brest-Litovsk signed in 1918 with Wilhelmine Germany, Lenin answered them by boasting of the treaty provisions he had already violated. It was Lenin who transformed opportunism—sign anything to save your neck—into a principle—ignore the piece of paper whenever possible. To quote his own words: "Yes, of course we are violating the treaty; we have already violated it thirty or forty times" (Triska and Slusser 1962, 221).

Lenin Tells Truth, Chicherin Lies

When he made his statement, Lenin was speaking to a secret party meeting. The statement is recorded in his Moscow-published collected works. For public consumption, however, his foreign minister, Georgi V. Chicherin, said:

> Even the Brest-Litovsk Treaty which was imposed upon Russia by violence was faithfully observed by the Soviet Government. Whenever it was accused of violating its diplomatic obligations, a frame-up by enemies of the Russian Soviet Government was shown to be at the bottom of the charges. (Goldwin 1959, 162)

During the Brest-Litovsk negotiations, the Bolshevik delegates "violated all approved procedure and protocol" (Whelan 1979, 48). Russia was a defeated power. Instead of seeking the best terms in a bad situation, Trotsky negotiated only for time—"time to permit the upsurge of revolution abroad" (Ibid.). As Trotsky wrote later:

> We began peace negotiations in the hope of arousing the workmen's parties of Germany and Austria-Hungary as well as those of the Entente countries. For this we were obliged to delay as long as possible to give the European workmen time to understand the main fact of the Soviet revolution itself and particularly its peace policy. (Whelan 1979, 48-49)

In other words, Trotsky and his delegation repudiated traditional behavior norms; as Joseph Whelan writes, "they negotiated as revolutionaries, directing their speeches not to their negotiating adversaries across the table but to the revolutionary working classes across their borders to Central and Western Europe" (Ibid.).

Trotsky and his delegation's behavior was extraordinary compared to past diplomatic behavior among nations. His delegation dined alone, rejecting invitations from its German hosts. Trotsky's purpose in "this seemingly petty behavior [was] designed to establish the Bolshevik reputation for commonsense, love of truth, and plain speaking that presumably would appeal to the masses everywhere." (Craig 1962, 6)

Importance of Brest-Litovsk Treaty

The importance of Brest-Litovsk in studying Soviet treaty diplomacy is that it set the pattern for the future. As Whelan (1979, 50) writes about the nascent Soviet diplomatic style:

> It ignored the premises and the values, the style and the ethics of traditional European diplomacy and declared its own based on a uniquely designed revolutionary Marxist-Leninist ideology. It set for itself revolution as a primary goal and linked this ultimate purpose to a radical negotiating style. In brief, it made diplomacy an instrument of revolution, and negotiations one more weapon in the arsenal of the class struggle.

John Wheeler-Bennett (1963, xii) in his history of the treaty writes that:

> with the opening of the negotiations, there emerged that new and potent factor in world diplomacy, Bolshevik propaganda; propaganda carried on by the party which formed the government of the Soviet state, but of whose activities that government professed official ignorance. 'The Party does not sign the treaty,' said Lenin, 'and for the Party the Government is not responsible.' It was upon this policy of 'parallel diplomacy', first used at Brest, that the activities of the Third International were based after its organization in 1919.

The importance of the treaty in Soviet history and strategy was noted by a long, front-page commentary in *Izvestia*, the Soviet government newspaper, on 20 September 1987. The author, Alexander Bovin, is a leading Soviet journalist and a strong supporter of Gorbachev. The Soviet émigré analyst Dmitri Simes ("Is Gorbachev Like Lenin Pausing to March Later?" *Los Angeles Times* 15 October 1987, II:7) said that the Bovin article is "a thinly disguised attempt to explain the strategic rationale behind Gorbachev's international conduct."

Under the treaty, a defeated Russia had to accept German peace terms—the surrender of 500,000 square miles of territory populated by 56 million inhabitants. Most Bolsheviks opposed signing such a treaty, but Lenin persuaded them otherwise. (In the early years of the Bolshevik Revolution, disagreement with the leader was not, as was inevitable under Stalin, punctuated by a Lubianka bullet in the back of the neck.)

Bovin says that Lenin "considered the struggle for peace as a part of a comprehensive struggle against imperialism in the name of interests of the revolution" (Ibid.). Lenin had seen, says Bovin, that "peace with Germany would provide a peaceful pause and would allow—if one acts intellectually— to enhance positions of the revolution, to gain strength, and to continue revolutionary influence on bourgeois Europe" (Ibid.). Bovin then describes Lenin's reaction when he was given the bound text of the treaty received from the German government: "Lenin ... kept the booklet in his hands for a moment and said laughingly that in less than six months this pretty piece of paper would disappear without a trace" (Ibid.).

Simes believes, and I agree with him, that the moral of the Bovin article is a message to those in the party leadership who are discomforted by all the talk "about the Kremlin's new, more moderate international conduct." And the message is that just as Lenin used the Brest-Litovsk Treaty as part of his "retreat the better to leap forward" strategy, so Gorbachev realizes, according to Simes, that "a pause today may be a precondition for marching further tomorrow" (Ibid.).

Lenin's Reaction

Earlier in 1987, extracts from Mikhail Shatrov's latest play, *The Brest Peace*, were published in a Soviet magazine, *Novoye Vremya*. The editors introduced the play with a full-page article emphasizing the relevance of the treaty to the present situation. Shatrov is a strong supporter of Gorbachev. The magazine called Brest-Litovsk "a classic example of political wisdom," because Lenin had realized that "only peace, a peaceful respite, could safeguard the victory of October" ("Mikhail Shatrov on Treaty of Brest Litovsk," *Radio Liberty* 124/87 [25 March 1987], page 1). Of course, it meant accepting "the exceptionally humiliating" terms. Just to be sure that the readers get the point, *Novoye Vremya* quotes Gorbachev as saying: "Peace is necessary not only as a political slogan but also as the basis for successful development, for dynamic building" (Ibid.). So we have not only the Bovin article but the *Novoye Vremya* article written in that special Bolshevik code language for the benefit of party members. And we also have Lenin's extraordinary statement:

He is no Socialist who does not understand that the victory over the bourgeoisie may require losses of territory and defeats. He is no Socialist who will not sacrifice his fatherland for the triumph of the social revolution. (Wheeler-Bennett 1963, 163)

From Outcast to Participant

International treaties helped to transform the status of the Soviet Union from outcast to participant in the affairs of the international community. Soviet treaty diplomacy has thus become one of the most important components of Soviet foreign policy; it has permitted the Soviet Union to introduce or successfully defend radical innovations in international relations. As Triska and Slusser (1962, 1) point out:

> International treaties, in these terms, have been especially significant for the Soviet Union: they have proved to be a convenient, useful and permissive vehicle for Soviet tactical and strategic objectives throughout its existence, and are likely to continue so to serve the Soviet Union in the future.

In the early years after the Bolshevik Revolution, some U.S. diplomats, who had assigned themselves or been assigned to specialize in Soviet affairs, believed that we should have as few dealings with the Soviet Union as possible. In 1953, George Kennan wrote that the United States "should never have established *de jure* relations with the Soviet government" (Stephanson 1989, 349 n. 1). Loy W. Henderson, a longtime career diplomat and one of the principal architects of twentieth-century U.S. diplomacy, opposed the establishment of diplomatic relations with the Soviet Union until it gave credible guarantees not to interfere in U.S. internal affairs.[35]

Loy Henderson's Concern

Henderson was concerned that Lenin's revolutionary ambitions had rendered the Soviet Union institutionally incapable of fulfilling the international accords it signed, let alone of abiding by the private assurances it gave. He wrote:

> It was my belief that since leaders of the Kremlin eventually were intending to contribute to the violent overthrow of all the countries with which the Soviet Union maintained relations, they considered Soviet relations with every country to be of a temporary or transitional character, subject to change at any moment. (Henderson 1987, xx; 227ff.)

---

35   In his memoirs, Charles Bohlen (1973, 125) says that Henderson "led the quiet struggle in the [Roosevelt] administration against the soupy and syrupy attitude toward the Soviet Union. A man of the highest character, absolutely incorruptible, he always spoke his mind, a practice that did not make him popular."

As the editor-annotator of Henderson's memoirs put it:

Throughout his [thirty-seven] years of service in the diplomatic corps, Henderson asked a fundamental question about our relations with the Soviet government: "Can the Soviets be trusted?" His answer, consistently, was "no." (Henderson 1987, xxix)

The fundamental continuity of Soviet foreign policy vis-à-vis the Western democracies from Day One of the Bolshevik Revolution may be luminously clear in the ninth decade of the twentieth century. It was not so clear half a century earlier to President Roosevelt and those around him, like Harry Hopkins, who simply did not, could not, or would not understand the meaning of Marxism-Leninism.[36]

For diplomats like Henderson, however, and for those he served with in the State Department's Eastern European Division, the Soviet design for world domination was no diplomatic secret. The utmost caution, he insisted to no avail, was needed in negotiating the initial recognition agreement between the two powers, one of which boasted openly of the inevitable realization of its global ambitions and was doing everything possible—legally or illegally— to hasten the day of ideological triumph.

A Prescient Memorandum

A few months after the 4 March 1933 presidential inauguration, the Eastern European Division presented a paper to President Roosevelt on how he might proceed in the negotiations for recognition. This prescient memorandum contained a paragraph as valid today as it was fifty-seven years ago:

The fundamental obstacle in the way of the establishment with Russia of the relations usual between nations in diplomatic intercourse is the world revolutionary aims and practices of the rulers of that country. It is obvious that, so long as the Communist regime continues to carry on in other countries, activities designed to bring about ultimately the overthrow of the Government and institutions of these countries, the establishment of genuine friendly relations between Russia and those countries is out of the question.... It would seem, therefore, that an essential prerequisite to the establishment of harmonious and trustful relations with the Soviet Government is the abandonment by the present rulers of Russia of their world revolutionary aims and the discontinuance of their activities designed to bring about the realization of such aims. More specifically and with particular regard to the United States, this prerequisite involves the abandonment by Moscow

---

36 Chapter 4 deals with the Roosevelt-Hopkins unwillingness to confront the reality of Soviet treaty diplomacy.

of direction, supervision, control, financing, et cetera, through every agency utilized for the purpose, of communist and other related activities in the United States. (Henderson 1987, 230)[37]

FDR's Determination

Little attention was paid in the White House to this memorandum that dealt with other bilateral issues as well. President Roosevelt was as determined to recognize the Soviet Union as he was to ignore the purpose of the Communist International, the Comintern. Even though the documents leading up to recognition contained a Soviet concession that it would refrain from subversive and propaganda activities in the United States, the document failed to mention the Comintern by name. And, within a week after the announcement of the establishment of diplomatic relations, the *Daily Worker*, the voice of the Comintern in New York City, was boasting that any claim that "the Litvinov Pact applies to the Communist International will meet with defeat" (Henderson 1987, 257).

It was an ominous event—the Soviet Union flouting its agreements before even the ink was dry. In the ensuing decades, Soviet disregard of its agreements would be repeated over and over again, events that American policy makers usually shrugged off with a what-can-you-do-about-it frown, often seeking to conceal the violations from the American public.

The U.S. Government was fully warned, almost prophetically, by its diplomats, who had studied the Soviet Union and understood what recognition entailed. Yet FDR embarked on a course with no quid pro quo. American recognition of the Soviet Union, formally announced 16 November 1933, only strengthened a regime whose existence has brought unprecedented misery and premature death to millions upon millions of people in and out of Russia.

Was Recognition Inevitable?

Although it can be argued persuasively that U.S. recognition was inevitable and that nonrecognition of the Soviet Union might not have accomplished anything very much, who knows? Delay of recognition or insistence on Soviet quid pro quos and self-enforcing provisions against

---

37 The memorandum of 27 July 1933 is entitled "Problems Pertaining to Russian-American Relations Which, in the Interest of Friendly Relations Between the United States and Russia, Should Be Settled Prior to the Recognition of the Soviet Government."

noncompliance might have prevented some of the calamities that have befallen the world.

What President Roosevelt accomplished by his recognition of the Soviet Union in the form he approved was to grant de facto legitimacy to the Leninist purposes of the revolution, whose achievement had been openly assigned to the Comintern. Because of the Comintern, other countries—England, China, Mexico—had earlier broken diplomatic relations with the Soviet Union. U.S. recognition in the face of the admitted and continuing interference in foreign countries by the Comintern was a blow to those statesmen who understood the threat of communism and who were prepared to resist subversion of their constitutional regimes.

When President Roosevelt ignored the purposes of the Comintern and its imperative—the export of the Soviet revolution throughout the world—he granted a legitimacy to Marxism-Leninism and its strategies for which the Free World has paid and is paying a heavy price. And this, in my opinion, is where and when it all began: Soviet exploitation of treaty diplomacy and its transformation into a weapon against the free world.

The Old Redefinition Game

I plan to ignore the old redefinition game about how the United States and other Western countries have broken treaties when it suited them. It's true that the United States ignored the 1986 censure of the International Court of Justice for supplying weapons to the Contras in Nicaragua and, further, it's true that a Pentagon spokesman once said a government had the right to lie. But in a world where the Soviet Union not only reserves to itself the right to live by its own "proletarian" code of morality but also proposes to impose that code on its neighbors far and near, in such a world treaty violations of the one must be judged differently from those of the other.[38]

By and large, the United States or some other Western democracy can rarely violate a treaty or attempt to do so or lie without being caught, either through some media exposé, a congressional or parliamentary investigation, or a whistle blower's leak. (In fact, the Western media assumes in many instances that when the government is not caught lying it is only because it

---

38 It could be argued that the manumission—without bloodshed, so far—of Czechoslovakia, East Germany, and Poland should demonstrate that the Soviet Union has annulled its right to impose its "moral code" on its neighbors. However, as I cited earlier, under the Brest-Litovsk treaty, Lenin surrendered 500,000 square miles of Czarist territory. When the time came, that territory was returned to Lenin's Russia.

has cleverly hidden its tracks.) In modern history, no other country in the world has so exposed the inner workings of its intelligence and foreign policy machinery as has the United States, either through Senate and House committee probes or through Freedom of Information Act suits.

What Kierkegaard Foresaw

The role of the media in modern times was amazingly foretold by Sören Kierkegaard, who wrote:

> Complete publicity makes it absolutely impossible to govern. No one had understood that better than the daily press; for no power has watched more carefully over the secret of its whole organization, who its contributors are, and its real aims, etc., as the daily press, which then continually cries out that the *government* should be quite public. Quite right; the intention of the press was to do away with government—and then itself govern. (*National Review* 2 April 1982, page 349)

To judge the United States and the Soviet Union by the same standard of morality would be like judging the traffic ticket scofflaw and the hard-core gunman (or gunperson) as equally degenerate. To anybody who wants to take off a few years to track the vexatious aspects of U.S. treaty diplomacy since 1945 and make invidious comparisons, my blessings.

What about conclusions, amendable or unamendable, and policy recommendations? In the words of Lenin's little pamphlet, What Is To Be Done? The Bush administration must develop a policy of deterrence in treaty diplomacy.[39] Essentially, deterrence means preventing those contingencies that threaten national security from arising. To achieve this objective, it becomes necessary to communicate in some way to a prospective antagonist what is likely to happen to him should he create a threatening situation. The expectation is that, confronted with this prospect, he will be deterred from taking the action that is regarded as inimical—at least so long as other less intolerable alternatives are open to him (Kaufman n.d., 25).

---

39   Henry Kissinger (1969, 15) defines deterrence as "the policy of preventing an action by confronting the opponent with risks he is unwilling to run—[which] depends in the first instance on psychological criteria. What the potential aggressor believes is more crucial than what is objectively true. Deterrence occurs above all in the minds of men." Then there is "mutual deterrence" (or "existential deterrence" or "mutual assured destruction") that argues that since nuclear weapons are so powerful, superiority in them is not strategically meaningful or necessary for deterrence ("Nuclear Revisionism," *Commentary* 87[3] [March 1989], page 43).

3

Would You Believe?

GÉRONTE. Il me semble que vous les placez autrement qu'ils ne sont; que le coeur est du côté gauche, et le foie du côté droit.

SGANARELLE. Oui, cela était autrefois ainsi, mais nous avons changé tout cela.

Molière, *Le Médecin malgré lui*, Act II[40]

The most fateful dilemma before the world today is not the existence of thousands of nuclear missiles. Rather, it is whether a seventy-two-year-old Marxist-Leninist dictatorship with startling military power can so will itself as to alter fundamentally its structure of one-party rule; whether such a dictatorship can become a peace-loving partner in a world of war, hot and cold.[41]

---

40   GÉRONTE. It seems to me that you have located them where they are not. Isn't the heart on the left side and the liver on the right?
      SGANARELLE. Yes, that's the way it used to be, but we've changed all that. (Molière, *The Pretend Doctor*)
41   According to the *London Economist* of 13 March 1988 (pages 19-22), as of 1988, 17 million people have been killed in wars since 1945; 4 million of these deaths occurred in the 1980s. There were something like 25 big wars going on. President Nixon (1988, 121) has written that since the end of World War II, there have been 120 wars in which 18 million people have been killed; forty of these wars were being waged as of 1988.

A Soviet ideologist has said:

... Communists are not willing to make fundamental concessions and are not about
to repudiate their belief in the ultimate universal triumph of communism; they do
indeed consider coexistence as something that will not last forever, but only until
the day that capitalism ceases to exist.... It is, therefore, just as absurd to demand
that Communists issue a guarantee that capitalism will be preserved as it would be
to seek assurances that the earth will stop its movement around the sun. (Kintner
1987, 17)[42]

Need for Imaginative Solutions

There is no indication in present-day Soviet political literature, despite
Mikhail Gorbachev's *glasnost* and *perestroika*—that the foregoing passage
misrepresents the Soviet ethos.[43] In fact, Gorbachev himself in December
1989 was arguing that there could be no change in the Soviet Communist
Party's monopoly of power. "At the present complex stage," he wrote in
Pravda, "the interests of the consolidation of society ... prompt the
advisability of keeping the one-party system" ("Doing It Their Way," *London
Economist* 2 December 1989, page 57). Two months later, Gorbachev seemed
to have changed his mind (see page 2).

It may well be that we are at the end of the postwar era and that we must
find more imaginative solutions to new problems—unless, of course, we are
entering a prewar era. Whichever it is, seventy years of Soviet imperialism,
military and ideological, is still with us in a modern world in which, with the
possible exceptions of Communist China and Vietnam, it is the only
functioning imperialism. If the Soviet Union still adheres to outmoded ideas
of world dominion—ideas that not even other communist countries (notably
the People's Republic of China, Yugoslavia, and Albania) accept as
legitimate—then the dangers to world peace multiply.

Whether the Soviet Union can change, in fact whether this superpower-in-
crisis can even modernize its socioeconomic structure, is a crucial question
for this reason: The Soviet Union is at present a military but not an economic
superpower. Gorbachev's domestic priority is to ensure that the Soviet Union
becomes an economic superpower without for a moment ceasing to be a
military superpower ("Gorbachev: New Man in the Kremlin," *Problems of
Communism* xxxiv[3] [May-June 1985], page 21). If the Soviet Union,
despite its floundering economy, has managed to become the most powerful
imperialism in the world today, what would it be like if it were to become an

---

42   This passage was originally cited in Bratov 1972, 189-190.
43   The Russian word *peredyshka*, or "breathing space," was also in current use as
part of latterday Gorbachevism. For more on *peredyshka* see chapter 9.

economic superpower like the United States or Japan while continuing to practice the tenets of Marxism-Leninism? When Prime Minister Margaret Thatcher said, "I like Mr. Gorbachev. We can do business together" (*Financial Times* 22 December 1984, page 26), what kind of business did she have in mind with a superpower whose military supremacy has been paid for by an economy in the final stages of decomposition?

The free world must think the unthinkable: The Soviet Union under its present rulership and ideology may be able to change for the better in the short run—but in the long run?[44] Rather, the Soviet Union must, in order to bolster its own legitimacy, continue to behave like an old-fashioned pre-1914 European imperialist power.[45] Just as once the European colonial powers sent a few gunboats upriver to quell the restless natives, so today, in the era of advanced technology, the Soviet Union used helicopter gunships, napalm and chemical warfare during its aggression against Afghanistan. Despite Soviet troop withdrawals and a new treaty, Afghanistan will always be in danger from Soviet subversion.

Soviets Can Change, Some Say

There is also an "on the other hand": namely, that the Soviet system can change dramatically, especially when it comes to arms control. The *London Economist*, for example, believes that "to its credit, Russia now understands that, if people are to trust disarmament agreements, the deals have to be checkable" ("One Roof, Two Houses Still," *Encounter* 23 April 1988, page 12).

For the first time the Russians are willing to submit themselves to real checking, including on-site inspections of some of their military installations and a watching Western eye on some of their army's maneuvers. They are also prepared to talk about nonsymmetrical disarmament (meaning that the side with the most weapons cuts the most) and "defensive defence," the idea that both sides' armies could be more convincingly equipped and positioned for defence, not attack. Little of this,

---

44   See Bauer et al. 1956, 211 in which the author writes that Soviet ideology "is an amalgam of formal and openly expressed principles, informal and covertly held ideas which are nevertheless consciously shared by the elite, principles of action which are merely implicit and often not consciously formulated by the leadership, and lessons learned from experience in the hard school of Soviet politics. Correct interpretation of Soviet behavior, adequate assessment of their intentions, or accurate prediction of their probable behavior cannot be made without weighing the role of ideological factors together with 'objective conditions' as an influence on the actions of the leaders."

45   For a discussion of Soviet imperialism see Feuer 1986.

alas, has yet been put down on paper; but Russia's apparent new open-mindedness does hold out some hope of making disarmament more than a propaganda word. (Ibid.)

But how can one check essential armaments data about the Soviet Union when our highest officials admit they do not know for certain what the Kremlin spends on arms? Gorbachev announces cuts in the Soviet army and its tanks, but what meaning do these numbers have when nobody in the West knows what the Soviet defense budget is?

Then Defense Secretary Frank C. Carlucci, after a visit to Moscow in 1988 and the third in a series of meetings with Soviet Defense Minister Dmitri Yazov, made a startling admission. He said that it is public knowledge that the U.S. military budget has declined in real terms by 10 percent since 1985. The result—also public knowledge—is that the United States is cutting the size of its armed forces by a number of ships, three aviation wings, several army and marine corps units, and about 45,000 personnel over the next two years. Said Carlucci:

> Far less about Soviet military capabilities is made public. Our estimates indicate that actual Soviet military spending is *at least six* [my emphasis] times the publicly announced budget figure. During my meetings, I suggested that the Soviets open their military budget for public scrutiny, and explain how it might change and how that would affect Soviet force structure. ("Soviet Military Candid Talk But No Action," *Wall Street Journal* 30 August 1988, page 18)[46]

Another Big Lie

The Soviet answer to Carlucci's suggestion was another one of those Big Lies. Carlucci was told that the Soviet government couldn't supply such information "for technical reasons having to do with the fact that the Soviet military budget is scattered across several different government departments, making it difficult to produce a budget breakdown resembling our own" ("Soviet Military: Candid Talk But No Action," *Wall Street Journal* 30 August 1988, page 18).

The proof of the Big Lie came a few months later in a speech by Yuri Dubinin, the Soviet Ambassador to the United States. He told his audience

---

[46]   For the text of the speech "Prospects for the U. S. -Soviet Dialogue" upon which this article was based, see Frank C. Carlucci's "Remarks prepared for delivery August 1, 1988 at the Voroshilov Military Academy of the General Staff of the Armed Forces of the Soviet Union in Moscow," U. S. Dept. of Defense news release No. 381-88. For the tremendous difficulties in assessing Soviet defense costs, see "The Economics of Soviet Defense Spending," *Radio Liberty* Supplement 4/88 (17 August 1988).

that "President Gorbachev recently announced the pending cut in the Soviet military budget by 14.2 percent and 19.5 percent cut in the production of military hardware" ("More than a 'thaw' needed, Soviet Ambassador Dubinin says," *Campus Report* [Stanford University] 8 February 1989, 17).

Now, if the West cannot be told by top Soviet military officials what the Soviet military budget is, what do Dubinin's figures mean? Zero. They are fraudulent figures. Why? Because what does 14.2 percent of the Soviet military budget mean when we are not allowed to know the base figure—that is, the total Soviet defense budget? What does a 19.5 percent cut in the production of Soviet military hardware mean when we don't know the base figure—that is, how much is being spent on military hardware? Ambassador Dubinin's figures are intended to gull the true believers in Gorbachev's policies.

The defense secretary's annual and final report to Congress reflected his skepticism about Gorbachev's policies and referred to the conflict between Soviet rhetoric and action. He cited air attacks against Pakistan; naval base construction at Tartus, Syria; military transfers to Nicaragua; SA-5 missiles to North Korea; support for Cuban forces in Angola, Ethiopia and Mozambique.

> These activities raise questions about the real meaning and influence of Soviet "new thinking" on their foreign policy. For the foreseeable future there will be great uncertainty about Soviet intentions. The current Soviet leadership's ultimate objectives are known only to them, and the duration of their authority is uncertain. (Carlucci 1989, 11-12; "Carlucci Says Soviets Still Seek Conquests, *Washington Times* 18 January 1989, page A5)

Understated Military Spending

The same argument about understated Soviet military expenditures was made by Kenneth L. Adelman, director of the Arms Control and Disarmament Agency (ACDA) from 1983 to 1987. In 1985, the U.S. military budget was about $250 billion. The United States estimated that the Soviets had spent a similar amount. Yet all that showed up in the Soviet military budget was the equivalent of $35 billion, a ridiculously small sum for a military superpower. And this continued Soviet secrecy comes at a time when, said Adelman, "it is tougher, not easier, than it was ten years ago to guarantee effective verification of arms control agreements we may sign with the Soviet Union"[47] (Adelman 1987b, 9).

---

47 Adam Ulam has described Soviet secrecy as "probably the most potent weapon that the twenty-odd people at the very top of the Kremlin hierarchy dispose of in warding off any attempt by outsiders to interfere with their rule" (*National Review* 19 August 1983, page 1022).

The "disinformation" component of the Gorbachev-Dubinin arms expenditure statistics were confirmed, astonishingly, in an article on page 56 of *Izvestia* 21 March 1989:

> It was announced that we [Soviets] are cutting our military budget by 14.2 percent. The degree of accuracy—down to tenths of a percent—is striking. Down to the last kopeck, so to speak. Yet none of us can name an accurate figure for our military expenditure, and consequently no one really knows what these percentage points mean in financial terms.

A Startling Admission

What I have quoted is a startling admission by a Soviet critic writing in a leading Soviet newspaper that President Gorbachev's announcement of arms expenditure percentage cuts is unintelligible without publication of the total Soviet arms budget. In other words, we have here a disinformation ploy by Gorbachev himself. Not only did Gorbachev announce the 14.2 percent cut but, according to Yuri Dubinin, Soviet ambassador to the United States, Gorbachev also announced a 19.5 percent cut "in the production of military hardware." Without knowing what the Soviet Union spends on military hardware, the advertised cut is meaningless.

And now we know from the official pages of *Izvestia* that arms budget expenditures do not come under the heading of *glasnost*. The *Izvestia* article was written by Albert Plutnik under the title, "The Military Lesson: A Civilian's Polemical Notes on Restructuring in the Army." Plutnik's sardonic reflections on the power of the Soviet military over the domestic front make fascinating reading. For example, he describes Western television scenes showing mass protests outside military bases and near nuclear testing ranges. Such protests mean that Western constituencies know where the bases and ranges are located while in the Soviet Union such information is considered "military secrets."

Plutnik ("The Military Lesson: A Civilian's Polemical Notes on Restructuring in the Army," *Izvestia* 21 March 1989, page 85) describes the arms budget process in the United States in glowing terms:

> Over there the Defense Department's budget is published in the press. And also there is the defense secretary's annual report to Congress, which covers in some detail all defense matters and the main provisions of military policy.... Could it be, perhaps, that in our country it is nothing more than a tradition—to allow the Defense Ministry to keep its programs in absolute secrecy? And is it the only such ministry anyway? What do we know about the activities of other ministries [that] exist more or less in secret [and] the vast complexes that are subordinate to them?

He concludes his long article with an unusual appeal to the Soviet military:

Despite our age-old inclination to seek the enemy within, we have only now realized that the main enemy within is the low living standard. This enemy cannot be stopped with a rocket launcher or annihilated with machine gun rounds. The Army by other means can make a very weighty contribution to peaceful transformations. That is what is needed now.

Can you, then, have genuine arms control with a superpower whose defense expenditures are unknown to the world, and where guessing what those expenditures are is described by the *London Economist* ("Roubles, Roubles Everywhere," 28 January 1989, page 46) as "a western sport (to call it a science would be too kind)"? The magazine estimated that the Soviet Union spent somewhere between 13 and 19 percent of GNP on defense compared to about 6 percent for the United States. The Soviets claim they spend no more than 3 percent of their GNP.

Colossal Soviet Arms Outlays

What explains this extraordinary Soviet expenditure on arms? In fact, what explains such swollen military expenditures in *all* Marxist countries, even those not necessarily allied to the Soviet Union? Third World countries like Libya, South Yemen, Syria, and Tanzania, as well as the Soviet Union and its East European allies, spend more of their GNP on arms than do NATO members. Marxist Ethiopia, Cuba, Nicaragua, and Mozambique spend more per capita on arms than does the United States. Vietnam, strapped for everything needed to build an economy, ranks among the world's top military machines. India has an enormous military machine, thanks to Soviet largess.

An important answer to explain Soviet arms expenditures and the reason for secrecy came from Robert Gates, then deputy director of the CIA ("Distrust, But Verify," *New Republic* 6 March 1989, page 13):

1. Despite a twenty-year relationship between the two superpowers based on mutual vulnerability, "the Soviet Union has been working to eliminate its own vulnerability and consolidate a unilateral advantage."
2. The Soviet Union has spent $150 billion on strategic defense (almost fifteen times what the United States has spent) in the past ten years because Moscow believes the United States "can develop a highly effective strategic defense, in part because they are doing large elements of such a program themselves."

3. Elimination of the Strategic Defense Initiative (SDI) would preserve the Soviet monopoly in strategic defense, "but would be a key indicator of a loss of U.S. will to compete militarily."

4. Failure to proceed with SDI "would hand the Soviets a unilateral advantage of historic consequences with awesomely negative implications for strategic stability and peace."

Gates the Pessimist

In his new post as deputy assistant to the president for national security affairs, Gates delivered a speech 1 April 1989 that certainly puts him into the class of "pessimists." (See chapter 7 for a discussion of "optimists, pessimists, and realissimists.")

Gates is of that school of analysts that believes that ideology, even in the Gorbachev era, plays a major role in the formulation of Soviet foreign policy. For U.S. policy makers to ignore or to minimize the importance of Marxism-Leninism in the Kremlin's operational code is to shackle policy interpretation to current cultural chic.

In the early months of his administration, President Bush was the target of domestic critics as well as of Gorbachev spokesmen for having shunned, since his inauguration, negotiations with the Soviets. To anybody to whom Bush-bashing is not a priority, the Administration position has been fairly clear: Past U.S. policies vis-à-vis the Soviet Union needed careful review, and that takes time.

Dr. Gates laid out a strategy agenda for U.S.-Soviet meetings. The strategy was described in a too little noticed address he made 1 April at the Center for Strategic and International Studies. Salient concepts from that 4,000-word speech must be interpreted as reflecting, in whole or part, the thinking of President Bush. These are some of the highlights of the Gates (1989, passim) analysis:

- "We in government, as a rule, spend too little time thinking about and planning for the future. We spend too little time reflecting on history and experience; we neglect strategy for tactics. The Bush Administration is trying to resist this. Accordingly, our reviews of the international setting and our polices are focused on the development of long-range strategy."
- "Regardless of the substantial odds against him, we take seriously Gorbachev's determination to modernize the Soviet economy."
- The Soviet system of rule over a seventy-year period "has brought to the peoples of the old Russian empire suffering on a scale previously unknown in human history.... I believe it essential for us today to

understand that this record is not confined to the Stalin era alone, was not the doing of a single demented leader, but covers the entirety of Soviet history, and is the product of the very nature of the system itself."

- "The popular impression of the Brezhnev period, reinforced by Gorbachev, is one of doddering old men presiding ineffectively and incompetently over a stagnating economy.... This is Western historical amnesia and Soviet selectivity, if not disinformation."

- In the "doddering" Brezhnev era, the following events occurred: the 1968 invasion of Czechoslovakia, the Soviet attack on China along the Ussuri river, and hints of a Soviet nuclear attack to come. The Soviets helped provoke the 1967 Middle East war. In the mid-1970s, the Soviets supported Cuban surrogate forces in Angola and Ethiopia. The Soviets supplied the wherewithal for North Vietnam's final conquest of South Vietnam. The Soviets underwrote the Sandinista revolution in Nicaragua. They sold $12 billion worth of weapons to Libya. They invaded Afghanistan. In 1980-81, they imposed martial law in Poland and suppressed Solidarity. They destroyed the dissident and human rights movements. "And all this," says Dr. Gates, "took place against the backdrop of the greatest peacetime military build-up in history."

- Dr. Gates said he offered this sketch of Soviet history "to underscore that our view of the Soviet Union cannot be based on the personality of one or another leader, but must be based on the nature of the Soviet system itself.... It is the Soviet system itself, and the 70 year continuity we see from leader to leader, from Lenin to Chernenko, and even Gorbachev, that shapes our view of the Soviet Union."

- "[W]e cannot make long-term decisions and devise strategies affecting freedom and the future that depend on the continued political (or even physical) survival of one man.... Unlike any Western or other modern state, politics at the highest level in the Kremlin today are as hidden from public view as in generations past. Much has changed, but more that is fundamental remains the same."

- "[W]hat Gorbachev has set in motion represents a political earthquake... He is a figure of enormous political importance. The forces he has unleashed are powerful but so are the people and institutions he has antagonized—thus setting in motion a tremendous power struggle and purge no less dramatic for the absence of show trials and terror."

And here comes the crucial finding by Gates—one of the highest policy-making officials in the Bush Administration, one who when he speaks says "we":

However, elections notwithstanding, Gorbachev's Leninism still means the continued political monopoly of the Communist Party. Gorbachev's dictatorship of the Communist Party remains untouched and untouchable. He seeks still a system based on the same Leninist political principles that guided his predecessors. As he said in 1987, "We will not retreat an inch from the path of socialism, of Marxism-Leninism." (Ibid.)

What, then, does President Bush seek from Gorbachev's Soviet Union? Nothing more than a counterrevolution. Or, according to Dr. Gates, a Soviet Union that is pluralistic internally, noninterventionist externally, observes basic human rights, contributes to international stability and tranquillity, "and a Soviet Union where these changes are more than an edict from the top and are independent of the views, power and durability of a single individual" (Ibid.).

I read the Gates speech as a basic state paper from President Bush for Gorbachev's study. Unfortunately for world peace, the Soviet response will be a repudiation of President Bush's hopes for a gentler, kinder Soviet Union.

In the meantime, we must keep in mind that since President Gorbachev assumed power in March 1985, the Soviet Union has fielded more tanks and artillery pieces than currently (June 1989) exist in the combined armies of Britain, France, and West Germany. General John Galvin, Supreme Allied Commander in Europe, has revealed that each month the Soviets produce enough tanks to outfit an entire division and enough artillery to equip four artillery regiments ("Soviet Nuclear Blackmail," *New York Times* 17 May 1989, page E3).

Edwin Luttwak summed it up:

The fact is that Soviet military production continues almost undiminished: Advanced aircraft, huge submarines, etc. keep appearing on satellite photographs. And the much publicized new doctrine of "sufficiency" has yet to change the sharply offensive character of the Soviet Union's military power, with its massed armor, vast commando forces for surprise attack and heavy "counterforce" ballistic missiles. ("The Alliance, Without an Enemy," *New York Times* 3 February 1989, Op-Ed page)

How to Measure Militarism

One way of measuring a state's militarism is by its "force ratio," that is, the number of full-time regular military personnel per 1,000 population. The U.S. Arms Control and Disarmament Agency has compiled such data that have been analyzed by Professor James L. Payne (1989, 113; "Marx's Heirs Belie the Pacifist Promise," *Wall Street Journal* 5 April 1985, page 34).

The analysis discloses that the average "force ratio" for Marxist countries (13.3) is twice as large as those of non-Marxist countries (6.1). For example, pairing divided countries confirms this thesis:

Force Ratios, 1985 (by country)

Non-Marxist	Marxist
South Korea, 14.7	North Korea, 38
North Yemen, 3.9	South Yemen, 12.5
West Germany, 7.8	East Germany, 14.0

Using the same table format, startling disparities appear when Marxist and non-Marxist states are grouped separately ("Militarism and the Soviet state." *Daedalus* 109[4] [Fall 1980], page 3)[48]:

Non-Marxist	Marxist
United States, 9.1	Soviet Union, 16.3
17 European, 7.6	8 European, 13.3
31 African, 2.1	9 African, 5.9

When compared separately, before Marxism and after Marxism, these are the results:

	Pre-Marxist	Marxist	% Increase
Ethiopia	1.8 (1973)	8.2	+356
Cuba	3.2 (1957)	23.5	+634
Nicaragua	2.6 (1977)	14.6	+462

---

48 The article by Richard Pipes demonstrates that, for the Soviet Union, there may be a historical continuity in its militarism. Under Peter the Great, there were three professional soldiers for every 100 inhabitants, a ratio three times higher than the ratio which obtained in much richer countries in the West. In some years virtually the entire national budget had to be turned over to the military. The Russian historian, Kliuchevskii, has shown that Peter's reforms, which laid the foundation of modern Russia, had been dictated largely by military demands.

Scraps of Paper

In the years ahead, the United States and the Soviet Union will be meeting again and again to negotiate all kinds of treaties, arms agreements, economic pacts, perhaps even a treaty of friendship (a favorite Soviet instrument). What meaning will these scraps of paper possess if one side seeks the other side's ruin because of some fraudulent nostrums which go by the collective name of "scientific socialism"? What meaning has conventional treaty diplomacy (the kind the noncommunist world routinely engages in) if one side, the Kremlin, believes that the doom of the other side is foreseeable and inevitable and that, indeed, it is duty-bound to hasten it? Such diplomacy has about as much meaning as the aforementioned 1929 Kellogg-Briand Pact in which all the signatories agreed to "The Renunciation of War as an Instrument of National Policy."

It may be that the many theses about the doom of capitalism that Soviet ideologists published in the past are no longer repeated with the same strident frequency as was the case during the Khrushchev-Brezhnev-Andropov era. If they no longer say these things too loudly, the question remains: Do they still believe and act upon them?[49]

Coexistence Through Expansion

Two Soviet historians now residing in the West, Mikhail Heller and Aleksandr Nekrich, in their important history in which they describe Soviet foreign policy as "coexistence through expansion," have written:

> The most virulent Western critics characterized [Soviet foreign policy] as follows: "What is ours is ours; the rest is negotiable." But they are mistaken; "What's ours is ours; what's yours will be ours" would better correspond to their real view. (Heller & Nekrich 1986, 563)

In the far reaches of the Pacific and in the frigid waters of the Baltic, huge Soviet fleets, especially missile-bearing submarines, intrude into waters that are within the territorial limits of other sovereign countries despite their protests, and Soviet bombers intrude into Japanese air space. Communist rebel groups in the Philippines, Indonesia, Chile, and El Salvador are supplied with arms by Soviet submarines and Soviet fishing vessels and, when safe

---

49   After the French defeat at the hands of the Prussian Army in 1870 and the loss of Alsace-Lorraine, the French military, informed by a revanchist ethos, adopted as its slogan: *Pensons-y toujours, n'en parlons jamais* or, "Always think about it; never talk about it."

from possible exposure, also by surface Soviet warships. All these activities go on while the United States talks arms control with a nation that in one respect could be characterized as uncontrollable.

"After Detection, What?" Iklé Asked

The problem of Soviet violations evoked a question from Fred Iklé, former deputy secretary of defense, more than a quarter of a century ago, a question which became the title of a famous article, "After detection, What?" Soviet treaty violations occur because the answer to Iklé's question then as now is Adelman's concession—nothing: "We never really found anything much to *do* about Soviet cheating."[50]

Iklé, who served as undersecretary of defense for policy for almost two terms of the Reagan presidency, is a former director of the U.S. Arms Control and Disarmament Agency. He is a leading strategic thinker. I would like to summarize his 1961 essay, "After Detection, What?" since it clarifies the reason why the Soviet Union can violate its treaties with impunity.

The strategist begins his seminal paper with this portentous theme: Detecting violations of arms control agreements is not enough. He writes: "What counts are the political and military consequences of a violation once it has been detected, since these alone will determine whether or not the violators stand to gain in the end" (U.S. Arms Control and Disarmament Agency n.d., 43).

Iklé argues that the potential violator of an arms control agreement isn't going to be deterred simply because of the risk of discovery. Deterrence results from the violator's fear that whatever gain he makes from the violation may be outweighed by the victim's reaction to it. If the violator of an arms control agreement thinks he can "discourage, circumvent or absorb our reaction," he will not be deterred no matter how superb our detection technology may be.

Four Categories

Iklé then sets up four categories for studying a detected arms control agreement evasion: (1) reaction of world opinion; (2) political reaction of the

---

50 Senator Malcolm Wallop (R., Wyo.) has suggested that the Senate be required to reaffirm by a two-thirds vote U.S. adherence to a treaty whose violation the president has certified. He also suggested an arms control version of the Gramm-Rudman-Hollings Act by which Congress is forced to enforce arms control agreements ("How I'd Testify on an Arms Treaty," *New York Times* 8 June 1987, page 21).

injured country; (3) military measures the injured power might undertake to restore the situation that would have existed without an arms control agreement; and (4) military and political measures that might go beyond this "restoration."

As for the first category—the bar of public opinion—how can its toothless verdict be useful? Supposing the violator is contemptuous of "world opinion"? As an example, Iklé recalls how the Soviet Union shocked world opinion with its sanguinary suppression of the 1956 Hungarian revolution. There was nothing complicated about what the Red Army was doing in Hungary. Whereas evidence of an arms control agreement violation might be equivocal, might involve technicalities difficult for a lay public to understand, what the Hungarian crisis meant was tragically clear: A popular rebellion by a small nation against a totalitarian regime was defeated by the military invasion of a large power. Moreover, agreements made with the Hungarian rebels were broken by the Soviet Union. At least thirteen resolutions were passed at the United Nations against Soviet intervention in Hungary. The Soviet Union ignored them all, as a quarter of a century later it ignored for almost a decade similar resolutions to get out of Afghanistan. "World opinion" even on lesser evils—say, the Iran-Iraq war—took a long time to be effective, if indeed it was; exhaustion by both sides was more likely the cause of the outbreak of peace. The amorphousness of "world opinion" makes that concept an inadequate sanction.[51]

The Injured Country

As for political reaction by the injured country, in the case of democratic governments the most important question is whether the injured government would even acknowledge that there had been a violation, especially when the violator plays dumb or denies the violation. The injured government must be willing to increase military expenditures, which might be difficult or impossible if domestic public opinion inhibits sanctions against an agreement violator. Then, too, allies may have to be consulted before sanctions are imposed.

Soviet immunity from sanctions for treaty violations didn't begin just yesterday, nor can the fault be laid to one party or one statesman. What we see is a dereliction of moral duty as well as a failure of strategic thinking that has characterized our presidents from Roosevelt to Reagan.

---

51   Hungary, the UN, and traditional diplomacy are discussed in chapter 5.

Let me offer another example of such dereliction and the concomitant admission by an American statesman that nothing can be done about Soviet nonobservance.

Building of the Berlin Wall

The building of the Berlin Wall on 13 August 1961—and here I am quoting Secretary of State Dean Rusk (1976, 253) during the Kennedy administration—was "in direct contravention of the four-power agreement of 1949, and we protested vigorously."

Rusk continues: "President Kennedy paid a memorable visit to Berlin to reassure West Berliners of America's firm commitment to their freedom, but short of going to war over Berlin, there wasn't much else we could do" (Ibid.).

Which, of course, is why Khrushchev could say, "When I want the West to scream, I squeeze on Berlin" ("Germans Are Debating an Unthinkable Idea: Removing Berlin Wall," *Wall Street Journal* 25 November 1987, page 12)[52] And when Gorbachev wants the West to adore him, the Berlin Wall loses its forbidding character and Western television shows moving scenes of East and West Germans fraternizing at East German-sponsored breaks in the wall.

Similar Candor

Rusk, secretary of state in the Johnson administration, spoke with similar candor about the Soviet occupation of Czechoslovakia in 1968. The West had become inured to the Berlin Wall; it was a part of international life. Rusk looked back upon his address to the UN General Assembly in October 1968 in which he had said that the United States "did not accept the authority of the Soviet Union over the East European countries as a matter of international law or international politics" (Rusk 1976, 253). And now the heart of the problem, according to Rusk:

[B]ut when you come up against the question of using force to back up your opinions, you have to decide whether, if you take the first step, you are also

---

52   But there came a time when the squeezing on Berlin had to stop. It is believed that Khrushchev's cave-in on Cuba in the 1962 missile crisis seriously undermined Khrushchev's power position in world affairs because Europe perceived that the frightening Soviet nuclear threat was a paper tiger. Result: "the relentless and frightening Soviet pressure on Berlin, which had defined the reality of the cold war since 1958, suddenly died down" ("Nuclear Revisionism," *Commentary* 87[3] [March 1989], page 43).

prepared to take the second and the third and the fourth, and, quite frankly, we were not prepared to fight a war over the Berlin Wall or Czechoslovakia. (Ibid.)

That was the cry in Europe in 1939—*pourquoi mourir pour Danzig?* (why die for Danzig?) But is that the only alternative? I am not suggesting that we should have gone to war over the Berlin Wall or over the Red Army invasion of Czechoslovakia. But is that, I repeat, the only alternative? Has anyone considered the question of not negotiating treaties with a power that is prepared to break them whenever it suits its policy? I have never heard a rational explanation as to why we should negotiate treaties when the Soviet Union has shown over and over again that these agreements, as the Soviet Union in practice sees it, have no realistic status in international law. If treaty provisions undertaken by the Soviet Union are unenforceable, short of going to war, why then do we negotiate?

Implication of Rusk's Conclusion

The implication of Rusk's summing up of the U.S.-Soviet situation is that it is the Soviet Union that decides when it's time to negotiate a treaty and what the negotiation is going to be about. In short, when the United States embarks upon a negotiation with the Soviet Union the United States tacitly accepts the right of the Kremlin to break the Soviet commitment at times and places of its own choosing.

The problem of U.S.-Soviet negotiations is even further complicated today because of the apparently irreversible intrusion of Congress into the president's foreign policy prerogatives, hitherto regarded as his privileged constitutional sanctuary. Thanks to President Reagan's or his staff's blindness, the White House permitted the Senate in 1988 to introduce into the ratification of the INF treaty with the Soviets a "condition" whereby, said the Senate, treaties are to be interpreted according to the "common understanding … shared by the president and the Senate at the time the Senate gives its advice and consent to ratification" ("How Ronald Reagan Weakened the Presidency," *Commentary* 86[3] [September 1988], page 28).[53]. This provision passed overwhelmingly in the Senate even though it is of dubious constitutionality. The Senate can bind the U.S. government with "implicit understandings" but it can't bind other nations, particularly the Soviet Union that does not consider itself bound by treaty commitments to begin with.

---

53   The reason for the challenge to the president's negotiating powers was the Democratic Senate majority's debate, led by Senator Sam Nunn, over whether or not the 1972 ABM treaty permits testing SDI in space.

Immunity from Sanctions Guaranteed

Can an arms treaty with a superpower whose violations are guaranteed to be immune from any sanctions satisfy the security needs of a nation such as the United States whose own treaty observance is guaranteed by an ever-watchful media and a passionately oversightful Congress? The ever-watchful media is not always concerned about cheating when the Soviet Union is involved. The *New York Times*, for example, in an editorial endorsing the Intermediate Range Nuclear Forces Treaty, conceded that despite the "extensive verification procedures ... the Soviet Union could still cheat—but not in militarily significant ways" ("Some Arms Cheating May Not Matter," *New York Times* 30 March 1988, page 22). The *Times* added that the INF verification measures "are adequate to discourage or detect significant evasion" (Ibid.). Insignificant evasion doesn't seem to matter to the *New York Times* even, apparently, as a criterion of character. More to the point, if the violations are so insignificant as not to be a threat to the United States and the NATO alliance, why should the Soviet Union bother to cheat and risk sullying its reputation?

A similar indulgence by the *New York Times* was granted the Soviet Union when Moscow announced it was prepared to scrap the thirty-story, phased array radar near the Siberian city of Krasnoyarsk that a *Times* editorial had characterized as "a hefty (*sic!*) contravention of the 1972 Antiballistic Missile Treaty" (Ibid., page 24). What the editorial failed to mention were four other Soviet violations or serious possible violations of the ABM treaty. All these violations or "maybe" violations were listed in the U.S. Arms Control and Disarmament Agency's Report *Soviet Noncompliance*, published in February 1986 (Wallop & Codevilla 1987, 128). And then, of course, there were the violations of SALT I, SALT II, the Helsinki Accords (of which more later), the Geneva Protocol of 1925, and the 1972 Biological and Toxic Weapons Convention (Adelman 1989, 150).

An Admitted Treaty Violation

In return for scrapping the Krasnoyarsk radar—a clear and now admitted treaty violation—the Soviet Union asked that the United States agree that the ABM treaty remain in force for ten more years and also agree not to press for space-based testing under that treaty. The *New York Times* repudiated such linkage on the grounds that the Soviet Union should not be "permitted to secure this by an offer to stop violating the treaty" ("Waltzing Round Krasnoyarsk," *New York Times* 21 July 1988, page 24; Also see "USSR Admits Krasnoyarsk Radar Violates ABM Treat," *Radio Liberty* vol. 1, no. 44 [3 November 1989], pages 18-20). But then in the spirit of *tout comprendre, on se rend indulgent,* the *Times* generously explained that Mikhail Gorbachev "does need a fig leaf behind which to divest himself of this embarrassment." As for a Washington plan to declare the Krasnoyarsk radar a clear violation of the ABM agreement, such a formal Washington declaration "can only make it harder for Mr. Gorbachev to persuade his hawks to tear the radar down" (Ibid.).

It must have been quite an embarrassment for critics of the Reagan administration who had first noticed in 1983 the Krasnoyarsk radar on U.S. satellite photographs, when Soviet Foreign Minister Shevardnadze formally announced on 23 October 1989, that "the construction of this station, equal in size to the Egyptian pyramids, constituted an open violation of the ABM treaty" ("Moscow ... Admits Breaking Pact," *New York Times* 24 October 1989, pages 1, 4). For six years—1983 to 1989—the Soviet Union had gotten away with a treaty violation, and the lying which accompanied that violation, without U.S. retaliation.

On 10 June 1988, when *glasnost* was in full spate, Shevardnadze said in a letter to the UN Secretary-General Perez de Cuellar:

> The USSR has taken unprecedented unilateral measures of openness, by giving American representatives a possibility to inspect the building site of the Krasnoyarsk radar as well as radar vans in the areas of Gomel and Moscow so as to see for themselves *that there are no violations of the ABM treaty of 1972 on the part of the Soviet Union* [my emphasis]. (*Wall Street Journal* 25 October 1989, page A14)

No Compliance Policy

What U.S. decision makers failed to create under the Carter and Reagan administrations was a compliance policy—something quite different from verification. According to Dr. John Lenczowski ("Dissent on INF Pact.," *Washington Times* 23 May 1988, page E1), former director of European and Soviet Affairs at the National Security Council, the Soviet Union has "violated or circumvented every agreement to date" with the exception of the atmospheric test ban. Moreover, even though President Reagan has publicly declared that the United States would "accept nothing less" than full compliance, he has in fact had no compliance to accept.

Dr. Lenczowski, who served during the Reagan administration, said: "Not only has the administration failed to undertake proportional responses to violations, but it has failed to develop any disincentives to deter future violations. The result is that the Soviets have nothing but *incentives* to cheat" (Ibid.).

Dr. Lenczowski opposed ratification of the INF treaty that was finally signed in Moscow by Reagan and Gorbachev until, he said, "a compliance policy is developed, funded and implemented" (Ibid.). He called for an Arms Control Insurance Fund with prepaid contingency responses to violations.

President Reagan, who was so enthusiastic about Gorbachev's good intentions, nevertheless submitted to Congress as one of his last official acts as president a full accounting of "Soviet noncompliance with arms control agreements." Such an annual report (this was the seventh) is required by law.

Continuing Soviet Violations

Despite his upbeat view of Gorbachev, President Reagan said in one of his last outgoing official statements that "when taken as a whole, this series of reports provides a clear picture of continuing Soviet violations" ("New Report Documents Soviet Arms Violations," *Human Events* 7 January 1989, page 8). There was a continuity to this 1988 presidential finding. His 1985 report to Congress had charged the Soviet Union with violating "its legal obligations under, or political commitment to, the SALT I ABM Treaty and Interim Agreement, the SALT II agreement, the Limited Test Ban Treaty of 19 Anticipating Critics, the Biological and Toxic Weapons Convention, the Geneva Protocol on Chemical Weapons, and the Helsinki Final Act. In addition, the Soviet Union has likely violated provisions of the Threshold Test Ban Treaty" (Ibid.).

The president said that the Soviet Union had corrected some of the violations, but only after the United States had objected, and, he added, other violations "are in the process of resolution" (Ibid.). But how meaningful can such agreements be if the U.S. government knows that its treaty partner is dedicated to violating agreements whenever possible?

Resolutions Ignored

The questions that the United States government refuses to answer—at least publicly, thereby putting freedom at permanent risk are:

1. Can treaties with a superpower hoping to fulfill its self-defined Marxist-Leninist destiny have any meaning?
2. What has been the history of Soviet treaty diplomacy?
3. What is the purpose of Soviet treaty diplomacy?
4. What value has a treaty with the Soviet Union without self-enforcing provisions against violations?

Professors Triska and Slusser (1962, 397, 392, 391) formulated the overriding, cardinal question: "[C]an the Soviet leaders be trusted to honor the commitments they voluntarily assume in international treaties?"

The answers to such questions may lead to policy answers. The answers may also help to explain how an economic and industrial cripple like the Soviet Union has in seventy years amplified its power, its influence, and its territory to a degree unprecedented in modern history. And how a party-government whose leadership killed its fellow citizens by the tens of millions and whose purges affected one in every three Soviet families still rules with little threat to its endurance.

Anticipating Critics

This is as good a place as any to anticipate those critics who will say that all I've accomplished with my many quotations from authoritative Soviet spokesmen, from the time of Lenin on, is to demonstrate that I have read Lenin and his epigones. Yet what else except examination of the canonical writings is there to go on in analyzing Soviet history and politics? Intuition? Warm handshakes with Kremlin inhabitants? Ballerina exchanges? Signatures on treaties?

If it is argued that what Stalin or Lenin said is dated, why isn't what Jefferson, Hamilton, or Madison said also dated? There are seminal, leading ideas that are fundamental to any society, polity, state, or party. The ideas of Tocqueville or Burke still retain their validity. We still debate Aristotle, Hegel, Plato. Why can't communism's patristic writings have a similar validity for Gorbachev today?

In his funeral oration over Lenin's tomb, Stalin said:

> Lenin never regarded the Republic of Soviets as an end in itself. He always looked on it as an essential link for strengthening the revolutionary movement in the countries of the west and the east, an essential link for facilitating the victory of the working class of the whole world over capitalism. Lenin knew that this was the only right conception, both from the international standpoint and from the standpoint of preserving the Republic of Soviets itself. (Voslensky 1984, 325; Stalin n.d. 6:12)

What do we do? Laugh it off and say along with the the Gorbachev upbeaters, paraphrasing Molière's *médecin*, "Gorbachev has changed all that"? How is one to judge Soviet foreign policy or, more exactly, the coherence of Soviet foreign policy and its pursuit of what can be called absolute security? There are certain data upon which one's research and conclusions depend: (1) the spoken or written words of Soviet actors; (2) officially adopted policies and programs; (3) the actual, describable Soviet conduct of foreign relations; and (4) the accumulated knowledge in the West about the Soviet Union, especially quantitative data (Volten 1982, 15).

Certain Presuppositions

But it cannot be denied that the analyst begins with certain presuppositions, just as I have done in referring to the Soviet Union's quest for absolute security. By establishing relationships or linkages among these data, especially their ordering, it then becomes possible not only to analyze the present direction of Soviet foreign policy and treaty diplomacy—the Soviets' own goals and intentions toward adversaries—but even to predict their future direction.

Some will argue that it isn't fair or particularly relevant or useful to quote articles in the *Great Soviet Encyclopedia* written twenty years ago—B.G.E. (Before the Gorbachev Era). Yet, as I will try to show in my chapter on the "Brezhnev Doctrine," Marxism-Leninism has certainly been the backbone of Soviet treaty diplomacy. It is the theoretical underpinning for delegitimizing "bourgeois diplomacy," for trampling on the sovereign rights of nonsocialist countries like Afghanistan. It has meant the sanctification of Soviet treaty diplomacy and, therefore, of Soviet foreign and military policy. The uses of Marxism-Leninism are many and the inevitable concomitant of a worldwide strategy. The official *Great Soviet Encyclopedia* says under "Diplomacy":

> The program of the Communist Party of the Soviet Union emphasizes that the CPSU considers the main goal of its activity in the area of foreign policy to be ensuring peaceful conditions for building a communist society in the Soviet Union. (*Great Soviet Encyclopedia* 1975, 8:277ff.)

Even Soviet academic studies of international relations show or emphasize the importance of ideology—specifically, the emphasis on the illegitimacy of noncommunist systems of governance. As Allen Lynch (1987, 147) has written, the Soviet theory of international relations urges Soviet citizens to seek "ways of bringing about its [the capitalist system] demise, so long as this does not threaten the hard-won achievements of socialism."

Professor J. David Gillepsie, who reviewed Lynch's book, wrote that "Soviet international relations theory, divested of orthodoxy, has moved in the direction of theory in the West. But in this normative sense, it remains distinctly Leninist, and full convergence is most unlikely in the foreseeable future" (*American Political Science Review* 82[3] [Summer 1988], page 1042).

It seems to me to be perfectly sensible and prudential, until such time as there is hard evidence to the contrary, to assume that authoritative Soviet spokesmen, whether vintage 1918 or 1990, are to be regarded as authoritative. Open repudiation by the Soviets of Leninist dogmas openly implemented by Gorbachev and his successors is the only way I know of judging whether fundamental change in the Soviet system has occurred. Those analysts who would not have accepted a weather prediction by President Reagan without careful checking and documentation should at least apply a similar standard to Mikhail Gorbachev's *coup de théatre* pronouncements.

4

What's a Little Ideology Among Friends?

I never thought we could make peace with the system; because it was not for the sake of an object we pursued in rivalry with each other but with the system itself that we were at war. As I understood the matter, we were at war not with its conduct but with its existence; convinced that its existence and its hostility were the same.

Edmund Burke (1867, 2:343)

Burke's words describe the irreconcilability of Britain's constitutional system with the French Revolution. It is probably the first contemporary statement of the dangers to peace and freedom of a unique transcendental faith, promulgated by utopians with gun and guillotine, by those who insist upon its universal application in order to perfect the human condition (Burke 1960, 480).

Ideology, a serious and weighty factor in U.S.-Soviet relations, is frequently disregarded by Western policy makers. Yet there is no understanding Soviet treaty diplomacy without understanding the ideology behind it.[54]

The insistence is widespread, especially among foreign policy publicists and many Sovietologists, that when Soviet leaders nowadays quote the

---

54 Kenneth Minogue (1985, 128) defines ideology as "a doctrine whose special claim upon the attention of its believers rests much less upon its supposedly scientific or philosophical character than upon the fact that it is a revelation."

trinity—Marx, Engels, and Lenin—it is all strictly for home consumption; they don't really believe in it anymore. Therefore, it is argued, for a Western analyst to cite what Lenin said, or what Gorbachev said Lenin said, is really not only meaningless but seriously misleading—that is, if we are to understand the sources of Soviet conduct or the aims of Soviet foreign policy.

Somehow, it is regarded in some quarters as "Cold War" propaganda to cite some awful revelational passage in Lenin when Gorbachev is trying so hard to de-Stalinize the Soviet Union. Gorbachev's efforts are much like the *soi disant* purifying argument among Soviet apologists that Stalin and Stalinism were an aberration from Lenin and Leninism—nothing more than a problem called the "cult of personality."

But the new breed of Soviet publicists, the Gorbachev *arrivistes*, concede that the Soviet Union B.G.E. (Before the Gorbachev Era) was "often blinded to the realities of international relations by its own ideology ... and as a result acted in ways that heightened or prolonged tension with the West" ("Soviets Admit Foreign Policy, Defense Errors," *Los Angeles Times* 26 June 1988, Part 1, page 8).[55] Said Yuli M. Vorontsov, first deputy Soviet foreign minister:

> In diplomacy we allowed ourselves to be carried away by polemics. We placed a high value on scoring polemical propaganda points, and often the propaganda stood in the way of real work. (Ibid.)

Repudiated Conventional Wisdom

In 1977, the historian Professor Richard Pipes, of Harvard University, wrote an article titled "Why the Soviet Union thinks it could fight and win a nuclear war" (*Commentary* 64[1] [July 1977], pages 21-34). He was sharply attacked because his view flew in the face of the widely held belief among liberals in Congress, the media, and the scientific academy that the MAD (Mutually Assured Destruction) Doctrine precluded any nuclear attack on the United States by the Soviet Union. But his thesis was confirmed eleven years later by a leading Soviet spokesman, Vadim V. Zagladin, thereby effectively repudiating the conventional wisdom of the liberal left. Pipes based his article on Soviet military literature and its supporting ideology. (I deal with this Soviet revelation in chapter 9.)

---

55   This statement was made at a press conference on the eve of the Communist Party's special conference that began 28 June 1988.

Alexander Solzhenitsyn, for his part, has argued that there has been no "end of ideology" in the Soviet Union. In a 1975 BBC interview he said:

> Today the leaders of the Soviet Union may not seem to attach so much importance to ideology. They may appear to be thinking only of power. But ideology directs all their actions, it compels them to try to expand their influence against all reason and necessity. (Solzhenitsyn 1975, 3)

"Ideologically Driven"

"Soviet actions—various Russian traditions and state interests apart—are ideologically driven," writes Zdzislaw M. Ruarz, a thirty-six-year veteran of the communist movement. A former Polish ambassador, Dr. Ruarz (1988, 97) says:

> Having embraced Leninism as gospel, the Soviets genuinely believe that this ideology can explain anything happening in the world and can even predict the future.... It is wrong to dismiss their frequent quotations of Lenin as mere rhetoric. Any such quotations ... should be taken most seriously. At the same time, the importance of Soviet political considerations should not be underestimated as they may outweigh even Lenin's teachings.

Those who minimize ideology as a crucial factor in Soviet policy making ignore its function: a method of control arising from two precepts. The first is "proletarian internationalism," which means everything must be subordinated to the interests of the Soviet Union;[56] it stands in contrast to "bourgeois nationalism." Mikhail Gorbachev has said that "Never is the importance of proletarian internationalism greater than it is today" (*Pravda,* 9 September 1984, page 1).

The second precept asserts the inalienable right of the party to rule—a right that can only come out of ideology ("The Eagle and the Small Birds," *Encounter* 358 [September-October 1983], page 23). Marxism may be a corpse, but the ideology which justifies party rule is the exclusive property of the Soviet Communist Party. The ideology is essential because, adapting Max Weber's typology, the Soviet Union has no other legitimacy, either through

---

56 In Stalin's view, "A revolutionary is he who without arguments, unconditionally, openly and honestly ... is ready to defend and strengthen the USSR, since the USSR is the first proletarian, revolutionary state in the world.... An internationalist is he who, without reservation, without hesitation, unconditionally is ready to defend the USSR because the USSR is the base of the world revolutionary movement, and this revolutionary movement cannot be defended and promoted unless the USSR is defended" (Stalin 1954, 10:61).

traditionalism, or democratic elections, or through some kind of charismatic authority.

Alain Besançon, the French historian of Bolshevism, has argued that Gorbachev's book *Perestroika* demonstrates that he has "preserved intact the Leninist vision" ("Gorbachev Without Illusions," *Commentary* 85[4] [April 1988], page 54).

Joseph L. Nogee and Robert H. Donaldson have provided us with a view of the function of Marxism-Leninism at a time when its tenets never seemed more pointless:

> Communism may not be a guide to Soviet behavior, but it is a creed that continues to infuse Soviet policy with dynamism. It identifies a cause, defines the enemy, and inspires the faith. Without an enemy and a cause, there would be no justification for a Soviet claim to world leadership. Without the doctrine there would be no basis for the dictatorship of the Communist party internally. Indeed, the whole logic of domestic repression is based upon a foreign threat. Thus, the very nature of the Soviet system sets limits on how far détente can go. ("World War I, World War II, WW III," *Commentary* 83[3] [March 1987], page 36)

A Maquillage?

Now, if Leninist ideology is only a form of maquillage to Gorbachev's apologists in the West, and if Lenin's writings are not to be interpreted as an essential part of Soviet praxis, and if Soviet foreign policy is not based on Leninist ideology, what *is* it based on? Traditional czarist imperialism? Perverted Tolstoyan pacifism? Caesaro-papism? Security needs, however defined? Russian nationalism?

If Marxism-Leninism is a trivial variable in Soviet decision making, then why do Soviet leaders *always* refer to Marxism-Leninism in their pronouncements? A legitimizing principle? Hasn't Marxism-Leninism justified party control of everything in the Soviet Union and in those East European lands coterminous with the Soviet Union? What else, if not this paranoid allegiance to ideology, can explain more than seventy years of mismanagement of the Soviet economy? And if Marxism-Leninism successfully legitimizes the party monopoly of power, isn't Marxism-Leninism then an important factor in comprehending Soviet thought and behavior? All one need do to understand the importance of Leninism to Gorbachev is to read the speech he delivered 19 April 1990 on the 120th anniversary of Lenin's birth. Quite clearly, Gorbachev was not planning a retreat from Leninism.

When *Izvestia* (11 October 1987) enumerates the official party slogans on the seventieth anniversary of the Russian Revolution—"Proletarians of the world, unite!", "Warm greetings to the communist and workers' parties!" or "Fiery greetings to the fighters against imperialist exploitation, oppression, and neocolonialism for freedom and independence"—are these slogans to be interpreted as party policy or written off as the usual propaganda fluff and not taken seriously? The first issue of *Kommunist*, the Soviet Communist Party theoretical journal, wrote: "The organizational principles of the political system fixed in the Soviet constitution retain their importance, the Marxist-Leninist ideology remains dominant." More propaganda fluff? Lip service to passé ideals?

Henry Kissinger (1969, 34) has written: "Whatever the ideological commitment of individual leaders, a lifetime spent in the Communist hierarchy must influence their basic categories of thought—especially since Communist ideology continues to perform important functions."

A Test of Soviet Intentions

I want to offer a test of Soviet intentions in these days of *glastroika*: There are some eighty Communist Parties in the noncommunist world. Of this total, twenty-two are in the Pacific area, twenty-five in the Americas, eleven in Africa and twenty-two in Western Europe. But in virtually every country of the noncommunist world, there are also Labor, Socialist, or Social Democratic Parties. Either they are ruling parties—as in Sweden, Norway, or Australia—or they are members of a ruling coalition, or they are the opposition party. Such parties are normally supported by the votes of the working classes and frequently middle-class intellectuals—what Communist Parties regard as their natural constituency.

Certainly nobody in his right mind, including the leadership of Western Communist Parties, would dare peddle the Soviet system—now in a terminal phase—in any West European country. The Soviet system has been mortally wounded in Eastern Europe. A Communist Party power monopoly in any country west of the Iron Curtain could not be achieved in any democratic election, as we saw in Nicaragua in February 1990; nor, without electoral fraud, could such a monopoly be achieved in Hungary or Poland. In fact, no Communist Party has ever come to power through an election. And where they were in power—however shakily, as in Eastern Europe—it is because of Soviet Red Army garrisons permanently stationed in supposedly sovereign countries. In political terms, international Kremlin-controlled communism has been a failure.

Even Soviet spokesmen concede that Communist Parties outside the Soviet bloc are a failure. Wrote Alexander Bovin in the 11 July 1987 issue of *Izvestia* :

Both in capitalist countries and in Third World countries, the Communist Parties, with few exceptions, have failed to become mass organizations, to win for themselves the support of the bulk of the working class, of the toilers. (*Radio Liberty* 292/87 [29 July 1987])

West European trade unions want no part of communism or its parties. Some left-liberal intellectuals or Marxist academics might, perhaps, have some umbilical affinity to Marxism-Leninism, but they are a disappearing lot, especially in France. There are some exceptions, of course. In the United States, there are a few coelacanths like the Harvard historian Professor John Womack, who is proud of being a communist, or Angela Davis, whose *glasnost* impels her to broadcast from the Soviet Union that there are no civil liberties in the United States. There are even a couple of dozen in the U.S. House of Representatives. In Western Europe, there are two large Communist Parties—one in France, the other in Italy—and some Communist Party legislators.

Why Communist Parties Today?

In view of the inarguable failure of communism and its leading practitioners—the Soviet Union and Communist China—what possible reason can there be for the existence of Communist Parties in, say, Western Europe, where the sun of economic prosperity and political stability has never shone more brightly?

In the 1970s, there was an ideological flurry in Western Europe over something called "Eurocommunism." It was an attempt by the Communist parties of the southern tier—Greece, Italy, France, Spain, and Portugal—to improve their ebbing fortunes by allegedly distancing themselves from the Kremlin, becoming "westernized." Looking back, it can be said that the decline of the communist movement began with the March 1977 "Eurocommunist" meeting in Madrid that was attended by the Communist Party leadership in Italy, France, and Spain. The meeting was a flop because nobody, especially Moscow, accepted the reality of "Eurocommunism." This was the era during which Marxism transformed itself from corpus to corpse.

Now, if the present Communist Party leadership in Western Europe no longer openly preaches class warfare or seizure of the state by revolution and subversion, and if after five summit meetings it dutifully cheers the "era of good feeling" between Presidents Reagan and Gorbachev, what do these parties stand for? If they no longer denounce democratic socialists as renegades, and if they treat social democrats with a modicum of respect, what remains of communism's ideological message? And if there isn't a country in the world today which can be labeled "fascist," and if capitalism and the free market can no longer be attacked with any credibility, what purpose do communists serve? In the light of all the talk about the "new thinking" in the era of Gorbachev the Good, these are important questions.

To a skeptic like me, who stubbornly discounts the possibility of fundamental change in the Soviet system, the answer is that Communist Parties exist, primarily, to enhance, as they always have, Soviet foreign policy either by propaganda through Kremlin-controlled and Kremlin-funded front groups, like the World Peace Council, or through agents of influence in the Western world of banking, labor, the media, science, and industry. By making Soviet foreign policy more acceptable, they weaken and divide Western foreign policies. The purpose of Soviet foreign policy is to weaken and eventually triumph over capitalism.[57]

The Secret Battalions

For international communism, the Soviet Union and its policies are, in the end, always right. Even when Communist Parties ritualistically criticize such Soviet actions as the 1968 intervention into Czechoslovakia or the 1979 invasion of Afghanistan, "reconciliation" with Moscow inevitably follows. And, of course, Communist Parties are also recruiting agencies for the secret battalions of Soviet intelligence.

The Soviet Union is not and never has been a state in the ordinary definition. Whatever the so-called "new thinking" may be, the Soviet Union also represents a self-defined movement, a self-defined force marching with history on the road to a classless society. Special departments within the Central Committee of the Soviet Communist Party are entrusted with the work of promoting "proletarian internationalism" among nonruling Communist Parties—that is, to ensure their acceptance of Soviet discipline over international communism. Another department supervises East European Communist Parties and yet another department exists for the purpose of promoting Soviet foreign policy initiatives. These activities have not been perestroiked out of existence. They function on a daily basis to weaken the Free Market Democracies and the capitalist system.

A testing ground for Gorbachev the Good is in the continued existence of eighty Communist Parties and myriads of Communist fronts, controlled in greater or lesser degree from the Kremlin. A little *perestroika* on the international front might help Gorbachev's credibility. (A commentary on the

---

57 George Kennan (1966, 74-75) says that "Moscow desires to retain them [Communist Parties] as instruments. It wants to use them for the reduction of competing political strength, for the sowing of discord and distrust among other countries, for the weakening of political and military potential elsewhere, for the sabotaging of resistance to the Kremlin's own foreign policies."

viability of the Gorbachev reform program is the current Moscow pun that *perestroika* will be followed by *perestrelka*, a shootout.)

A Driving Ideology

It is a fact of political life that we ascribe the national policies of most countries to a driving ideology, religious belief, or ethos, as in the Moslem fundamentalism of the Ayatollah Khomeini, the conservatism of President Reagan and Margaret Thatcher, the Catholicism of Pope John Paul, the emperor worship of the Japanese, or the social democracy of Scandinavia. Only Gorbachev, to his admirers in the West, seems to be free of impediments such as ideology. He cites Lenin; he doesn't mean it. He's forced to call himself a Marxist-Leninist; it's just rhetoric.

If ideology has no meaning in the Soviet Union, why is Marxism-Leninism taught as a compulsory subject in all Soviet schools, from first grade to postgraduate classes? The importance of Marxism-Leninism in Soviet rulership was described in 1983—true, before Gorbachev took power—by Roy Medvedev (1983, 62) in these words:

> No one can hold an important post in any social or state organization if he does not adhere to the Party ideology of Marxism-Leninism. The foundations of Marxism-Leninism are taught in all schools and institutions of further education, regardless of their type. No higher degree, be it in physics, mathematics, astronomy, literature or law, is awarded before the candidate has sat a preliminary exam in Marxist philosophy.

In 1984, a school law was introduced that contained this strategic goal: "The unchanging foundation of the Communist upbringing of pupils is the development in them of a Marxist-Leninist outlook on the world" (Heller 1988, 162-67). It also called for "military-patriotic training of the pupils ... for service in the armed forces of the Soviet Union, teaching them to love the Soviet Army, and the development in them of a strong sense of pride in belonging to a socialist society...." (Ibid.).

Marxism-Leninism is most assuredly a major subject of study in the Soviet military establishment. As Jan Triska has written: "The Soviet system by its very nature attempts to secure the universality of its absolutes, as stipulated by Soviet ideology" ("A Model for Study of Soviet Foreign Policy," *American Political Science Review* LII [March 1958], page 70). This was written more than three decades ago. Despite all the protestations of Gorbachev's friends in the West, I think Triska's words may well have been carved in stone.

Ideological Basis

General William E. Odom[58] argues that the "ideological basis for Soviet military needs cannot be discounted lightly (because) a body of Marxist-Leninist thought about military science and doctrine has been articulated and imbued in both the officers corps and the party leadership...." ("Soviet Military Doctrine," *Foreign Affairs* 67[2] [Winter 1988], page 116).

Even more important, the question of ideology in Soviet treaty diplomacy must always be kept in mind, because one of the basic tenets of Marxism-Leninism is that war is the result of the existence of private property that divides men into classes: the exploiters and the exploited. So long as the capitalist class exists, and so long as it owns not only the means of production but also the means of making war, the "objective conditions" for peace are nonexistent. War becomes inevitable. As General Odom has put it:

> True peace can come only with the demise of capitalism. Thus the task of the Soviet military and all "peace-loving forces" is to ensure such an overwhelming correlation of forces in favor of the socialist camp that the class struggle can be pursued successfully—preferably without resort to war, especially nuclear war, but with the victory of socialism in any event. (Ibid.)

The argument will be made that all this was said before Gorbachev's reforms began in earnest. The answer lies in the words of Gorbachev himself. To the question—If the Soviet Union must join with imperialism to help prevent war, what happens to Lenin's "international class struggle" doctrine?—Gorbachev (1987, 144-48) has this to say:

> Does this imply that we have given up the class analysis of the causes of the nuclear threat and of other global problems? No. It would be wrong to ignore the class heterogeneity of the forces acting in the international arena or to overlook the influence of class antagonism on international affairs and on the approaches to the accomplishment of all other tasks of mankind.

If Not Marxism-Leninism, What Then?

Well, if not Marxism-Leninism, what does explain Soviet support of Castro, however lukewarm it may appear, and the Angolan communists, the "wars of national liberation" (as in Afghanistan), the Soviet destruction of the

---

58 Lieutenant-General Odom, U.S. Army (ret.), was the director of the National Security Agency from 1985 to 1988.

Korean airliner in 1983, the support for Jaruzelski's suppression of Solidarity, the crushing of Czechoslovakia's 1968 Spring, the perversion of psychiatry and pharmacology, and the unwillingness to share *ultimate* power with other groups in a party-controlled society?

Those who reject the ideological component in Soviet treaty diplomacy should be faced with these questions:

- If the Soviet Union were not a Marxist-Leninist political system, would the United States be negotiating differently with President Gorbachev? If yes, how?
- Is negotiating with Britain and France different from negotiating with the Soviet Union? If yes, what makes the difference? All these countries have nuclear weapons.
- Why do the Western countries arm and against whom? Does not the essential fact that the West must continually upgrade its weaponry, competing in quality as well as quantity, distort negotiations with the Soviet Union because the essential element of mutual trust is zero?

A Successful Strategy

We are again witnessing a successful communist strategy exploiting the West's will-to-believe: using personality to overwhelm and replace history not only in the Western media but also even among sober academic analysts.

A recent beneficiary of this will-to-believe in the virtues of Soviet leaders was Yuri V. Andropov, and before him, of course, Josef Stalin ("The Andropov Hoax: The Americanization of Yuri," *The New Republic* 7 February 1983, pages 18-21). Ignored was Andropov's *cri de coeur,* uttered during his 23 April 1982 Lenin Day speech: "The name of Leonid Ilyich Brezhnev is linked ... to the triumph of the magnificent cause: the victory of communism throughout the world.".[59]

Today's Western pro-Soviet choristers hold that it is not the system that is bad but a sociopath named Stalin. Peculiarly, these apologists for the Soviet Union never apply a similar sociological standard of the personality variable in analyzing the capitalist system. It is the capitalist system, per se, that is rotten whether saint or sinner is at the helm.

Seweryn Bialer, a onetime high communist official in Poland and now at Columbia University, credits Marxism-Leninism with motivating Soviet leaders because "if they were simply cynics they could be bought off by their

---

59   Seven months after these words, Andropov succeeded Brezhnev as Party General Secretary to the thunderous acclaim of Western publicists.

wealthier adversaries" (Bialer 1986, 349). Not even the severest critics of the Soviet Union have accused Gorbachev and Company of maintaining secret Swiss bank accounts.[60]

Congressional Support for Communist Dictators

It is certainly ideology that explains the support in the U.S. Congress for communist dictatorships and the opposition to noncommunist juntas—an indulgence toward an infinitude of Soviet human rights transgressions and stern, unforgiving moralizing about South African apartheid. After all, there was little support in Congress for Pinochet's Chile, for Angola's Savimbi, or for struggling El Salvador. For representatives like then House Speaker Jim Wright, Ron Dellums, and George Crockett, and for senators like Christopher Dodd, totalitarians like Fidel Castro are admirable, but a General Pinochet is beyond the pale. These congressmen and their allies in and out of Congress have embraced a left-liberal pro-Soviet ideology regardless of its malignant influence on American security. Such an indulgence is what has been called "ideological thinking." [61]

For such men who live by a double standard—one that consistently favors Soviet foreign policy and Marxism-Leninism and as consistently abuses rightist regimes—George Orwell's (1965, 178) point about the intelligentsia applies:

> There is no crime, absolutely none, that cannot be condoned when "our" side commits it. Even if one does not deny that the crime has happened, even if one knows that it is exactly the same crime one has condemned in some other case,

---

60 "What can you tell us about the fact that Comrade Gorbachev is building a dacha in the Crimea and is receiving honoraria for his books in Switzerland?" That startling question was addressed to Boris Yeltsin, ousted Politburo member, when he spoke on 20 November 1988 at the Higher Komsomol School. Yeltsin replied: "The dacha has been built. And there were hardly sufficient personal funds for its construction. Concerning the honoraria, I will not elaborate" (*Russkaya mysl* 6 January 1989, page 8). It may be, after all, that Gorbachev has a Swiss bank account. The report of the speech appeared in the dissident Moscow journal, *Glasnost*, and was reprinted in the Paris-based Russian language émigré publication, *Russkaya mysl'*. It was brought to my attention by Dr. John R. Dunlop at the Hoover Institution.

61 Karl Mannheim (1936, 50) defined ideological thinking thus: "The ideas expressed by the subject are thus regarded as functions of his existence. This means that opinions, statements, propositions, and systems of ideas are not taken at their face value but are interpreted in the light of the life situation of the one who expresses them."

even if one admits in an intellectual sense that it is unjustified—still one cannot feel that it is wrong. Loyalty is involved, and so pity ceases to function.

Dangerous Illusions

The late Leonard Schapiro, one of the giants in the field of Soviet studies (along with the late Philip Mosely and Merle Fainsod), wrote that the illusion that:

> at bottom the Soviet Union is reasonable and basically motivated by the same aims as Western nations—such as security, extension of its influence, trade and cooperation—has at times influenced U.S. or British policy. It is, I believe, the most dangerous illusion that Western statesmen can suffer and is caused by ignorance of Soviet history,[62] by the failure to attach any importance to Soviet party literature and *by an underestimation of the influence of ideology on Soviet aims* [my emphasis]. Washington Times 30 April 1987, page E6).

Not to understand the self-declared enemy is to lose sight of the reality and purpose of totalitarian militarism. The words of Neville Chamberlain (Colvin 1971, 173) on 31 October 1938 became the unwritten epitaph on the tombstones of tens of millions of people during the following seven years: "Our foreign policy is one of appeasement. We must aim at establishing relations with the Dictator Powers which will lead to a European settlement and a sense of stability."

Yearning to Appease

This yearning to appease applied earlier to arms control. In 1936, a new Italian cruiser, the *Gorizia*, was found to have breached agreed-upon cruiser weight limits by 10 percent. The Chamberlain government overlooked Mussolini's noncompliance in the hope that eventually he would stick by the 1936 London Naval Treaty (Wallop & Codevilla 1987, 41).

It should not be forgotten that the Western world, except for Czechoslovakia, cheered Chamberlain and the other Munich men upon their

---

62 Ignorance of Soviet history was never more apparent than during the Washington summit in December 1987. In remarks to the press corps, Gorbachev said that "the American and the Soviet people elected their respective governments," the Soviet people in October 1917 (*Washington Times* 4 July 1988, page E7). Not a single reporter or television commentator knew enough about Soviet history to refute his statement. In fact, the Bolsheviks were defeated in the 1917 election, the first and last popular election in Russian history. Having lost the balloting, they seized the government with machine guns.

return home. Those who uttered warnings that Hitler's treaties, and particularly the Anglo-German Pact of Friendship, were meaningless were looked upon as warmongers.

It is astonishing that so much of what the Bolshevik leaders have described as their hopes have become the present reality. For example, a year or so before the 1917 Bolshevik seizure of power, Lenin published *State and Revolution*. In it, he wrote that he hoped to see the day when:

> the majority of the people will exercise ... control over the capitalists and the intellectual gentry, who still retain capitalistic habits. This control will really become universal, general, national; and there will be no way of getting away from it: there will be nowhere to go. The whole of society will have become one office, and one factory, with equal work and equal pay. ("Marxism-Leninism—and After," *Soviet Analyst* 16[16] [19 August 1987], page 4)

With the exception of the last six words, Lenin's nightmarish dream is the Soviet Union today, even under the ineffable Gorbachev. Then as now there is little discrepancy between Soviet rhetoric and Soviet deed. There is a noteworthy consistency of Soviet views on almost every major aspect of foreign policy. People who believe there are "hawks" and "doves" in the Kremlin probably also believe in the Tooth Fairy.

Soviet Ideological Commitment

In foreign policy decision making vis-à-vis the Soviet Union, it is always dangerous to ignore or to underestimate what has been called "the significance of the Soviet ideological commitment" ("The Soviet Decision for war against Finland, November 1939: A Comment," *Soviet Studies* XXXIV[34] [April 1987], page 314). Dr. Hannes Adomeit, in a scholarly study of Soviet foreign and military policies since World War II, has asked a question whose answer should provide the basis for a realistic foreign policy for the democratic powers. Asks Adomeit (1982, 3):

> Has Soviet ideology been eroded to such an extent that it has ceased to be a factor of any consequence? Or have objective requirements of crisis behavior consistently relegated ideological considerations to a place of lesser importance?

Dr. Adomeit's answer (Ibid., 121):

> Soviet foreign policy has not been that of a traditional nation state; it has always been characterized by a mixture of national *and* ideological elements.

Marx's First Principle

How could Soviet treaty diplomacy be that of a traditional nation-state when the Soviet leadership is informed by Karl Marx's thunderous first principle that:

> The Communists ... openly declare that their ends can be attained only by the forcible overthrow of all existing conditions. Let the ruling classes tremble at a communistic revolution. (Marx & Engels 1967, 120)

In a book cited earlier, Messrs. Bauer, Inkeles, and Kluckhohn[63] (1956, 211) write:

> Correct interpretation of Soviet behavior, adequate assessment of their intentions, or accurate prediction of their probable behavior cannot be made without weighing the role of ideological factors together with "objective conditions" as an influence on the actions of the leaders.

The tragedy of the West is that its leaders steadfastly decline to learn from the writings and actions of Soviet leaders—from Lenin to Stalin to Gorbachev—the meaning of communism, its strategy, its tactics, and its ultimate aims. A sophisticated politician may understand that he may be living in a Hobbesian universe. Yet when it comes to the Soviet Union he will behave, as Orwell described William Butler Yeats in another context, in the manner of the "natural born innocent."

Obsessed by Communism?

An integral part of American sports culture is the vocation of "scout," the well-paid sports expert who spends his time in the stands studying the on field behavior of opposing baseball or football teams so as better to prepare his home team for future confrontations. Yet in Washington, to insist that a statesman ought to know everything about his opponent, especially the ideology by which the opponent operates his actions, is regarded as being obsessed by communism. In the absence of such "scouting," Western

---

63   The same authors also write that Soviet ideology "is an amalgam of formal and openly expressed principles, informal and covertly held ideas which are nevertheless consciously shared by the elite, principles of action which are merely implicit and often not consciously formulated by the leadership, and lessons learned from experience in the hard school of Soviet politics" (Bauer, Inkeles & Kluckhohn 1956, 211).

statesmen got into the habit of substituting, as Eric Hoffer once put it, mythology for history. It is astonishing to realize how little most Western statesmen and politicians know about the strategies of the Soviet Union for world conquest and the motor (Marxism-Leninism) that drives those strategies. As Richard Pipes has written, "Ignorance of Russia places Western statesmen at a great disadvantage vis-à-vis their Soviet counterparts, who, emerging from the background of an international revolutionary movement, have always had a keen interest in Western societies" ("Militarism and the Soviet State," *Daedalus* 109[4] [Fall 1980], page 2).

Alain Besançon argues that "most of communism's successes occur because the adversaries of communism are incapable of making a precise and realistic evaluation of it" (Besançon 1984, ix).

> If our statesmen are social democrats, they think that communism will evolve toward social democracy. If they are liberals, they predict a Soviet liberalization. If they are conservatives, they see, behind the Soviet Union, eternal Russia, a great power with its unalterable imperial goals and respectable interests. Policies formulated on such assumptions are all the falser for their appearance of being true. And these policies have consistently failed. (Ibid.)

What else but willful ignorance would account for the foolish White House statements about Stalin during World War II? Charles Bohlen, the distinguished U.S. diplomat and expert on the Soviet Union, wrote a sharp criticism of FDR at Yalta:

> I did not like the attitude of the president, who not only backed Stalin but seemed to enjoy the Churchill-Stalin exchanges. Roosevelt should have come to the defense of a close friend and ally, who was really being put upon by Stalin.... [Roosevelt's] apparent belief that ganging up on the Russians was to be avoided at all cost was, in my mind, a basic error, stemming from Roosevelt's lack of understanding of the Bolsheviks.... In his rather transparent attempt to dissociate himself from Churchill, the president was not fooling anybody and in all probability aroused the secret amusement of Stalin.[64] (Bohlen 1973, 146)

---

64 Far worse was Bohlen's further judgment of FDR: "As far as the Soviets were concerned, I do not think Roosevelt had any real comprehension of the great gulf that separated the thinking of a Bolshevik from a non-Bolshevik and particularly from an American. He felt that Stalin viewed the world somewhat in the same light as he did, and that Stalin's hostility and distrust, which were evident in wartime conferences, were due to the neglect that Soviet Russia had suffered at the hands of other countries for years after the Revolution. What he did not understand was that Stalin's enmity was based on profound ideological convictions. The existence of a gap between the Soviet Union and the United States, a gap that could not be bridged, was never fully perceived by Franklin Roosevelt" (Bohlen 1973, 211).

Harriman Also Critical

W. Averell Harriman, Roosevelt's ambassador to Stalin, was also critical of the president, describing him as a statesman who had "no conception of the determination of the Russians to settle matters in which they consider that they have a vital interest in their own manner, on their own terms.... The president still feels he can persuade Stalin to alter his point of view on many matters that, I am satisfied, Stalin will never agree to" (Harriman & Abel 1975, 369-70).

Had political leaders like President Roosevelt (who, at war's end, held the world in his hands) and his *eminence grise*, Harry Hopkins, understood Lenin's revolution, they would have understood Stalin's resolution (Demosthenes warned the Athenians that "close alliances with despots are never safe for free men" [Byrnes 1976, 86]). Thus, they would not have mindlessly miscalculated the imperialist treaty diplomacy of the Soviet Union, quondam ally of Nazi Germany, when Britain stood alone against the threat of Hitlerian conquest. Here, for example, are the words of Harry Hopkins after Yalta 1945:

> In our hearts we really believed a new day had dawned, the day we had for so many years longed for and about which we had talked so much. We were all convinced we had won the first great victory for peace, and when I say we, I mean all of us, all civilized mankind. The Russians had proved that they could be reasonable and far-sighted and neither the president nor any one of us had the slightest doubt that we could live with them and get on peaceably with them far into the future. I must, however, make one reservation—I believe that in our hearts we made the proviso that we couldn't foretell how things would turn out if something happened to Stalin. (Sherwood 1948, 870)

And listen to the words of FDR[65] himself talking about Stalin:

---

65   It is little known that FDR (or someone in the White House did it for him) accepted election as an "honorary member" into the communist-front League of American writers in 1938. He remained a member for two years, even after the signing of the Nazi-Soviet Pact. Sidney Hook learned about this "honorary" membership in 1940 and warned FDR that he ought publicly to disown the organization that like other communist organizations was busy denouncing the war against Hitler as "imperialist" (Beichman 1987, 18-19). The 1930s were an era that, as George Orwell pointed out in his essay on Arthur Koestler, intellectuals might be antifascist but not antitotalitarian. Even during the Nazi-Soviet Pact, there were "no enemies on the left."

I think that if I give him everything I possibly can without demanding anything in return, then *noblesse oblige*, he will not attempt to annex anything and will work to build a peaceful and democratic world.[66] (Iklé 1964, 89)

Impossible Solutions

FDR's words remind me of something Reinhold Niebuhr once described as "the strategy of fleeing from difficult problems by taking refuge in impossible solutions" (Gilmour 1971, xi). How could a political leader like Stalin with a record of blunder after blunder in foreign policy have left behind at his death in March 1953 a Russia which was militarily and diplomatically stronger than it had ever been?[67]

Professor Adam Ulam blames a good part of the success of Soviet foreign policy on the Roosevelt-Churchill diplomacy. They failed, he argues, to grasp the complexities of Soviet foreign policies and its messianic Leninist-Stalinist-czarist roots. There never would have been "mystery and awe" had our policy makers understood the man, the system, and pre-Bolshevik history (Ulam 1974,). [68]

---

66 President Roosevelt's prewar diplomacy was at a poorly planned level as well. His inauguration in 1933 occurred a few weeks after Adolf Hitler came to power. When FDR learned that Neville Chamberlain was heading off to Munich in 1938 for the sellout of Czechoslovakia, he cabled the British prime minister: "Good man" ("The Munich Men: How Chamberlain and Roosevelt Invited World War II," *Policy Review* 45 [Summer 1988], page 20). Professor Francis L. Loewenheim, a member of the Historical Division of the State Department in the Eisenhower administration, has disclosed that the supportive telegram was never delivered to Chamberlain by then U.S. Ambassador Joseph P. Kennedy, despite instructions ("Munich: What Remains To Be Said," *Washington Times* 30 September 1988, page F1).

67 Among Stalin's failures in foreign policy: involving the Soviet Union in the most calamitous war in its history; permitting a renascent Reichswehr after World War I to train on Russian soil for a decade so that when Hitler took power in 1933, he took possession of a ready-made instrument for military dominance; losing his Berlin blockade bluff to the United States; losing Yugoslavia as a Soviet satellite; wiping out the Red Army General Staff on the eve of World War II; and, preventing a "united front" between the German Socialists and the German Communist Party to defeat Hitler in the early 1930s.

68 By the time FDR realized he had failed at Yalta, it was too late to do anything about it. On 23 March 1945, nineteen days before he died, President Roosevelt confided to Anna Rosenberg, "Averell is right. We can't do business with Stalin. He has broken every one of the promises he made at Yalta" (Harriman & Abel 1975, 344). Thirty-five years later, President Carter publicly evidenced the same pained disillusion with the Soviet Union (see chapter 7).

Willful Blindness

Another example of willful blindness to Stalin's cruel dictatorship was in ignoring the implications of the following facts: 5.24 million Russian officers and men surrendered to the Germans, hundreds of thousands of Soviet subjects in military units were working—voluntarily—for the Nazis in 1943 and toward the end of the war more than a million men had been organized by former Red Army generals and staff officers into an anti-Stalin army—the Russian Liberation Army, or the Vlasov Army ("The Other Russian Army," *New York Review* 24 November 1988, page 7).[69]

President Truman must have forgotten the meaning of the Truman Doctrine ("to support free peoples who are resisting attempted subjugation by armed minorities or outside pressure") when, in 1949, he said:

> I like Stalin.... He is very fond of classical music.... I got the impression Stalin would stand by his agreements and also that he had a Politburo on his hands like the 80th Congress. (Taubman 1982, 100)

In his recently published private journals, however, President Truman wrote:

> [Stalin] broke twenty agreements he'd made with Roosevelt and he broke thirty-two with me. I don't know how you're going to be able to tell in advance that a man is going to make agreements and then break them; I guess you just can't....
>
> The trouble, of course, was that Russia didn't live up to the agreements but nobody could really have predicted that in advance. (Truman 1989, 368-69)

"Nobody could really have predicted that in advance"? Absurd. There were dozens of Soviet experts who, had he been willing to listen to them in and out of the State Department, could have enlightened him about Stalin as treaty breaker.

Another example of willful blindness was FDR's ambassador to Moscow—the egregious Joseph E. Davies. He even endorsed treason on behalf of the Soviet Union. In 1946, he was quoted by the *New York Times* as saying: "Russia in self-defense has every moral right to seek atomic-bomb secrets through military espionage if excluded from such information by her

---

69   In the first volume of *The Gulag Archipelago*, Alexander Solzhenitsyn described the Vlasov Army as signalling "a phenomenon totally unheard of in all world history: that several hundred thousand young men, aged twenty to thirty, took up arms against their Fatherland as allies of its most evil enemy" ("The Other Russian Army," *New York Review* 24 November 1988, page 7).

former fighting allies" ("Davies Says Soviet Has Rights to Spy," *New York Times* 19 February 1946, page 2).[70]
And in 1942, Ambassador Davies said:

> In my opinion the Russian people, the Soviet government and the Soviet leaders are moved basically by altruistic concepts. It is their purpose to promote the brotherhood of man and to improve the lot of the common people. They wish to create a society in which men may live as equals, governed by ethical ideals. They are devoted to peace. (Hudson 1967, 25-26)

Let me not in my condemnation of Rooseveltian autodidactism about Stalin ignore the fact that well-informed publicists also fell for the dictators. I am thinking of a Walter Lippmann column three months after the Nazis came to power. As his biographer writes, Lippmann was "[e]ager to believe that the dictator was now willing to moderate his revolutionary nationalism" (Steel 1980, 331, 416). Lippmann described a Hitler speech as a "gentlemanly statesmanlike address" that offered "evidence of good faith." Twelve years later, Lippmann hailed Yalta with the sentence, "There had been no more impressive international conference in our time, none in which great power was so clearly hardened to the vital, rather than the secondary, interests of nations" (Ibid., 416). John Foster Dulles, later President Eisenhower's secretary of state, greeted Yalta as opening a "new era" in which America "abandoned a form of aloofness which it has been practicing for many years and the Soviet Union permitted joint action on matters that it had the power to settle for itself." It was, indeed, the Age of Credulity. (Ibid., 331, 416)

Kissinger's Obtuseness

Probably one of the most egregious examples of obtuseness about Soviet communism came from Secretary of State Henry Kissinger himself. He successfully advised President Ford to bar Alexander Solzhenitsyn from the White House in 1975.[71] Kissinger with Brent Scowcroft, then as now the

---

70   Davies' memoirs of his diplomatic service were published as *Mission to Moscow*. In 1943, with President Roosevelt's encouragement, the book was made into a Warner Brothers Hollywood movie. The movie critic James Agee described the film as "the first Soviet production to come from a major American studio" ("The Cycles of Western Fantasy," *Encounter* 402 [February 1988], page 11; Snow 1958).

71   It will be recalled that Solzhenitsyn, having been charged by the Soviets with treason on 13 February 1974 and expelled from the Soviet Union with his family, eventually came to live in the United States. It should also be recalled that Solzhenitsyn was never invited to the White House either by Presidents Ford, Carter, or Reagan and at this writing by President Bush. (Nevertheless, with what

president's National Security Adviser, prepared a servile memorandum in June 1975 to warn President Ford against receiving Solzhenitsyn at the White House or from attending a dinner in Solzhenitsyn's honor tendered him by then AFL-CIO President George Meany. The memorandum said in part:

> The Soviets would probably take White House participation in this affair as either a deliberate negative signal or a sign of Administration weakness in the face of domestic anti-Soviet pressures. We recommend that the invitation to the president be declined and that no White House officials participate....
>
> During Solzhenitsyn's Washington visit another problem may arise: Pressure may be generated by Meany, members of Congress or others for the president to receive Solzhenitsyn in the White House. He is a Nobel Prize winner, he is widely admired in the United States and the Senate has passed a resolution granting him honorary United States citizenship (if the House follows suit he would be the only person except Churchill so honored).... The arguments against such a meeting are as compelling as those against accepting the banquet invitation, but more difficult to defend publicly. (Dunlop et al 1985, 28)

Sickening Servility

And then came these sickening sentences:

> Solzhenitsyn is a notable writer, but his political views are an embarrassment even to his fellow dissidents. Not only would a meeting with the president offend the Soviets but it would raise some controversy about Solzhenitsyn's views of the United States and its allies.... Further, Solzhenitsyn has never before been received by a Chief of State and such a meeting would lend weight to his political views as opposed to his literary talent. (Ibid.)

There is more of this prose that, when the memorandum leaked, impelled George Will to write in the *Washington Post*:

> The United States government may have to expel Alexander Solzhenitsyn from the republic, not only as a hands-across-the-barbed-wire gesture of solidarity with its

---

must have been unconscious irony, President Reagan quoted from the writings of Solzhenitsyn to Soviet audiences during the May 1988 summit in Moscow "Solzhenitsyn: Back in the Soviet Union," *Christian Science Monitor* 9 September 1988) While the Senate unanimously adopted a resolution conferring honorary U.S. citizenship on Solzhenitsyn, the House of Representatives, acting on the formal request of Kissinger's State Department, killed the resolution in the House Judiciary Committee, chaired to his everlasting shame by former Rep. Peter Rodino (Dunlop 1985, passim).

détente partner, the Soviet government, but also to save the president and his attendants from nervous breakdowns.... Détente has conferred upon Brezhnev a veto over the appointments calendar of the president of the the United States. (Ibid., 29; *Washington Post* 11 July 1975, Op-Ed page)

It should be added that in the era of the Bush-Reagan-Gorbachev détente, the Kissinger-Scowcroft policy over the president's appointments calendar was still in effect, at least where Solzhenitsyn was concerned.

What Eisenhower Didn't Know

According to the historian Paul Johnson (1983, 433), General Dwight D. Eisenhower, the supreme commander in 1944, "refused to accept the salient point that the degree to which his troops penetrated into Central Europe would in fact determine the postwar map." He quotes Eisenhower as saying: "I would be loath to hazard American lives for purely political purposes."[72]

John Colville, Churchill's private secretary during World War II, describes how when U.S. military forces were poised to seize Berlin, well before the Red Army, Eisenhower forbade his commanders to move. He told General Montgomery, "As far as I am concerned Berlin is nothing but a geographical expression" ("How the West Lost the Peace," *Commentary* 80[3] [September 1985], page 46).[73] As Robert Nisbet put it: "Berlin was a gift to Stalin by Eisenhower in the name of Franklin D. Roosevelt" ("Roosevelt and Stalin," *Modern Age* [Spring and Summer-Fall 1986], page 210).

Although Eisenhower ran for president in 1952 on a proposed U.S. foreign policy of rollback rather than containment of the Soviet Union, he ignored the uprising on 17 June 1953, in Soviet-occupied East Germany, the demonstrations by Polish workers in Poznan, and the climactic rebellion of Hungarians in October 1956. President Eisenhower abided by an unspoken understanding with the Soviet Union about spheres of influence in Europe.

---

72 During one of the toasts at the Teheran conference, Roosevelt said, looking at Churchill and Stalin, "I do not doubt that the three of us lead our people in accordance with their desires, in accordance with their aims" (Solzhenitsyn 1975, 4). FDR was saying this about a tyrant like Stalin who at the height of the 1937-38 terror had been shooting 40,000 persons a month!

73 When General Patton pressed Eisenhower to allow the Ninth Army, having crossed the Elbe, to move on Berlin, Eisenhower asked: "Who would want it?" Patton replied, "I think history will answer that question" ("How the West Lost the Peace," *Commentary* 80[3] [September 1985], page 46).

"The Greatest Foreign Policy Blunder"

Former President Nixon, writing in 1988, said that Eisenhower's "opposing British and French efforts to defend their interests in Suez was the greatest foreign-policy blunder the United States has made since the end of World War II." And, adds Nixon, "I have reason to believe that Eisenhower shared the assessment after he left office" (Nixon 1988, 205).

Years later (in 1945), Maxim Litvinov, Stalin's longtime foreign secretary, was quoted by Edgar Snow as saying privately: "Why did you Americans wait until now to begin opposing us in the Balkans and Eastern Europe? ... You should have done this three years ago. Now it's too late" ("The Cycles of Western Fantasy," *Encounter* 402 [February 1959], page 11 n. 17).

George Kennan, watching what was going on during and after the war, deplored "the inexcusable ignorance about the nature of Russian communism, about the history of its diplomacy" (Topitsch 1987, 129). He wrote at the time:[74]

> I mean by that F.D.R.'s well-known conviction that although Stalin was a rather difficult character, he was at bottom a man like everyone else; that the only reason why it had been difficult to get on with him in the past was because there was no one with the right personality, with enough imagination and trust to deal with him properly; that the arrogant conservatives in the Western capitals had always bluntly rejected him, and that his ideological prejudices would melt away and Russian cooperation with the West could easily be obtained, if only Stalin was exposed to the charm of a personality of F.D.R.'s caliber. There were no grounds at all for this assumption; it was so childish that it was really unworthy of a statesman of F.D.R.'s standing. (Ibid.)[75]

And Churchill, Too?

What could Winston Churchill have been thinking about when he said in the House of Commons on 27 February 1945: "I know of no government which stands to its obligations, even in its own despite, more solidly than the Russian Soviet government" (Triska & Slusser 1962, 392)? And after the Nazi attack on the Soviet Union, Churchill "ordered all anti-Soviet

---

74 Earlier, Kennan said that "FDR and others found charitable and comforting explanations for Soviet behavior" (Kennan 1966, 25). For a comprehensive analysis of the FDR-Stalin relationship, see Nisbet 1989 and "Roosevelt and Stalin," *Modern Age* Spring and Summer-Fall 1986.

75 The original of this quote is to be found in Kennan 1960, where the author's strongest criticism is directed at coalition or summit diplomacy. He rejects multilateral diplomacy and the idea of "negotiation with a single hostile political entity."

intelligence work to cease during the wartime alliance..." (Wright 1987, 231). Yet he wrote a letter to Sir Stafford Cripps on 28 October 1941, well before Pearl Harbor, responding to Stalin's reproaches about lack of British aid:

> [The Russians] brought their own fate upon themselves when by their pact with Ribbentrop, they let Hitler loose on Poland and so started the war. They cut themselves off from an effective second front when they let the French army be destroyed. If prior to June 22nd they had consulted with us beforehand, many arrangements could have been made to bring earlier the great help we are now sending them in munitions.... We were left alone for a whole year, while every communist in England, under orders from Moscow, did his best to hamper our war effort.... That a government with this record should accuse us of trying to make conquests in Africa or gain advantages in Persia at their expense or being willing to "fight to the last Russian soldier" leaves me quite cold. If they harbor suspicions of us, it is only because of the guilt and self-reproach in their own hearts. (Topitsch 1987, 121-22)

Western leaders have uniformly ignored Soviet foreign policy aims and the meaning of Marxist-Leninist ideology. Almost from year one of the Bolshevik Revolution, it was clear that the democratic world was the Kremlin's target. This deliberate ignorance of Soviet intentions was multiplied during World War II "when Britain and the United States erroneously terminated or reduced their surveillance of Soviet operations within their borders after 1941 on the mistaken assumption that Russia was an ally in the struggle against Hitler" (Costello 1988, 619). The full extent of Soviet espionage against the democracies only came to light well after the end of the war. The misperceptions of our wartime leaders toward Stalin led to costly defeats and staggering human losses at the hands of Stalin and his successors.[76]

Massacre at Katyn

The history of Soviet relations with the Western democracies resembles Edward Gibbon's definition of history in his *Decline and Fall of the Roman Empire*: "little more than the register of the crimes, follies, and misfortunes of mankind." And in this case the victims of Soviet crimes were 14,500 Polish officers murdered by the Soviet NKVD in 1940 near Smolensk and in other parts of Western Russia (Zawodny 1962, passim; Fitzgibbon 1975, passim).

---

76 In 1929, Secretary of State Henry L. Stimson vetoed the continued funding for the Black Chamber, a cryptographic unit which had broken the Soviet, Japanese, and German codes before World War II. His reason? "Gentlemen do not read each other's mail" (Jeffreys-Jones 1977, 128).

That this hecatomb occurred at Stalin's command was not surprising in view of the even worse horrors that he had perpetrated against his own people. And Churchill's memoirs tell us that at the Allied conference at Teheran in 1943, Stalin suggested that, after the German defeat, 50,000 German officers be shot (Churchill 1951, 374).

What was unforgivable was the cover-up of the Katyn massacre, above all, by the British government. This obsequiousness before Stalin, this willingness of the democracies to play the role of coconspirator in genocide with Stalin will forever stain Churchill's and especially Eden's place in history. For they did know that Stalin's troops—not Hitler's—had committed the Katyn massacre. They said nothing in the face of a report from Owen O'Malley[77], British ambassador to the Polish government-in-exile, that said:

> In handling the publicity side of the Katyn affairs we have been constrained by the urgent need for cordial relations with the Soviet government to appear to appraise the evidence with more hesitation and lenience than we should do in forming a common sense judgment on events occurring in normal times or in the ordinary course of our private lives; we have been obliged to appear to distort the normal and healthy operation of intellectual and moral judgments; we have been obliged to give undue prominence to the tactlessness or impulsiveness of Poles, to restrain the Poles from putting their case clearly before the public, to discourage any attempt by the public and the press to probe the ugly story to the bottom. In general we have been obliged to deflect attention from possibilities which in the ordinary affairs of life would cry to high heaven for elucidation, and to withhold the full measure of solicitude which, in other circumstances, would be shown to acquaintances situated as a large number of Poles now are. We have in fact perforce used the good name of England like the murderers used the little conifers to cover up a massacre. ("Katyn," *Encounter* 284 [May 1977], page 88)

Years later, in the summer of 1976, a memorial to the Katyn martyrs was unveiled in the London section of Hammersmith. A Labour government was in power, but it acted no differently from the Conservatives. The government declined to be represented at the unveiling ceremony.

So Monstrous a Crime

Was there anything more that Stalin and his epigones needed in order to be assured that anything they did during and after the war would meet with the silence of approval by Western governments? If so monstrous a crime against humanity could be given the mantle of cover-up by Churchill, what need the

---

77 O'Malley's report can be found in the Public Record Office, London, reference FO 371 24467.

Soviets fear of future violations of agreements with Western countries, let alone observance of ordinary decencies? Not to be forgotten, too, is the forced repatriation of Soviet POWs by British and U.S. military complements. Under the Gorbachev dispensation, *glasnost* has finally forced out a confession that Katyn was, indeed, a crime committed by the Soviet Union.

It was President Nixon who in 1972 characterized détente as "the new foundation [that] has been laid for a new relationship between the two most powerful nations in the world" (U.S. Government Printing Office 1974, 661). Sixteen years later, he was writing: "Diplomatic treachery, military intimidation, and aggression by proxy are standard operating procedures for the Kremlin leaders" (Nixon 1988, 98). How do you arrange détente with a superpower guilty of diplomatic treachery, if of nothing else?[78]

An Eerie Echo of the Past?

And when the history of the Reagan administration is written, will some of President Reagan's statements made at the Moscow summit in May-June 1988 have the same eerie echo then as the Roosevelt-Hopkins post-Yalta quotations have for us today? How will we regard the statement about Andropov and the KGB by then Vice-President George Bush? Shortly after the bloody-minded ex-chief of the powerful secret police succeeded Leonid Brezhnev as general secretary of the Soviet Communist Party, Bush, then our vice-president, said:

My view of Andropov is that some people make this KGB thing sound horrendous. Maybe I speak defensively as a former head of the CIA. But leave out the operational side of KGB—the naughty things they allegedly do.... (*Christian Science Monitor* 20 December 1982, page 20)

One of the most cogent commentaries on American foreign policy was made privately by Andrei Gromyko, the Soviet Union's long-time foreign minister. He was asked what he regarded as the greatest weakness of U.S. foreign policy. The question was posed by Arkady N. Shevchenko, Gromyko's aide and the UN official who later defected to the United States. Referring to American statesmen, Gromyko said:

---

78 For the international communist movement, détente and peaceful coexistence did not mean "the maintenance of the political and social status quo in the various countries, but on the contrary [they] create the optimum conditions for the development of the struggle of the working class and all democratic forces" (Light 1988, 60). This was the statement issued in 1976 at the Conference of the Communist and Workers' parties of Europe.

They don't comprehend our final goals and they mistake tactics for strategy. Besides they have too many doctrines and concepts proclaimed at different times, but the absence of a solid, coherent, and consistent policy is their big flaw. (Shevchenko 1985, 279)[79]

The Need for Policy Conception

A similar criticism has been made by Western spokesmen not only about the United States but about the NATO alliance. Jean-François Revel[80] has shown that when it comes to one of the five necessary elements in a successful foreign policy—conception—the behavior of the NATO allies makes conception and, consequently, decision making, difficult. When President Reagan in May 1983 announced the Strategic Defense Initiative, the European allies (with the temporary exception of Britain) "immediately assumed hostile positions.... Politics, not strategic priorities, often leads allies to disown one another" ("The Crisis in Western Democracy," *Imprimis* 17[4] [1988], page 2). The split among the allies over intervention in the Persian Gulf was another example of an alliance operating without a "consistent policy."

What Gromyko said with great accuracy about the United States (and Revel about the NATO alliance) is that it was the Soviet Union that had a solid, coherent, and consistent policy—one intended to achieve the final goals as outlined by V. I. Lenin. We can assume that Gromyko was speaking for the Soviet leadership. Therefore the question which must be asked is this: Can the Soviet Union be trusted as a treaty partner?[81]

New Political Thinking?

Since the accession of Gorbachev to the Kremlin throne, much has been heard about the "new political thinking" and the "new philosophy" of Soviet

---

79   Anthony Eden, Churchill's foreign secretary and later prime minister, noted just before the Yalta conference that among the three heads of state, Stalin was the only one "who had a clear idea of what he wants and is a tough negotiator" (Eden 1965, 583)

80   Alexander Hamilton said the four elements of a successful foreign policy should embody decision, activity, secrecy and dispatch. Revel has added a fifth element: conception.

81   Alexander Solzhenitsyn believes that to guarantee that the Soviet Union will comply with a treaty, the Soviet Union must create a new system whereby the government's actions will be subject to public opinion, to the press, and to a freely elected parliament ("Conversation with Solzhenitsyn," *Encounter* 258 [March 1975], page 68). In 1989, such a system seemed like a distinct possibility. Also see Andrei Sakharov's prescription in chapter 11.

foreign policy. The *Neue Zuercher Zeitung* of 15 July 1987 noted that, while Soviet commentators discuss a "new philosophy" of foreign policy, they have not outlined a new foreign policy ("'The New Political Thinking' and the 'Civilized' Class Struggle,"[82] *Radio Liberty* 292/87 [29 July 1987], II:2-6).[83]

Similarly, much has been heard about the new "military thinking" in the Red Army, the new "defensive doctrine", the principle of "reasonable sufficiency." Defense Secretary Frank C. Carlucci raised the "new thinking" question in discussions with Soviet Defense Minister Dmitri Yazov "because we in the West have yet to see any slackening in the continued growth of Soviet military power."[84] Carlucci offered this documentation in a Defense Department news release (no. 381-88) 1 August 1988:

- Twenty years after the Prague Spring, the Red Army had more divisions in Czechoslovakia than the United States has in all of Europe.
- The Red Army had more divisions in East Germany than the United States has in its entire active army.
- On the Kola Peninsula in northern Europe, opposite Norway's three light infantry border battalions, the Soviets have stationed three divisions, a navy fleet, and a naval infantry brigade.
- Off the Japanese coast, the Red Army maintains large numbers of ground forces supported by the Soviet Air Force "to guard against what they claim is the threat of invasion from the Japanese home defense force."
- The Soviet force structure—heavy emphasis on tanks, motorized artillery, forward-based bridging equipment, heavy SS-18 nuclear missiles with first-strike potential—"stood in stark contrast to Soviet statements on defensive doctrine."

---

82 The analysis in this article is based on articles in leading Soviet publications by official Soviet commentators. They agree that "civilized forms of class struggle is on the agenda" but they do not rule out "armed struggle" in the realization of world revolution.

83 Genrikh A. Borovik, head of the Soviet Peace Committee, complained in June 1988 that (according to the *Los Angeles Times*) "while Moscow's foreign policy now benefits from 'new political thinking' their partners in the West have not caught up and are still thinking in the old stereotypes" ("Soviets Admit Foreign Policy, Defense Errors," *Los Angeles Times* 26 June 1988, I:8).

84 The *New York Times* report of 2 August 1988 (page 1) on the Yazov-Carlucci meeting described Carlucci's visit to the Soviet Union as "part of an expanding relationship between American and Soviet military establishments that has accompanied the general improvement in relations between Washington and Moscow."

Soviet Military Expansionism

The defense secretary could have listed another example of Soviet military expansionism: increasing Soviet naval operations in the Mediterranean accompanied by renovation and enlargement of a Soviet military installation on the coast of Syria. He could also have referred to the Soviet Union's violation of the Geneva accord on Afghanistan in mid-August 1988. The agreement was signed in April 1988 and became effective 15 May 1988, but it didn't stop the Soviet Union from sending Soviet aircraft from Soviet territory to bomb guerrilla positions inside Afghanistan.[85]

Since the agreement was signed, Pakistan has been coerced by the Soviet Union into cutting off most of the military aid to the Afghan freedom fighters. By July 1988, the Soviet government and its puppet Kabul government had filed more than thirty formal protests and statements claiming more than four hundred violations by Pakistan. The Kabul communist regime jointly declared with Moscow that if Pakistan continued to aid Afghan resistance "it would be necessary to undertake the most resolute retaliatory steps." And, on 17 August 1988, the Pakistani military aircraft carrying President Mohammed Zia ul-Haq, the U.S. ambassador to Pakistan and the chief of the U.S. military aid mission, and a number of Pakistani generals mysteriously crashed. Not a bad haul for, from the Soviet view, a serendipitous coincidence about which one could ask, *cui bono*?

Despite all the talk about "new doctrine" and "new thinking," *glasnost* and *perestroika*, the fact remains, Carlucci said, that the Soviet Union has neither announced nor undertaken the destruction or decommissioning of a single ship, tank, or plane, nor any withdrawals of troops from Europe or East Asia. Carlucci added: " Soviet forces are still organized and equipped to initiate powerful offensive strikes to seize and hold territory" ("Soviet Military: Candid Talk But No Action," *Wall Street Journal* 30 August 1988, page 18; "Carlucci, on Soviet Union Visit, Casts Doubts on Reported Strategy Shift," *New York Times* 2 August. 1988, page 1).

Treadmill of Negotiations

So what is Carlucci's answer to the Soviet problem as a conegotiator? More meetings with Defense Minister Yazov and negotiations to reduce

---

85   The 28 August 1988 front-page headline of the *New York Times* read: "U.S. Says Soviets Are Expanding Base for Warships on Syrian Coast." Three days later, the headline of a page four article read: "U.S. Says Moscow Bombings Violate Afghan Pact."

strategic and conventional forces. I suppose there's not much else that Carlucci could say. The West is on the treadmill of negotiations with a military superpower that seeks victory over the West by maintaining military dominance. How reminiscent of Churchill in 1946: "I do not believe that Soviet Russia desires wars. What they desire is the fruits of war" (*Washington Times* 24 June 1988, page F4).

What has been discussed in Soviet journals is "the question ... of civilized forms of class struggle" (Radio Liberty 292/87, part 2, pages 2-6). Armed "class struggle" may be off limits between superpowers, but it is, according to Soviet commentators, not off limits in developing countries. In the Third World, it is "the use of armed struggle that in many respects determined the success of the anti-imperialist movement of the oppressed peoples" (Ibid.) The possibility of a "peaceful evolution from capitalism to socialism" (Ibid.) is examined by one Soviet commentator who, citing Lenin's words, writes that "as communists, we do not much believe in its chances" (Ibid.), but it may be worth trying. The writer concludes that even peaceful revolution will contain an element of "non-peaceful" revolution.

Common Sense, Not Ideology

One of the leading scholars of Soviet affairs—Vera Tolz of Radio Liberty—argues (and quite cogently) that the Soviet Union is retreating from Marxism-Leninism. Its tenets are undergoing revision under the leadership of Alexander Yakovlev, who "has called for his country to be guided by common sense rather than ideology," she writes ("The Soviet Union Retreats from Marxism-Leninism," *Radio Liberty* 1[42] [20 October 1989], page 11). Despite earlier citations in this chapter of Roy Medvedev and others on the importance of Marxism-Leninism in Soviet institutions of higher learning, Vladimir Kuptsov, head of the government department responsible for the teaching of social sciences in the Soviet Union, announced that, as of fall 1989, courses in Marxism-Leninism have been abandoned.

On the other hand, we read that in a television broadcast 16 November 1989, Gorbachev told the Soviet people that the Soviet Union "is not ready for private property or competing political parties, but is leaving the door open for both in the future" ("Gorbachev Says It's Not Time for Soviet Private Property," *New York Times* 17 November 1989, page 8).

At a time when Gorbachev's *offensive du charme* has made him one of the most popular foreign leaders since the end of World War II and when he seems to have won the trust of ex-President Reagan, President Bush, the Congress, and American elites, it is paddling upstream against endless rapids of muddy water to raise questions and suspicions about Gorbachev's policies. An acceptable challenge.

5

'A Paradox, a Paradox,
a Most Ingenious Paradox ...'

Man is free if he needs to obey no person but solely the laws.

Immanuel Kant[86]

While the purpose of this volume is to examine the Soviet record since 1945 on bilateral or multilateral instruments of agreement, the earliest records from the first years of the Bolshevik Revolution must also be examined. My purpose in doing so is to show that the origins of Soviet treaty diplomacy already incorporated the innate Leninist will and ideological drive to exploit treaties so as (1) to lull powerful enemies and (2) to legitimize on the international scene the Soviet operational code in treaty diplomacy. My major concentration, however, will be on Soviet treaty diplomacy since the end of World War II.

This cutoff date has been adopted because:

1. It is from 1945 on that the great Soviet military-political build-up begins—one intended to buttress the Marxism-Leninism that has still to be repudiated by Gorbachev. The Soviet Union has enjoyed extraordinary success in constructing a collective security system comprising Warsaw

---

86   Hayek 1944, 82

Pact countries and countries beyond the Soviet-bloc periphery (Haselkorn 1978, xii).

2. This post-1945 buildup has allowed the Soviet Union the freedom to project its military-political-nuclear power anywhere in the world.

3. In other words, Soviet treaty diplomacy that in the early stages had been at least arguably defensive, and that was uneasy about a possible *cordon sanitaire* by Western and Central European states, became aggressive treaty diplomacy in the aftermath of World War II. Official Soviet publications claim that in contrast to "bourgeois" diplomacy, the diplomacy of the Soviet Union is "scientific diplomacy [since] it is constructed on the foundation of Marxist-Leninist theory and knows how to use the powerful weapon of a Marxist, i.e., truly scientific, analysis of reality and the knowledge of regularities of historical development" (U.S. Senate 1969, 77).

Examination of Soviet Record

The examination of the Soviet treaty record will necessarily be based on the answers to three questions:

1. What is the historic relationship of the Soviet system to contemporary international diplomacy?

2. How does the nature of the Soviet system affect or relate to the history of Soviet compliance with international agreements?[87]

3. What is the short- and long-range purpose of Soviet treaty diplomacy in contrast to conventional treaty diplomacy among nontotalitarian societies?

The assumption that underlies this study is that the Soviet Union is animated, as it has been since 1917, by a belief system aimed at the conquest of the West or the noncommunist sector of the world through military or other means, and that Soviet treaty diplomacy is designed to facilitate this conquest.

The core of the Leninist credo, that after seventy years of application may still drive Moscow's revolutionary strategy, was summarized by Lenin (1902, 41-42) in his typical exclusionary fashion as far back as 1902:

---

87 Professor Chayes says that a treaty is "a legal instrument [that] defines a range of prohibited conduct and gives the prohibition the force of law. In so doing it imports a whole set of attitudes and inhibitions associated with law into what, absent the treaty, was a purely prudential decision" ("An Inquiry into the Workings of Arms Control Agreements," *Harvard Law Review* 85[5] [March 1972, page 906 n. 1).

[T]he only choice is either bourgeois or socialist ideology. There is no middle course (for mankind has not created a "third" ideology) and, moreover, in a society torn by class antagonisms there can never be a nonclass or above-class ideology.[88]

Dogma Demands Subversion

This dogma demands and legitimizes subversion by Lenin's heirs of existing Western alliances and of countries aligned to that alliance, like Japan and some members of the ASEAN organization. To effectuate that strategy, which aims to institute a global Marxist-Leninist new order, the Soviets have adapted treaty diplomacy as one of their tactical weapons. To paraphrase Clausewitz, treaty diplomacy for the Soviet Union is the extension of political war by other means. Or, perhaps Lenin's formulation is more immediately apposite:

We have the great experience of the Revolution and from this experience we have learned that it is necessary to conduct a policy of merciless onslaught when the objective conditions permit it ... but we must resort to the tactic of temporizing, the slow gathering of forces, when the objective conditions make it impossible to issue appeals for a general merciless repulse. (Horelick 1986, 279; Lenin 1917 23: 12-13)

"Détente" Better Than Confrontation

"Temporizing," "slow gathering of forces"—these phrases are ingredients in the formula known as détente or peaceful coexistence. While Lenin justified violence or revolutionary violence, there could be "objective conditions" which would preclude violence however legitimate it might be. Said Lenin:

Not a single question pertaining to the class struggle has ever been settled except by violence. Violence when committed by the toiling and exploited masses against exploiters is the kind of violence of which we approve. (Fainsod 1963, 135)

---

88 Alfred Meyer (Adomeit 1982, 329) has summarized Soviet ideology as comprising a philosophy called dialectical materialism; historical materialism or generalizations about man and society, past and present; an economic doctrine called political economy, which seeks to explain capitalism on the one hand and socialism on the other; and, last, political guidelines called "scientific communism," which deals with the strategy of communist revolutions and the political problems of socialist states.

For the Western powers, negotiations with the Soviet Union are exponentially different from negotiations among themselves or with other noncommunist powers. When the United States confers with, say, Canada over the problems of acid rain or free trade, there is nowhere any hidden, let alone visible, agenda item calling for the destruction of one of the conegotiators. When the United States treats with Britain, Greece, or Argentina, those countries do not doctrinally characterize the United States as the *glavni vrag* (Russian for the "main enemy"), a favorite epithet of the Soviets about the United States.[89] Those powers on the other side of the table from the United States may not like doing business with the United States, and the United States may not like doing business with them, but surely neither side seeks the ruin of the other.[90] Indeed, negotiations among noncommunist states are based on an all-but-forgotten historical fact and tradition: Democracies don't fight each other.

Although there have been between 100 and 200 wars and conflicts (depending on definitions) fought since the end of World War II, not a single war has been fought between two free market democracies, the FMDs. Actually, no wars have ever been fought between nations with freely elected governments since the "first new nation" was created in 1787 at Philadelphia ("A Force for Peace," *Industrial Research* [April 1972], page 55).[91]

Lewis F. Richardson, author of the pioneering work *Statistics of Deadly Quarrels*, a statistical investigation into the causes of war, suggested that "similarity, equality and cooperation generally make for amity rather than enmity" (Charles S. Gochman, review of David Wilkinson's *Deadly Quarrels, Lewis F. Richardson and the Statistical Study of War*, *American Political Science Review* 75, page 570).

And today, despite all kinds of competition among the democracies, there is little possibility of war between any of them for any reason. What possible

---

89 For the Soviet image of "the enemy," see Fainsod 1963, 341-42.

90 The U.S.-Canada trade pact was the subject of much U.S. Senate criticism after the accord was signed 3 January 1988, but no one suggested that Canada was, to use the Soviet phrase about the United States, the glavni vrag—the main enemy—or any other kind of enemy.

91 Owen Harries ("Is the Cold War Really Over?" *National Review* XLI[21] [10 November 1989], pages 40-45) argues that while the fact that democracies do not go to war with each other "has some validity as a historical generalization," it can be explained by special circumstances rather than "the intrinsic nature of democratic states." Until the end of the nineteenth century, he points out, democratic states did repeatedly threaten each other with force; he offers, however, only two examples: the Venezuelan crisis (1895) between Britain and the United States, and the Fashoda crisis (1898) between Britain and France. In any case, threats of wars are not wars.

scenario can be envisaged which would bring about armed conflict between France and Germany, or the United States and Japan, or Italy and Norway, or Spain or whatever? The only wars that exist today are those launched by terrorist *groupuscules* against the democracies. So much for Lenin's "scientific" socialism that foresaw imperialist wars for markets and raw materials as inevitable under capitalism. There is no need for democracies to preach "peaceful coexistence" among themselves.

As Edmund Burke foresaw in his "Letters on a Regicide Peace":

Nothing is so strong a tie of amity between nation and nation as correspondence in law, customs, manners and habits of life. They have more than the force of treaties in themselves. They are obligations written in the heart. (Burke 1960, 476)

Unwritten Agreement That Binds

The U.S.-Israel relationship is an example of two countries, in no way explicit allies, who over forty years have established a moral commitment to each other—the unwritten agreement that binds, "obligations written in the heart."[92] And this applies not only to Israel but even where there may be signed agreements, as with Western Europe and Japan or any country whose citizens enjoy democratic freedom.

When, however, the United States or any other noncommunist state meets with the Soviet Union, it is negotiating not merely with a state but with a politically esurient system: Marxism-Leninism, the system's propellant.[93] The Soviet Union asserts a legitimacy putatively granted to it by the so-called laws of history *à la* Marxism-Leninism—a legitimacy that, in accord with its doctrines, cannot be granted to the United States or any other capitalist

---

92   The Pollard espionage case was a damaging blow to the the U.S.-Israel relationship. See Blitzer 1989, passim.

93   Marxism-Leninism is defined as an ideology with five components: (1) the doctrine of class struggle; (2) a conception of world society as having passed through five historical stages; (3) contemporary existence of two camps—capitalist and socialist; (4) the belief that planning and collective property constitute superior forms of social organization; and (5) the inevitable world victory of communism. The function of an ideology, in its broadest context, is to concretize the values, the normative judgments that are made implicitly or otherwise by members of the society as to what is moral or desirable, as to what is the good society (Bell 1966, 78). Samuel Huntington's definition of an ideology is that it represents "a system of ideas concerned with the distribution of political and social values and acquiesced in by a significant social group" ("Conservatism as an Ideology," *American Political Science Review* June 1957, page 454).

democracy.[94] To quote Lenin: "[A]s soon as we are strong enough to defeat capitalism as a whole, we shall immediately take it by the scruff of the neck" (Lenin 1943, 282).

"We Will Bury You"

Three and one-half decades later, Nikita Khrushchev was reported by *Time* magazine (26 November 1956) as saying to a group of NATO envoys at a Kremlin reception: "Whether you like it or not, history is on our side. We will bury you."[95]

The following year, Khrushchev, less belligerently, prophesied on American television (CBS's *Face the Nation* 2 June 1957) that "your grandchildren in America will live under socialism" ("A Model for Study of Soviet Foreign Policy," *American Political Science Review* LII [March 1958], page 70).

Mikhail Gorbachev has argued in his book, *Perestroika,* that the West misinterpreted Khrushchev's threatening prediction.[96] Gorbachev's denial, while understandable, is without foundation. The truth is that Khrushchev meant what he said. At the Sixth Conference of the East German Communist Party in East Berlin (14 January 1963), in a speech at the railroad station on 6 January, Khrushchev said: "I will shout for joy at the funeral of capitalism." Turning to Western correspondents, he said: "Make a note of it, gentlemen, your time is up. You are waiting for the GDR [German Democratic Republic]

---

94   Even socialist states like the People's Republic of China or Yugoslavia which reject Soviet hegemony represent legitimacy problems for the Kremlin. But that's another story about which more later.

95   Senja 1982, 89 describes how Khrushchev once defined peaceful coexistence as "leading America to the grave with one arm around her shoulder." Senja served as chief of staff to the Czech Minister of Defense until 1968. The Khrushchev quote has been explained by indulgent commentators in the West (*New York Times Book Review* 27 March 1988, page 6) as having meant that in time the Soviet Union would outproduce the West or the United States economically. I prefer to take Khrushchev, never known for his tact, literally. Khrushchev's bitterness against the United States is to be seen in his speech at the adoption of the 1960 communist and Workers' Parties' Manifesto. The "bury" metaphor is a favorite of Soviet communism, as noted in the October 1960 article in International Affairs by Major-General Nikolai Talensky who wrote, "There is no doubt that, in the case of a new war, capitalism will be finally buried" (U.S. Senate 1961a, 14).

96   In his memoirs, Nikita Khrushchev claims that "[e]nemy propaganda picked up the slogan and blew it all out of proportion." He has an elaborate explanation for what he meant by "We will bury the enemies of the Revolution" (Crankshaw 1970, 512).

to disappear, while we are waiting for them [capitalists] to perish from the face of the earth" (U.S. Senate 1961b, 52ff.). And, of course, Lenin said pretty much the same.[97]

According to Khrushchev himself, "the basis for the beginning of all wars will be finally eliminated only when the division of society in hostile antagonistic classes is abolished." The Soviet Union, as the first "Socialist" country, is participating in "a great historic process in which various revolutionary and democratic movements united, work in concert under the determining influence of Socialist revolutions. Until these movements are victorious—namely, until democratic and all other noncommunist societies are overthrown—world peace is unattainable" (Ibid.).

The Communist theory of war has gone from the original Marxist view of internal uprisings for the seizure of power, to the need of war to create Communist revolution, to the Khrushchevian "revisionist" view that war is not essential to the victory of Communism and that new techniques can be developed for seizing power. However, Lenin did add a proviso—if the "ruling classes" refuse to surrender "to the will of the people, the proletariat must break their resistance and start a resolute civil war."[98]

"Now They Say 'Détente'"

A few years later, with Leonid Brezhnev on top of the heap, a sardonic Alexander Solzhenitsyn, speaking in the United States in 1975 after his exile from his homeland, remarked: "Now, of course they have become more clever in our country. Now they don't say, 'we are going to bury you' any more, now they say 'détente'."

In practical terms, when a free nation-state meets with the Soviet Union, the former is only negotiating a few trucial moments in what the Kremlin regards as an inevitable conflict with only one possible outcome: victory for

---

97 One of the most significant of Lenin's statements on coexistence begins: "We live not only in a state but also in a system of governments and the existence of the Soviet Republic alongside the imperialist states over the long run is unthinkable. In the end either the one or the other will triumph. And until that end will have arrived a series of the most terrible conflicts between the Soviet Republic and the bourgeois governments is unavoidable. This means that the ruling class, the proletariat, if it only wishes to rule and shall do so, must demonstrate this also with its military organization" (Lenin 1932, 24:122).

98 As Henry Kissinger (1958, 66-67) has written: "[T]he most substantial Communist contribution to the theory of war has been in the area of limited war—the conflict in which power and policy are most intimately related, in which everything depends on gearing the psychological to the physical components of policy."

the Soviet Union in accordance, presumably, with the "scientific" laws of history embodied in Marxism-Leninism (Lenin 1932, 122).[99]

In 1958, Khrushchev told Adlai Stevenson:

> You must understand, Mr. Stevenson, that we live in an epoch when one system is giving way to another. When you established your republican system in the 18th century the English did not like it. Now, too, a process is taking place in which the people want to live under a new system of society; and it is necessary that one agree and reconcile himself with this fact. The process should take place without interference. (*New York Times* 28 August 1958)

This Soviet rhetoric reflects its hardened political belief system that, by the use of psychological warfare,[100] it has "affected the inner coherence of the territorial state ever since the rise to power of a regime that claims to represent, not the cause of a particular nation, but that of mankind, or at least of its suppressed and exploited portions" ("Rise and Demise of the Territorial State," *World Politics* IX [July 1957], page 487).

Articles in Soviet journals talk disparagingly about people who regard nuclear war as feasible. Western commentators rarely attend to the real Soviet view of the use of nuclear military power or to the nature of Soviet military thinking in the nuclear space age ("The New Soviet Military Encyclopedia," *Survey* 26[2] no. 115 [Spring 1982], page 533[101]).[102]

One of the first acts of the Bolsheviks was not merely to repudiate all legal relationships established by the czarist regime with other countries but also to announce that "it would refuse henceforth to conform to the rules and procedures that had been obtained in international relations" (Degras 1951, 1-3). This announcement was contained in the Bolshevik Decree on Peace passed by the Second All-Russian Congress of Soviets on 8 November 1917.

---

99   This mystical concept that history is on the side of revolutionaries is not confined to communists alone. Other tyrannies have made the same claim—the Nazis, for example. In a speech at the Berliner Sportspalast, Josef Goebbels said (*Voelkischer Beobachter* 4 October 1943): "We shall conquer because it lies in the logic of history, because a higher destiny wills it ... because without our victory, history would have lost its meaning and history is not meaningless" (Wight 1966, 29).

100   Soviet "active measures," of which more later, are a good example of psychological warfare.

101   Also see Douglass & Hoeber 1979 for an earlier but still relevant study of Soviet "war-fighting" and "war-winning" strategies.

102   In chapter 9, I discuss a statement by Vadim V. Zagladin, deputy head of the international department of the Communist Party Central Committee, confirming that the Soviet Union had based its policy on winning a nuclear war. This statement was made at a Moscow press conference of 25 June 1988.

Lenin's Own Words

What we ignore at our peril is the disparity in negotiating with a superpower whose moral behavior is totally contrary to that of the democracies. This difference was underscored by Lenin in words which have, unfortunately, been forgotten: "Our morality is deduced from the class struggle of the proletariat ... Communist morality is the morality which serves the struggle" (Lenin 1943, 9:475-79).

Stalin made a clear distinction between treaties signed with capitalist countries and those signed with socialist countries. And when he made this statement in 1927, no other socialist country was yet in existence:

> International agreements of the Soviet Union with countries with capitalist systems must inescapably be of a different character [from Soviet agreements with socialist states] because the basic content of [Soviet-capitalist] international relations is determined by the struggle of the two systems. (Triska & Slusser 1962, 223)

The paradox referred to in the title of this chapter consists in the fact that, despite this Marxist-Leninist eschatology, the free market democracies and those countries not under Soviet rule must live side-by-side in what the Soviets call "peaceful coexistence"—pretending that the Soviet Union is like any other country (*le pays légal*) yet knowing full well that the Soviet Union (*le pays réel*) is a sworn enemy whose behavior is based upon its own moral code that is called "History." As Bernard Brodie (n.d., 7) wrote:

> The communist philosophy explicitly and systematically rejects the previously accepted norms of international conduct. The principle of expediency in the approach to the existing pattern is not simply indulged, it is avowed and exalted.

Subservient to the Soviet Union

Thus, the free nations have negotiated thousands of agreements, treaties, conventions, pacts, commercial understandings, and protocols. This they have done with a nation-state whose legitimacy stipulates the ineluctable transition of democratic (or any other noncommunist politicoeconomic) systems by infiltration, coup, subversion, or aggression, into totalitarian societies subservient to Marxism-Leninism and to the rules of "proletarian internationalism"—a euphemism definable as subservience to the Soviet Union as the first and leading Marxist-Leninist power. Or, in the words of Stalin:

> The Soviet Union is the base of the world revolutionary movement and to defend, to advance this revolutionary movement is impossible without defending the USSR. ("What the Russians Mean," *Commentary* October 1962, page 316)

The Soviet Union signed hundreds and hundreds of economic agreements, protocols, treaties of friendship and mutual assistance, and nonaggression pacts with Afghanistan over more than six decades. According to *Pravda* of 11 December 1978, the Soviet Union and Afghanistan even signed a protocol on 10 December 1975 extending their treaty of neutrality and nonaggression for ten years. None of these bits of paper meant anything when the Kremlin decided in 1979 that the time was ripe for aggression against Afghan independence. One of Brezhnev's lieutenants interpreted Soviet-Afghan treaties as legitimizing the Soviet invasion. On 24 March 1980, Moscow Radio (and *Pravda* the next day) quoted Andrei Kirilenko as saying:

> [T]he Soviet Union responded to the request by the legal government of Afghanistan and, in accordance with our treaty obligations to this, our neighbor country, and with the provisions of the UN Charter, granted military aid to the Afghan people.

An Overkill of Legitimacy

A veritable overkill of legitimacy: the pseudolegal government of Afghanistan, a Kremlin puppet government, "asked" for the invasion. And, anyway, the Soviet Union was only fulfilling its treaty obligations and it was all being done within the UN Charter. So what's all the excitement? Seven years later, 5 million refugees had fled Afghanistan. At the time, they represented half the refugees of the world and a third of the country's preinvasion population. Roughly 2 million more of those remaining in the country had to flee their homes because of Soviet bombings ("A Profound Test," *New York Times* 10 March 1987, page 25). As of spring 1988, one out of fifteen Afghans had been killed in the war—the equivalent of 13 million American dead (*London Economist* 12 March 1988).[103]

---

103 For a later tally of the human costs of the ongoing war to the Afghan people, see chapter 11.

A number of economic aid packages the Soviet Union offered Afghanistan while it still enjoyed its freedom, such as building airports and runway extensions and hard-surfacing roads, obviously were intended as Soviet military assets in some future but inevitable invasion.

As part of Gorbachev's *glasnost* program, the real story about Afghanistan was beginning to emerge in 1989. According to a Soviet specialist on the Afghan war, the Soviet invasion of Afghanistan had nothing to do with treaty obligations and was nothing more than an act of aggression. Soviet troops played a direct part in the 1979 coup in Kabul. The coup, in which Hafizullah Amin, the Afghan leader, was assassinated and replaced by the Soviet puppet, Babrak Karmal, was then employed to justify the Soviet intervention.

This revision of Soviet history was made public in *Izvestia,* which interviewed Yuri V. Gankovsky, chief researcher of the Institute of Oriental Studies. The scholar said he had been allowed into Kabul two weeks after the coup in December 1979 and had interviewed Red Army officers from whom he learned that Soviet units had participated in the coup. Ten years later the story of what had really happened was emerging ("Soviet Scholar Links Russian Army to Kabul Coup," *New York Times* 5 May 1989, page A6)[104]

Afghanistan Was a "Mistake"

The Soviet writer Aleksandr Prokhanov published an article in a leading magazine, *Literaturnaya Gazeta,* saying that the invasion of Afghanistan had been a mistake. The experts—the diplomats, the specialists in Islam, the politicians and the military—were wrong. He omitted to mention the role played by journalists and writers like himself who had celebrated the war. Academician Oleg Bogomolov, director of the Institute of Economics of the World Socialist System, had made public a memorandum prepared by his Institute which warned against invading Afghanistan ("Bogomolov Reveals Opposition to Afghan Invasion," *Radio Liberty* 116/88 [1988], page 1).

It is not always so simple as all that when the Soviets decide to "revise" their history. Another version of the aggression against Afghanistan surfaced in 1989: namely, that the invasion by the Soviet Union had been due to a

---

104 For another belated revisionist confession, see chapter 8 on the aggression against the Republic of Georgia in 1921, supposedly at the request of the Georgian workers.

disinformation campaign initiated secretly by the CIA. This disinformation was channeled to Soviet correspondents in Kabul. Their news dispatches to Soviet newspapers warned that a threatening internal crisis could bring into power an anticommunist government. These reports so alarmed the senior members of the Politburo—Foreign Minister Gromyko and Defense Minister Ustinov—that they persuaded the ailing Leonid Brezhnev to cosign a written decision to invade its neighbor. Since a fourth Politburo signature was needed, they prevailed upon Yuri V. Andropov, then head of the KGB, to add his name to the order. Thus, the United States could be held equally culpable for the invasion with the Soviet Union. This story was told to me by Vitaly Kobysh, an *Izvestia* political analyst, during a journalist delegation visit to Washington, D.C. in 1989.[105]

The 1980 Soviet *Philosophical Dictionary* defines "state" as "the political organization of an economically dominant class that seeks to preserve the existing order and to suppress opposition from other classes" (Frolov 1980, 77). This clearly means that states other than the Soviet Union, which defines itself as a classless society or on the road to becoming one, are illegitimate, and it would follow, therefore, that treaties with capitalist democracies are not necessarily binding ("Doublethink in the Soviet Union," *Problems of Communism* January-February 1985, page 68).[106]

The Vanguard of History

On 9 December 1982, *Firing Line* (no. 534, page 2) quoted Richard Pipes as saying:

> The present [Soviet] regime maintains itself in power fundamentally on the grounds that it represents the vanguard of history, by which it means that it marks

---

105   Kobysh also said that Soviet authorities had opened archives in an attempt to unearth the relationship of Walter Duranty, the *New York Times* Moscow correspondent during the 1930s, with the Soviet Communist Party. Duranty's coverage was solidly pro-Stalin, especially his reporting of the Stalin-induced famine in the Ukraine. And since Stalin is by now a more or less despised figure, the examination of the Duranty file presumably is intended to uncover any possible devious or unsavory relationship between the *New York Times* correspondent and the Stalin dictatorship. The Kobysh report was confirmed by another Soviet journalist, Igor Tronin, head of the foreign information department of *Sovetskaya Moldavia*, a daily newspaper published in Kishinev ("Moscow Aims at Journalists in Probe of Afghan Disaster," *Washington Times* 27 March 1989, page 1).

106   Cf. Max Weber, who defines a state as "a human community that (successfully) claims the monopoly of the legitimate use of physical force within a given territory" (Gerth & Mills 1958, 78).

the first stage in the world revolution toward abolition of classes—the creation of a communist, classless society. That involves, or implies, a continuous external spread. It also implies that once a territory has gone communist, it cannot revert to the older system.

Obviously, a political order that regards the idea of "peaceful coexistence" as a stratagem for ultimate conquest cannot negotiate in good faith. A Soviet handbook, *Diplomaticheskii Slovar* (Diplomatic Dictionary), defines communist diplomacy as:

> invariably successful in exposing the aggressive intentions of the imperialist governments.... It does this from the tribunes of diplomatic conferences, in official diplomatic statements and documents, as well as in the press. [This] is one of the important methods of socialist diplomacy by means of which it mobilizes democratic social opinion and the masses of people all over the world against the aggressive policies of the imperialist governments. (U.S. Senate 1969, 51; *Diplomaticheskii Slovar* 1960, I:466)

The problem of treaties with the Soviet Union is that we are dealing with an adversary that plans to coexist with its capitalist neighbors no longer than is necessary. As Soviet ideologist V. Kortunov has written: "International agreements cannot alter the laws of class struggle" (*Soviet Analyst* 8[13] [28 June 1979], page 2; "The Leninist Policy of Peaceful Co-existence and Class Struggle," *International Affairs* May 1979). He continued:

> In their efforts to avert a nuclear war and to develop economic, scientific and technical ties, countries with different social systems are, at the same time, pursuing far different class goals in their foreign policy. For the Soviet Union and other socialist states, the policy of détente constitutes a struggle to create favorable conditions for communist construction and therefore the development of the world revolutionary process; for the capitalist countries, it is an effort to protect the bourgeois setup in a new historical situation. (Ibid.)

The American Dilemma

Such an ideological message by a Soviet spokesman creates a trying dilemma for the United States about the meaning of international law and the Charter of the United Nations in a world of nations where the Soviet Union is a dominant superpower. The dilemma was posited by George Kennan in his essay "Diplomacy in the Modern World":

> The American concept of world law ignores those means of international offense, those means of the projection of power and coercion over other peoples which bypass institutional forms entirely or even exploit them against themselves. Such things as ideological attacks, intimidation, penetration, and disguised seizure of the institutional paraphernalia of national sovereignty. It ignores, in other words, the

device of the puppet state and the set of techniques by which states can be
converted into puppets with no formal violation of, or challenge to, the outward
attributes of their sovereignty and their independence. (Kirkpatrick 1984, 3)

And there is perhaps something else less tangible than clashing views on
international law: the good faith that is essential to establishing enforceable
agreements but that is lacking in the Soviets. As Henry Kissinger wrote in
1957:

> The emphasis of traditional diplomacy on "good faith" and "willingness to come to
> an agreement" is a positive handicap when it comes to dealing with a power
> dedicated to overthrowing the international system. For it is precisely "good faith"
> and "willingness to come to an agreement" which are lacking.... (*Wall Street
> Journal* 17 December 1984, Op-Ed page)

Years later, as secretary of state, Kissinger forgot that admonition. As the
London Economist wrote at the time (11 August 1975), "The nub of
[Kissinger's] argument is that it's desirable to sign lots of agreements with
the Russians—even agreements from which Russia gets more immediate
benefit than America does—because this gives future Soviet governments an
investment in continued good relations with America; they won't want to lose
the benefits they have won" (Besançon 1978, 58). The *realpolitik* version of
this approach is that if you feed the shark, his teeth will eventually wear out
and he'll lose them.[107]

Lloyd George Had It Wrong

The founder of "linkage" policy was British Prime Minister Lloyd George,
who formulated "the principles of a policy that was to become standard for
the West vis-à-vis the Soviet Union: to smother Bolshevism with generosity"
(Heller & Nekrich 1986, 97). In 1922, Lloyd George said, "I believe we can
save her [Russia] by trade. Commerce has a sobering influence ... trade, in
my opinion, will bring an end to the ferocity, the rapine and the crudity of
Bolshevism more surely than any other method" (*Free Trade Union News*
[Washington, D.C.] October 1978, page 10).

The ghost of Lloyd George still wanders around the corridors of the U.S.
Government. During the Carter administration, Marshall Shulman, the State

---

107 Unfortunately, the shark's teeth regenerate a row at a time, according to research
findings at the Mote Marine Laboratory in Sarasota, Florida. The shark is never
without three functional rows of teeth, says Perry Gilbert, former director of the
lab ("Sharks' Teeth Arrive a Row at a Time," *Insight* 19 September 1988, page
59). So much for *realpolitik* and its misleading metaphors.

Department adviser on Soviet affairs, wrote that "the measured development of economic relations can reasonably be made conditional upon Soviet restraint in crisis situations and in military competition" (*London Economist* 26 March 1977, page 15). So the Soviet Union marched into Afghanistan.[108]

The same "linkage" tactic surfaced in 1989, this time under the aegis of the Trilateral Commission. Three of its members—Henry Kissinger, former French President Valéry Giscard d'Estaing, and former Japanese Premier Yasuhiro Nakasone—supported Soviet global economic integration. The Commission endorsed Soviet observer status in the GATT (General Agreement on Tariffs and Trade) and in the International Monetary Fund. Full membership would be considered only after the Soviet economy became market-oriented ("Bush's Soviet Policy: No Surprises." *Christian Science Monitor* 24 April.1989, page 7).

Jean-François Revel has pointed out that this linkage—the idea of economic détente—"has been turned upside down." In 1984, he said:

At the beginning of the seventies we initiated economic, financial, and technological trade—help in various forms to the Soviet Union and to other Communist European countries because, we reasoned, "They will become dependent on us and this means that they will become more peace-minded and nice and less aggressive."

But in fact, ten years later, what do we see? That *we* are dependent upon *them*, upon Eastern markets even as we subsidize them, you see? So that you have the Germans, the French, the British telling the Americans, "We cannot stop the gas pipelines because it means so many jobs for us." So the whole philosophy of détente, accelerated by economic pressures, is completely turned around.... We have given the Soviet Union a tool to use against us. (Buckley 1989, 119)

Traditional Treaty Diplomacy

Traditional treaty diplomacy is a handicap when confronted by a superpower dedicated to overthrowing the international system. As an example of what I mean, let me recount the following episode that I witnessed as observer-participant:

Anna Kethly was the only member of the Imre Nagy cabinet to get out of Hungary during the anti-Soviet uprising in October 1956. Ordered by Nagy to New York, she was finally, after weeks of waiting, granted an audience by a deputy secretary-general at the United Nations. Neither Dag Hammarskjold nor the then U.S. ambassador to the UN, Henry Cabot Lodge, would see Madame Kethly. Nor was she allowed to address the UN General Assembly.

---

108 See chapter 7 for Shulman as human rights strategist.

The UN was not only seized by the Hungary crisis but also by the British-French-Israeli assault on Suez and Egypt.

Thirteen resolutions had been passed in the General Assembly calling upon the Soviet Union to get out of Hungary. The Soviet Union ignored the resolutions, and the Red Army crushed the rebellion at the cost of tens of thousands of Hungarian lives. At the same time, resolutions were calling upon Britain, France, and Israel to halt their aggression against Egypt. These resolutions, with President Eisenhower's intense support, helped end the Suez miniwar. Madame Kethly asked the UN official: Why has the UN been so effective in Suez and so ineffective in Hungary?

The UN official's answer was simple and cruel: Because the countries concerned in the Suez aggression are democracies, they have legal oppositions, they have freedom of the press and speech, and they are open to persuasion—pressure from domestic and world opinion. Their borders are "permeable." Ergo, the UN is effective in Suez.

Madam Kethly then asked the UN official: "Aren't you then saying that democracies can be penalized for their actions while dictatorships are rewarded for their actions?"

There was no answer.

There was, however, an answer from Soviet spokesmen. There had to be some kind of "clarification" from the Kremlin to explain how an assault against a sovereign nation like Hungary fitted into Khrushchev's pronouncement on "peaceful coexistence." And this was the "party line":

It should be emphasized that giving help to a friendly government who asks for it against an attack by armed bands ... is not interference. As the recent Hungarian events showed such aid serves the purpose of defending international peace and security. (Light 1988, 48)

A Mug's Game

Because of the history of the Western democracies, traditional treaty diplomacy—a mug's game to the Soviets—is all we have. Such a diplomacy can occur only under particular circumstances.

Even if the United States wanted to discard traditional treaty diplomacy vis-à-vis the Soviet Union, it would be difficult to do so because of leaks to the media and congressional scrutiny. We have only to recall the Iran-Contra affair. As a piece of covert action, it was clearly not within the bounds of contemporary diplomacy. That venture ignored Congress, the Cabinet, the media, and was as secret as any initiative ever handled by a president—an enterprise comparable to the ill-fated Bay of Pigs invasion during President Kennedy's early days in office. Yet the Iran-Contra exposure ended with a congressional investigation and the certainty that no president would soon attempt to go outside traditional treaty diplomacy. Under the rules of American political culture today, covert action has become difficult, if not impossible.

To a political organization like the Soviet Union, repudiation of or noncompliance with a bilateral or multilateral agreement like the United Nations Charter is as normal as an attempted subversion of a neighboring state.[109] And while democratic countries have been known to repudiate or to "re-interpret" seemingly binding treaties, I would argue that such Western actions are *episodic*—not *systemic,* as in Soviet treaty diplomacy.[110]

The Hong Kong Case

Hong Kong, especially since the 5 June 1989 massacre, is an example of where the West plays by the rules and dares not challenge a treaty partner who doesn't. Britain must obey its treaty with the People's Republic of China by returning the colony to Mainland China by 1997. Of course, the word "colony" hardly applies to Hong Kong's 6 million Chinese who, in the words of John Hughes ("Hong Kong: Another Look," *Christian Science Monitor* 24 May 1989, page 18), "have long been free [and] are faced with the loss of that freedom." The communist regime has pledged that, for fifty years after Hong Kong is returned to the PRC, its Western-style institutions and capitalist

---

109 A Resolution adopted by the UN General Assembly on 12 December 1957 (A/Res/424) said: "2. Condemns the violation of the Charter by the Government of the Union of Soviet Socialist Republics in depriving Hungary of its liberty and independence and the Hungarian people of the exercise of their fundamental rights...."

110 Nazi Germany, whose ideology was arguably an offshoot of Marxism-Leninism, was also a "systemic" violator of treaties, among them the 1934 nonaggression pact with Poland, the June 1935 naval agreement with Britain, and, of course, the Nazi-Soviet Pact of August 1939. Even before Hitler marched into the demilitarized Rhineland, the Weimar governments had been violating almost every clause written into the Versailles Treaty intended to keep Germany disarmed (Brown 1987, 142). Whether the People's Republic of China ought to be included in a roster of "systemic" treaty violators will emerge when Hong Kong is transferred to Beijing's jurisdiction in 1997. Reports of violations of the Sino-British agreement were already being reported in 1987 and 1988 ("Hong Kong's Hopes of Freedom are Fading Fast," *Wall Street Journal* 28 December 1987, page 13; "Hong Kong: Down to Basics," *London Economist* 12 March 1988, page 35; "Exodus," *The New Republic* 23 May 1988, pages 12-13; "Hong Kong Gone," *National Review* 21 April 1989, pages 22-23). And, of course, in the aftermath of the 5 June 1989 massacre in Tiananmen Square, doubts about Hong Kong's future under the Beijing slogan, "One country, two systems," seem dubious indeed.

economy will remain untouched. Yet there is no question that Britain, if it dared, would try to renegotiate the treaty.

Alexander Solzhenitsyn is correct in saying that, to guarantee that it comply with a treaty, the Soviet Union must create a new system where the government's actions will be subject to public opinion, to the press and to a freely elected parliament. In other words, a rule of law.

There has always been a question as to whether there is a rule (not a system) of law in the Soviet Union. A rule we take for granted exists in the democracies, with such attributes as legal equality and legalized opposition. The Polish philosopher Leszek Kolakowski has written that Lenin "laid the foundations for the system of law characteristic of totalitarianism, as opposed to the laws of a despotic system" (Heller & Nekrich 1986, 142).

In despotism, the characteristic feature is the severity of the law. What is characteristic of a totalitarian system is the fictitious nature of the law. In reality, the law does not exist. Nor for that matter does the penal code (Ibid., 142). Signing agreements with the Soviet Union inevitably raises the question of compliance because that country lacks a system based in law or, for that matter, a constitutional system freely arrived at.[111]

Meliorism Mocked

For decades, a school of Western specialists in Soviet politics has insisted that a definable rule of law operates in the Soviet Union. While the Soviet version of the rule of law, it was argued, could not be described as a Western sibling, still there were points of similarity. But it took Gorbachev's *glasnost* to make a mockery of the melioristic view of Soviet jurisprudence and of all the scholarship that had gone into trying to prove the existence of nonexistence.[112]

Congruent with the extraordinary Nineteenth Party Conference that began in Moscow 28 June 1988 was the publication by the Soviet Communist Party Central Committee of "theses"—an agenda for delegate discussion—in *Pravda* 27 May 1988. Section eight of the "theses" dealt with the rule of law. The formulation contained the implicit admission that the rule of law had not played much of a role in the Soviet political system. The "thesis" text read:

---

111 Constitutionalism is defined by Alexander Bickel ("Notes on the Constitution," *Commentary* 60 [1975], pages 53-57) as "a special kind of law which establishes a set of pre-existing rules within which society works out all its other rules from time to time." The purpose of constitutionalism is to balance an efficient exercise of government power with some control of that power.

112 For Natan Shcharansky, the émigré Jewish activist from the Soviet Union, *glasnost* "is not a form of freedom. It's just a new set of instructions on what is and isn't permitted" (*Washington Post* 14 December 1987, page A15).

A major legal reform must be implemented with a view to improving radically the work of all bodies which are obliged to strengthen legality and defend the democratic principles of state life and citizens' rights and freedoms. The priority measures ... include the radical enhancement of the role of justice, and strict observance of the democratic principles of the legal process, the adversarial nature and equality of both sides, openness and the presumption of innocence. ("Conference Theses: The Way Ahead," *Soviet Analyst* 17[12] [15 June 1988], pages 3, 8)

What does a rule of law mean? Everything that the proposed Thesis Section eight covers, meaning that none of these protections embodied in a rule of law has existed in the Soviet past nor exist now. If they did, what would there be to reform? Perhaps a more useful benchmark would be a political system based on majority rule—a republican form of government. As described by Thomas Jefferson:

The first principle of republicanism is that the *lex majoris partis* is the fundamental law of every society of individuals of equal rights. To consider the will of society enunciated by a single vote, as sacred as if unanimous, is the first of all lessons in importance. This law, once disregarded, no other remains but the use of force. ("Education in Defense of a Free Society," *Commentary* 78[1] [July 1984], page 17)

Preventing Party Influence

In 1988, the chairman of the Soviet Union Supreme Court, Vladimir Terebilov, called for amendments to the Soviet Constitution to guarantee the independence of the Soviet courts. Such a guarantee was essential to prevent state or party officials from influencing the decisions of the courts (*Literaturnaya Gazeta* 27 April 1988).[113]

What I am saying is old hat to Soviet citizens. On 8 June 1988, in advance of the party conference, The Soviet literary weekly *Literaturnaya Gazeta* held a roundtable discussion on the concept of "the socialist state, ruled by law," a concept equivalent to the *Rechtstaat* ("lawful state").[114] The participants

---

113 In 1989, *Glasnost*, the dissident Soviet journal, reported that when Vladimir Terebilov had been minister of justice and later chairman of the Soviet Supreme Court, he had ordered the destruction of Soviet legal files dating from Stalin's bloody 1930s to the 1950s—5,000 dossiers a month. *Tass* reported on 12 April 1989 that Terebilov had retired from his judicial post. He had also been accused by Nikolai Ivanov, deputy head of the commission investigating Uzbek corruption, of using his position to protect officials from prosecution. (*Soviet Analyst* 18[11] [31 May 1989], page 8)

114 Professor Harold Berman of Harvard University has been a leading exponent of the existence of a "rule of law" in the Soviet Union. See Berman 1983.

agreed that the *Rechtstaat* could only function if the government and the party could be subordinated to the law. The legal experts called for a separation of powers, trial by jury, and a Constitutional Court, presumably like the U.S. Supreme Court. The most shocking statement in the roundtable discussion was made by the magazine's legal expert, Arkadii Vaksberg. Referring to the "Theses" to be presented at the Nineteenth Party Conference, he said:

> I think that those who called in the Theses for the "completion" of the socialist lawful state were, to put it mildly, not entirely sincere. What kind of "completion" can we talk about when *our state has not been lawful in the true sense of the word for a single day in the whole history of its existence*? [my emphasis] ("Legal Reform Debated in *Literaturnaya Gazeta*," *Radio Liberty* 255/88 [15 June 1988], page 4)

The Soviet Communist Party Central Committee "theses" parodied the idea of the rule of law.[115] The Central Committee's Thesis Section 8 demanded "strict observance of the democratic principles of the legal process." But how can you have this without a democratic, constitutional system of government to turn rights on paper into rights in life? Who's going to ensure the "strict observance"? The KGB, the Politburo, the Central Committee?

A New Decree

On 8 April 1989, the Presidium of the Supreme Soviet passed a decree that was presented to the world as part of the move to establish a rule of law. The decree replaced two crimes in the RSFSR legal code: "Anti-Soviet agitation and propaganda" and "Dissemination of deliberate fabrications besmirching the Soviet state and social system" (Articles 70 and 190(1)).

Izvestia admitted that these articles "gave broad scope for reprisals against dissidence since they allowed legislators to interpret as anti-Soviet agitation and propaganda, as they saw fit, any actions reflecting criticism of the

---

115 Writes Ambassador Max M. Kampelman, "When we speak of the 'rule of law', we mean not only procedural guarantees that provide specific consequences flowing from violation of well-established laws; we also speak of human values. Following the rules is not enough. One of this century's most imaginative political thinkers loaned his name to the danger of adherence to rules without values—we shudder at the word 'Orwellian'. There are, therefore, those who believe, understandably, that the term 'Soviet law' is a contradiction in terms. The widespread use of terror as an administrative tool in the Soviet Union justifies this belief" ("The Rule of Law in the Soviet Union," *Freedom-at-Issue* November-December 1989, pages 23-24).

negative aspects of our life or actions by specific leaders" (*Soviet Analyst* 17[2] [15 June 1988]).

Anti-Soviet agitation and propaganda (Article 70) was replaced by a new definition, as cited in *Izvestia*:

> Public calls for the overthrow of the Soviet state and social system or for its change by methods contrary to the Soviet Union Constitution, or for obstructing the execution of Soviet laws for the purpose of undermining the Soviet Union political and economic system, and equally the preparation for purposes of dissemination or the actual dissemination of material containing such calls.... (Ibid.)

Punishment of such crimes runs from three to seven year terms.

The definition which replaced the 190(1) article read:

> The public insulting or discreditation of the Soviet Union supreme bodies of state power and government, other state bodies constituted or elected by the Congress of People's Deputies of the Soviet Union or the Soviet Union Supreme Soviet, or officials appointed, elected or approved in office by the Congress of People's Deputies or the Soviet Union Supreme Soviet, or public organizations and their all-union bodies constituted according to law and acting in conformity with the Soviet Union Constitution is punishable by deprivation for a period up to three years or a fine of up to R(ubles) 2000. (Ibid.).

Pravda made it clear in articles published 11 and 14 April that these decrees would be directed against dissident individuals or groups. The decree shows how far the Soviet Union has yet to travel before one can describe it as a land that enjoys a rule of law in a democratic sense ("Anti-State Crimes—What Has Changed?" *Soviet Analyst* 18[9] [3 May 1989], pages 7-8).

No Rule of Law Possible

There can be no rule of law when the state and the party, through the KGB, can invoke the severest penalties against those citizens who, according to the KGB, violate the laws against revealing state secrets. Since it is the KGB that defines the state secrets, the definitions can include restrictions on personal freedoms such as the freedom to publish. Gorbachev himself has defended censorship of the Soviet media in order to prevent the revelation of state and military secrets ("State and Official Secrets in the Soviet Union," *Radio Liberty* 113/88 [16 March 1988], pages 1-4).[116]

In June 1988, The KGB appealed to the party (not to the Soviet State) to speed up drafting of a law defining the status of the KGB, the Committee for State Security, within the Soviet political system.

---

116 Gorbachev addressed himself to the secrecy matter in an interview with *L'Humanité,* which was republished in *Izvestia* 8 February 1986, page 2.

The KGB "has no true counterpart, either in history or in the contemporary world," John Barron (1974, 1) has written. The KGB combines the functions of the CIA, the FBI, the National Security Agency, the Coast Guard, the Immigration and Naturalization Service, and the Secret Service, plus political and ideological control over everybody as well as a network of informers.

The network of informers has been openly admitted by a KGB official. On 1 March 1989, *Izvestia* reprinted a letter from a local newspaper in the Mariiskyaya Autonomous Republic. The writer said that "we often hear of secret employees of the KGB in almost every major collective. Please would you explain how the concept of *glasnost* squares with the activity of the system of state security" ("The KGB Is Always with Us," *Soviet Analyst* 18[1] [31 May 1989], pages 3-4)? The reply came from the head of the local KGB:

> In accordance with the Soviet Union constitution, every citizen is obliged to render any necessary help and cooperation in guaranteeing state security.... As regards employees, our operatives work openly, and many people know them. Apart from this, within the Committee [KGB] there is a so-called institution of free-lance KGB employees. They exist mainly in large enterprises and there are not many of them. The activity of free-lance employees is regulated by the corresponding regulations. (Ibid.)

The memoirs of Kevin Klose, a former U.S. correspondent in Moscow, contain an unforgettable and explosively meaningful sentence uttered by a Russian friend: "When Westerners think of the KGB, they think of spies. When we think of the KGB we think of our neighbors," the free-lance informers (Klose 1984, 116).

Who Controls the KGB?

It is little realized that the KGB is controlled not by the Soviet state and its officials as provided by the *Soviet Constitution* (1985, articles 32, 131 and 136) but by the Communist Party. What rule of law could possibly exist in the Soviet Union where the KGB—with powers over the life, liberty, and property of the Soviet population, a virtual *imperium in imperio*—is responsible only to twenty or so individuals in the Politburo and Central Committee, some of whom themselves are onetime KGB officers? There is no law nor any provision in the constitution that legitimizes the relationship between the Politburo leadership and the KGB. That is why presumably the KGB, after seventy years of existence, now says it wants to legitimize itself in the eyes of the people ("Reform of the Soviet Political System: The KGB Calls for a Law on State Security," *Radio Liberty* 358/88 [5 August 1988], pages 1-8).

Whatever games the KGB wants to play and whatever changes it seeks for itself, there is no genuine rule of law in the Soviet Union and there will be none until the monopoly power of the Soviet Communist Party is dismantled, which is what Solzhenitsyn was saying. What exists today in the Soviet Union and what will continue to exist even under Gorbachev the Reformer is what is called "instructive law" or "secret instructions." This system, invisible to the naked eye, affords party officials, *nomenklatura* appointees, and their friends the protection of the law denied to ordinary citizens. According to Soviet students of what passes for the rule of law, top officials instruct judges and prosecutors how to decide specific cases. There is no appeal from these instructions, which have been described by Professor Robert Sharlet of Union College by the oxymoron "legal arbitrariness."

This finding is confirmed by the on-the-spot observation of Michael Voslensky (1984), whose book on the *nomenklatura* describes crimes committed with little or no risk by these top officials within the party apparatus. As Peter Reddaway pointed out, "The worst that can befall them in normal times is to be pensioned off to a comfortable retirement amid a measure of public disgrace." ("More Equal Than Others," *New Republic* 2 December 1985) [117]

Yet to Be Disproven

Writing in 1985, shortly after Gorbachev's ascension as party general secretary, Professor Sharlet predicted that "if past experience is any guide, odds are that many years will pass before legality overcomes political expediency in the Soviet Union" ("Politics of Soviet Law," *Problems of Communism* January-February 1986, page 60). And in 1988 his prophecy has yet to be disproved. Since the Politburo has "historically defined itself as a meta-juridical institution above and outside the law," and since it frequently "adopt[s] a cavalier attitude toward their own laws," there is little possibility of a rule of law, writes Sharlet. (Ibid.).

Writing about the Soviet judiciary, Professor Eugene Huskey ("Soviet Justice in the Age of *Perestroika.*," *Christian Science Monitor* 22 August 1989, page 18) said that for "some segments of the bench" there is dissatisfaction with "the Communist Party's interference in judicial decision making." As Professor Huskey wrote: "Although officially condemned,

---

117 Wolfgang Leonhard writes: "What distinguishes a *nomenklatura* official is not his professional qualifications or his sense of initiative but his absolute loyalty to the regime, which he has to express time and again, just like the bond of personal loyalty between a vassal and his suzerain" (*Freedom-at-Issue* [New York, N.Y.] March-April 1988, page 33).

politicians' oral instructions to judges, known as telephone justice, remain a part of Soviet legality" (Ibid.).

He reported that in Sverdlovsk, several judges protested against what one of them called "the illusion of judicial independence." Despite official communist pressure for a conviction, a judge, Leonid Kudrin, dismissed charges of illegal assembly against a group of protesters. Two other judges followed Kudrin's lead. What Professor Huskey called "this judicial strike" spread to the office of the State prosecutor, which refused to appeal these "politically-errant court decisions" (Ibid.).

Professor Eugene Kamenka ("Marxism and the Law," *Times Literary Supplement* 5 June 1981, page 637) has contended that the work of the well-known Soviet jurist E. B. Pashukanis and "his vision of a socialist society in which Law is replaced by Plan can and did lead to and justify the horrors of Stalinism." Wrote Professor Kamenka:

> ... Pashukanis's rejection of the right and duty-bearing individual in socialist administration resulted in the fact that there was no anti-Stalinist Marxist theory of law to present a principled rejection of the concepts of "social danger" and "social harm" replacing the "bourgeois" concept of "guilt"; that there was no rejection of indeterminate sentencing, that there was no elevation of the social role of law, legal ideology and the legal profession, let alone of independence of the judiciary....

> Pashukanis's work fits better with the lawlessness and contempt for law of the Stalinist purges and of the Great Proletarian Cultural Revolution than it fits with the predictability, regularity and fairness that Soviet and Chinese people long for. (Ibid.)

That there is no genuine rule of law in the Soviet Union is now openly admitted. For example, David K. Shipler, the former Moscow correspondent of the *New York Times*, reported after a recent visit to the Soviet Union that Gorbachev's reformism has inspired "intensive battles" in the party hierarchy "over how far to go" (*New York Times* 4 November 1988, page A19). Some Soviet officials (unnamed), wrote Shipler, "recognize the hypocrisy of the country's constitutional guarantees of various rights and freedoms." He quoted one senior Soviet official as saying that "We had a great constitution under Brezhnev, but it had no practical value. There was no law, only empty phrases." Judges, the Soviet official admitted, were so beholden to the communist Party apparatus that they simply did what the politicians told them.

For years, we have heard from U.S. specialists in Soviet "law" that the Soviet Union was moving toward a genuine rule of law. Now Shipler reported that "in a tentative step toward an independent judiciary, judges' terms may be lengthened and party officials may be subject to criminal penalties for pressuring judges." Trial by jury "in the most serious cases" may be introduced. There are "some" who are even urging that the accused be allowed a lawyer at the time of arrest rather than having to wait until after the police investigation.

A Genuine Rule of Law?

In other words, as I said earlier, everything that might point to a genuine rule of law is now just being considered. A genuine rule of law has never existed in the Soviet Union despite all the Western political pilgrims who told us otherwise. One analyst has written that "the police and criminal law systems have the function not merely of repressing crime, but of contributing to the labor supply" (Westoby 1989, 219). Timber extraction and mining, for example, depend on forced labor which the criminal law supplies.

Without a genuine rule of law, the question arises: To whom does the state and the property it claims as its own belong? If the working class and the peasantry are effectively excluded from participation in law-making, what greater fictional title can there be than to call the Soviet Union "a worker's state"? As it stands now, when a handful of individuals control everything in real property, they can be said to be the owners, but with no responsibility to anybody except themselves. In the meantime, however, we have the Central Committee's Thesis Section 8—a tacit admission that some seven decades after the Bolshevik Revolution the Soviet Union is still without the rule of law and that the Communist Party leadership, wealthy in privilege and affluent in property, is still beyond the law. Without a rule of law, what meaning do legal instruments like bilateral or multilateral agreements have to the Soviet Union? Earlier I cited the definition of a treaty as "a legal instrument [that] defines a range of prohibited conduct and gives the prohibition the force of law" ("An Inquiry into the Workings of Arms Control Agreements," *Harvard Law Review* 85[5] [March 1972], page 906 n. 1). How, then, can a state, which defines and therefore repudiates the rule of law as a bourgeois invention, be expected to abide by it?

A Welcome Back

In his 24 May 1989 Coast Guard Academy speech, President Bush said the United States must aim at "integrating the Soviet Union into the community of nations" (Associated Press 24 May 1989). He said that the U.S. objective "is to welcome the Soviet Union back into the world order" (Ibid.). Such a welcome back, such integration, presupposes an agreed-upon sharing of values if a democratic community with a Soviet Union as a member is to remain viable. One of the *sine qua non* values of a democratic world community is the rule of law.

In 1989, Soviet spokesmen were making the claim that the country was moving toward the rule of law. Gvido Zemribo, chief justice of the Supreme Court of Latvia and a member of the Soviet Union Supreme Soviet, says that the country is moving toward just such a happy condition. Mr. Zemribo was interviewed during a visit to the United States where he addressed the University of Maine Law School graduating class. He quoted Alexander N. Yakovlev, regarded as President Gorbachev's "alter ego," as saying: "For a thousand years, Russia was ruled by men. It is time that the country must be ruled by law" ("Soviets Shift Toward a Rule of Law," *Christian Science Monitor* 5 June 1989, page 12). Mr. Zemribo said that "telephone justice," where party officials call judges requesting particular verdicts, is declining, which of course means that in the era of *glastroika*, "telephone justice" still exists. Since it is difficult independently to confirm Mr. Zemribo's claims, we shall have to wait and see.[118]

What Is the Soviet Union?

Milovan Djilas, the one-time Yugoslav communist ideologue, holds out little hope for a recognizable rule of law in the Soviet Union. He is quoted in a spring 1987 interview with the *South Slavonic Review* as saying:

> The Soviet Union is in essence a military empire. It is too immature to indulge in economic competition. It can only advance its aims by arms and ideology, by armed support for all kinds of conflict and all sorts of revolutions. (*Soviet Analyst* 11 November 1987, page 8)

The Soviet contempt for a rule of law is reflected in the leadership attitude toward its international agreements. Soviet treaty diplomacy regards agreements with other countries as never more than temporary because Marxism-Leninism emphasizes, in Lenin's words, the need to exploit "the contradictions and opposition between two imperialist power groups, between two capitalist groups of states and [to] incite them to attack each other" (Topitsch 1987, 15). Such a theory leads inevitably to rejection of the status quo anywhere in the world to which the Soviet Union applies its Marxist-Leninist yardstick. Leonid Brezhnev said at the Twenty-fifth Party Congress that "our revolutionary conscience," rather than respect for national borders or international law, would guide Soviet foreign policy ("Two Hundred Years of American Foreign Policy," *Book Forum* III[4] [1978], page 533).

The paramount reason why treaty diplomacy is part of the Soviets' grand strategy of conquest stems from what Professor Merle Fainsod has described

---

118   On Yakovlev, see Safire, "A Second Yalta," *New York Times* 6 March 1989, A19.

as the Soviet image of "the enemy." He has argued that the greatest single difference between the Soviet Union and the Western democracies in foreign affairs "derives from the image of 'the enemy' which is deeply imbedded in Marxist-Leninist patterns of thought." Writes Fainsod (1963, 341-42):

> The politics of communism are built around the concept of the implacable capitalist adversary who has to be disarmed and defeated lest he in turn annihilate communism. The Leninist dialectic which the leadership has been trained to apply is essentially a vision of progress and triumph through conflict and struggle. Such a *Weltanschauung* reduces any accommodation to a negative virtue. Compromise becomes at best a disagreeable necessity rather than a creative achievement.... The essence of politics becomes the clash with the capitalist enemy.

Writing in the early Gorbachev era, Milovan Djilas said:

> The Soviet system, personified in the party bureaucracy, has no capacity to accept the idea of a world that would not be hostile. Through the system that it has created, the Soviet bureaucracy has condemned itself to thinking conspiratorial thoughts and to living in fear for its existence. (Voslensky 1984, xv)

Typically, Soviet spokesmen argue that it is the West that hardens the image of the *glavni vrag*, the main enemy, as exemplified by the Soviet Union. Ignoring the vatic pronouncements of Lenin, Stalin, Khrushchev, Brezhnev, Andropov, and lesser spokesmen about the doom of capitalist states, Oleg T. Bogomolov, director of the Institute of Economics of the World Socialist System, said in 1988 that U.S. foreign policy has as an underlying assumption that the Soviet Union is the Number One Enemy:

> Anti-Soviet propaganda is a major mistake for the West because those shaping the destiny of the world fell victim to their own propaganda. Now, they can't see beyond that "enemy image" they have created. ("Soviets Admit Foreign Policy, Defense Errors," *Los Angeles Times* 26 June 1988, page 8)

"The Counterintelligence State"

In other words, noncommunist states must negotiate with, as John Dziak (1987, xvi) has written, "a counterintelligence state, an enterprise perpetually in search of enemies, foreign and domestic."

If such is the foundation of Soviet treaty diplomacy, it follows that there can be no common ground between the Soviet Union and those with whom it negotiates. Today's "ally" is, for certain, tomorrow's enemy.[119]

---

119 Despite this Leninist warning, Stalin couldn't have been more surprised when his ally of some twenty-two months, Nazi Germany, invaded the Soviet Union in June 1941. Yet what greater proof of the validity of "today's ally-tomorrow's enemy" totalitarian dogma than the Nazi onslaught? Perhaps it was Hitler's treaty

Table 1

Results of 1989 Wall Street Journal/NBC News Poll

	Favor	Oppose
Remove trade restrictions so Soviet Union could sell more to United States	51%	41%
Allow Soviet Union to join international lending institutions so that they could borrow more money from West	45%	48%
Provide direct economic aid to Soviet Union	26%	66%
Allow U.S. companies to sell high-tech products to Soviet Union even if they have potential military use	17%	77%

The historic question in Soviet-Western treaty diplomacy is: How can you negotiate with the Soviets and hope for observance of agreements? During peacetime we normally do not look upon conegotiators as potential war makers. When Winston Churchill said it was better to "jaw-jaw" than "war-war," surely he didn't have in mind the Western democracies as potential war makers. As pointed out earlier, they have never gone to war with each other. Yet we continue to negotiate with the Soviet Union as if the Kremlin were either dedicated to peace and freedom or could be persuaded to pursue such a pacific path, as was the hope of Dr. Kissinger, quondam practitioner of *realpolitik.* [120]

diplomacy applying the Leninist dialectic that surprised Stalin. (After all, in December 1939, Stalin told Hitler's foreign minister, von Ribbentrop, "The friendship of the peoples of Germany and of the Soviet Union, sealed by blood, has every reason to be lasting and firm."

120 In 1980, Alexander Solzhenitsyn described what he called the "Kissinger syndrome" as one where "individuals, while holding high office, pursue a policy of appeasement and capitulation ... but immediately upon retirement the scales fall from their eyes and they begin to advocate firmness and resolution. How can this be? What caused the change? Enlightenment just doesn't come that suddenly! Might we not assume that they were well aware of the real state of affairs all along, but simply drifted with the political tide, clinging to their posts" ("Misconceptions About Russia Are a Threat to America," *Foreign Affairs* Spring 1980, pages 806-7).

Compulsion to Negotiate

That compulsion upon the West, especially the United States, to negotiate, establishes a moral equivalence between the Soviet Union and the United States in public opinion and puts an open society at a great disadvantage. After all, there is such a phenomenon as "world opinion." The democracies must worry about the drift of this public opinion just as the Soviets, using Gorbachevite public relations and disinformation techniques against the United States, seek to absorb that opinion into their arsenal. In fact, in 1989 it was clear that it was Gorbachev and his public diplomacy that were setting the agenda in Soviet-American diplomatic negotiations. Under the Gorbachev party dynasty, the Soviets have demonstrated unusual skill at manipulating opinion by their secret and not-so-secret battalions in the West, and with excellent results.[121]

In fact, news polls in 1989 demonstrated that there had been a significant change in American public opinion vis-à-vis the Soviet Union in the decade from 1979. To take but one example: to the question, "If the United States and the Soviet Union reached an agreement on arms control this year, do you think the Soviet Union would live up to the agreement, or would it cheat?" the answers were as follows: In September 1987, 27 percent of respondents thought that the Soviet Union would comply while 61 percent said the Soviet Union would cheat. In 1989, 41 percent thought that the Soviet Union would live up to the agreement while 46 percent said they would cheat ("Americans Are Warming to Soviet Union, Poll Finds," *New York Times* 3 December 1989, page 15).[122]

---

121 In response to the question "Who is more trustworthy, President Reagan or Soviet leader Gorbachev?" then Secretary of Education William Bennett was quoted (*Washington Times* 11 August 1987, page D-1) as saying that 29 percent of those polled in Britain said President Reagan was more trustworthy while 21 percent said Gorbachev; in France, 47 percent said President Reagan while 10 percent said Gorbachev; in West Germany, 26 percent said President Reagan was more trustworthy while 33 percent said Gorbachev. About a year later, the *Wall Street Journal* (21 October 1988, page A6) reported that an October 1988 German opinion poll by the Friedrich Ebert Foundation showed the following: In 1970, 70 percent of West Germans saw the Soviet Union as a threat to world peace; today only 11 percent do. Less than a year after that poll, the *Washington Times* (13 June 1989, page A10) reported that 90 percent of West German respondents to a public opinion poll say they trust President Gorbachev and his policies while President Bush received a 58 percent approval rating, Chancellor Helmut Kohl 50 percent.

122 The favorable-unfavorable view of the Soviet Union went up from 15 percent favorable in 1979 to 30 percent in 1989. The favorable-unfavorable view of Gorbachev increased from 38 percent favorable in November 1987 to 47 percent favorable in 1989. To the question as to whether respondents thought that the

Despite this change over time in the popular view of Gorbachev, the Soviet Union was still an object of suspicion. A 1989 *Wall Street Journal/NBC* news poll presented these results ("Summit, Changes in East Bloc Leave Americans Hopeful but Skeptical About Soviets, Cold War," *Wall Street Journal* 6 December 1989, pages A16) (see table 1 page 118).

But even without Gorbachev, Soviet propaganda did well, particularly under Brezhnev. Henry Kissinger said in 1981:

> It is an amazing phenomenon, less than two years after Afghanistan, less than four years after Cuban troops under a Soviet general appeared in Ethiopia, six years after the same thing happened in Angola and while thirty-plus Soviet divisions are constantly bringing pressure on Poland, that at this moment there should be mass demonstrations all over Europe—affirming what?—the desirability of peace and implying that it is the United States which is the obstacle. (National Strategy Information Center 1981, 46)

Soviet Union was trying to dominate the world, in May 1989 the ratio was 50 percent trying to 43 percent not trying. In November 1989, five months later, the ratio had gone to 34 percent trying to 58 percent not trying ("Americans Are Warming to Soviet Union, Poll Finds," *New York Times* 3 December 1989, page 15).

6

The Protracted Confrontation: Forever?

The Soviet Union and the United States have probably had more face-to-face treaty negotiations than any other two countries in modern times. There is always a negotiation going on between the two superpowers somewhere in Europe or in Washington. Yet, despite these thousands and thousands of meetings between the United States and the Soviet Union, danger still exists—although, admittedly, at an unprecedentedly low level.

In all of modern history there has never been as protracted, intense, and *globally perilous* a confrontation between two countries and even two systems of nation-states as has existed for seventy years between the noncommunist world, chiefly the United States, and the Soviet Union, or what Andrei Gromyko calls the "Socialist Commonwealth."[123]

What makes this confrontation, the unilateral inspiration of Marxism-Leninism, so extraordinary in the post-World War II era is that it exists for one and only one reason: The Soviet leadership, no matter who the party general secretary may be, is driven to fulfill the, for them, immutable Marxist-Leninist prophecies of ultimate victory; and it insists, for reasons

---

123 Andrei Gromyko: "The commonwealth of socialist states is an indissoluble entity.... For the Central Committee of the communist Party of the Soviet Union and the Soviet government, for the Soviet people, there is no more sacred cause in the field of foreign policy than strengthening the commonwealth of socialist countries" (*Pravda* 28 June 1968, page 3). Twenty years later, the "Socialist Commonwealth" was in ruins.

concerning the legitimacy of the Bolshevik regime, on accelerating the fulfillment of these prophecies. The Kremlin regards any fundamental (as against temporary) amendment to these prophecies of victory over the capitalist West as an act of apostasy, usually called "revisionism"—unless, of course, such an amendment is authorized by Kremlin ideologists. As Irving Kristol wrote in 1985, "A Marxist-Leninist regime that actually declared its intention to live in peace with 'capitalist' powers would inflict a mortal wound on its own legitimacy" ("Coping with an 'Evil Empire'," *Wall Street Journal* 17 December 1985, Op-Ed page).

Four years later, Professor Kristol was arguing that the legitimacy of the Soviet Union had, indeed, suffered a "mortal wound" and might in 1989 no longer be called the "Soviet Union" but rather "Greater Russia, a different kind of imperial power."[124]

Thriving Amidst Crises

A state like the Soviet Union can only thrive amidst crises, whether real or fancied. As John Dziak (1987, 51) has pointed out, "Conspiracies presuppose enemies and a conspiracy come to power must perpetually justify itself by exposing threats to its own exclusive claims."

This confrontation—the Soviet Union vs. the world—had in some seventy years become a Soviet geopolitical success story, as one can easily see by comparing a map of the world in 1917 to one in 1987. In 1919, 7.8 percent of the world's population and 16 percent of the world's territory lived under socialist control. Half a century later, in 1969, those figures had increased to 34.4 percent of the world's population and 25.9 percent of the world's territory. And in 1969, "socialist control" did not include Afghanistan, Angola, Cambodia, Ethiopia, Laos, Libya, Mozambique, Nicaragua, or South Yemen. Twenty years later, the Soviet empire was unravelling.

Or, one can do a census of communism in power. According to a Soviet spokesman, the world communist movement has expanded from eighty-eight countries with parties and some 50 million members during the early 1970s to almost 100 countries with one or more parties and over 82 million members in the mid-1980s. Of the 82 million, more than 77 million, almost 95 percent, live in the sixteen communist-ruled states of what Moscow calls "the world socialist system." The remainder, fewer than 4.7 million, live in eighty other countries ("Checklist of Communist Parties in 1987," *Problems of Communism* January-February 1988, pages 60-81).

---

124 From a personal communication by Kristol to the author, 18 October 1989.

Until the beginning of the Soviet empire breakup in 1989, communist parties ruled in sixteen countries; Marxist-Leninist regimes controlled twenty-three others. Some eighty movements are active in the rest of the world. The core communist states are not all pro-Soviet—witness Albania, China, North Korea, Yugoslavia—but they may be states that the Soviets hope will one day come around to accept "proletarian internationalism," the Stalinist euphemism for Soviet mastery. The number of communists in the world has increased from 82.2 million members in 1986 to 89.8 million in 1987 (*Washington Times* 14 July 1987, page A5).

However, according to the census of Communist Parties prepared annually by the Hoover Institution's Richard Staar (1990, xii-xxxi), total worldwide party membership declined from an estimated 90.5 million to 82.6 million at the end of 1989, almost a 9 percent drop. Half the decline was due, of course, to the overnight dissolution of the Romanian Communist Party, which went from a membership of 3.8 million to zero. Total party membership for Eastern Europe as a whole declined by 25 percent. Party membership in Western Europe dropped 41 percent.

Even with the repudiation of Communist rule both in Eastern Europe and in non-Communist parts of the world, such as Nicaragua, the international movement still remains a formidable force, capable of being roused at times and places of the Soviet Party's International Department's own choosing.

From the inception of a formally structured Soviet foreign policy in 1924 following the Treaty of Rapallo, when the Soviet Union opened up "normal" diplomatic relations with the European capitalist powers, Soviet diplomacy has operated on two levels: traditional diplomatic activity, a maquillage; and the Soviet Union's real foreign policy exemplified in Comintern/Cominform/International Department activities (Heller & Nekrich 1986, 209).

Two-Tier Diplomacy

This two-tier diplomacy is still at work, as seen in a 1986 speech by Central Committee Secretary Anatolii Dobrynin, at the time one of Gorbachev's top policy advisers. Whatever the Soviet Union may think of the fate of the capitalist system, said Dobrynin, "it, as a state did not set itself the aim of overthrowing capitalism in other countries" ("Dobrynin urges U.S. to Adopt New Foreign Policy," *Radio Liberty* 218/86 [1986], page 5).[125] In other words, capitalism, presumably damned by the lapidary laws of

---

125 For example, the *Neue Zuercher Zeitung* (15 July 1987) wrote that Soviet spokesmen might be writing about "a new philosophy" of foreign policy without outlining a new foreign policy.

Marxism-Leninism, would inevitably perish one day but not—heaven forfend!—because the Soviet state did anything to hasten the day. [126]

Dobrynin, of course, was speaking with forked tongue. (In chapter 2, I quoted Lenin as saying about the Brest-Litovsk treaty that "The Party does not sign the treaty and for the Party the Government is not responsible.") Dobrynin is saying that *as a state* the Soviet Union is not seeking to overthrow capitalism. But the Soviet Union and its "parallel diplomacy" is not a state as ordinarily defined. The Soviet Union also represents a movement, a self-defined force marching with history on the road to a classless society. There are special departments within the Central Committee of the Soviet Communist Party to whom the work of promoting "proletarian internationalism" among nonruling communist parties is entrusted. Another department supervises East European Communist Parties and another department exists for the purpose of promoting Soviet foreign policy initiatives intended to weaken and eventually destroy the democracies. So much for Dobrynin's assurances.

Treaties of friendship and Soviet pledges of noninterference in a country's internal affairs mean little to the Soviet Union. For example, a clause in the fifty-year Anglo-Soviet Treaty of 1942 provided that both powers would refrain from intruding into the internal affairs of the other. The treaty was violated by the Soviet Union even before negotiations had been concluded ("The Brezhnev: the Soviet Supercarrier," *Armed Forces Journal International* [April 1987], pages 473, 134).

Soviet Propaganda Assets

When the Soviets engage in treaty diplomacy, they begin with an edge: They have important political and propaganda[127] assets in almost every country of the world to bolster their treaty diplomacy.

First, there are the Communist Parties in the capitalist countries whose principal task is to organize support for Soviet foreign policy.

---

126 Unfortunately for Dobrynin's assurances (the first tier of Soviet diplomacy), an earlier Soviet leader had spoken more frankly (the second tier). Leonid Brezhnev put it neatly in 1970: "Imperialism will not collapse by itself, automatically. Active and determined action by all the revolutionary forces is needed to overthrow it" (Brezhnev 1972, 296].

127 Paul Kecskemeti defines propaganda as "streams of instrumentally manipulated communications from a remote source that seek to establish resonance with an audience's predispositions for the purpose of persuading it to a new view that the propagandist prefers" (de Sola Pool et al. 1973, 844).

Second, there are the Moscow-controlled international fronts linked to the CPSU International Department that directs their activities and provides them with financial support. These fronts with regional branches involve youth, labor, women, church, scientists, lawyers, and journalists.[128]

Third, there are the intellectual classes for whom there exist no "enemies on the left." With all that has happened and all the ghastly revelations about the real story of the Soviet Union, and the repudiation of socialism and communism by Eastern Europe, the Soviet Union still represents to large sectors of Western and Westernized intellectuals all that is good (or potentially good) in socialism. Nothing changes or alters this consciousness about socialism, the belief that socialism is prospering and that capitalism is dying. In Western High Culture,[129] to be anti-American is to be progressive; to be anti-Soviet is to be against history.

As a force to support Soviet treaty diplomacy, such international fronts are invaluable, especially in influencing the always susceptible media in democratic countries.[130] As Professor Gordon A. Craig put it, the Soviets can pursue "multiple channels of negotiation" (Craig 1962; Craig 1961, chapter 4).

One of the great achievements of Soviet propaganda in the early 1980s was the Soviet proposal for a "nuclear freeze." Sucked into this scam was none other than Massachusetts Governor Michael Dukakis, who in 1988 became the Democratic Party's candidate for U.S. president. As a historical fact, Leonid Brezhnev called for a nuclear freeze on 23 February 1981, and soon the phrase was on the lips of every nuclear disarmer. Prominent among those arms control parishioners was Doctor Helen Caldicott, who described the other Mike—Mikhail Gorbachev—as "the only sane leader in the world." He "is like Jesus Christ," she said. Ted Turner, the TV tycoon, also sees the Soviet president as a savior. "Gorbachev has probably moved more quickly,"

---

128 For an invaluable case history of how the Soviet propaganda network operates and the power of Soviet fronts in the Western democracies, see Alexiev 1985.

129 By High Culture, I mean a system of patterned beliefs that seeks a dominant, indeed a monopolistic, role in determining societal values so as to replace prevailing values. It is represented by a self-styled politico-literary avant-garde in democratic societies. See Beichman 1987, 80.

130 For an up-to-date organizational chart of the Soviet Active Measures apparatus, see "Soviet Active Measures and Disinformation Forecast," *Disinformation* 11 (Winter 1989), pages 10-11. The chart diagrams these fronts in horizontal and vertical linkages and relates them to the CPSU International Department and to the concentration of power represented by President Gorbachev. For an earlier organizational chart, see U.S. Department of State 1983. For a more recent study, see "Communist Fronts in 1987," *Problems of Communism* January-February 1988, pages 82-88; Spaulding 1988, 403-9.

he said, "than any person in the history of the world. Moving faster than Jesus Christ did. America is always lagging six months behind" (*Time* magazine 22 January 1990, page 58).

A Psychoanalytic Fantasy

Dr. Caldicott is the author of *Missile Envy*. Her book provides a psychoanalytic fantasy about America's military leaders. Because of their feelings of sexual insecurity and inadequacy, U.S. military chiefs have developed the nuclear deterrence arsenal. It is not clear from her book whether the existing huge Soviet nuclear arsenal is due to feelings of similar sexual inadequacy among the Soviet marshals and generals. Dr. Caldicott is described as president of Physicians for Social Responsibility.

It was with this Helen Caldicott, whose lectures and interviews have made her a slavish supporter of Soviet foreign policy, that Governor Dukakis held a joint press conference in 1982 to announce his support for a nuclear freeze (*Human Events*, 20 August 1988). In reply to the freeze campaign, then Assistant Secretary of Defense Richard Perle wrote:

> With a freeze implemented, the Soviet Union would find itself in a commanding strategic position. Two of the three legs of our strategic deterrent would be vulnerable—our ICBMs and bombers—and Soviet resources could be concentrated on consigning our submarines to a similar peril. That is why Moscow wants the freeze resolutions to pass—and why we do not. (*New York Times*, 7 September 1982, Op-Ed page)

Charles Krauthammer, writing in the *New Republic* (28 April 1982), said that "when taken seriously as a plan, the freeze continually fails on its own terms. It seeks safety, but would jeopardize deterrence; it seeks quick action, but would delay arms control; it seeks real reductions, but removes any leverage we might have to bring them about."

The Blame-America-for-Everything Brigade

Now, whatever can be said for supporting a nuclear freeze, the fact that a pro-Soviet propagandist like Dr. Caldicott is for it should make any responsible individual, especially an ambitious politician, cautious about a joint appearance with Dr. Caldicott, an undisputed leader of the Blame-America-for-Everything brigade.

What is troublesome about Dr. Caldicott's psyche is that there is something savagely vengeful about her. Some of her recent opinions reminded me of Madame Defarge in Charles Dickens' novel *A Tale of Two Cities*. There is one statement Dr. Caldicott made in 1986 right after the frightening disaster at the Chernobyl nuclear reactor station in the Soviet Union that has never received the attention it deserves. Said Dr. Caldicott, this lover of humanity, in words recorded for all time by the *St. Louis Globe-Democrat:*

> I think the [Chernobyl] accident should have happened here [in the United States]. I hate to say that as a physician, but unless there are thousands of American martyrs, nothing will be done.

Dr. Caldicott's sensibility is, perhaps, an extreme case of what is meant by *pas d'ennemis à gauche* (no enemies on the left); it is also an example of the effectiveness among some liberals of the Soviet claim to a higher morality.

The Will to Mastery

The Soviet ethos—an insatiable will to mastery—is a political phenomenon which, with the end of World War II, dominated its treaty diplomacy with the democracies. The ambition to dominate was born out of the ideological aspirations of Marxism-Leninism-Stalinism, a doctrine that is luminously clear in its rhetorical self-assurance: that ultimate triumph over the non-Marxist world is predestined.[131]

That this credo vis-à-vis the noncommunist world has changed little in seventy years can be seen over and over again in the officially promulgated Soviet "party line." Whether, in the era of glastroika, the "party line" has changed for good remains to be seen. Over and over again, Soviet leaders have made clear that as far as Marxism-Leninism is concerned, its aims are uncompromisable. The language, the syntax, the jargon changes, but the message is always clear. Even when a "new" military doctrine is announced, examination of the rhetorical fallout shows that the words may have changed but there's always the wink-and-the-nod to ensure that the intent of the writer is clear. For example, here is an article by Lieutenant General of Aviation Vladimir Serebryannikov in 1987:

---

131 Some students of Soviet affairs argue that Leninism is not true Marxism. Stalin, however, said that "Leninism is the further development of Marxism. Leninism is Marxism in the epoch of imperialism and proletarian revolution" (Stalin 1933, 1:8-9). Zbigniew Brzezinski has written that "Stalin consummated the marriage of Marxism-Leninism and Soviet (particularly Russian) nationalism" ("The Soviet Past and Future," *Encounter* March 1970, page 7).

Of course, we are not pacifists. We cannot count on the regeneration of the imperialists, on their "goodwill" or on their desisting from making militaristic plans. As long as an imperialistic bourgeoisie remains armed, and, above all, increases its military might and hatched plans for getting revenge by force, socialism must know how to defend itself with arms. Any diminution of the role of military might means capitulation to reaction.... At the present time Lenin's counsel fully applies: that the toilers must master military affairs ... otherwise we will be treated like slaves. This great idea of Lenin's has not lost its force, nor has the Leninist criticism of those who console themselves with sterile and cowardly dreams of a disarmed existence alongside an armed bourgeoisie. ("Soviet Military Doctrine," *Global Affairs* III[1] [Winter 1988], page 185)

In 1955, Nikita Khrushchev said:

Our smiles are genuine. We wish to live in peace and tranquility. But if anyone believes that our smiles involve abandonment of the teachings of Marx, Engels and Lenin, he deceives himself poorly. Those who wait for that must wait until a shrimp learns to whistle. (Staar 1986, 33; *International Affairs* [Moscow] January 1956, page 2)

Addressing the Twenty-fourth Communist Party Congress on 30 March 1971, Leonid Brezhnev expanded:

Conscious of its internationalist duty, the communist Party of the Soviet Union will continue to pursue a line in international affairs which helps further to invigorate the world-wide anti-imperialist struggle and to strengthen the fighting unity of all its participants. The total triumph of the socialist cause all over the world is inevitable. And we shall not spare ourselves in the fight for this triumph, for the happiness of the working people![132]

Andropov's Minatory Words

Brezhnev's successor, Yuri V. Andropov, said in June 1983 that our time is "marked by a confrontation, unprecedented in the entire postwar period by its intensity and sharpness, between two diametrically opposed world outlooks, the two political courses of Socialism and Imperialism. A struggle

---

132 Brezhnev's speech was published 30 March 1971 by the Novosti Press Agency Publishing House (Moscow) under the title "Report of the CPSU Central Committee to the 24th Congress of the Communist Party of the Soviet Union." The salient passage cited here and that appeared on page 28 of the Report, was quoted by Prime Minister Margaret Thatcher in an address to a joint meeting of the U.S. Congress on 20 February 1985 (British Information Services PR4 21 February 1985, page 3).

is going on for the minds and hearts of billions of people on our planet" ("Can We Negotiate with the Russians?" *Encounter* no. 15 [1985], page 9).

Georgi Arbatov, a member of the Soviet Communist Party Central Committee and one of the most important spokesmen for the Soviet leadership, said in 1973: "There can be no question as to whether the struggle between the two systems would or would not continue. The struggle is unavoidable" ("World War I, World War II, WW III," *Commentary* 83[3] [March 1987], page 36; *The Communist* [Moscow] [February 1973], page 110; Ulam 1983, 48).

More recent is the 1984 statement by Andrei Gromyko, speaking then as a member of the Politburo of the CPSU and Soviet minister of foreign affairs:

Peaceful coexistence is a specific form of socialism's class struggle against capitalism. This struggle is going on and will continue in the field of economics, politics and, of course, ideology, because the world outlook and the class goals of the two social systems are opposite and irreconcilable. ("A Lenin Peace Policy," *Moscow News* 16 [1984], page 5).

Compare the Arbatov and Gromyko statements on the communist meaning of coexistence with the following statement from Lenin:

We live not only in a state but also in a *system of governments*, and the existence of the Soviet Republic alongside the imperialist states over the long run is unthinkable. In the end either the one or the other will triumph. And until that end will have arrived a series of the most terrible conflicts between the Soviet Republic and the bourgeois governments is unavoidable. This means that the ruling class, the proletariat, if it only wishes to rule ... must demonstrate this also with its military organization. (Lenin 1932, 24:122)

The words in 1931 of Dmitri Z. Manuilsky,[133] Comintern secretary for fifteen years, were pure Leninism:

War to the hilt between communism and capitalism is inevitable. Today we are not strong enough to attack. Our time will come in twenty or thirty years. To win we shall need the element of surprise. The bourgeoisie will have to be put to sleep, so we shall begin by launching the most spectacular peace movement on record. There will be electrifying overtures and unheard-of concessions. The capitalist countries, stupid and decadent, will rejoice in their own destruction. As soon as their guard is down, we shall smash them with our clenched fist. (Weeks 1987, 202)

---

133 The current edition of the *Soviet Military Encyclopedia* honors Manuilsky with an extraordinarily long write-up and photo.

Stalin's "Two Camp" Theory

It was not long after World War II that the "two camp" theory received concrete expression by one of Stalin's closest spokesmen, the egregious Andrei Zhdanov. The first organizational meeting of the Cominform (Communist Information Bureau), held in Poland 22-27 September 1947, assembled Communist Party leaders from Bulgaria, Czechoslovakia, France, Hungary, Italy, Poland, Rumania, and Yugoslavia. They came to listen to Zhdanov deliver the main political report, whose key passage read:

> The more the war recedes into the past, the more distinct become two major trends in postwar international policy, corresponding to the division of the political forces operating in the international arena into two major camps: the imperialist and anti-democratic camps, on the one hand, and the anti-imperialist and democratic camp, on the other. The principal driving force of the imperialist camp is the U.S.A.... The anti-imperialist and anti-fascist forces comprise the second camp. This camp is based on the Soviet Union and the new democracies. (Jaffe 1975, 221)

It was being argued among Western commentators at the end of the 1980s that the Gorbachev policy of *glasnost* and *perestroika* foreshadowed a changed Kremlin view about the inevitability of communist revolutions in noncommunist states and, therefore, foreshadowed changes in Soviet foreign policy. Yet, examination of Soviet journals in this period demonstrated that the so-called new thinking in Soviet foreign policy would in no way affect the aim of Marxism-Leninism: namely, the ultimate goal of world revolution.

How confused (but only temporarily) the Western academic and editorial pro-Soviet meliorists among these commentators must have been to read that Gorbachev's important seventieth anniversary speech 2 November 1987, contained this statement:

> In October 1917 we parted with the Old World, rejecting it once and for all. We are moving toward a new world—the world of communism. We will never swerve off this road. (*New York Times* 3 November 1987)

Six Decades Earlier

In more sectarian language, Lenin had said the same thing six decades earlier: "We are internationalists. We aim at the firm union and full fusion of the workers and peasants of all the nations of the world into a single, worldwide Soviet Republic" (Lenin 1924, volume 34).

The key to understanding the meaning of Gorbachev's political rhetoric with its soothing vocabulary is to read what his predecessors have said in less tactful language and then to compare it with what he is saying today.

For example, in his book *Perestroika,* Gorbachev writes:

We want freedom to reign supreme in the coming century everywhere in the world. *We want peaceful competition between different social systems to develop unimpeded* [my emphasis], to encourage mutually advantageous cooperation rather than confrontation and an arms race.... ("Gorbachev Speaks Out on the Roots of Perestroika," *Washington Post* 6 December 1987, page D2)

The crucial sentence in that passage is "We want peaceful competition between different social systems to develop unimpeded...." Despite the seeming utopianism, Gorbachev is emphasizing that there can be no compromise between the free world and its rooted market economy and Soviet monopoly socialism. He wants the competition to be unimpeded and "peaceful," but in the same way that Karl von Clausewitz[134] wrote: "The conqueror is always peace-loving, since war comes from the resistance which the defender offers to his offensive" (Keep 1967, 139). V. M. Molotov modernized the concept minus Clausewitzian irony: "We should like the [global] change-over to communism to be as painless as possible" ("Soviet Foreign Policy—New Methods, Old Aims," *New York Times* 30 January 1956, Editorial page).

The Same Rhetoric

The rhetoric remains the same no matter who the Soviet spokesman is. Here are the words of Georgi Chicherin, the Soviet foreign minister in 1922, as he spoke in Genoa at what George Kennan called "the first great summit conference of the century":

... The Russian delegation recognizes that in the present period of history, which permits the parallel existence of the old social order and of the new order now being born, economic collaboration between the States representing the two systems of property is imperatively necessary for the general economic reconstruction. (Kennan 1960, 217).

There is an Italian saying: *Si cambia il maestro di capella ma la musica é sempre quella,* or, while the orchestra conductor may change, the music always remains the same. One might apply these words to the present direction of Kremlin moves on the international scene. While much has happened since Gorbachev's assumption of leadership to justify an optimism

---

134 Lenin much admired the Prussian strategist and read him frequently. His copy of Clausewitz has this marginal annotation in the text cited: "Ha, ha, that's witty" (Keep 1967, 139).

about the future course of Soviet treaty diplomacy, there is for me a great uncertainty about the Soviet future because the essential duplicity which informs Soviet strategy is still there.

Here is a sample of how Gorbachev sells his prepackaged *glasnost*. The opening sentences of the U.S. edition of his *Perestroika* read:

> The purpose of this book is to talk without intermediaries to the citizens of the whole world about things that, without exception, concern us all. I've written this book because I believe in their common sense. I am convinced that they, like me, worry about the future of our planet. ("Which Gorbachev Do You Read?" *New Republic* 21 December 1987, page 8)

From the opening sentences of the Hungarian edition of what presumably is the same book:

> In our work and worries, we are motivated by those Leninist ideals and noble endeavors and goals which mobilized the workers of Russia seven decades ago to fight for the new happy world of socialism. *Perestroika* is a continuation of the October Revolution. (Ibid.)

Which Gorbachev—and in what language—do you read? *Autres temps, autres moeurs.*

A Good Question

Discussing arms control in general between the United States and the Soviet Union, the *Wall Street Journal* recently said that the prospect of "a Soviet ABM breakout raises once again the question of why we are negotiating new treaties with them when they are breaking the old ones" ("Breakout," *Wall Street Journal* 25 February 1988, page 20). Or, one can ask, why negotiate with a superpower that quite clearly has no intention of living peacefully with its neighbors or its rivals and, provably, has no intention of honoring for long its international commitments? After all, the United States and its allies are wedded to a democratic status quo in which change must come about peacefully, or at least not by internal subversion and/or external aggression. What U.S. alliances remain are defensive.

The Soviet Union, on the other hand, favors its own status quo; its alliances are most certainly not defensive. The Soviet Union is informed by a doctrine that, in rejecting a democratic status quo, seeks eventual destabilization of those areas in the world that neither follow Soviet foreign policy nor indulge Soviet definitions of national security.

A Nonshooting War

Vladimir Bukovsky has argued that the Soviet Union, "seeing itself as the hub of 'world socialism,' has been conducting, as its *raison d'être* demands, a nonshooting war against the rest of the world over the last seven decades" ("Hope and Despair in the Soviet System II," *Encounter* 40[1] [January 1988], page 22). He continued:

> Since Watergate and the U.S. debacle in Vietnam, Soviet expansionism and the Soviet nuclear buildup have accelerated, and after a careful weighing of the "correlation of forces" the Soviets seem to have come to the conclusion that they could now undermine the United States as a world power by making trouble for it in its soft underbelly in Central America. (Ibid.)

Bukovsky also pointed out that Article 28 of the Soviet Constitution says that the Soviet Union supports revolutionary and national "liberation" struggles throughout the world.[135] He added, "So long as this stipulation remains one of the governing principles of the Soviet state, the Kremlin will go on having an excuse for expansionism." (Ibid., pages 25, 22).

Why Negotiate?

The question persists: Why negotiate with a superpower whose aim is to disrupt existing international agreements among the nations of the free world; a superpower that conducts a permanent—overtly, covertly, or both— political offensive against all noncommunist countries anywhere and everywhere? Why not a policy of "masterly inactivity" or "benign neglect" as far as treaty diplomacy with the Soviet Union is concerned, especially when we know from Lenin's own words what Soviet treaty diplomacy intends? Said Lenin:

> It is necessary to be able to use the contradictions and differences which exist among the imperialists. All diplomacy strives to take advantage of the contradictions between opponents. But unlike the diplomacy of exploiting states,

---

135 Article 28 of the Soviet Constitution occurs in chapter 4, under "Foreign Policy" and declares, *inter alia*, "The foreign policy of the Soviet Union is aimed at ensuring international conditions favorable for building communism in the Soviet Union ... consolidating the positions of world socialism, supporting the struggle of peoples for national liberation and social progress...." (Soviet Constitution 1985, 23). The clause, "consolidating the positions of world socialism," could certainly be extrapolated to justify the presumably repudiated Brezhnev Doctrine.

which in a majority of cases tries to use the contradictions between other states—and even artificially provokes or exacerbates them—in order to increase international tension and create a situation which would be favorable for the execution of its own aggressive schemes, socialist diplomacy uses the contradictions between imperialist states in the interests of peace, for the purpose of destroying the aggressive blocs slapped together by the imperialists and preventing their aggressive actions, and consequently, for strengthening the general security. (U.S. Senate 1969, 82)

In other words—and minus the spurious moral indignation—Lenin's theory of treaty diplomacy was to exploit the normal differences that exist between nation-states with different traditions and political cultures and thus prevent the formation of an alliance that might threaten Soviet ideological and military thrusts. Democratic diplomacy no doubt also seeks occasionally to exploit the normal differences that exist between nation-states, but for limited ends, not for the extinction of a constitutional republic and its recreation into a satellized nation.

NATO Disintegration

As we watch a much weakened NATO, and as we watched the earlier disintegration of SEATO and ANZUS, it would appear that Lenin's theory works, his strategy has been highly successful. After all, during the wartime alliance of the Soviet Union with the Western powers against a common enemy, negotiations with the Soviet Union "were extremely difficult and frustrating," in the words of Professor Philip Mosely (U.S. Senate 1969, 25), who was personally involved in negotiations with the Russians. Why should the atmosphere be any better in a time of nonshooting war between the Soviet Union and the NATO powers?

Using a discussion of the Helsinki negotiations as a springboard, Ambassador Max Kampelman ("Can We Negotiate with the Russians?" *Encounter* no. 15 [1985], passim) has given several reasons why U.S.-Soviet negotiations are essential:

1. There is no "realistic alternative" to such negotiations.
2. The West European members of the Western alliance, that would be in the forefront of any military confrontation, are concerned about "a nuclear catastrophe" and are, therefore, in no position to ostracize the Soviet Union.
3. For the United States to go it alone on a policy of ostracism of the Soviet Union would have isolated this country and weakened the Western alliance.

4. If the West hopes to achieve a thaw and a liberalization of the communist system, "we must try to achieve them in ways that are open to us: and that means using the international political process."
5. It is important to win over West European public opinion and neutralize the influential "peace" movement in West European countries.
6. The West cannot hope to influence Soviet policy without "great military strength and military strength cannot be had without the support of public opinion."

Kampelman's interlocutor, George Urban, then posed his question: "Can we negotiate with a global superpower whose words we cannot trust, whose entire ideology lifts amorality to the level of principle, and whose very reading of human nature and man's destiny is entirely different from our own?" (Ibid. page 16)

Kampelman's answer was no answer at all: "... [D]o we sign a treaty banning bacteriological weapons with the Soviet Union when we know perfectly well that the Soviets used chemical and bacteriological weapons in Afghanistan?" (Ibid.)

Then why, one asks, do "we" sign such a treaty? Deponent sayeth not.

Theory of Soviet Treaty Diplomacy

Jean-François Revel and Branko Lazitch ("Heritage of the Dialogue Culture," *Wall Street Journal* 7 January 1985, Op-Ed page) have outlined a theory of Soviet treaty diplomacy that, they say, follows these principles:

1. "Lies and deception are normal tools in international relations since international relations are essentially war."
2. "Compromise is often inevitable but, as Lenin said, there are several kinds of compromise." In other words, there are good compromises and bad compromises.
3. Treaty violations are normal behavior in treaty diplomacy.

According to Revel and Lazitch, between 1925 and 1941 the Soviet Union signed fifteen nonaggression or neutrality treaties. It broke, denounced, or violated eleven of these treaties. Germany and Italy violated two, and two others were abrogated. Between 1950 and 1980, the Kremlin signed eighteen alliances; it violated fifteen, among them the Helsinki agreements.

Some of George Kennan's State Department dispatches from Moscow could be cited today with profit for our national leadership. Writing in 1946, Kennan said:

Their (the Russians'] history had known many armistices between hostile forces; but it had never known an example of the permanent peaceful coexistence of two neighboring states.... The Russians therefore have no conception of permanent friendly relations between states. For them, all foreigners are potential enemies. In examining a position taken by a foreign state, the Russians make no effort to look at it from the standpoint of the foreign state in question or from any fancy community of aims on the part of themselves and the state involved. They assume it is dictated by purposes which are not theirs, and they examine it only from the standpoint of its effect on them. If the effect is favorable, they accept it without gratitude; if it is unfavorable, they reject it without resentment. We could make it much easier for ourselves if we would face these facts. (Urban 1982, 358; for an explanation by Kennan himself for his later change of view about the Soviet Union, see Urban 1982, 398ff)

7

Optimists, Pessimists, Realissimists

In the Soviet Union we have a saying, "a pessimist is someone who believes things can't get any worse. An optimist thinks maybe they can."

Abel G. Aganbegyan, Soviet economist[136]

Western diplomats who negotiate with Soviet diplomats, as well as publicists or scholars who observe and analyze U.S.-Soviet negotiations, are of two kinds: optimists and pessimists.

The optimists believe that dialogue and negotiation with this superpower, a totalitarian state with an aura of authoritarianism, is an unavoidable necessity precisely because it is the kind of regime it is—powerful and unscrupulous. It can be taken as a law of international life that optimists about the Soviet Union, even in the Gorbachev Era, are forever doomed to find that their sunny prophecies and rational analyses about the course of Soviet events are wrong, misguided, and of no use to anyone.

One of the best examples of the optimist who was done in by events at the Kremlin and as a result became a pessimist (but only for a little while) is Jimmy Carter. Shortly after he became president in May 1977, he said:

Being confident of our own future, we are now free of that inordinate fear of communism which once led us to embrace any dictator who joined us in our fear. For too many years we have been willing to adopt the flawed principles and tactics

---

136 *Fortune Magazine* 2 January 1989, page 47.

of our adversaries, sometimes abandoning our values for theirs. (*The Guardian* 24 January 1982, page 10)[137]

By the end of his term, President Carter appeared to have learned that, where the Soviets are concerned, things are seldom what they seem. Brezhnevian kisses and bearhugs at the Vienna summit meeting may have meant something to Carter; they meant nothing to Brezhnev. In due course, confronted by the invasion of Afghanistan—to him an utterly unpredictable action—President Carter told a TV interviewer on New Year's Eve 1979: "This action of the Soviets has made a more dramatic change in my own opinion of what the Soviets' ultimate goals are than anything they've done in the previous time I've been in office" (*American Spectator* April 1981, page 32).[138]

Pessimists and Their Prototypes

The pessimists, on the other hand, believe that without some internal upheaval, little in the Soviet Union can be changed for the better, even when the current Soviet party general secretary pledges improvements. Like Leszek Kolakowski's phrase in a Polish context, the Russians will get "a milder hangman." In other words, the pessimists believe that the West can only lose to the Soviet Union in any negotiation because of the sensible Soviet policy of incremental gains on the West. These gains reach a point where a return to the *status quo ante* is impossible, given the power of public opinion in the democracies. The prototypical pessimist would be someone like Senator Malcolm Wallop of Wyoming who with his coauthor, Angelo Codevilla of the Hoover Institution, recently wrote:

[I]n the 1980s, after twenty years of the arms control process, the United States is left with a radically worsened strategic situation, with an impaired ability to judge military developments at home and abroad, with a near-total reliance on arms control for our safety and independence, as well as with a growing realization that Americans have precisely zero means for enforcing the terms of any agreement, good or bad. (Wallop & Codevilla 1987, 132; *Commentary* 85[4] [1988], page 70)

---

137 In 1989, Jimmy Carter described Gorbachev as "the most humanitarian of the world's leaders" ("For Good or Evil," *Washington Post* 21 May 1989). I suppose for Carter, Pope John Paul isn't a world leader and George Bush is less of a humanitarian than Gorbachev.

138 President Carter was frequently wrong in his perceptions. For example, during a state visit by the Shah of Iran in 1978, he toasted the about-to-be-toppled monarch with the statement, "I can see how you are loved by your people" (Menges 1988, 26). In January 1979, the Shah fled, and a month later the Ayatollah Khomeini took over.

"Biggest Collective Delusion"

Norman Podhoretz, editor of *Commentary* magazine, is another prototypical pessimist. He has described the Western belief in arms control agreements with the Soviet Union as "the single biggest collective delusion or superstition that the world has known at least since the Middle Ages" (Podhoretz 1987, 34ff.).[139] To paraphrase his reasons:

1. Disarmament negotiations during the 1920s and 1930s increased the danger of war. The democracies were delighted to disarm and save money while the dictatorships were able to increase their arms expenditures and to do a little cheating on the side as well. In the postwar era, the arms control process enabled the Soviet Union to forge ahead in the competition while preventing the United States from catching up.
2. The arms control process is based on self-deception in the West about the "nature of the totalitarian enemy." The Soviet threat is created by a "revolutionary actor [who] is seeking a new world order in which it would enjoy hegemony." It is argued that because it has lost its ideological appeal as a model society, the Soviet Union is no longer the danger it once was. In other words, all that is left to the Soviet Union is its military power. Then all the more reason for the Kremlin to hold on to that power.
3. The arms-control process is "based on fraud, and in the simplest sense: the Soviets cheat. The agreements are fraudulent."[140]

Soviet Arms Control Strategy

Edward Rowny has been chief arms adviser to five presidents and currently to President Bush. He has summarized the strategy of Soviet arms

---

139 During the interwar years, Walter Lippmann observed that "the disarmament movement was, as the events have shown, tragically successful in disarming the nations that believed in disarmament."

140 Another pessimist is the British publicist Anthony Hartley, who also dealt with arms control. He recently wrote: "Contrary to what is usually assumed, disarmament is a consequence of political agreement rather than its cause. Without any prior accord on specific political disputes, Arms Control, if realized prematurely, must have the result of upsetting that balance of military power which provided a limiting framework to hostility. Any treaty which brought about an imbalance of military power in Central Europe would intensify, rather than diminish, the psychological disquiet which distinguishes Cold War" ("The 'Cold War' for Beginners," *Encounter* LXXX[3] [February 1988], page 11).

control, that is always at the top of the East-West agenda ("Moscow's Process Emphasis," *Washington Times* 30 May 1989, page C1):

1. By encouraging a Western "fixation" on arms control the Soviets will be able best to direct East-West relations in their interest.
2. Such preoccupation with arms control diverts attention from the underlying causes of East-West tensions: namely, the difference in the values of the Soviet and U.S. social systems.
3. By advocating vague "agreements in principle," the Soviets give the false impression that a full bilateral agreement is at hand, even though critical issues remain unresolved.

The pessimist frequently has good reason for his mood. In May 1989, Soviet Foreign Minister Shevardnadze threatened that the Soviet Union would quit dismantling SS-23 missiles, as required by the INF (intermediate-range nuclear forces missiles) treaty, if the United States decided to replace its vestigial Lance short-range missiles, which the INF treaty allows. The U.S. idea was to triple the Lance short-range missiles to more than 250 miles ("Moscow Faulted on Missile Threat," *New York Times* 15 May 1989, page 15).

Shevardnadze's threat was, said Richard Perle ("How the PR coup evolved?" *Washington Times* 5 June 1989, Op-Ed page), "the unscrupulous tactic of unilaterally revising the terms of an agreement by deliberately violating one of its obligations—a tactic easy for the Kremlin, which is unburdened by coalition politics or public opinion, but unthinkable for any Western democracy."[141]

One could well ask, Whatever happened to President Gorbachev's cry in his United Nations speech, *"Pacta sunt servanda"* (treaties must be observed)?

Why would Shevardnadze have attempted such a coup, obviously with Gorbachev's blessing? It could be part of that built-in Soviet disregard for treaty obligations plus part of its cold war strategy that also implies a sense of adventurism and opportunism: If you can get away with it, fine; if not, what do you lose? It could explain the sale to Libya of 15 Sukhoi-24D bombers, supersonic planes never before sold to anybody. Qadaffi now possesses a

---

141 The "Lance" issue became moot in November 1989 when the West German government decided that in view of the changes in Eastern Europe the short-range nuclear modernization program could no longer be justified ("Bonn Aides, in Washington, Say Modernizing Missiles Is Dead Issue," *New York Times* 11 November 1989, page A6).

missile delivery system to Israel and southern Europe. It could explain Shevardnadze's visit to Teheran during the world uproar over the late Ayatollah Khomeini's death sentence of Salman Rushdie and the ceremonial visit of an Iranian delegation to Moscow in late June 1989 ("Red Mischief," *New Republic* 1 May 1989, pages 10-11)

Any Lessons for Bush or State Department?

Of overriding importance is: What lesson did the Bush Administration or the State Department draw from this attempted missile coup? Or did these institutions go right on negotiating as if nothing had happened, as if it were just a naughty child acting up? Are there no penalties for such Soviet threats, as there would be if the U.S. government had made a similar démarche?

Another example of treaty violation that was ignored has to do with the Montreux Convention of 1936 that governs the right of transit and navigation through the Bosporus and Dardanelles Straits to the Mediterranean. Article ten of the Montreux convention provides that, in time of peace, light surface and minor war vessels enjoy freedom of transit through the Dardanelles. Annex two to the Convention is quite clear in its distinction between "capital ships" and aircraft carriers. There is no article in the Convention covering aircraft carriers.

In 1976, when the first of the Soviet Union's 43,000-ton Kiev-class warships sailed through the Straits, Moscow classified the vessel as an antisubmarine cruiser. It was clearly an aircraft carrier. When it made its first trip through the Straits, the vessel carried only helicopters on deck. The Soviet Union noted that there were no catapults or arresting gear for aircraft. As soon as the ship reached open sea, the Soviet Union reclassified it as a "tactical aircraft-carrying cruiser." The ship now carries 36 Yak-36 vertical- or short-takeoff and landing aircraft (Brown 1987, 40).

Still another example of how the Soviet Union profits from the deliberate obliviousness by American policy-making elites to Soviet treaty behavior was the U.S. Senate's refusal to enact into law a provision to protect the country against Soviet treaty violations. On 20 May 1988, Senator Steve Symms (R., Idaho) presented an amendment to the INF treaty that would require the president to certify that the Soviet Union has ceased violating treaties signed in the past before the INF treaty became effective.

Symms Amendment

The Symms amendment was divided into five parts at the Senator's request, a division that corresponded to the five existing arms control treaties between the United States and the Soviet Union:

1.   ABM treaty.
2.   Nuclear test ban treaty.
3.   Biological and chemical weapons treaty.
4.   Salt I interim agreement.
5.   Salt II.

Now this was no "have-you-stopped-beating-your-wife" trick proposal. President Reagan had on numerous occasions in the past submitted, as required by law, findings that the Soviet Union had violated *every one of these arms control agreements*. Nevertheless, the five parts of the amendment were defeated in the Senate by 8-to-1 majorities ("INF Treaty: Soviet Violations of Past Treaties," *Human Events* 4 June 1988, page 19). If Soviet violations (and nobody argued that they didn't exist) can be ignored by the United States Senate, what is there for the Soviet Union to worry about?

Incremental Gains

The pessimist realizes that what he feels would prove to be a step backward for the United States is a step backward forever, whereas a step backward for the Soviet Union might well lead to two or more steps forward.

An example of incremental gains over the democracies by the Soviet Union is the unusual, even unprecedented leftist composition of the U.S. House of Representatives. Who would have predicted ten or twenty years ago that by 1989, without causing much of a stir, there would be sitting at least two dozen pro-Soviet congressmen who would be either documented Marxists or open communist collaborators? And that among these, several would have authentic political clout and be in a position to decide almost invariably within a pro-Soviet context such great issues as defense, arms control, and international security? This collaboration had become so notorious that two journalists, J. Michael Waller and Joseph Sobran ("Congress's Red Army," *National Review* 39 [31 July 1987], page 40), wrote: "It's getting harder and harder for all sides to tell the Democratic line from the Soviet one."[142]

When President Reagan was asked by Arnaud de Borchgrave, editor-in-chief of the *Washington Times,* "about the number of hard-left members of

---

142 Also see Fossedal & Lieberman 1988, 39ff. The authors have found that "in many areas of foreign policy, the Democrats and the Kremlin seem to have reached a remarkable consensus.... [A] large number of Democratic leaders support the Soviet position most of the time."

the House who are now acting as pro-Soviet agents of influence,"[143] Reagan replied:

> Well, Arnaud, that is a problem that we have to face. It would be easy enough to just stand up and start shouting. But some years ago—I happen to know because I've been a student of the communist movement for a long time, having been a victim of it some years ago in Hollywood—the Communist Party was to call upon their "willing idiots"—their term—not just liberals who weren't communists, but ... they were to engage in a campaign that would make anti-communism unfashionable. And they have succeeded. (*Washington Times* 30 September 1987, pages 10-11)[144]

The "Realissimist" Negotiator

There is actually a third category of negotiator—what I call the "realissimist." He is the statesman who signs agreements with the Soviet Union, suspecting all the while that the Soviet Union will violate the agreement at the first chance. Knowing full well that noncompliance is inevitable, he hopes that this time it will be different.

Former Secretary of State Dean Acheson was a realissimist. He tells the story (Acheson 1959) of the May 1949 meeting in Paris of the foreign ministers of Britain, France, the Soviet Union, and the United States. The

---

143 The pro-Soviet caucus in the House of Representatives hasn't changed much as of November 1989. The House voted 379-29 on 2 November 1989 (along with the Senate, which voted 95-0) to condemn the Ortega regime's decision to end the cease-fire in Nicaragua and "to reaffirm U.S. support for peace and democracy in Central America" (*Human Events* 1989, page 3). The twenty-nine were all Democrats.

144 The remaining text of President Reagan's comment on this subject is worth pondering: "You know that today even among the people that are anti-communist, there is a tendency to say, 'Oh, you know, enough of that, hey, don't, this is old-fashioned McCarthyism,' and so forth, and all of that. Well, they're taking advantage of this now. Remember, there was once a Congress in which they had a committee that would investigate even one of their own members if it was believed that that person had communist involvement or communist leanings. Well, they've done away with those committees. That shows the success of what the Soviets were able to do in this country with making it unfashionable to be anti-communist. So you have to be careful in opposing them not to trigger that reaction on the part of your own people that you're depending on to support you. And it's no fun, but it is true—there is a disinformation campaign, we know, worldwide, and that disinformation campaign is very sophisticated and is very successful, including with a great many in the media and the press." De Borchgrave interposed: "And on the Hill?" President Reagan replied, "And on the Hill" (*Washington Times* 30 September 1987, pages 10-11).

Soviet military authorities had instigated a strike on the Russian-operated railroad in West Berlin. Nothing was moving; in other words, the Soviet blockade of West Berlin was on again. The Soviet minister, the egregious Andrei Vishinsky, under great pressure finally agreed on 20 June 1949 on some *modus vivendi* on trade and traffic with Berlin. The most important agreement concerned a treaty for an independent Austria.

The conference broke up with the usual champagne toasts and buffet sandwiches. As the conferees—minus Vishinsky—were downing a last glass, they were told that Vishinsky was reconvening an emergency meeting of the ministers. He had received a phone call from Andrei Gromyko, using what the French described as "brutal language," that the agreements on Austria, which had been concluded earlier in the day, had to be reopened for some new provisions. Until the agreement was revised, it was null and void.

When the meeting of the foreign ministers resumed, the British Foreign Secretary, the tough-minded and "realissimist" Ernest Bevin, "congratulated [Vishinsky] on a new record. Soviet agreements were fragile things, but today's was the frailest yet. It had not even survived the day" (Ibid., 46). The joint Allied policy adopted by Bevin and Acheson as they walked through the corridors to the meeting was that they would tell Vishinsky "to go to hell." And they did. In the event, the Austrian State Treaty was not signed until 1955.

The consummate exemplar of a realissimist is President Reagan, who once said about the Soviet Union that "a government that breaks faith with its own people cannot be trusted to keep faith with foreign powers" (*Washington Times* 30 September 1987, page 10).[145]

British Prime Minister Margaret Thatcher is another realissimist who once said, "If a country persists in putting people into prison because of their political and religious views, that's something you have to take into account when you gauge whether they are going to keep any agreements you reach on arms control" (*American Foreign Policy Newsletter* [Washington, D.C.] December 1987, page 10).[146]

---

145 A memorable example of how the Soviet regime breaks faith with its citizens is the story of Academician Petr Kapitsa, Nobel laureate in physics in 1979 (he died five years later). From 1921 to 1934, Kapitsa worked in Britain at the Cavendish laboratories in Cambridge. In 1934, the Soviet government invited him to return to the Soviet Union in order to "acquaint" himself with Soviet physics. Kapitsa was given a guarantee, underwritten by Maxim Gorky, of return to England. The promise was broken. Kapitsa was not allowed to leave the Soviet Union (*Radio Liberty* 232/88 [7 June 1988], page 3).

146 How Mrs. Thatcher can reconcile this statement with an earlier one that Mikhail Gorbachev is a man she can do "business" with remains a mystery that she may someday explain in her memoirs.

The realissimist, however, never answers the question: Why, if you believe that the Soviet Union is a treaty violator by virtue of its Marxist-Leninist faith, do you negotiate at all? Why keep hoping that this time the Soviet Union will abide by the agreement?

The answer is that the realissimist is always· in danger of being transformed into an optimist. As an optimist, he can view the Soviet Union as a putatively sated superpower, and in consequence will then negotiate arms control treaties which his realissimist side realizes would imperil national security.

A Fundamental Change?

The eight Reagan years afford an extraordinary case history of the transformation of a president from pessimist to realissimist to optimist ("Has Reagan Gone Soft? The old Anti-Communist has a new, more complex view of Russia." *Time* 13 October 1986, page 27). Ronald Reagan's remarkably stern views of the Soviet Union under Leonid Brezhnev, Yuri Andropov, and Konstantin Chernenko turned 180 degrees when the Soviet Politburo chose a less moribund general secretary. In his pre-election campaign speeches and in his first term, Reagan viewed the Soviet Union as a world revolutionary state seeking world domination. Four years later all had changed ("Reagan and the Russians: Crisis Bargaining Beliefs and the Historical Record," *American Political Science Review* 78[2] [June 1984], pages 339-40).

For example, a few days after the third Reagan-Gorbachev summit in December 1987, President Reagan was interviewed by four U.S. journalists. In the course of the interview he said:

Possibly the fundamental change is that in the past, Soviet leaders have openly expressed their acceptance of the Marxian theory of the one-world communist state.... Their obligation was to expand and make the whole world [communist]. I no longer feel that way; I think we're dealing with an [Soviet] administration that—and this doesn't mean that I'm dropping my guard or anything, but that we have a potential here of a recognition that we have two systems that are competitive, that aren't alike, that have different values, but a desire to prove that we can live in a world together in peace. And this is what I've been seeing in these three meetings, and more in this last meeting with the general secretary. ("Aren't the Soviets Sill Expansionist at Heart? No, Says Ronald Reagan," *Los Angeles Times* 10 December 1987, page E1)

What Happened to the Big Chill?

And yet two years earlier, in an address to a joint session of Congress 21 November 1985, he said: "We cannot assume that their [Soviet] ideology and purpose will change. This implies enduring competition. Our task is to ensure that this competition remains peaceful" (Reagan 1986, 42).

On 26 February 1988, an interview with President Reagan was published in the *Washington Post* under the byline of Lou Cannon. The president was asked whether he believed that Gorbachev "really is a different kind of leader than the Soviets have had before." Replied President Reagan:

> Yes, I do, having met most of them.... I think that one difference is that he is the first leader that has come along who has gone back before Stalin and that he is trying to do what Lenin was teaching ... with Lenin's death, Stalin actually reversed many of the things. Lenin had programs that he called the new economics and things of that kind. And I've known a little bit about Lenin and what he was advocating, and I think that this, in *glasnost* and *perestroika* and all that, this is much more smacking of Lenin than of Stalin. And I think that this is what [Gorbachev] is trying to do. (*Washington Post* 26 February 1988)[147]

Changed Perceptions

In the same interview, the president was asked whether his perception of the Soviet Union today was different from his perception seven-and-a-half years ago when he entered the Oval Office. Referring to Brezhnev, Andropov, and Chernenko—Gorbachev's predecessors—President Reagan said they were "of a different philosophy than this one [Gorbachev]"

---

147 A difference of opinion between President Reagan and the CIA surfaced publicly in 1988. In a speech on 19 January, Robert Gates, deputy director of Central Intelligence, declared that quite possibly Gorbachev was embarking on a Leninist road. But, Gates added: "I, for one, do not find a return to Leninism comforting" ("What Is Going on in the Soviet Union?" *National Security Record* [Heritage Foundation] April 1988, 1ff.). Gates's speech pointed out that "there has been no repudiation" of the Brezhnev Doctrine by Gorbachev's Soviet Union, "whose aggressive objectives abroad and totalitarianism at home remain largely unchanged" (Ibid.).

An offended State Department demanded in vain Gates' dismissal. He became deputy national security adviser in the Bush Administration in 1989, resigning his CIA post. However, his troubles did not end. Secretary of State James Baker rejected two speech drafts by Gates on the grounds of "timing." At a meeting with Gorbachev in Moscow, attended by Baker and Gates, the Soviet leader suggested that their two countries so improve their relations as "to put Mr. Gates out of a job" ("Baker Bars Expert's Speech About Gorbachev's Chances," *New York Times* 27 October 1989, page 1). Obviously, Gorbachev was signalling to the White House not only his disapproval of Gates but making it clear that the Soviet Union would not look kindly upon a promotion to National Security Adviser should the incumbent, General Brent Scowcroft, move on to another and more important post—say, director of Central Intelligence ("Baker Launches Drive to Get Gates," *Washington Times* 2 November 1989, page E1).

("Excerpts from Interview with Reagan," *Washington Post* 26 February 1988, page A18).

President Reagan's benign view of Lenin and Leninism as more pacific than Stalin and Stalinism contrasted sharply with an anti-Leninist cult that in 1989 was beginning to take shape in the Soviet Union itself. Until then, Soviet commentators and publicists had avoided attacks on Lenin himself. He was the holy ikon. Say anything you want but leave Lenin out of it. If someone is to blame, let it be Stalin, Khrushchev, or Brezhnev. Never Lenin.

Now, on 10 February 1989, a full-blown assault on Lenin accompanied by a peculiar exoneration of Stalin appeared. In an article in *Moskovskaya Pravda*, Colonel-General Dmitri Volkogonov, a leading Soviet historian, charged that the epithet "enemy of the people," that was fatally applied to millions of Soviet citizens during the Stalin dictatorship, was first used by Lenin himself as far back as November 1917, within a month of the Bolshevik Revolution. The epithet itself was first heard during the French Revolution to justify Robespierre's Terror (Reuters 10 February 1989).

Stalin Voted Against

Volkogonov, who is writing the first Soviet biography of Stalin,[148] told Reuters in an interview that the minutes of a meeting of the Soviet leaders read as follows: "A draft decree was introduced by Comrade Lenin calling for the arrest of prominent members of the party Central Committee as enemies of the people and for them to be tried by a revolutionary tribunal" ("Soviet Historian Says Lenin Coined Term 'Enemy of the People'," *Reuters* Moscow 10 February 1989; "Soviet historian criticizes Lenin," *Washington Times* 13 February 1988, page 6). The minutes said that the decree was adopted by the Council of People's Deputies with only Stalin voting against.

Volkogonov wasn't whitewashing Stalin, since he told Reuters that Stalin "went through a grotesque change in his development; he was not always a vampire" (Ibid.). He contrasted Stalin's vote against Lenin's "enemy of the people" decree with the day of 12 December 1937 when Stalin and the then Prime Minister V. M. Molotov sanctioned the execution of 3,167 people and then went off to the movies in the evening.

Lenin's 1917 decree that initiated his terrorist policies was followed by another decree, "The Socialist Fatherland in Danger!" of 21 February 1918. The document provided for execution "on the spot" for what Lenin called "counterrevolutionary agitators." According to Richard Pipes' manuscript history of the Russian Revolution, there were objections to such a sweeping

---

148 Although the biography was to be published in the summer of 1988, as of June 1989 it had not yet appeared (Byrnes 1989, 37).

decree, one whereby Lenin's opponents could be killed. When one of his critics said, "Then why do we bother with a Commissariat of Justice? Let's call it frankly the Commissariat for Social Extermination and be done with it," Lenin replied, "Well put ... that's exactly what it should be ... but we can't say that" (Steinberg 1953, 145).

"Made My Blood Run Cold"

Bertrand Russell's low opinion of Lenin, whom the British philosopher met in 1920 on a trip to Moscow, is to be found in a collection of Russell's papers called *Unpopular Essays*. One of the essays is called "Eminent Men I Have Known." Calling Lenin "cruel," he goes on to describe his meeting with Lenin: "When I put a question to [Lenin] about socialism in agriculture, he explained with glee how he had incited the poorer peasants against the richer ones 'and they soon hanged them from the nearest tree—ha! ha! ha!.' His guffaw at the thought of those massacred made my blood run cold" (Russell 1950, 170-71).

The postrevolutionary critical writings of Maxim Gorky, suppressed since 1917, were recently made public in the Soviet Union. In one of his essays he says about Lenin and Trotsky, "Now in cold blood they bring dishonor on the Revolution, on the working class, forcing it to conduct bloody murders and inciting pogroms and arrests of innocent people" ("Maxim Gorky's Criticism of Bolshevik Terror Revealed in Soviet Union,"[149] *Radio Liberty* 1[11] 17 [March 1989], page 2). He described Lenin as a person who "has all the qualities of a 'leader,' including a lack of morals, which is necessary for this role, and a lordly, merciless attitude toward the life of the people" (Ibid.).

Lenin's writings are replete with frank, uninhibited, cynical, and occasionally cruel statements; so much so that his published writings, it is now openly admitted in the Soviet Union, have undergone considerable censoring by Soviet ideological authorities. The Soviet press recently discussed how the Lenin corpus has been so manipulated that one Soviet writer said that it was "incredible" that there should be in the Soviet Union "a forbidden Lenin" ("Censorship of Lenin in the Soviet Union," *Radio Liberty* 328/88 [1988], page 4).

Embarrassing Cross-Examination

While we cannot expect a president to become an instant Sovietologist upon occupying the Oval Office, still one would expect that before

---

149 The article is a summary of Gorky documents published in a new Soviet journal, *Izvestia TsK KPSS*, that show him to have been critical of the revolution and the aftermath through 1927.

pronouncing on Lenin and his successors, especially when important treaty negotiations are inevitable, a president would consult with scholars who could inform him, for example, that the practice of terrorism, forced labor, and concentration camps was begun by Lenin. It should be noted, too, that while the liberal media, particularly television news broadcasters, were always on the prowl for some Reagan gaffe to exploit, none of them so much as grimaced at the Reagan nonsense about Lenin, the kindly statesman who inspired Gorbachev to undertake his good and wondrous deeds.

It became particularly embarrassing when President Reagan allowed himself to be cross-examined by tongue-in-cheek Soviet journalists on his knowledge of Leninism and Soviet ideology, I offer the following colloquy between President Reagan and two Soviet television interviewers at the White House on 28 May 1988, just before the Moscow summit:

> Q. Mr. President, I can't help but ask you a question which is very interesting to Soviet people.... You, in your speeches, many times have quoted the works of Lenin, you've made reference to his works, you quoted him about expansionistic aims of Soviet communists. Soviet specialists, insofar as I know, in the U.S. press and people who work in the Library of Congress, have studied all of the compositions of Lenin's, and they haven't found one similar quotation or anything that's even close to some of those quotations. So I would like to ask you what works of Lenin did you read, and where were those quotations that you used taken from?
>
> THE PRESIDENT: Oh, my. I don't think I could recall and specify here and there. But I've had a—I'm old enough to have had a great interest in the Soviet Union and I know that in the things I studied at college ... that the declarations of Karl Marx, for example, that Karl Marx said your system, communism, could only succeed when the whole world had become communist.... Now, as I say, I can't recall all of the sources from which I gleaned this, and maybe some things have been interpreted differently as in modern versions, but I know that Lenin expounded on that and said that that must be the goal. But I also know ... that every leader, every general secretary but the present one had ... reiterated their allegiance to that Marxian theory that the goal was a one-world communist state. This man [Gorbachev] has not said that. So I wasn't making anything up; these were the things we were told. (U.S. White House press release #14,383, 1988, page 3)[150]

---

150 Some months earlier, Gennadii Gerasimov, the Soviet spokesman, brought Lenin's collected works to a press briefing. It seems that President Reagan had in a speech to American publishers attributed to Lenin the sentence, "the road to America leads through Mexico." Gerasimov said that if anyone at the briefing could find such a remark in Lenin's works, "I am ready to eat my hat" ("Kremlin Reinterprets and Re-emphasizes the Legacy of Lenin," *New York Times* 10 May 1987, page E3).

Melioristic Interpretations

Melioristic interpretations of the new Soviet leadership and of Leninism as somehow superior to Stalinism are far different from the harsh and hardheaded judgments made by President Reagan during his first years in office. For example, at his very first press conference 29 January 1981, when Brezhnev was still alive, President Reagan said:

> I know of no leader of the Soviet Union since the revolution ... that has not more than once repeated in the various communist congresses they hold their determination ... of world revolution and a one-world socialist or communist state.... Now, as long as they do that, and as long as they reserve unto themselves the right to commit any crime, to lie, to cheat, in order to attain, and that is moral, not immoral, and we operate on different set of standards, I think when you do business with them ... you keep that in mind. (*New York Times* 30 January 1981)

On 8 March 1983, in a speech to the National Association of Evangelicals, he said of the Soviet leadership:

> Let us beware that while they preach the supremacy of the state, declare its omnipotence over individual man, and predict its eventual domination over all the peoples of the earth, they are the focus of evil in the modern world.... I urge you to beware the temptation ... to ignore the facts of history and the aggressive impulses of any evil empire, to simply call the arms race a giant misunderstanding and thereby remove yourself from the struggle between right and wrong, good and evil. (*New York Times* 9 March 1983)

The Mysterious Transformation

What accounted for this dramatic alteration of President Reagan's perspective has yet to be explained. President Reagan seemed unaware of a major Gorbachev address 14 March 1987 to the Central Committee of the CPSU celebrating the seventieth anniversary of the Bolshevik Revolution in which the general secretary said:

> We live in a world which has changed profoundly under the influence of our Revolution. More than one-third of mankind has already cast off the fetters of capitalist exploitation. Socialism exists, it is developing, it is growing stronger as a world system. There are no more colonial empires—there are dozens of young sovereign states. The forces of the international proletariat have multiplied and their interests are expressed by Marxist-Leninist communist and workers' parties. Mass democratic, anti-imperialistic and anti-war movements are developing. The general crisis of capitalism is deepening.

Martin Anderson's book, *Revolution*, makes the point that history judges a presidency inevitably on his performance in foreign policy. Since U.S. foreign policy in the broadest sense has focused since the end of World War II largely on the Soviet Union, an administration will be evaluated on how its president made out vis-à-vis the Soviet Union. From that standpoint, as David Brock has written, "Ronald Reagan has not only proved unequal to the challenge, but he has also left a legacy of détente that may turn out to be more dangerous than its precursor of the 1970s" "What the Kiss-and-Tell Books Tell," *Commentary* August 1988, page 27).[151]

When the history of the Reagan Administration is written, President Reagan's misperceptions about Lenin and about the course of Russian history will be seen as one of the most monumental errors ever made by an American president in fashioning a foreign policy toward the Soviet Union.

Fruitful Negotiations

Talleyrand once said that negotiations are more fruitful when based on fact rather than on principle. Helsinki is a sad example of how right Talleyrand was. The Western powers negotiated a "principle"—human rights—without determining how that agreement would work in practice.

In 1975 in Helsinki, in lieu of a peace treaty formally ending World War II, the participating nations signed the Helsinki Final Act, including three separate "baskets" of agreements: on arms, on economic exchange, and on human rights and humanitarian affairs. The Final Act called for a sequence of future meetings, thereby creating a novel sort of institution: a floating "family" of negotiators, with no permanent headquarters, no staff, and no budget.[152] Almost every year, experts meet somewhere, and every five years or so there is a major follow-up meeting on all three baskets. According to Michael Novak, a U.S. delegate:

---

151 During the waning days of his administration, President Reagan seemed to have cooled a little in his enthusiasm for Gorbachev and the new Soviet Union. The then national security adviser, Gen. Colin Powell, said: "The danger has not gone.... We are still dealing with another superpower and ... we should not hyperventilate at every statement that comes out of Moscow" ("Danger not gone from Soviet Relations, Reagan Warns,," *Washington Times* 19 December 1988, page A7). President Reagan himself talked more cautiously in a speech 16 December 1988, at the University of Virginia.

152 The U.S. State Department publishes semiannual reports on "Implementation of Helsinki Final Act" (Washington, D.C.: U.S. Government Printing Office). See, for example, Special Reports nos. 130, 134. 146, and 154.

The first of these major meetings was in Madrid. It almost collapsed over the Soviet invasion of Afghanistan, and lasted nearly three years. The Vienna followup meeting, just begun, is of the same importance.

That the Soviets apparently had signed Helsinki with no intent of compliance was shown in the arrest, torture, banishment and even killing of Soviet citizens who took the Helsinki Accords seriously, and called themselves "Helsinki monitors." It was a decision which must have been taken deliberately since anyone would have known that enforcement of the human rights provisions of Helsinki would be exceedingly difficult if not downright impossible. (*International Herald Tribune* 29 November 1986, page 4)

Good Faith Shattered—Again

It can be argued that Helsinki, or the CSCE (Conference on Security and Cooperation in Europe), is not a treaty. True, the document is not legally binding on the signatories. It is "a good-faith international agreement to perform certain specific functions in order to advance objectives perceived as general improvements in human relationships" ("Statement," *Freedom House* no. 58 [November-December 1980], page 8).

By the time of the 1980 Madrid review conference called for by the Helsinki agreements, President Carter had conceded that the "behavior of the Soviet Union, in particular, has dishonored the principles of the Helsinki accords, both inside and outside its own borders" ("Continuing the CSCE Process," *Current Policy* no. 204 [29 July 1980], page 2). He was referring, *inter alia*, to the "brutal occupation" of Afghanistan. And if Soviet troops were still in Afghanistan at the time of the Madrid conference (a few months later), U.S. pressure on the Soviet Union to get out of Afghanistan would continue.

Senator Malcolm Wallop wrote scathingly about Helsinki:

I am familiar with the Americans who signed that act, and know of none who believed for one moment that the Soviets would abide by its provisions on human rights. Yet they did believe that the Final Act was one of mutual acceptance for the long haul.... This process, in the long run, was to lead us, slowly, to a comfortable division of the world in which we would all enjoy ourselves. *In other words, the Helsinki Final Act was our formal acceptance of the Brezhnev Doctrine, coupled with our expectation that its application would be limited to places then already under communist rule* [my emphasis]. ("American Partnership in the Brezhnev Doctrine," *Global Affairs* Winter 1986, page 28)[153]

---

153 For a further discussion of the Helsinki relationship to the Brezhnev Doctrine, see chapter 10.

Schifter's Remarkable Statement

During the waning days of the Reagan administration, a State Department executive made a remarkable statement that demonstrated how our government indulges continued and premeditated violations of treaties or other agreements by the Soviet Union. And while a State Department spokesman's words are not necessarily the equivalent of probative evidence, they cannot be regarded as disinformation *à la Russe*. Assistant Secretary of State Richard Schifter said in Vienna in January 1989 at the conclusion of the "Helsinki" conference and the signing of still another document:

> What's important about this document is not only what's in it, but the fact that the Soviet Union shows a more serious intention to live up to its commitments. *The Soviets told us they had to scrutinize the language more closely than before because there was every intention to abide by it* [my emphasis]. ("35 Nations Issue East-West Pact to Protect Broad Human Rights," *New York Times* 17 January 1989, page A-9)

We have here a remarkable confession—and it is a confession—by a high State Department official. The italicized sentence tells us that the Soviet Union in the past had signed an agreement (or agreements) with which it had no intention of complying. For almost fifteen years it had openly flouted or selectively obeyed a multilateral agreement, admittedly not binding legally. The agreement surely implied a good-faith understanding that the signatories would do certain things to enhance human rights and, in the absence of a rule of law, to right historic wrongs committed against their citizens. If that good-faith understanding was not implicit, then why did the United States sign that agreement?

That these continued violations of Helsinki were premeditated was obvious. Yet during all those years, the Reagan Administration did nothing more than to protest during "Helsinki" review sessions. Now, in 1989, Mr. Schifter said about the new agreement, the Soviet Union had "every intention to abide by it" (Ibid.). Until now, the Soviet Union had behaved like a deadbeat who signs checks with smiling insouciance knowing full well he will never have to pay up. Now the deadbeat has reformed; no more bad checks. The United States and the other democratic signatories were expected, of course, to abide by the Helsinki Final Act provisions, which included recognizing as permanent the post-World War II frontiers attained by Soviet imperialism in Eastern Europe. Such dismal results represent "treatyism" with a vengeance, "treadmill diplomacy" at its worst.[154]

---

154 The importance of treatyism in American political culture can be seen in how President Reagan handled the arrest and jailing of Nicholas Danilov, the U.S.

Abrogate the Helsinki Process?

A few years ago, Freedom House raised the question of whether the CSCE (Conference on Security and Cooperation in Europe) process should be abrogated. And why on earth not? In 1980, with the invasion of Afghanistan, the Soviet Union had violated six of the ten principles of the CSCE agreement:

Principle I: **Sovereign equality.** The Soviet Union had violated its neighbor's "territorial integrity" and "freedom and independence." And in 1990, the three Baltic countries still sought sovereign equality.

Principle II: **Refraining from the use of force.** The Soviets did not "refrain from the threat or use of force against the territorial integrity or political independence" of Afghanistan.

Principle VI: **Nonintervention in internal affairs.** The Soviet Union supported and in turn withdrew support from one puppet ruler and then put into power an Afghan not even living in the country at the time his predecessor was overthrown.

Principle VIII: **Equal rights and self-determination of peoples.** By manipulating successive regimes in Afghanistan, the Soviet Union had violated the self-determination of ethnic groups in Afghanistan.

Principle IX: **Cooperation among states.** The Soviet Union, by use of military forces and oppressive controls over Afghanistan, had violated the CSCE spirit of "cooperation with one another and with all states in accordance with the purposes and principles of the Charter of the UN."

Principle X: **Fulfillment in good faith of obligations under international law.** The Soviet Union had clearly flouted international law, as witness the UN General Assembly annual resolutions condemning the Soviet Union's invasion of Afghanistan.

Other violations cited by the Freedom House paper included increasingly repressive treatment of human rights activists in Eastern Europe, despite Principle VII, "to respect the equal rights of peoples and their right to self-determination."

News correspondent. Says Donald Regan (1989, 376-381) in his memoirs, "For his part, [President] Reagan knew the [Danilov] case had to be resolved in a way that did not undercut Gorbachev's position with the KGB and other important constituencies within the Kremlin." The cult of treatyism brings us to this pass: a U.S. president must agree that his Soviet adversary is to be treated circumspectly even in a blatant miscarriage of justice so that treatyism may flower in the cloudless climes of détente. L'affaire Danilov was finally resolved in an exchange of prisoners: Danilov for a Soviet spy named Zakharov.

Wherein the Remedy?

What, then, is the remedy for such obviously premeditated violations by Soviet policy makers? Marshall D. Shulman, adviser on Soviet affairs to Secretary of State Cyrus Vance, wrote early in the Carter administration: "It should be clear that the effort to compel changes in Soviet institutions and practices by frontal demands on the part of other governments is likely to be counterproductive" ("Sudden Diplomacy," *New York Times* 30 January 1977, page 29; "On Learning to Live with Authoritarian Regimes," *Foreign Affairs* 55 [January 1977]).

Assuming that Dr. Shulman is correct, then all the more reason to ask, Why, oh why, do we sign such agreements and why, oh why, do we helplessly watch these violations? Can we be sure that a "nonfrontal" demand will work? It took fifteen years before a State Department executive could say with some conviction that *this* time the Soviet Union had every intention of abiding by the Helsinki process. Until now, the Soviets didn't care what language was put into the agreements since they weren't going to abide by the language anyway. And, if it turns out that they do not in the future abide by the Helsinki process, what then?

When the Soviet Politburo reads such a preemptive pardon for Helsinki violations, is there any need to concern itself seriously with Western public opinion? Even more important, why do we engage in such futile negotiations when there is no way that individual human rights can coexist, can be imbedded within the confines of a totalitarian regime? In a UN general debate, an Eastern bloc foreign minister made a statement that nullifies any protection of human rights: "[A]n individual may exercise his rights *only as a member of a broader community*" (U.S. Mission to the UN 1976, 5). That is a thought that President Gorbachev would enthusiastically endorse.

Secretary of State Baker's Testimony

Here is an area that President Bush has promised to do something about, judging from Secretary of State Baker's testimony at his Senate confirmation hearing: "Human rights means full compliance with the Helsinki Accords. There can be no relaxation of our standards on this issue" (*New York Times* 18 January 1989, page A10).

And if there is no "full compliance," will the human rights conference, endorsed by the Reagan administration, go on as scheduled in 1991, assuming Gorbachev's *offensive de charme* is still charming the West? Undoubtedly, it will—just another example of the enchanting effects of "treatyism."

Columnist William Safire scoffed at the Baker testimony and implied that the secretary of state had actually endorsed the 1991 human rights conference but was avoiding a public commitment, preferring to place the responsibility and commitment on the outgoing administration. Safire put his finger on what has been a continuing problem in U.S. treaty diplomacy vis-à-vis the Soviet Union—being drawn into "a long-range negotiating framework" that benefits the Soviets and disadvantages the FMDs. U.S. diplomacy is suddenly "hip-deep in the molasses of multilateralism" ("Chameleon on Plaid," *New York Times* 19 January 1989, page A19).

Nothing so distorts Western political consciousness as to hold out the possibility that, as the result of a negotiation process with the West, the Soviet Union will so fundamentally alter the monopoly power of the Soviet Communist Party that it will permit freedom of expression, of assembly, of religion, of travel, and other human rights. It is not in the nature of a communist or other dictatorship to allow such freedoms, either singly or collectively, except as part of a temporary, expediential *coup de théatre* such as occurred in 1986 and that goes by the Russian word *glasnost*.

As Ambassador Kampelman described the Helsinki process, the West was saying about the Soviet Union, "A country that makes war on its own people cannot be trusted not to make war on its neighbors" ("Can We Negotiate with the Russians?" *Encounter* no. 15 [1985], page 11)

Public Relations Triumph

In 1989, the fourth year of the Era of Glasnost, there occurred one of the greatest public relations triumphs in Soviet history. Not since Josef Stalin had promulgated his Constitution in the 1930s to the cheers of useful idiots in the West have similar cheers been heard, this time for Mikhail Gorbachev.

Yet unmentioned midst all the huzzahs was an extraordinary phenomenon about the Soviet Union, one which had existed openly for decades: Almost 98 percent of the territory of the Soviet Union in 1988 has been and is off limits to foreign travelers, including East Europeans and other Soviet allies. That is, of the Soviet Union's 8.6 million square miles (the United States contains 3.6 million square miles), only 172,000 square miles is accessible to visitors. That's the equivalent of saying that travel for foreigners in the United States is confined to Minnesota and Utah, with the rest of the country off limits.

"The Soviet Union is the only country in the world," says Harry F. Young (1987) in a State Department geographic study, "in which virtually the entire inhabited and physically accessible countryside is, as a rule, closed to foreigners.... In practice the open area also is limited to larger towns reachable by prescribed routes (in some cases only by air)."

These areas are also closed to Soviet citizens. To travel to sensitive zones, the Soviet citizen must have a visa and his internal passport. To arrive at a forbidden zone without the visa means you will be barred entry. Even if you have relatives you would visit, you must get a written invitation, then a visa. The formalities take so long that, said an article in *Izvestia* of 7 September 1987 (page 8), "it is as if you are undertaking a journey not in your native Odessa region but to the banks of the Amazon."

Closed Cities

Even more striking is the fact that seven Soviet cities, each with a population of more than one million persons, are closed to foreigners— Chelyabinsk, Dnepropetrovsk, Gorkiy, Kuybshev, Omsk, Perm, and Sverdlovsk. That would be as if Dallas, Detroit, Houston, Philadelphia, Cleveland, Miami, and San Diego were closed to visitors.

Now, practitioners of "moral equivalence" will say that the United States also has its closed areas for the Soviets. The answer is that Stalin began to restrict foreign diplomatic travel in May 1941 but the United States did not begin to retaliate until 1955. Even under the rule of that earlier *glasnost* reformer, Nikita Khrushchev, the Soviet Union refused to remove its travel restrictions or to abolish the closed areas. So today about one-fifth of the United States is closed to Soviet diplomatic and journalistic personnel. Except: The U.S. restrictions do not apply to travel by Soviet citizens involved in U.S.-Soviet exchanges, nor to those who are visiting friends and relatives or performing commercial or other nondiplomatic duties. While the Soviet restrictions apply to everybody, the mild and virtually unenforceable U.S. restrictions are limited to specific Soviet individuals.

Recently, a Soviet cartographer announced in *Izvestia* that secrecy directives in force since 1930 had been lifted and this, he added, would mean the end of intentional distortion of maps of the Soviet Union. The cartographer V. Yashchenko, head of the Main Administration of Geodesy and Cartography, said: "People could not recognize their motherland on the map. Tourists tried in vain to figure out where they were" ("Accurate Soviet Maps," *Radio Liberty* 401/88). On 15 March 1988, the magazine *Sovetskaya Kultura* published an article by Leningrad Professor Boris Egorov in which he said he had been unable to find an accurate map of Moscow in the Soviet Union. However, he had succeeded in Paris. Egorov also revealed that maps of Estonia are unobtainable in Estonia but that inhabitants of that unhappy Soviet republic can buy them in Stockholm (Ibid.).

Closed areas, restricted areas, and deceptive maps—all would seem highly incongruous in the Era of *Glastroika* (Glasnost+Perestroika). When Gorbachev takes down his "Berlin Wall" enclosing 98 percent of the Soviet

Union—when we can all go and visit Gorky, for example—it'll be time to take another look at *Glastroika*.[155]

In the meantime the West should ask: What kind of treaty diplomacy can we engage in with a country whose rulers have closed off 98 percent of its area and a huge percentage of its population from any contact with foreigners, even foreign communists? A rulership that mistrusts its own people, as well as the entire world outside, is difficult to trust as a negotiating partner.

Kenneth L. Adelman, until 1987 director of the U.S. Arms Control and Disarmament Agency, recently said:

> Why do you suppose we have a problem with Soviet noncompliance with arms control agreements? Can we be surprised when a nation that spends billions each year on a propaganda apparatus that systematically lies to its own people fails to comply fully with an arms control agreement it signs with us? Can we be surprised when a nation that subscribes publicly to an international human rights agreement—as the Soviets did by signing the Helsinki accords of 1975—and then makes no effort to abide by it—can we be surprised when such a nation violates its arms control commitments? (*Washington Times* 9 December 1987, page A11)[156]

---

155 My skepticism is shared, it seems, by Soviet citizens. Vadim Buzychkin, an editor of *Moscow News*, said in a 1987 interview: "Perestroika is a myth. Everything we print is wishful thinking. We are fooling the people, giving them a false sense of security. They believe that criticism is permitted and initiative encouraged. They stick their necks out, get in trouble, and we cannot even protect them. We are at war with bureaucracy. There are just a few people in the top leadership who are pushing for reform. Glasnost can end any moment and our heads will be the first to roll. We are the kamikaze of *perestroika*" ("Testing Glasnost: An Exile Visits His Homeland," *New York Times Magazine* 6 December 1987, page 122).

156 I am impressed how, even on small things, the party elites violate their own rules. For example, on 11 September 1957 a decree of the Presidium of the USSR Supreme Soviet prohibited giving the name of any living statesman to any "regions, cities, districts, and other communities, to any enterprises, railway stations, kolkhozes, administrations and teaching establishments" (Tatu 1980, 20). Such a step had to be taken following Khrushchev's successful purge of the so-called "anti-Party" group. His name, however, was not removed from a town in the Ukraine. Two years later, the Soviet press was trumpeting the fact that a famous kolkhoz in Kalinovka, Khrushchev's birthplace, had adopted a new name, "Khrushchev's Home."

As a further example of Leninist duplicity, after Lenin's seizure of power, treaties were signed between the Russian Soviet Federated Socialist Republic and the other Soviet republics. Each republic had the formal right to conduct its own foreign policy but in practice was denied the right to pursue even an independent domestic policy. Moscow constantly violated the treaties by intervening unceremoniously in the internal affairs of the republics (Heller & Nekrich 1986, 151).

Adelman is understating the situation, considering that Lenin wrote, "The scientific definition of dictatorship is a power that is not limited by any laws, not bound by any rules, and based directly on force" (Heller & Nekrich 1986, 62). How do you engage in credible treaty diplomacy with a state whose founder not only espoused such a ruthless strategy but charged his successors to follow that strategy until ultimate triumph? How do you engage in credible treaty diplomacy with a regime where a rule of law does not really exist, where lying is built into the system of rule?

When the Lying Began

The systematic lying began in the early hours of the Bolshevik Revolution. On the second day of the revolution, Lenin addressed the Second All-Russia Congress of Soviets as prime minister of the new revolutionary government. He said:

> In accordance with the sense of justice of democrats in general, and of the working classes in particular, the government conceives the annexation or seizure of foreign lands to mean every incorporation of a small or weak nation into a large or powerful state without the precisely, clearly and voluntarily expressed consent and wish of that nation, irrespective of the time when such forcible incorporation took place, irrespective also of the degree of development or backwardness of the nation forcibly annexed to the given state, or forcibly retained within its borders, and irrespective finally, of whether this nation is in Europe or in distant, overseas countries. (Lenin 1917, 26:250)

The above can be regarded as the "First Principle" of Lenin's Doctrine. In content, it is exemplary. And in the same speech came what could be regarded as the "Second Principle," equally exemplary:

> If any nation whatsoever is forcibly retained within the border of a given state, if in spite of its expressed desire—no matter whether expressed in the press, at public meetings, in the decisions of parties, or in protests and uprisings against national oppression—it is not accorded the right to decide the forms of its state existence by a free vote, taken after the complete evacuation of the troops of the incorporating or, generally, of the stronger nation and without the least pressure being brought to bear, such incorporation is annexation, i.e., seizure and violence. (Ibid., 250)

A year later, in January 1918, the Third All-Russian Congress of Soviets proclaimed that "the Soviet Russian Republic is established on the basis of a free union of free nations, as a federation of Soviet national republics" (Conquest 1967, 25).

The two principles, that today can be described as an inseparable part of the democratic ethos, were quickly violated by Lenin. And, of course, "the free union of free nations" was a total lie, as I will show in the following pages.

Machiavelli's Advice

The question of Leninist lying in the 1920s may also affect the meaning of *glasnost* and *perestroika* in the 1990s. I know it runs against the received wisdom of our time to suggest that in *glastroika* (my preferred neologism) we may be witnessing another example of the historic czarist (yes, czarist) and Bolshevik tradition of deceiving the enemy. Lenin and his dedicated secret police chief Feliks Dzerzhinski (the "sword of the Revolution"), possessed the records of the czar's Okhrana police, who knew how to exploit the *agent provocateur* tactic. Lenin must also have known Machiavelli's writings and, if he did, he and Dzerzhinski put Machiavelli's advice to good use.

Machiavelli believed that deceit was a worthy substitute for brute assault by violence. In *The Art of War* he argued that the commander who conquered by stratagem was as praiseworthy as he who conquered by force. In *The Prince* he advised the ruler on how to "confuse men's brains" and employ cunning in politics. As he wrote: "[F]or some time I have never said what I believed and never believed what I said, and if I do sometimes happen to say what I think, I always hide it among so many lies that it is hard to recover" ("Trapping the Prince: Machiavelli and the Politics of Deception," *American Political Science Review* 80[3] [September 1986], page 777 ff.).

Soon after the Bolshevik Revolution, Lenin initiated his first "sting" operation. So-called defectors appeared in the West to announce that the Soviet Union was on the verge of collapse, that a counterrevolutionary operation was operating in Russia itself, and that anti-Bolshevik elements outside of Russia ought to work together with the internal opposition. This deception maneuver, which worked for eight years, was finally exposed by the Bolsheviks themselves, and the pseudoconspiracy, that had been run by Moscow from its inception, is today known in the West as "The Trust." Its major accomplishment was to prevent organization of any extramural émigré resistance to the Bolshevik regime.

Disinformation Strategy

This disinformation strategy was "carefully calculated to dupe the West into believing the Communist revolution was moribund—and therefore no threat. It resulted in Britain, France, and other European nations extending trade credits, technological transfers and diplomatic recognition to what they assumed would quickly evolve into a non-Communist Soviet Union," according to Raymond Rocca, a one-time CIA executive who worked with James J. Angleton, the cashiered head of CIA counterintelligence (Epstein 1989, 25-40).

Another "sting" operation like The Trust was organized by the Soviets during the Cold War. This one was called WIN, a Polish acronym for "Freedom and Independence." It was a smashing success for the Soviets. However, in December 1952, the Polish government told the story of WIN in a two-hour radio broadcast and boasted about how they had used American-supplied gold coins to finance the deception. The purpose of these exposés, according to Angleton, was to distract U.S. attention "from the real weaknesses in the Soviet system of control in Eastern Europe, and to focus its attention as well as its limited intelligence resources on fake weaknesses instead" (Ibid.). While the reasons for the 1970s Soviet foreign policy initiative called "détente" may have been several, it should be remembered that it was during "détente" that the Soviet Union engaged in the greatest rearmament program in human history.

Does *glastroika* mean that the leopard can, assuming he would like to, really change his spots?

8

When Is a Treaty Not a Treaty?
The Lenin Doctrine

Upon my tongues continual slanders ride,
The which in every language I pronounce,
Stuffing the ears of men with false reports.
I speak of peace, while covert enmity
Under the smile of safety wounds the world.

Shakespeare[157]

Every one of the countries that came under Soviet domination in the twentieth century came to that tragic pass despite treaties, agreements, pacts, accords, conventions, declarations, protocols, and accords. The *de facto* annexation all came about as a result of Soviet violence or threat of violence: East Germany, Poland, Bulgaria, Romania, Hungary, Czechoslovakia, the Ukraine, Georgia, Mongolia, Estonia, Latvia, and Lithuania. Afghanistan is only the latest victim of Soviet aggression. Had not Finland twice defied the Soviet Union in World War II, Finland might have become a Bolshevik colony just as, for more than a century until 1917, it had been a czarist duchy.

"Every state has the right to choose freely its own political and social system" (*New York Times* 14 June 1989, page 1). So read the "Joint Declaration on June 13, 1989," signed by President Gorbachev and West

---

157 King Henry IV, Part II, spoken by Rumour as the curtain rises.

German Chancellor Helmut Kohl. There are also unilateral Soviet statements supporting the right of states "to choose freely" their own way of life, including the right of secession. There are long-forgotten statements by V.I. Lenin such as:

- "Why should we Great Russians, who have been oppressing more nations than any other people, deny the right of secession for Poland, Ukraine or Finland?" (*Pravda* 15 May 1917)
- "The freedom to unite implies freedom to secede. We Russians must emphasize the freedom to secede" (Lenin 1937, 24:298).
- "If Finland, Poland or the Ukraine secede from Russia, there is nothing bad in that" (Ibid., 24:300).
- "Anyone who disagrees is an annexationist and a chauvinist.... Any Russian Socialist who does not recognize Finland's and the Ukraine's right to freedom will degenerate into a chauvinist" (Ibid., 24:301).

The right of secession written into Soviet law by treaty 30 December 1922 was titled "Treaty Concerning the Establishment of the Union of Soviet Socialist Republics." The treaty was signed by such Communist worthies as Stalin, Trotsky, Molotov, Kalinin, Frunze, Kirov, and Ordzhonikidze. Some signed as representatives of the Russian Socialist Federal Soviet Republic (R.S.F.S.R.), others for the Ukrainian Socialist Soviet Republic, the Byelorussian Socialist Republic, and the Caucasian Socialist Federal Soviet Republic, comprising Georgia, Azerbaijan, and Armenia. This treaty set up what we now know today as the Soviet Union. It was signed while Lenin was still alive and functioning.

Paragraph No. 26, the last, of the 1922 treaty says: "*Each Allied Republic retains the right to leave the Union*" (Schapiro 1950, I:201). Here, then, we have, as quoted above, Lenin's own words offering moral encouragement to secessionists and dispraise for those who oppose secessionists. And, the very fundamental law upon which the Soviet Union today stands gives any one of the constituent Soviet Republics the right to secede. And on top of that we have a statement by President Gorbachev made 7 December 1988, before the forty-third session of the United Nations General Assembly in which he upheld the sanctity of treaties.

Georgia, A Sovereign Country

One of the earliest Soviet treaties with a sovereign country was signed with the Independent Georgian Republic on 7 May 1920. With the fall of the czarist regime, which had annexed the country in 1801, Georgia became independent on 26 May 1918. The treaty contained an unqualified Soviet recognition of the independence of Georgia. Let me cite Article I of that treaty:

> Proceeding from the right, proclaimed by the RSFSR, of all peoples to free self-determination up to and including separation from the State of which they constitute a part, Russia unreservedly recognizes the independence and sovereignty of the Georgian State and voluntarily renounces all the sovereign rights which had appertained to Russia with regard to the People and Territory of Georgia. (Conquest 1967, 24-25)

Article II of the treaty reads:

> Proceeding from the principles proclaimed in Article I above of the present Treaty, Russia undertakes to refrain from any kind of interference in the internal affairs of Georgia. (Ibid.)

In return for this treaty guarantee, the Georgian government, whose ruling party was Menshevik (Social Democrat), agreed in Article X to cease prosecuting communists and to release immediately all who had been imprisoned for crimes relating to communism. In less than a year, in February 1921, the Red Army invaded Georgia and entered Tiflis. A Soviet regime was established. So much for the Soviet-Georgian treaty guarantee.

A Warning Ignored

The case of the Independent Georgian Republic is important since it foreshadowed the character of Soviet treaty diplomacy. It should have served as a warning to Western powers with whom the Soviet Union, shortly thereafter, began to negotiate for recognition, trade, and credits.

The reasons the Soviets gave for the invasion of the Georgian Republic were that Georgia's Menshevik government had sought to restore the "bourgeoisie" to power and that it had ignored the "Socialist interests of the peasants." The invasion, according to Soviet historians (one is always tempted to put the noun in inverted commas), was in response to a plea for help that followed an armed uprising by Georgia's workers.[158]

But recently the wave of *glasnost* history refuted the Georgian worker uprising legend. Ironically, the refutation is written by the same historian,

---

158 The Soviet Union is always responding to the pleas of the working class. On 22 March 1957, a Colonel Federor wrote in Red Star: "Trained by the Communist Party, the armed forces of the USSR live up to their international duty. This was demonstrated by the aid they gave to the working people of Hungary...." ("The Challenge of Democracy," *Encounter* pamphlet no. 10, page 26).

Akaki Surguladze, whose 1982 monograph described the alleged Georgian worker revolt as a truly historical event. In April 1988, Surguladze proclaimed: There had been no uprising at all; in fact, it would have been impossible at that juncture to organize one. Says the prominent Soviet historian: "The Menshevik government was overthrown by the Red Army, which was summoned at the initiative of I. Stalin and S. Ordzhonikidze" ("Georgian Historians Reassess 1918 Declaration of Georgian Independence," *Radio Liberty* 251/88 [12 June 1988], pages 1-4).[159]

The seizure and continued occupation of the Baltic States is a further disturbing example of Soviet treaty diplomacy. Although, technically, the West still does not recognize the legitimacy of the Soviet Union's Baltic occupation, the Sonnenfeldt Doctrine has effectively reduced Western nonrecognition to meaninglessness.[160]

Occupation in the Baltic

In 1920, the Soviet government signed a treaty with Lithuania, Latvia, and Estonia renouncing "all rights of sovereignty forever" (Schapiro 1950, 54-55). Later, nonaggression pacts were signed between the Soviet Union and the three states. A convention defining aggression, signed in 1933, stipulated that "no political, military or other considerations shall serve as an excuse or justification for aggression" (Ibid 1955, 69, 74).

Six years later, the Soviets and Nazis made the first moves against the Baltic States. Under the Secret Additional Protocol and Secret Supplementary Protocol of the Nazi-Soviet Pact, the Baltic countries were to fall within the sphere of influence of the Soviet Union.[161]

By the end of October 1939, the Soviet government had forced the three Baltic States to sign mutual assistance pacts, granting the Soviet Union naval and military bases on their territory. These pacts still guaranteed the independence of the three states and promised that the Soviet Union would

---

159 The Soviet Red Army reoccupied the Ukraine in spring 1920. It then ordered the entire Ukrainian Communist Party Central Committee out of the region, even though the Ukraine was at the time an independent Communist state (Daniels 1988, 88).

160 "[T]he Sonnenfeldt Doctrine did relate to the supreme political fact of the post-World War II era, the guarantee of general peace by the standoff between the nuclear armed Superpowers and the inviolability of the frontier between East and West as the necessary conditions for that general peace" (*Presidential Studies Quarterly* xviii[4] [Fall 1988], page 835).

161 For texts of Secret Additional Protocol and other relevant documentation, see Sontag & Beddie 1948, 78ff.

"not in any way affect their state organization, economic and social systems, military measures, and in general, the principle of nonintervention in internal affairs" (Conquest 1987, 129). In fact, Foreign Minister Molotov said on 31 October 1939: "We declare that all the spreading of the nonsense about Sovietizing the Baltic countries is only to the interest of our common enemies, and of all anti-Soviet provocateurs" (Ibid.). Six months later, after ultimata, Soviet troops occupied the three countries. They were then annexed to the Soviet Union. As Robert Conquest has written:

> The principles under which the Soviet Union occupies the Baltic States contrary to solemn treaty obligations are central to the Kremlin's whole attitude to treaties, and we need not be surprised at recent breaches of arms agreements.... [I]n one sense the whole of Soviet foreign policy is definable in terms of a deployment of force and fraud. (Ibid.)

Soviets Admit Baltic Takeover

On 16 August 1988, according to an Associated Press (AP) Moscow dispatch, the Soviet Union admitted—and defended!—the 1940 takeover of the Baltic States. The takeover, the reasoning went, was necessary for the survival of the Soviet Union at a time when it was isolated and insecure and at the brink of World War II. In the words of Valentin M. Falin, at the time Novosti press agency chairman, as quoted by AP: "It had to be decided 'to be or not to be.' We had an opportunity to choose the least of the evils and understandably we opted for the 'to be' part."

Or, as Stalin once told Charles Bohlen: "The Soviet Union always keeps its word ... except in cases of extreme necessity" (Bohlen 1973, 219). Or to quote Machiavelli: "A prudent ruler cannot, and should not, honor his word when it places him at a disadvantage and the reasons for which he made his promise no longer exist" (Machiavelli 1960, 72).

At the news briefing, the AP report said that Falin never acknowledged that the three Baltic countries had been forcibly incorporated into the Soviet Union. Instead, he referred to the "transfer of the Baltic States to the north." Nor did he acknowledge the existence of the Molotov-Ribbentrop Pact signed 23 August 1939, which paved the way for the Soviet takeover of the independent Baltic States and the German invasion of Poland.

What Justifies Occupation Now?

Despite the concession that the seizure of the Baltic countries had been the result of the Nazi-Soviet Pact, there was no indication at the briefing that the three victims would now be allowed to return to their former independence. The Falin excuse for the Soviet action might conceivably be defended as *raison d'état*: plus the "Gromyko Doctrine," once a member of the "Socialist Commonwealth," always a member. But without an operating Brezhnev Doctrine, what could justify the continued and present occupation of the Baltic States half a century after the infamous Stalin-Hitler pact?

Gorbachev himself seemed to be endorsing the Brezhnev Doctrine (although at the December 1989 Malta summit, he reportedly repudiated it) as far as the occupation of the Baltic countries was concerned. On 19 February 1987, in Riga itself, he defended the occupation of the Baltic countries with words that were hardly conducive to belief in the "new thinking" in Soviet foreign policy. Said Gorbachev: "The Russian warrior-liberator has helped the Baltic peasant and fisherman to defend his native land against desecration and servitude and to protect it against the foreign invader." Soviet statehood had guaranteed the "freedom and democracy for the working people" of the Baltic countries. Obviously, only "anti-Soviet provocateurs," to use Molotov's phrase, would be agitating to secede from the Soviet Union.

Finland Didn't Quite Work Out

Finland is an example where things didn't quite work out as Lenin had expected. With the collapse of the czarist regime, the Parliament of the once Grand Duchy of Finland proclaimed its independence on 15 November 1917. The Bolshevik government recognized the independent republic of Finland on 1 December 1917. Lenin anticipated a socialist seizure of power in Finland and was prepared to concede Finnish independence "to nullify Finnish bourgeois claims that the Finnish identity and freedoms were under threat from Great Russian chauvinism" (Allison 1985, 6). The civil war that broke out in Finland in 1918 saw Russia supporting its Finnish Red contingents.

Things were different on the Afghanistan front. On 20 February 1922, Soviet ambassador Roskolnikov wrote to the Afghan Ministry of Foreign Affairs:

> The Government which I represent has always recognized and respected the independence of the two Governments of Khiva and Bukhara. The presence of a limited contingent of troops ... is due to temporary requirements expressed and made known to us by the Bukharan government ... whenever the Bukharan Government so requests, not a single Russian soldier will remain on Bukharan soil....
>
> The extension of our friendly assistance in no way constitutes an interference against independence.... If the government of Bukhara should ... prove dissatisfied with the continuation of such brotherly assistance, then the Government I represent shall most immediately withdraw its troops. ("U.S. Must Reassess Afghan Policy," *Wall Street Journal* 18 October 1988, F4)

In 1924, the two emirates Khiva and Bukhara were incorporated into the Soviet Union.

In May-June 1955, Khrushchev and Bulganin traveled to Yugoslavia. The visit was intended to heal Stalin's five-year rupture with Tito that Stalin had engineered. On 18 September 1949, the Soviets used an interesting tactic to legitimize breaking a treaty that had outlived its suitability for Soviet strategy. Stalin charged prior violation by a Soviet treaty partner—"a transparent legal maneuver"—to justify treaty breaking.[162] In denouncing the Soviet-Yugoslav Treaty of Friendship, Mutual Assistance and Postwar Collaboration of 11 April 1945, the Soviet Union used the charge of "prior violation," including the murder of innocent men, to show that Yugoslavia had already transgressed the treaty *de facto* (Triska & Slusser 1962, 392, 391).

Journey to Canossa

At the end of the Khrushchev and Bulganin "journey to Canossa," a joint Soviet-Yugoslav statement—the Belgrade Declaration—was issued. It defined the basis on which relations between the two countries would be conducted. George Kennan described the declaration as a "high-minded document, speaking of such things as 'respect for the sovereignty, integrity, and equality of states in their relations with each other,' of peaceful coexistence among nations 'irrespective of ideological differences and of differences in their social systems,' and of noninterference in the other's internal affairs 'for any reason'" (Micunovic 1980, ix-x). The crucial paragraph in the declaration approved the:

> observance of the principle of mutual respect and of noninterference in internal affairs for any reason—whether of an economic, political or ideological nature— because questions of internal structure, of different social systems, and of different ways of advancing to socialist development are exclusively a matter for the peoples of the individual countries.... (Ibid., 3)[163]

---

162 Stalin used the "prior violation" maneuver on 5 April 1945 in denouncing the Soviet-Japanese Neutrality Pact of 13 April 1941. It was preliminary to a declaration of war against Japan. According to Herbert Feis, the Soviets had decided in 1943 to attack Japan. Stalin used the same maneuver against Finland. On 28 November 1939, he charged that Finland had "systematically violated" its obligations under the Soviet-Finnish Nonaggression Treaty of 21 January 1932, and that the Soviet government considered itself "released from the [treaty] obligations" under the treaty. Then followed the attack on Finland (Triska & Slusser 1962, 392).

163 Soviet acceptance of the proposition that socialism is to be achieved as "exclusively a matter for the peoples of the individual countries" is one of the

Then Came Hungary

Just a year later—June 1956—Khrushchev was interfering in the affairs of Poland with threats of Soviet military intervention. Four months later, the Red Army was killing Hungarian insurrectionists by the tens of thousands. And in 1957, despite the Belgrade Declaration, Khrushchev launched a crusade against Yugoslavia, accusing Tito of "revisionism."

The Belgrade Declaration, that said that interference in the internal affairs of a country was barred no matter what the reason, was ignored in Poland, Hungary, and Yugoslavia. This 1955 self-imposed restriction on Soviet behavior seems to have been reinstated in Eastern Europe and in Africa, but have the Soviets repudiated the Brezhnev Doctrine in Afghanistan? Whether the Soviet troop withdrawal from Afghanistan in February 1989 meant an annulment of the Brezhnev Doctrine or whether the retreat was another of those zigs and zags in Soviet foreign policy is yet to be seen. Earlier, Professor Richard H. Ullman wrote that Gorbachev had "not disavowed the Brezhnev Doctrine, which proclaimed Moscow's duty to intervene there to assure ideological conformity" ("Ending the Cold War," *Foreign Policy* 72 [Fall 1988], page 135).

What About the Helsinki Accords?

Why shouldn't Britain or the United States have sought to reopen the 1945 Yalta agreement, one of whose clauses stipulated free elections in Poland? Why shouldn't the democratic signatories to the Helsinki Accords have suggested (on the basis of the Lenin Doctrine, the Yalta agreement, and the Belgrade Declaration) the renegotiation of the "forcible incorporation" into the Socialist Commonwealth and the Warsaw Pact of the once free nations of Central Europe and the Baltic? After all, point eight of the "Guiding Principles" of the Helsinki agreement provides:

---

hoariest legends in Soviet ideology. As far back as 1920, Georgi V. Chicherin, the first people's commissar for foreign affairs, in a diplomatic note to the then U.S. Secretary of State Bainbridge Colby, said that "the Soviet Government clearly understands that the revolutionary movement of the working masses in every country is their own affair. It holds to the principle that communism cannot be imposed by force..." (Goldwin 1959, 162). At the time of the note, dated 4 October 1920, Chicherin had just dropped his activities as a founding member of the Comintern, the Kremlin's highly effective international agitprop organization, whose assignment it was to establish communism worldwide by whatever method necessary (Lazitch & Drachkovitch 1972, 60).

By virtue of the principle of equal rights and self-determination of peoples, all peoples always have the right, in full freedom to determine, when and as they wish, their internal and external political status, without external interference, and to pursue as they wish their political, economic, social and cultural development. Accordingly, the participating States will refrain from any acts constituting a threat of force or direct or indirect use of force against another participating State. Likewise they will refrain from any manifestation of force for the purpose of inducing another participating State to renounce the full exercise of its sovereign rights. Likewise they will also refrain in their mutual relations from any act of reprisal by force. (U.S. Department of State 1975, 81)

How to Legalize Imperialism

So concerned is the Soviet Union with establishing the legality of its imperialism that on 16 October 1968, even before Helsinki, the then Soviet Premier Alexei Kosygin signed a "treaty" with Czech Premier Cernik, legalizing the presence of Red Army troops in Czechoslovakia. The treaty followed the invasion of that country for daring to experiment with the idea of "socialism with a human face."

Not only has the West failed to raise, as part of a linkage process, questions of self-determination in negotiating even a nonbinding agreement like the Helsinki "Final Act," it has also tacitly accepted the Brezhnev Doctrine. This unilateral declaration brands in advance as illegitimate the attempted secession of any country under Soviet rule or tutelage.[164]

The Brezhnev Doctrine violates the program of the Soviet Communist Party that was adopted 31 October 1961 by the Twenty-second Party Congress. It declared:

The Communist parties are independent and they shape their policies with due regard to the specific conditions prevailing in their own countries.... The Communist Party of the Soviet Union ... regards it as its internationalist duty to abide by the appraisals and conclusions which the fraternal parties have reached jointly concerning their common tasks in the struggle against imperialism, for peace, democracy and socialism. ("Party Program," *New York Times* 2 December 1968)

---

164 Western optimists who think that the Brezhnev Doctrine may have disappeared in a cloud of *glasnost* should take note of a 1 July 1986 *Pravda* editorial that said: "To threaten the socialist system, to try to undermine it from the outside and wrench a country away from the socialist community means to encroach not only on the will of the people but also on the entire postwar arrangement, and, in the final analysis, on peace." Apparently the new party line has overrun the policy expressed in the editorial.

The West should ask over and over again: By what right (except by the right of ideological domain, I suppose) did Red Army troops occupy Poland, Czechoslovakia, Hungary, and Bulgaria? Even if the Soviet Union actually and verifiably reduces its occupation forces in Eastern Europe, the question remains: What justifies the Soviet military presence in countries like Poland, Czechoslovakia, and Hungary, that have demonstrated they do not want a foreign army of occupation within their borders?

It is tacitly assumed that in any negotiation the Soviet Union will lie, but that the Western powers, subject to public scrutiny, will not dare to lie or to violate their democratic criteria of behavior.

Yet, negotiation with the Soviet Union is exactly what Western diplomacy, with the United States in the lead, insists upon no matter what atrocity the Kremlin is *openly* guilty of: aggression in Afghanistan, imprisonment of Helsinki human rights activists and Russian workers who tried to organize independent trade unions, overt anti-Semitism and persecution of religion, assassination of an American army officer in the Soviet zone of Berlin, arrest and frame-up of an American journalist, and, most recently, the economic boycott of embattled Lithuania. Such human rights violations have persisted whether the party general secretary is Lenin, Stalin, Khrushchev, Brezhnev, Andropov, Chernenko, or (much less so under) Gorbachev.

Odious Libels Worldwide

I have italicized the word "openly" because, overtly, the Soviet Union disseminates odious libels against the United States as part of the KGB's "active measures" campaign. Some of these libels accuse the United States of having assassinated Sweden's Olaf Palme and India's Indira Gandhi, of attempting to kill Pope John Paul II and Corazon Aquino, and of being responsible for the AIDS pandemic[165] (*Disinformation* no. 6 [Summer

---

165 On 5 November 1987, the Associated Press reported (*New York Times* 5 November 1987, page 11) that two Soviet scientists, Roald Sagdeyev and Vitali Goldansky, had "disavowed" Soviet press charges that the AIDS virus was artificially cultivated at a secret American military base at Fort Detrick, Maryland. The disavowal had appeared a few days earlier in Izvestia. (Last year, *Pravda* ran a cartoon showing a U.S. officer handing a scientist money in return for a beaker labeled "AIDS Virus." Corpses surround them.) In the meantime, the AIDS libel had appeared all summer in newspapers in Kenya, Peru, Sudan, Nigeria, Senegal, and Mexico (*Wall Street Journal* 18 August 1987, editorial page). The AIDS story first surfaced at a Non-Aligned Movement summit meeting in Zimbabwe, in a fifty-two-page pamphlet titled, "AIDS: USA Homemade Evil, Not Made in Africa." Arthur A. Hartman, then U.S. ambassador to the Soviet Union, denounced the smear campaign in April 1987, two years after Gorbachev had taken power, to no avail.

1987], page 1). The Soviet journal *New Times* (no. 37 [1985], pages 28-30) reported that Jessica Savitch, the NBC-TV reporter killed in a 1983 auto accident, was "murdered" by "CIA agents" and American "Zionists" for narrating a documentary about unhappy Soviet émigrés in the United States. The Soviet daily *Izvestia* accused the U.S. government of murdering 918 members of the People's Temple in Guyana (in reality, a mass suicide) in 1978 to prevent them from migrating to the Soviet Union ("Gorbachev's 'Glasnost': Another Potemkin Village?" Heritage *Backgrounder* no. 571 [20 March 1987], page 9).[166]

When Soviet ambassador to the United States Yuri Dubinin denied that the Soviet Union was behind the worldwide campaign to blame the United States for AIDS, he was shown an article in *Izvestia* that made that charge. The Soviet ambassador then said that Soviet journalists, like reporters anywhere else, can publish what they like. He said: "To say that every journalist who signs his article was doing so on behalf of the government is not right" ("Soviets Suggest Experiment Leaks in U.S. Created the AIDS Epidemic," *Los Angeles Times* 9 August 1987).[167]

A story in the *Los Angeles Times* in 1988 (18 January, page 18) began as follows: "The Soviet Union has apparently renewed its disinformation campaign in the Third World against the United States, despite recent pledges by top Soviet leaders to end it."

The article reported Charles Z. Wick, then director of the U.S. Information Agency, as saying that following the December 1987 U.S.-Soviet summit in Washington, he "had been assured by Mikhail S. Gorbachev and other Soviet officials that Moscow would end anti-American disinformation" (Ibid.).

But, despite these Soviet "assurances," a report in the *Ghanaian Times* alleged that the United States had given South Africa chemical weapons that were then turned over to rebels in Angola and Mozambique; that the United States and South Africa were exchanging information on bacteriological weapons; and that the United States had developed a biological weapon designed to kill individuals of a particular ethnic group or race. On 9 January 1988, the report was picked up from Accra, the Ghana capital, by Tass, the Soviet news agency, and sent worldwide over the Tass English-language

---

166 Also see "Is 'Glasnost' a Game of Mirrors," *New York Times* 22 March 1987, Op-Ed, signed by Vasily Aksyonov, Vladimir Bukovsky, Edward Kuznetsov, Yuri Lyubimov, Vladimir Maximov, Ernst Neizvestny, and Aleksandr Zinoviev. The seven are dissident Soviet émigrés living in the West.
167 The Soviet magazine *Literaturnaya Gazeta* also ran a similar story (see "Glasnost Brings Little Change to Disinformation Activities," *Washington Times* 18 August 1987, page 6).

service the same day. Tass wrote: "The [Ghanaian] newspaper emphasizes that the greatest danger to Africa is posed by U.S.-South African experiments with ethnic weapons which possess selectivity in killing only people with dark color skin."

Gorbachev's audacity in dealing with official U.S. reports of Soviet "active measures" was reported by Kenneth Adelman at a presummit meeting in 1987 between the Soviet leader, Secretary of State Shultz, and then National Security Adviser Frank Carlucci. Gorbachev simply denied the documented State Department report, which he held in his hand, of Soviet libels of the United States (Adelman 1989, 213-14).

A Murmured U.S. Response

And what was the response of the U.S. government to these criminal libels? USIA Chief Wick murmured, through a spokesman, that the Tass report "was the kind of thing that undermines the move toward greater understanding between our two countries" ("Soviets Said to Renew 3rd World Disinformation Drive, *Los Angeles Times* 18 January 1988, page 18). State Department spokeswoman Phyllis Oakley denied "all these ridiculous allegations and regrets that the Soviet Union has chosen to repeat them" (Ibid.). And then, on behalf of the United States Government, Mrs. Oakley uttered this powerful threat that surely must have created fear and trembling in the Kremlin's inner sanctum. Even though, said the spokeswoman, the State Department has no plans to protest the libel to the Soviet Union—here comes the pop-gun—"It will not be forgotten" (Ibid.).

Mrs. Oakley is, after all, a voice programmed to speak whatever absurd prose is recorded for her. But isn't it sad that our only weapon of response to Soviet disinformation is memory? That's really harassing an enemy, that knows that its greatest ally is the collective amnesia of the democracies.[168]

Even though President Reagan and Gorbachev had just signed a treaty, had exchanged toasts, had had private discussions during which the president had found in Gorbachev a new and morally superior type of Communist leader, the ideological war of lies against the United States went on with little attempt at concealment. And summitry goes on regardless of Soviet violation

---

168 Former Secretary of State Dean Acheson put his finger on the reason for Soviet active measures when he said that "the Soviet Union is an aggressively imperialist state seeking to impose its domination where it can and to sow confusion and disintegration where its grasp falls short" (McLellan 1969, 6).

not merely of treaties but even of simple pledges. (For further on Soviet "active measures," see chapter 11.)

Summit diplomacy has become an inextricable part of American political culture. In the words of President Nixon, "summit meetings between leaders of the United States and the Soviet Union have become essential if peace is to be preserved" (*Wall Street Journal* 28 October 1985, Op-Ed page; Nixon 1988, 48).

Summit Meetings—Cui Bono?

Why? How does one prove such a statement? Or is it that summit meetings are really "essential" only for the Soviet Union alone and its never-ending "peace" offensive? As former Secretary of State Dean Acheson (1959, 25) has said:

> I have heard people who should know better, including a head of government, say happily, "As long as we keep them talking, they're not fighting." Nothing could be more untrue; they are fighting. They are adopting a tactic specifically prescribed by Lenin to delay the crises while demoralizing and weakening the enemy.

We have had summit meetings in the past—Geneva 1955, Camp David 1959, Paris 1960, Vienna 1961, Glassboro, N.J. 1967, Moscow 1972, Washington/San Clemente 1973, Moscow 1974, Vladivostok 1974, Vienna 1979, five summits between President Reagan and Mikhail Gorbachev in the second Reagan administration, and the Bush-Gorbachev Malta summit, 1989. What happened in the aftermath of such meetings as far as preserving peace or improving the lot of mankind was concerned? I suggest this as a legitimate criterion since summits seem to have become for some the cure-all therapy for the seventy-year-old world crisis.

The Yalta and Potsdam summits were followed by Stalin's seizure of Eastern Europe. The 1955 summit was followed by Soviet suppression of the Poznan uprising in the summer of 1956 and the bloody aggression against the Hungarian people in the fall of 1956. The 1959 and 1961 summits were followed by Khrushchev's nuclear bomb explosions, the building of the Berlin Wall in 1961, and, for good measure, emplacement of Soviet missiles in Cuba and the ensuing crisis over their removal in October 1962.[169] There is no question in my mind that the 1961 Vienna summit was a prelude to disaster for the Western democracies.

---

169 President Kennedy warned the Soviet Union on 4 September 1962 against introducing offensive missiles in Cuba. On 22 October 1962, he delivered his "quarantine" speech. On 20 November 1962, he lifted the "quarantine" blockade against Soviet vessels en route to Cuba.

The Lure of Summitry

The Kennedy-Khrushchev summit of 3-4 June 1961 came a few weeks after the pitiful April 1961 Bay of Pigs invasion of Cuba. That failure may have given the Soviet leader the idea that President Kennedy could be successfully bullied.[170] Khrushchev's premonition might have been strengthened by the irresolute, postsummit U.S. reaction to the building of the Berlin Wall in August-September 1961. It should also be remembered that Kennedy had at first resisted Khrushchev's call for a summit. Kennedy did not want a summit so early in his administration. He wanted nonsummit negotiations among experts, but he finally gave in. The lure of summitry was impossible to resist. JFK met with his advisers on Soviet affairs—Llewellyn Thompson, Charles Bohlen, George Kennan, and Averell Harriman—11 February 1961 to discuss the Khrushchev application for an early summit. Theodore Sorensen (1966, 610) writes:

> None of these men, least of all the president, wanted a formal 'summit' conference between the two heads of government. While such a conference, in Kennedy's long-held view, might be necessary when war threatened, or useful as "a place where agreements ... achieved at a lower level could be finally, officially approved ... a summit is not a place to carry on negotiations which involve details." Those had to be conducted through quieter channels and by full-time experts. Summitry raised undue hopes and public attention, thus producing unjustified relaxations, disappointments or tensions. It injected considerations of personal prestige, face-saving and politics into grave international conflicts.

The fall 1962 Cuban missile crisis might have resulted from what turned out to be an incorrect assumption by Khrushchev as to who would blink in a U.S.-Soviet Union confrontation. That incorrect assumption might have led to something more than a few minor skirmishes between both superpowers.[171]

---

170 In his memoirs, Khrushchev (1970, 458) speaks kindly about President Kennedy at Vienna. However, Theodore Sorensen's summary (1966, 612ff.) of the conversations between Kennedy and Khrushchev are sobering indeed. Khrushchev sounds like he's on a roll while JFK comes off, even in the hands of his Boswell, second best.

171 An example of bad faith is Khrushchev's behavior early in the Cuban crisis. During the summer and fall of 1962, Khrushchev pledged through intermediaries that: "Nothing will be undertaken before the American Congressional elections that could complicate the international situation or aggravate the tension," and that: "No missile capable of reaching the United States [will] be placed in Cuba" (Allison 1971, 40-41).

Brezhnev's Brinksmanship

Glassboro 1967 was followed a year later by the Red Army invasion of Czechoslovakia. The 1972 summit was followed by Brezhnev's brinkmanship in the Middle East during the 1973 Yom Kippur war. And, after a Carter-Brezhnev summit, there followed the genocidal invasion of Afghanistan in December 1979. From the resolution of the Cuban missile crisis in the early years of the Kennedy administration until President Carter's rude awakening in 1979, the Soviet Union engaged, with no American response, in an arms buildup, both conventional and nuclear, that placed the United States and its NATO allies in an inferior position lasting to this very day. Unbelievable but true, Secretary of Defense Robert McNamara said in 1965 that the Soviet Union would not challenge the U.S. lead in strategic nuclear weaponry ("Is Russia Slowing Down the Arms Race?" *U.S. News and World Report* 58[5] [April 1965], pages 52-61).[172] Four years later, the Soviet number of ICBMs exceeded that of the United States (Douglass 1988, 174).

It is too early to say what the five Reagan-Gorbachev summits will produce, but if we are to judge by the past record, very little good will accrue for the democracies. *Ex nihilo nihil.*

The Washington summit in December 1987 is an excellent case history of how, under the new Soviet leadership, little had changed for the better. On 30 October 1987, in a joint statement convening the summit, Gorbachev pledged to move forward on the question of human rights. At the conclusion of the summit, it was clear that the Soviet Union would do little if anything about human rights. At the end of the Moscow 1988 summit, during which President Reagan boldly raised the question of human rights both publicly and privately, Gorbachev counterattacked as he had at the Washington summit. In fact, Gorbachev said of the United States: "What right does it have to be the teacher; who gave it the moral right?" These rhetorical questions came in reply to questions about the Soviet Union's denial of the right of emigration.[173]

---

172 President Carter's Secretary of Defense, Harold Brown, who had been operating on the McNamara policy that the United States ought to let the Soviets achieve an arms balance with the United States, was forced to repudiate the McNamara policy and start an Operation Catchup of his own. As he wrote in his last annual report about the Soviet Union arms policy, "We arm, they arm; we stop, they arm" ("Soviet Military Doctrine," *Foreign Affairs* 67[2] [Winter 1988/89], page 115). Obviously, in 1980 it was no longer childish to be possessed by an "inordinate fear of communism."

173 Senator Daniel Patrick Moynihan (1980, 97) has said that "since the destruction of Nazism and the eclipse of Fascism as a school of political thought (Franco's

There is, of course, an answer to the question about "the moral right" to challenge the Soviet Union's attitude. The Soviet Union pledged in three separate international documents that "everyone shall have the right to leave any country, including his own" (*Wall Street Journal* 16 December 1987, Op-Ed page). The three documents are: the Universal Declaration of Human Rights, the International Covenant on Civil and Political Rights, and the 1975 Helsinki Accords. Nothing in these documents says anything about barring would-be emigrants from the Soviet Union on the grounds that they may have once been privy to state secrets, nor anything about setting up impossible conditions for obtaining an exit visa, practices that the Soviet Union has engaged in over the years.

Long-Range Soviet Plans

Many defectors from the Soviet Union and Warsaw Pact countries have testified to Soviet long-range plans for political warfare against the United States and the Western alliance. Books by General Major Jan Sejna (a highly placed Czech intelligence official), Ladislav Bittman of the Czech intelligence service, Anatoliy Golitzin, Arkady N. Shevchenko, and many others have revealed in documented fashion the continuing conspiracy of the Soviets against the very countries with whom they are in continuous negotiations.

In the light of such activities by a chiliastic Soviet Union, is it possible to have normal diplomatic relations and pursue normal treaty diplomacy with that country?

In 1924, the Treaty of Rapallo opened the era of diplomatic relations between the Soviet Union and the capitalist world. Great Britain, Italy, Norway, Austria, Greece, Sweden, China, Denmark, and France all recognized Soviet Russia. But, as the Russian historians-in-exile Mikhail Heller and Aleksandr Nekrich (1986, 210-11) have pointed out, Soviet foreign policy operates on two levels: traditional diplomatic relations and the activity of the Comintern, later the Cominform and the CPSU International Department.

"Quite often the two levels of foreign policy," they write, "functioned together and it was difficult to determine where one ended and the other began.... The lack of separation between traditional diplomatic activity and the innovative moves of the Comintern was indicated by the fact that quite often Soviet diplomatic representatives abroad were at the same time officials of the Comintern" (Ibid.).

Spain having been its last bastion), [the Soviet Union] remains the only major political doctrine that challenges human rights in principle."

Three Foreign Policy Precepts

Since the 1920s, Russian foreign policy has been based on three precepts:

1. The need to strengthen the Soviet Union in order to strengthen the world revolutionary movement;
2. The inevitability of conflict between the Soviet Union and the capitalist countries. (Therefore, the revolutionary movement in the capitalist countries represented a reserve force that could help Moscow in cold or hot war. The conflict, however, need not—inevitably—be war, according to a resolution adopted at CPSU Central Committee plenary session in 1980); and,
3. The nature of capitalist countries, which did not exclude the possibility of carrying on normal diplomatic and trade relations with them while conducting subversive revolutionary activity against them (the most important precept).

One could add here another Soviet concept that affects Soviet foreign policy. It was embodied in a statement made by Khrushchev to President Kennedy at their 1961 Vienna summit: "The continuing revolutionary process in various countries is the status quo, and anyone who tries to halt this process not only is altering the status quo but is an aggressor" (Nixon 1988, 48).

The only treaty with a noncommunist country that, it can be said, the Soviet Union under Josef V. Stalin observed over and above the letter was the Nazi-Soviet Pact of 23 August 1939.[174] As Heller and Nekrich (1986, 353ff.) put it: "In 1940 and 1941 the Soviet Union conscientiously abided by the terms of its agreement to supply Germany with strategic raw materials, in particular oil and grain. In this way the Soviet Union contributed significantly to the German preparations for war against—the Soviet Union itself." The Soviet side "honored its commitments with exceptional care and punctuality."

The Punctilious Stalin

Stalin's punctiliousness in observing the Nazi-Soviet Pact was unusual because he had little respect for treaties in keeping with this dictum:

---

[174] For a succinct scholarly monograph on the events leading up to the 1939 compact, see John Kolasky, *Partners in Tyranny: The Nazi-Soviet Non Aggression Pact* (Toronto, Canada: Mackenzie Institute, 1990). The book also contains key documents of the agreement.

With a diplomat words must diverge from acts—what kind of diplomat would he otherwise be? Words are one thing and acts something different. Good words are masks for bad deeds. A sincere diplomat would equal dry water, wooden iron. (Stalin 1933, 2:285)

9

Of Pitfalls and Booby-Traps

To the Bolshevik, politics is the craft of conflict; to the American, it is the art of compromise.

Brzezinski and Huntington[175]

Since treatyism with the Soviet Union is inevitable if not relaxing, U.S. negotiators should always keep in mind two questions:

1. Would the Kremlin ever negotiate a treaty that would weaken the Soviet Union militarily or politically or, conversely, strengthen the conegotiator? Did Gorbachev become the Politburo's "First Minister" in order to preside over the liquidation of the Soviet Empire or was he chosen by the Politburo to arrange, despite tactical detours, for the extension of that empire with all deliberate speed?

Liquidating a "social class," as Stalin did the Russian peasantry, is at worst a venial sin (Gorbachev has yet to denounce the Great Terrorist with Khrushchevian candor), but to liquidate the proletarian empire created by the same Stalin would be a mortal sin. When Gorbachev was asked by *L'Humanité* whether the vestiges of Stalinism had been overcome in the Soviet Union, he replied: "Stalinism is a concept thought up by the enemies of communism to discredit socialism as a whole" ("The Case of Nikolai

---

175 1965, 38.

Bukharin," *Encounter* 411 [January 1989], page 54). As President Nixon[176] wrote, "To a man [Stalin] who killed tens of millions of Soviet citizens Gorbachev gave a pat on the back and a slap on the wrist" (Nixon 1988, 43).[177]

2. Is Soviet treaty diplomacy intended in the long run to weaken the United States militarily and politically and to strengthen the Soviet Union?

Soviet Intentions Toward the West

In asking these questions, whose answers seventy years of Soviet geohistory have made all too obvious, U.S. negotiators would be seeking to assess the long- as well as the short-range Soviet intentions toward the West. Such an assessment should be regarded as an absolute prerequisite to negotiations. As Kenneth Adelman[178] wrote:

> The key issue for arms control has never been defenses or offenses *per se* but political intentions. We ask: are the Soviets willing to trade a genuine reduction in the threat to us in exchange for a genuine reduction in the threat to them? That has always been the nub of the problem. Thus far strategic arms control agreements have failed to achieve this goal: they have coincided with huge increases in offensive weapons in both arsenals and a disproportionate increase in U.S. vulnerability. ("Negotiating Arms Reductions," *New York Times* 19 January 1987, page 23)

---

176 President Nixon wrote that Gorbachev has endorsed Stalin's brutal collectivization program and quoted Gorbachev as praising "the tremendous political will, purposefulness and persistence, ability to organize and discipline the people displayed in the war years by Joseph Stalin" (Nixon 1988, 43). In fact, President Gorbachev still has to face up to the question of Stalin. In his speech November 1987 celebrating the seventieth anniversary of the October Revolution, he argued that there had been no alternative to Stalin's line. Interestingly, Aleksandr Yakovlev, President Gorbachev's top aide, argued that there could have been an alternative to Stalinism. (*Radio Liberty* 25 August 1988, page 3).

177 Soviet sociologist Igor Bestuzhev-Lada has suggested in an article in the Soviet journal *Nedelya* (*Radio Liberty* 167/88 [15 April 1988], page 15) that 38-50 million people were repressed under Stalin. Nineteen to 25 million of the 150 million peasants had died or had been left "semi-living" during collectivization. As many people had been repressed or killed during the purges from 1935 to 1953, the year of Stalin's death. Historian Roy Medvedev, in an article in the Soviet journal *Argumenty i fakty* (*Radio Liberty* 1[7] [17 February 1989], page 27), estimated that approximately 40 million people were repressed by Stalin. About 20 million of these died in labor camps, through executions, forced collectivization and famine.

178 Adelman was director of the U.S. Arms Control and Disarmament Agency when this passage was published.

A careful definition of Soviet intentions in bilateral or multilateral negotiations must be the only basis for a theory of U.S.-Soviet negotiations, as it would be, for example, for a theory of U.S. intelligence. If the Soviet Union is regarded as just another power (in the same way some historians and publicists regarded the Third Reich in its early years as an offshoot of Wilhelmine Germany), then the negotiating approach to the Soviet Union would be no different from the negotiating approach to France or Mexico ("Ethics and Intelligence," *Foreign Affairs* 56 [April 1978], page 629).[179]

A la Prochaine

The Soviet Union however, is like no other power in the world. Over and over again it has shown that it considers itself exempt from the normal rules of international behavior, and it frequently acts on that presumption. The Soviet Union is prepared to move militarily whenever its inner dynamics demand and whenever it feels secure that its aggression will meet ineffective resistance, if any.

The invasion of Afghanistan was a most recent example of Soviet inner dynamics at work that this time didn't quite come off. *A la prochaine....* There's always a next time. To further its policies, the Soviet Union is prepared to use any tactic as part of its strategy of world conquest. As Michael Voslensky has written about the Soviet caste system:

> The *nomenklatura* is a class of privileged exploiters. It acquired wealth from power, not power from wealth. The domestic policy of the *nomenklatura* class is to consolidate its dictatorial power, and its foreign policy is to extend it to the whole world. (Voslensky 1984, 441)

Undeniable Soviet Violations

In chapter 2, I discussed Yegor Ligachev's warning to strikers and their supporters in Armenia as an example of Soviet self-exemption from the normal rules of international behavior.

Another example of this self-exemption from treaty commitment can be seen in the undeniable violations by the Soviet Union of its treaty with the

---

179 To know what Soviet intentions really are, it isn't essential to engage in what the intelligence community calls "controlled penetrations." The intentions are all laid out in the canonical writings of Marx and Lenin. While it is difficult sometimes to understand the relationship between ideology and power drives, one can always assume that the Soviet Union, when it can, will seek to damage the United States and its allies.

occupying powers in Berlin, particularly the United States. For example, Point Ten of the Potsdam Agreement of 1945, underwritten by the United States, Britain, and the Soviet Union said:

> Subject to the necessity of maintaining military security, freedom of speech, press and religion shall be permitted, and religious institutions shall be respected.... The formation of free trade unions shall be permitted. (Shirer 1961, 94)

For more than four decades, there was no freedom of speech, religion, or press in East Germany, nor were there any free trade unions. What unions there were in East Germany were Communist Party fronts and so antilabor that their exploitative actions sparked the construction worker uprising on 17 June 1953. The strike that started in East Berlin spread throughout the country (Baring 1972, 6ff.).

The Berlin Blockade

Earlier, in June 1948, the Soviet Union had tried to take over all of Berlin by throwing a full blockade around the city following the Red Army takeover of Czechoslovakia in February 1948. (The blockade began after the Allied Powers agreed 6 March 1948 to merge the three Western occupied zones. Stalin lifted the blockade 12 May 1949.) Berlin, an excellent case history of the Soviet Union's attitude on treaty compliance, was under four-power control at the time of the blockade (Clay 1950, chapters 18-20; Adomeit 1982, passim).

As for the Berlin Wall, Gorbachev told NBC's Tom Brokaw in a TV interview 30 November 1987 that the wall was erected for three reasons: first, because East Germany wanted to prevent "any interference in its domestic affairs" (East Germany wanted to protect itself against "harm" from West Berlin); second, because the occupying Western powers had been first to violate the Yalta and Potsdam agreements by dividing Germany; and third, because Warsaw Pact troops are grouped in offensive formations for defensive purposes only ("Thank You, Mr. Gorbachev," *New York Times* 4 December 1987, page A39). All fictions.

The Nicholson Assassination

Attacks on U.S. service personnel and property occurred regularly in the Soviet occupation zone of East Berlin. These attacks culminated in the assassination, which is what it was, of Major Arthur D. Nicholson on 24 March 1985. It should be remembered that the United States has the legal right to enter East Berlin, just as the Soviet Union has the right to enter noncommunist West Berlin. These entries into each other's zones are allowed to treaty-constituted Military Liaison Missions, which were created after the war by the four occupying powers: the United States, Britain, France, and the Soviet Union. Under this quadripartite treaty (the Agreement on the Control Mechanism in Germany dated 14 November 1944), a Military Liaison Mission is allowed to observe Soviet military activity in East Germany. Soviet military liaison teams can and do legally range freely in the zones occupied by the Western powers.

The Soviet Union refused to make any restitution or to apologize for the killing of Major Nicholson. More than three years after the tragedy, in June 1988, Soviet Defense Minister Dmitri Y. Yazov finally apologized half-heartedly to Defense Secretary Frank Carlucci during the Moscow summit ("Soviets Regret Killing of U.S. Major in 1985," *New York Times* 15 June 1988, page 3).

A few months later, however, the Soviet Red Army paper *Krasnaya Zvezda* was trumpeting the old charges once again that the Allied missions were "procuring vital secret information" when they entered the Soviet zone (*Insight* 13 February 1989, page 37). No mention was made of Soviet spy activities by Soviet missions in the Allied occupation zones. Whether or not the official Soviet journal's accusation was to build up a record for future use in manufacturing a Berlin crisis anew remains to be seen.[180]

Even after the Nicholson killing, Soviet attacks on U.S. personnel continued. As of 17 September 1987, there had been thirteen Soviet-directed occurrences against U.S. personnel and property. More than half of these incidents—seven—occurred in 1987 alone at the height of the Gorbachev *glasnost* campaign. U.S. government response to these provocations and actual attacks were muted, ignored, or actually kept secret in the interest, presumably, of détente. It was only at the insistence of members of Congress that these incidents were finally made public ("Hidden Risks of Liaison Duty," *Washington Times* 25 September 1987, page F4; "Where Gunshots Drown Out Sounds of Glasnost," *Washington Times* 13 November 1987, page F3).

---

180 On the eve of the Bush-Gorbachev Malta summit, the Soviets arrested and detained for seven and a half hours a U.S. officer and a noncommissioned officer near Halle, about eighty miles southwest of Berlin. Later investigation showed that the U.S. officers had not been in a restricted area. This incident was the fifth in 1989. As tit-for-tat, the Western military forces have detained over the same period five Soviet military observer teams. The Pentagon announced that there would be no protests to the Soviet Union over these detentions (Associated Press 6 December 1989).

Secrecy Arouses Senator

The secrecy surrounding these hostile Soviet actions aroused then Senator Chic Hecht (R., Nev.), who objected in the Senate to the Reagan administration's penchant for classifying Soviet offenses against U.S. military personnel as top secret. Senator Hecht was a member of the Senate Intelligence Oversight Committee.

"We are keeping from the American people," Hecht said, "the whole story of top Soviet secret intelligence activities. And the time has come—and I feel this strongly—to tell the American people the true story of Soviet activities" (personal communication with the author 5 December 1987).

For example, we were keeping secret, according to Senator Hecht, Soviet laser and radio frequency energy military applications. The most recent example at the time of this flagrant exercise of Soviet laser power occurred 30 September 1987 off Hawaii. An Air Force Boeing 707, known by its military designation as WC 135, was on patrol observing the maneuverings of two "AGIs," as Soviet intelligence ships are designated. Suddenly, one of the ships shot a laser ray at the U.S. plane, blinding one of the two American pilots, a woman officer.

Had the other pilot not had his head down to look at the instrument panel, the plane with two blinded pilots would have crashed into the Pacific. And it would have been assumed, incorrectly, that the accident had been due to engine trouble or some other routine cause.

"The question we should be asking," said Senator Hecht, "is what makes this laser attack different from firing a machine gun or a missile at an Air Force plane? The net effect is just the same" (Ibid.).

The September 30 incident was downplayed by the Reagan administration. In fact, it was not until Senator Malcolm Wallop (R., Wyo.) charged that the Soviet Union had fired a laser beam at U.S. aircraft that the Pentagon finally confirmed the attack 2 October 1987.

Aggressive Laser Technology

This was not by any means the first time that the Soviets had used laser technology for provocative attacks against U.S. personnel. According to the Pentagon, as reported in the *New York Times* on 3 October 1987, "there had been previous episodes in which Western patrol aircraft had been 'irradiated' by Soviet laser devices on ships" (*New York Times* 3 October 1987, page 6).

On 9 November 1989, the Pentagon reported that Soviet ships were "suspected" of aiming laser beams at four American military aircraft in the Pacific, possibly injuring the eye of one crewman. These incidents occurred despite a U.S.-Soviet pact on averting dangerous military incidents signed in

Moscow by Admiral William J. Crowe, then chairman of the Joint Chiefs of Staff, and Gen. Mikhail A. Moiseyev, chief of the Soviet General staff.

Senator Hecht also disclosed (in a personal communication to the author 5 December 1987) that SPOT, the French satellite, had "accidentally" taken photographs of a huge Soviet laser factory. The installation is located on a mountaintop near Dushanbe, the capital of Tadzhikistan, where ethnic disorders broke out in February 1990. Photos taken by U.S. satellites have been classified. What the Soviets are doing at this installation, some 7,500 feet above sea level, is not being discussed publicly by the administration. What the Soviets are making, the scope of their laser research, and the military consequences are all being kept secret from the American people.

As part of President Gorbachev's "new thinking" reformism, the United States and the Soviet Union signed an agreement 12 June 1989, effective 1 January 1990, to reduce "dangerous military activities" and the chances of starting a war by accident. It took nine months of negotiations to reach an accord, said Admiral William J. Crowe, chairman of the Joint Chiefs of Staff, who signed on behalf of the United States during an eleven-day visit to the Soviet Union (Gen. Mikhail A. Moiseyev, Soviet chief of staff, signed on behalf of the Soviet Defense Ministry) ("U.S. Says Lasers Strike Its Planes," *New York Times* 13 June 1989, page A17).

The agreement covers hazardous use of laser range finders that could blind the other country's soldiers or sailors, and accidental straying of planes or military units into the other's territory. In other words, the United States is agreeing not to do something it hasn't done—using laser technology to blind the other's sides military—while the Soviet Union is agreeing not to do something it has been guilty of doing and shouldn't have done in the first place. What the new agreement does not deal with, ostensibly because there are other agreements to cover them, is an incident like the fatal shooting in 1985 of Major Nicholson or the shootdown of the South Korean airliner in 1983 that killed 269 civilians (Associated Press dispatch #1443 [12 June 1989]; "Avoiding Accidental Confrontation," *Christian Science Monitor* 13 June 1989, page 8).

Solzhenitsyn's View

Alexander Solzhenitsyn has written that "we would understand nothing about communism if we tried to comprehend it on the principles of normal human reason. The driving force of communism, as it was devised by Marx, is political power, power at any cost and without regard to human losses or a people's physical deterioration" ("The Soviet Union at the Moment of Brezhnev's Death," *National Review* 21 January 1983, page 28; "A General Theory of Sovietism," *Encounter* 60 no. 5 [May 1983], pages 19-21).

Over the past decades, while the Soviet Union was engaging in wide-ranging treaty diplomacy with the United States and the other democracies, nine new Leninist regimes arose in the Third World and aligned themselves with the Soviet Union. Several of these regimes threaten Western trade routes and security. The Soviet presence in Managua, Cam Ranh Bay, Aden, and both African coasts, according to James Billington ("Realism and Vision," *Foreign Affairs* 65[3] [Spring 1987], page 635), "provides a reminder that we are confronted not just by traditional Great Russian imperialism, but by the executors of a global ideology." Billington writes:

> Even the continuing atrocity of a classical imperial move into Afghanistan is justified by the Soviet *nomenklatura* ... as the necessary defense of a threatened revolution. By this reasoning, social processes are no less irreversible than Leninist regimes themselves; and the only limit on Soviet assistance is the capability of the Soviet economy to support military power, and of the Soviet political machine to convert that power into political advantage. (Ibid.)

Part of Long-Range Strategy

It is quite possible that the Soviet Union might, as part of a long-range strategy, surrender certain dearly-held ideological positions or favorable tactical situations. It has done so in the past, sometimes under military threat.

For example, the Soviets agreed in 1942 and 1943 to withdraw their troops from northern Iran. In the Teheran Declaration of 2 December 1943, Roosevelt, Churchill, and Stalin reaffirmed Iranian independence and territorial integrity. In September 1945, British Foreign Secretary Ernest Bevin and Soviet Foreign Minister V. M. Molotov agreed that all foreign troops would be out of Iran by 2 March 1946. In 1945, Stalin attempted to seize two Iranian provinces for eventual incorporation into the Soviet Union. The Soviet Union financed a separatist movement in Azerbaijan and instigated a Kurdish People's Republic. But under military threat by President Truman, Stalin finally withdrew Soviet troops (Acheson 1987, 197).

Following Stalin's death, the new Soviet leadership, as part of a post-Stalin strategy, negotiated agreements on issues that only a short time earlier had seemed to defy solution. In July 1953, there was a Korean armistice; in July 1954, an armistice in Indochina; and in May 1955, a long overdue treaty with Austria (Pipes 1972, 1). Then there was the Limited Nuclear Test Ban Treaty of 1962, the Berlin agreement of 1971, and SALT I in 1972.

The classic postwar example of Soviet surrender of a once tenaciously held position was the Austrian State Treaty. After eight years of negotiation involving 400 separate meetings, an agreement was finally reached. What is more, Austrian sovereignty was respected even when its border with Hungary provided an exit for Hungarian rebels fleeing their country in fall and winter

1956. How come? With Stalin's death, a new Soviet leadership felt changes were necessary. Not only was Austria freed in 1955 from Red Army occupation but, in the spring, a delegation headed by Khrushchev arrived in Belgrade to convey official apologies to Marshal Tito for the Soviet Union's policy against Yugoslavia after World War II. It is possible that similar considerations affected the Finno-Soviet treaty of 1948.

The *Peredyshka* Strategy

The West should realize that an important aspect of Soviet history is the *peredyshka* (or "breathing space") strategy, be it in foreign adventurism or domestic policy. Lenin's ready acceptance of the punitive Treaty of Brest-Litovsk over the objections of colleagues like Nikolai Bukharin and Leon Trotsky was *peredyshka* in operation. When Lenin saw what a disaster "war communism" had brought to Russia, he introduced the New Economic Policy, or NEP, another example of *peredyshka*. The "united front" policy enunciated by Stalin in 1936 was *peredyshka* at work, as was Stalin's China policy that provided the Soviet Union a ten-year truce in an ongoing conflict with Japan. President Gorbachev's *perestroika* (or my preferred neologism, *glastroika*) is but another example of the temporary *peredyshka* strategy ("The Collapse of World Revolution," *Working Papers in International Studies* [Stanford, Calif.: Hoover Institution] I-89-13 [1989]). However, one can always hope, in the words of the French aphorism, that *rien ne dure que le provisoire*, or nothing lasts as long as the temporary.[181]

In a recent book on the importance of arms control to U.S. foreign policy, Bruce Berkowitz has a chapter called "Arms Control That Works." He cites as examples of successes: first, the U.S.-Soviet Union agreements on Incidents at Sea and, second, the Hot Line (Berkowitz 1988). A critic of his book made the point that these two agreements were successful "because they cost no faction in either government much, verification was simple, and they dealt with 'practical issues on a day-to-day basis'." As for the Hot Line agreement, it merely guarantees that messages will "get through, not that they will be truthful" ("The Magic Kingdom," *Commentary* 85[4] [April 1988], page 70).

---

181 It should be noted that *peredyshka*, or Soviet-arranged periods of détente have customarily ended with Soviet military action (Berlin 1953, Hungary 1956, Czechoslovakia 1968, Afghanistan 1979) or by use of surrogate forces (Angola and Mozambique).

Permanent Concerns

Those realissimists who know the meaning of Soviet history and Soviet treaty diplomacy are cautious when they write about how to negotiate with the Soviet Union. The permanent concerns to Western negotiators are fundamental questions like: Can Soviet treaty diplomacy speak to the truth? Can the Soviet Union be trusted to keep its treaty commitments?

These are not emotive questions. The Polish philosopher, Leszek Kolakowski, a communist in his youth, insists that "mendacity is not an accidental blemish on the body of communism. It is the absolute condition of its health and its life.... So, in order to keep this legitimacy principle alive, they have to keep the mendacious facade without which they would fall apart" ("The Eagle and the Small Birds," *Encounter* 358 [September-October 1983], pages 38-39).

Some years ago, a Senate subcommittee issued a compendium (U.S. Senate 1969, passim) taken from the writings of U.S. experts on negotiating with the Soviet Union. Among those who were cited were George F. Kennan, Philip E. Mosely, Dean Acheson, Gordon A. Craig, Fred C. Iklé, Thomas W. Wolfe, and Robert Conquest.

Whether these men would still hold to the same views I do not know. But these students of Soviet behavior reached certain conclusions at the time. They are worth examining:

1. Soviet accommodation with the democracies is regarded by the Kremlin as a negative virtue. For the Soviets, the United States is the eternal "class" enemy. Whatever helps the "class" enemy to survive betrays Marxism-Leninism.

2. The essence of Soviet politics and Soviet military doctrine is the inevitable clash—not necessarily a military clash—between the United States and the Soviet Union and how, under such circumstances, to ensure a Soviet victory. If the Soviet Union can obtain that victory by intimidation or by inducing an opponent to adopt a policy of unilateral disarmament, all the better. Whether or not the Soviet Union believes war with the democracies is inevitable can be debated. However, it can be said that Mikhail Gorbachev, like his predecessors, would appreciate the reply of Bismarck who, when asked whether he wanted war, said: "Of course not, I want victory" (Thatcher 1985, 4).

3. The Soviet Union believes it can win a thermonuclear war, according to Soviet military doctrine at one time. More recently, Professor Richard Pipes of Harvard University, one of the West's leading students of Soviet history, wrote that the Soviet Union rejects mutual deterrence since it

regards "conflict and violence as natural regulators of all human affairs" (Pipes 1984, 29).[182]

4. So long as the United States remains a functioning, prosperous market economy, capitalism, despite all the propaganda directed against it from the Kremlin and from Marxist academics, is a living reproach to Soviet socialism. Thus, in the eyes of the Kremlin, the existence of capitalism endangers Soviet legitimacy.

5. Because the Soviet Union seeks ultimate victory for the Leninist revolution, an aspiration that remains unaltered by the present leadership, it is a superpower that is innately expansionist and that is determined to subvert democratic societies. To achieve that aim, the Soviet Union lives in a state of permanent mobilization, *glastroika* notwithstanding.

George Kennan's Warnings

In the subcommittee's citation, taken from his *Memoirs 1925-1950*, Kennan 1962 uttered these warnings about negotiating with the Soviet Union:

1. Don't get chummy with the Soviets.
2. Don't assume a community of aims with them that does not really exist.
3. Don't make fatuous gestures of good will.
4. Don't make requests of the Soviets unless you are prepared to make them feel your displeasure in a practical way should the request be denied.
5. Don't be afraid of unpleasantness and public airing of differences.[183]

---

182 When analysts like Richard Pipes and Joseph Douglass, among others, propounded the thesis that Soviet military doctrine accepts the idea that it could win a nuclear war, they were derided. Yet here are the words of Vadim V. Zagladin, deputy head of the International Department of the Communist Party Central Committee, that confirm that thesis: "While we rejected nuclear war and struggled to prevent it, we nevertheless based our policy on the possibility of winning one [my emphasis]" ("Soviets Admit Foreign Policy, Defense Errors," *Los Angeles Times* 26 June 1988, section 1, page 8). This statement was made at a press conference on the eve of the Communist Party's special conference that began 28 June 1988. Writing in 1988, President Nixon argues: "For the Kremlin, all that nuclear weapons have changed is the means through which it pursues its traditional ends" (Nixon 1988, 43).

183 In later years, Kennan, who had once expressed the hope that "never would we [Americans] associate ourselves with Russian purposes in the areas of Eastern Europe beyond her own borders," became a spokesman for wide-ranging accommodation with the Soviet Union ("The Cycles of Western Fantasy," *Encounter* 402 [February 1988], page 10 n.16; Kennan 1960, 352-53).

Professor Mosely (who is regarded, along with Professor Merle Fainsod, as the cofounder of Soviet studies in America) has made the point that the Soviet attitude toward negotiation differs totally from that of the democracies. We put great faith in negotiations. They do not (U.S. Senate 1969, 16ff.). President Nixon (1988, 102) has written that "for the Soviets the purpose of negotiation is not compromise but victory."

"Compromise" Is Not a Russian Word

Mosely's conclusions were embodied in a paper he wrote in 1951 describing Anglo-American negotiations with the Soviet Union during World War II. He stressed that the word "compromise" in Russian is not of native origin and "carries with it no favorable empathy. It is habitually used only in combination with the adjective 'putrid'" (U.S. Senate 1969, 211).[184] His summation declared:

1. Soviet diplomats and experts cannot participate in informal day-to-day negotiations until they have received the most detailed instructions from Moscow.
2. Each point at issue "then becomes a test of will and nerves" (Ibid.). Grievances, real or imaginary, are piled on by Soviet spokesmen with accusations of bad faith against the adversary. Such tactics have two purposes: first, to weary the adversary; second, to attenuate any real grievances against the Soviet Union that the adversary might raise.[185]
3. One of the main pitfalls in negotiations with the Soviet Union is "the tendency to rely upon reaching an 'agreement in principle' without spelling out in sufficient detail all the steps in its execution." Thus, "the Western powers sometimes gained the 'principle' of their hopes, only to find that 'in practice' the Soviet government continued to pursue its original aims" (Ibid.).

---

184 Alain Besançon (1984, xv) argues that "the first rule [to stay in power] of Leninism has as a corollary a second one: compromise. When continuity of power is in jeopardy because the state is exercising its ideological program too rigidly, the program simply has to be put aside for a time" (Gerson 1984, xv). Could this explain the Gorbachev *perestroika* strategy? *Peredyshka?*

185 John Wheeler-Bennett (1963, 138) has referred to "the incalculable capacity of the Slav for interminable conversation," At a meeting of foreign ministers of the United States, United Kingdom, France, and the Soviet Union in London in 1947, British Foreign Secretary Ernest Bevin said: "I did not dream we would have insults and abuse inflicted on our countries in the manner we have had them this afternoon" (*New York Times* 14 December 1947, page 10).

4. Since there are rarely informal channels of communication with Soviet diplomats, a U.S. delegation should try to determine whether the Moscow negotiating team has no instructions, has definite instructions, or has instructions to do nothing more than build up a pro-Soviet propaganda position.

A Wise Briton's View

One of the most interesting views of negotiating with the Russians comes from Sir William Hayter, former British ambassador to Moscow:

Negotiation with the Russians does occur from time to time, but it requires no particular skill. The Russians are not to be persuaded by eloquence or convinced by reasoned arguments. They rely on what Stalin used to call the proper basis of international policy, the calculation of forces.

So no case, however skillfully deployed, however clearly demonstrated as irrefutable, will move them from doing what they have previously decided to do; the only hope of changing their purpose is to demonstrate that they have no advantageous alternative, that what they want to do is not possible.

Negotiations with the Russians are therefore very mechanical; and they are probably better conducted on paper than by word of mouth. (U.S. Congress 1987, 29)

Former Secretary of State Dean Rusk had another view of treaty diplomacy with the Soviet Union. During the 1960s, he said the United States and the Soviet Union negotiated a Test Ban Treaty, Civil Air Agreement, Consular Treaty, Treaty on the Non-Proliferation of Nuclear Weapons, two important space treaties, and an agreement not to put weapons of mass-destruction on the sea bed. Said Rusk (1976, 247): "The most effective agreements with Russia would be those where performance on both sides can be easily checked and where the question of 'good faith' does not arise."

Iklé Sees Soviet Advantages

Former Undersecretary of Defense Fred Iklé (U.S. Congress 1987, 48-50) has pointed to the advantages that Soviet negotiators enjoy over their adversaries:

1. The United States cannot develop "a negotiating position on a major issue without letting the public in on some of the internal controversies." This strengthens the Soviets because they can thereby estimate the strength with which Western positions are held. But in the case of the

Soviet Union, no leaks ever appear detailing differences between officials of the Central Committee, the Politburo, or the Supreme Soviet, or indicating what might be a Soviet fallback position. And Soviet propagandists like Georgi Arbatov or Georgi Shakhnazarov are always available, of course, to discuss at private Georgetown dinners the struggle between "hawks" and "doves" in the Kremlin.

2. Soviet public opinion, unlike Western public opinion, places no constraints on Soviet policy makers. They can, therefore, choose negotiating tactics with a freedom denied Western negotiators, who are beset with domestic interference.

3. A further Soviet advantage is that Soviet strategy is often supported by Western political opposition leaders and media representatives. Soviet propaganda is, moreover, fully coordinated, whereas "Western countries speak always with many voices."

The Iklé analysis reminded me of a passage in the classic four-volume travel journal *Russia in 1839* by the Marquis de Custine. While it could be argued, Kennan (1971, 124) once wrote, that de Custine's report was not "a very good book about Russia in 1839, we are confronted with the disturbing fact that it was an excellent book, probably, in fact, the best of the books, about the Russia of Joseph Stalin; and not a bad book about the Russia of Brezhnev and Kosygin." And I would add it's not a bad book about the Russia of Andropov and, perhaps, even the Russia of Gorbachev.

Even as far back as the mid-nineteenth century, foreign observers marveled at the quality of Russian diplomats compared to those in the West. The Marquis de Custine (1951, 132) explained it:

> If better diplomats are found among the Russians than among highly civilized peoples, it is because our papers warn them of everything that happens and everything that is contemplated in our countries. Instead of disguising our weaknesses with prudence, we reveal them with vehemence every morning; whereas the Russians' Byzantine policy, working in the shadow, carefully conceals from us all that is thought, done, and feared in their country. We proceed in broad daylight; they advance under cover: the game is one-sided. The ignorance in which they leave us blinds us; our sincerity enlightens them; we have the weakness of loquacity; they have the strength of secrecy. There, above all, is the cause of their cleverness.

The negotiations trap for the United States exists not only vis-à-vis the Soviet Union but also vis-à-vis a Soviet ally like the Palestine Liberation Organization. As the *Wall Street Journal* put it:

> The State Department's willingness to talk with the PLO leads the United States toward a familiar trap that the Soviet bloc and its proxies set continuously around

the globe. Faced with a determined, U.S.-aligned adversary, all these opponents decide to go over the heads of their U.S.-aligned adversaries and communicate directly with the American public.... This tactic has been used in Korea, in southern Africa, in Central America and in the Middle East. It is used because it works. The insurrection on the West Bank, the PLO's "Intifada", has little to do with the Israeli government and everything to do with U.S. opinion. (*Wall Street Journal* 16 December 1988, page A14)

A Forgotten Example

One of the worst things for negotiators to do is to surrender a principle for opportunistic reasons. A forgotten example of such surrender was the indiscriminate forced repatriation of Soviet POWs in the aftermath of World War II, a policy ordered by the U.S. Joint Chiefs of Staff. The U.S.-Soviet agreement on this wanton betrayal of human rights demonstrated a "Western ineptitude" in negotiating with the Soviet Union, an ineptitude based on ignorance of Soviet practice by U.S. negotiators. Men like Dean Acheson and Joseph Grew, who knew what Stalinism meant, understood that repatriation would mean the use of force. Their criticism of the agreement was ignored by their superiors until more than 2 million Soviet POWs had been repatriated, many against their will ("The United States and Forced Repatriations of Soviet Citizens, 1944-47," *Political Science Quarterly* 99[2] [June 1973], pages 253-275; Tolstoy 1977).

In an editorial lamenting the energetic participation of British statesmen in this degrading behavior, the *London Economist* described one of the lessons to be learned from this episode:

> It can hardly be imagined that the British and Americans would have done what they did in 1944-47 if they had known more about the country to which they sent all those unfortunates. Today they know more about it, but the Soviet world is still intensely secretive and the ignorance and incomprehension between the two halves of Europe this leads to still pose the risk of dangerous blunders. (*London Economist* 25 February 1978, page 13)[186]

Circumventing International Law

Andrei Amalrik cites research showing that the British Foreign Office circumvented international law by pretending that the Russians outside of the Soviet Union were members of the Allied army whom they were returning to their homeland. Britain and the United States also ignored the right of

---

186 An editorial on this dishonorable episode in the *London Times* was titled, "The Nation's Shame" (*New York Times Book Review* 19 November 1978, page 85).

political asylum in their haste to appease Stalin ("Victims of Yalta," *Harper's* [May 1979], page 93).

Another case where the United States surrendered a principle for opportunistic reasons was the "Agreement Between the United States of America and the Union of Soviet Socialist Republics for Cooperation in Exchanges in the Scientific, Technical, Educational and Cultural Fields in 1960-61" (U.S. Secretary of State 1959, vol. 10, part 2, page 1946).

In signing that agreement, the Eisenhower Administration was propagating a lie. The Big Lie the U.S. government was peddling occurred in this sentence of the agreement:

> Both parties will encourage exchanges as may be agreed between them of delegations representing organizations devoted to friendship and cultural ties, labor, trade union, youth *and other nongovernmental organizations in the Soviet Union* [my emphasis] and the United States for the purpose of exchanging experience and knowledge of the cultural and social life of both countries. (Ibid.)

Now, the United States knew when it signed this agreement that it was propagating a fiction. In 1961, there were *no* "nongovernmental organizations in the Soviet Union," particularly trade unions. In a one-party, totalitarian state, there can be no autonomous voluntary organizations. Lenin himself destroyed the line between the state and society that exists in democratic and, usually, even in most authoritarian countries, by enunciating the principle, "We recognize nothing private." In a state where no autonomy exists legally and constitutionally in a state for trade unions, parent-teacher organizations, churches, synagogues or mosques, cultural groups, and other private organizations, that state can be properly defined as totalitarian.

Concern About Meany Reaction

So concerned was the U.S. government at having signed an agreement that included trade union exchanges that it ordered a U.S. embassy attaché in Brussels to look up then AFL-CIO President George Meany, who was attending an international labor conference in the Belgian capital, to explain the reasons for the treaty.

Meany later told me what went on when the American diplomat did his explaining in a hotel room. "What right," said Meany, "does the government have to put American trade unions and Soviet trade unions in the same category? Our unions are free," he said; "theirs are party-controlled. What right does the government have," he continued, "telling the AFL-CIO that our government is going to encourage American labor unions to meet with the Soviet groups as if they were morally equal?" It must have been quite a tirade.

The diplomat listened to Meany's nonstop denunciation in silence. When the AFL-CIO president finally stopped to light a cigar, the diplomat said, "I've been sent here to tell you why the government signed this treaty with this clause which we knew would be objectionable to the AFL-CIO. Khrushchev wanted something like this clause and he put on a lot of pressure to get it. But you can just ignore it."

You can just ignore it. Meany hit the roof at that: "You're telling me we can ignore it. You can bet your bottom dollar we'll ignore it and when I get back home I'm going to blast the State Department and the White House for this treaty."

It had been the State Department's hope that if it "explained" the reason for the lie, Meany would understand and say nothing publicly. It didn't work. When Meany returned to Washington, he loosed his attack. To this day, the AFL-CIO has never exchanged trade union delegations with the communists. (Nor, for that matter, when Franco was alive, did they exchange with the Falangist trade unions) ("Folded Inside Cultural Exchange, *Washington Times* 20 May 1988, F4).)

Why Propagate a Fiction

One may well ask, If American officials knew they were propagating a fiction about the existence of nongovernmental organizations in the Soviet Union, why did they sign such an agreement and then, guiltily, try to explain it away? So what if Khrushchev did want such a clause?

The real answer is that once you engage in the moral equivalency game in which everybody and everything in the Soviet Union is like everybody and everything in the United States, then the course is irreversible. Moral positions go down the tubes. The lies in ideology become truths in politics. In Lionel Trilling's words: "it is characteristic of a well-developed ideology that it can diminish or destroy the primitive potency of fact" (Trilling 1958, 3).

Practitioners of moral equivalence will argue that just as "they" have "their" ideology, we have ours—democracy, or freedom. Freedom is a series of interrelated values whose hierarchy varies from one political culture to another. The concept of freedom means tolerance of other views—adversary views. The concept of ideology means intolerance of opposing views. Ideology demands an enforced monopoly of its "truths." Freedom makes no claim to infallibility. The very *raison d'être* of an ideology is its claim to infallibility. I base this contention on Karl Mannheim's analysis:

The concept "ideology" reflects the one discovery which emerged from political conflict, namely that ruling groups can in their thinking become intensively interest-bound to a situation that they are simply no longer able to see certain facts which would undermine their sense of domination. There is implicit in the word "ideology" the insight that in certain situations the collective unconscious of certain groups obscures the real condition of society both to itself and to others and thereby stabilizes it. (Mannheim 1936, 40)[187]

Kampelman Strategy

Max Kampelman, during his service to the Reagan administration, offered this strategy for successful negotiations with the Soviet Union:

1. The negotiations must be based on candor and honesty about the nature of our opponent. Kampelman is all for confrontation. For us, he said, "not to engage in confrontation, for us not to be candid about our concerns, I think does not make an honest negotiation and cannot lead to any kind of constructive results" (*Intelligence Report* [American Bar Association] 7[2] [February 1985], page 3).

2. It is essential that the United States highlight the issue of Soviet violations of existing arms control agreements. "Even though they may yell like stuck pigs," he remarked, "that's unimportant. They should yell.... The Soviet act must not dissuade us from being honest and candid and consistent about our position" (Ibid.). Ambassador Kampelman did not, however, elaborate on what happens after the U.S. negotiators "highlight" the Soviet violations of arms treaties. Are there any sanctions against the violators?

3. "If we raise an issue eleven times and there is no response or rejection of that issue, and if it's important to us and if we don't raise it a twelfth time, that becomes significant to the Soviets. Because we have dropped the issue, the Soviets conclude that it's not important to us anymore. We must understand that, so we do not drop the issue the twelfth time. If it is an issue that is of real concern to us, we must continue to raise it, patiently, persistently, consistently" (Ibid.).

---

187 Who else but an ideologist like the embattled Leon Trotsky could have so humbled himself as to tell the 13th Soviet Communist Party Congress: "The Party in the last analysis is always right because the Party is the single historic instrument given to the proletariat for the solution of its fundamental problems.... I know that one must not be right against the Party. One can be right only with the Party, and through the Party, for history has created no other road for the realization of what is right" (Fainsod 1965, 149).

Need for Display of Strength

For example, President Lyndon B. Johnson proposed to the Soviet leadership that both sides rid themselves of antiballistic missiles. The Soviet leadership rejected the idea out of hand. President Nixon proposed to Congress deployment of an antiballistic missile, an ABM. Congress accepted the proposal and the bill was passed. Lo! the Soviet Union was suddenly prepared to talk about restraining ABM defense. Or, as Kampelman put it: "We had to engage in this display of strength before they had the incentive to negotiate" (Ibid.).

Another veteran of the negotiating process is Kenneth L. Adelman. Several of his guiding principles on arms control negotiations are:

1. Be patient. One of the most successful treaties ever concluded with the Soviet Union was the 1955 Austrian State Treaty. It took ten years to negotiate that treaty which guaranteed Austria's freedom and withdrawal of Soviet occupation forces.[188]
2. Bargain from strength. Unilateral concessions by the United States will not inspire Soviet reciprocity. Congressional giveaway "arms control" amendments inspire the hope in Soviet negotiators that Congress will deliver free of charge what the Soviets might otherwise have to pay for with their own concessions.[189]
3. Insist on compliance. Unless the United States can find some way to get the Soviets to rid themselves of their penchant for treaty violations, "the future of arms control is in jeopardy" ("Negotiating Arms Reductions," *New York Times* 19 January 1987, page A22).

Nixon's Views

In his book *1999: Victory Without War*, President Nixon devotes a chapter to negotiating with the Soviets. He makes these points:

---

188 It should be remembered that the Soviet "collective" leadership during the 1953-55 period was still trying to recuperate from the aftermath of Stalin's death. Khrushchev and Nikolai Bulganin had just returned from a "Canossa" pilgrimage to Yugoslavia's Tito, hoping he could be won back into the "Socialist camp." When the devil is sick, the devil a saint would be ... or, *peredyshka*.

189 In 1977 President Carter cancelled production of the B-1 bomber. Senator John Tower asked academician Aleksandr Shchuykin in Moscow what the Soviets would now do in return. Shchuykin replied: "Sir, I am neither a pacifist nor a philanthropist" (Adelman 1987a, 2).

1. He rejects the school of thought that argues that, in negotiating with Moscow, the less the better. However, he concedes that Soviet leaders use negotiations to win victory without war. "Too often we use negotiations only to achieve peace without victory," Nixon wrote.

2. A president who opposes negotiations *per se* would be opposed by Congress and a large sector of the American people.

3. Even with communists, "statecraft counts [and] negotiations can make a positive difference." He offers the successful negotiations with China as having made a better and safer world.

4. Without negotiation, NATO would fall apart because today in Europe the fear of nuclear war has "eclipsed" the fear of Soviet expansionism. Gorbachev's brilliant public relations "peace" campaign and "President Reagan's belligerent rhetoric about the Soviets have contributed to this problem," he says.

5. "[A] reduction in East-West tensions divides the East more than it does the West," according to Nixon. Confrontation makes a dictatorship stronger while contact and negotiation can weaken it.

A Great Mystery

We have here a great mystery. Point four says that, were it not for summitry that creates détente, the Kremlin could achieve its forty-year-old objective: the disintegration of NATO and, concomitantly, the withdrawal of U.S. troops from Europe. The mystery is: Since summitry presumably strengthens NATO, why does Gorbachev keep going to summits?

In détente we have a striking example of the dangers of Soviet treaty diplomacy to treaty partners. Détente meant cooperation between the two superpowers, according to the Nixon-Brezhnev declaration of May 1972. That paper charged the two superpowers with a "special responsibility ... to do everything in their power so that conflicts or situations will not arise which would increase international tensions." A document outlining twelve "basic principles of relations" between the United States and the Soviet Union was agreed upon as a code of conduct.

At the first opportunity, the Soviet Union violated those principles by its involvement in the events that led up to the 1973 Yom Kippur War. The Soviets knew the Arab attack was coming at least four days before it happened on October 6. Despite the "basic principles," they not only did not warn the United States of the attack, they also attempted to widen the war by transporting Moroccan troops to the front. Three days after the Arab attack on Israel, Brezhnev (President Nixon's partner in an agreement "to do everything in their power so that conflicts or situations will not arise which would increase international tensions" sent Algeria (and a day later all Arab countries) a message saying that "Syria and Egypt must not remain alone in their fight against a perfidious enemy" ("In Spite of Détente Talk, Trends Are Going Against America," *Washington Post* 28 July 1975).

Brezhnev's Contempt

Showing his utter contempt for détente and President Nixon, Brezhnev gave a speech in Moscow the day before the message was sent to Algeria expressing the hope that the Arab aggression against Israel would not disturb "détente." Well, it didn't, even though on 25 October 1973 President Nixon ordered a grade three nuclear alert and even though Brezhnev made it clear that he was prepared to send in Red Army airborne divisions to rescue the encircled Egyptian Third Army unless the Israelis withdrew. Admiral Elmo Zumwalt, chief of U.S. Naval Operations (1970-74) has written about that in great detail.

In 1972, President Nixon characterized détente as "the new foundation [that] has been laid for a new relationship between the two most powerful nations in the world" (Pipes 1986, 29). Today, he writes: "Diplomatic treachery, military intimidation, and aggression by proxy are standard operating procedures for the Kremlin leaders" (Ibid.). What President Nixon fails to answer is how come he didn't appreciate the perversity of Soviet communism in 1972. Why did he and Secretary of State Kissinger stake their political careers on détente? Why did President Nixon discourage intelligence estimates that stressed the omnipresent Soviet threat?

That these were not solitary perceptions can be seen in a statement made by Professor Eugene Rostow of the National Defense University in 1979: "Kissinger's policy was that the facts about Soviet power and policy of expansion must be 'concealed' from the American people while the government negotiates the 'best deal it can get'" (U.S. Congress 1987, 4842). President Nixon writes:

Our aspirations are in direct conflict. America wants peace; the Soviet Union wants the world. Our foreign policy respects the freedom of other countries; theirs tries to destroy it. We seek peace as an end in itself; they seek peace only if it serves their ends. The Soviets pursue those ends unscrupulously, by all means short of all-out war. For the Soviets, peace is a continuation of war by other means. (Nixon 1988)

Inherently Aggressive

The Soviet Union is, says Nixon, "an inherently aggressive power because its totalitarian system cannot survive without expanding. The Soviet system of internal repression is the root cause of its aggressive foreign policy" (Ibid.).

I could quote still harsher language Nixon uses to describe the Soviet

Union. What I don't fully understand is why the United States should negotiate with a country that, as he says, is guilty of "diplomatic treachery" and therefore, I assume, cannot be expected to live by the bilateral rules of détente.

President Nixon writes that while many anticommunists in the West "reviled the policy of détente ... the anticommunists in the East supported this approach wholeheartedly" (Ibid.).[190] Presumably the anticommunists in the East supported détente because it relaxed tensions between the superpowers. Therefore, by allowing the East European peoples a little more freedom, the Kremlin dictatorship would be weakened.

Now, here we have a bizarre paradox. President Nixon describes Gorbachev, whom he has met in Moscow, as a formidable opponent. If relaxation of tensions (glastroika?) weakens a dictatorship, why then does the dictatorship introduce such policies? Why would the Soviet Union with its "bicycle" ideology—stop pedaling and moving and down you go—allow itself to be weakened? Or is the risk, if any, worth taking because détente enfeebles the democratic will to resist communism?

Homicidal Stalin

A feral monster like Josef Stalin, as is now admitted in the Soviet Union, was able during an earlier détente (for which read "Cold War") to win prestigious recruits worldwide to his Stockholm "Peace" Campaign. The names that in 1948 and 1949 graced the Stockholm peace petitions were world famous and influential. There was a climactic Stalinist peace meeting at the Waldorf-Astoria Hotel in New York in April 1949.[191] Stalin's "peace

---

190   Among the anticommunists who denounced the Nixon détente policies was the AFL-CIO, whose 1975 convention passed a resolution that said that détente "has been a one-way street in which American concessions have not been reciprocated by the Soviet Union" (*AFL-CIO Free Trade Union News* 30[11], page 3). The labor federation's resolution also declared that the Soviet Union "understands détente not as a relaxation of tension or as cooperation to insure peace but as an intensification of ideological warfare and a stage in the 'international class struggle' brought about by growing Soviet power and Western decline" (Ibid., 4). Further, détente had "confused the American public's attitude on the need for a strong defense program, created uncertainty among our allies as to our commitment to their defense, and sown illusions about the intentions and character of the totalitarian regimes" (Ibid.).

191   For a firsthand description of this Stalin "peace offensive," see Hook 1987, 382-85, 474.

offensive" was going great guns until real guns began shooting in June 1950 in Korea.

Khrushchev enlisted his "peace" battalions in the West despite the 1956 Hungarian massacre, the Berlin Wall, and the missiles. Brezhnev had his "peace" transmission belt united fronts despite the bloody Soviet invasion of Afghanistan. Andropov sent dissidents to psychiatric hospitals and shot down a civilian Korean air liner, but to the U.S. media he was known to be a lover of Scotch, American novels, and tango dancing.

Kremlin's Détente Drama

And now, Mikhail Gorbachev and Raisa and her American Express Gold Card. Chernobyl, what's that? Nick Danilov frame-up? Forgotten. Watch the great détente drama in the Kremlin between the forces of light-and-glastroika and the forces of darkness-and-black-reaction, between the superhawks like Egor Ligachev and the superdoves like Boris Yeltsin and hard-headed détentistes like Gorbachev.

By 1999, this country (including our military establishment)[192] may well be a nation of pacifists, thanks to "détente." The magic of détente is that with it you can do anything, even make a wilderness and call it peace.

---

192 President Nixon says quite correctly that "the only battle the Pentagon seems ready to wage is the battle to get more money from the Congress" (Nixon 1988, 102). Reluctance by the military to risk combat did not begin with the U.S. defeat in Vietnam. Such reluctance was seen during the Soviet-imposed blockade of Berlin in 1948. "The most determined opposition to the use of force came from the J[oint] C[hiefs] of S[taff] who viewed the problem in purely military terms. Secretary of State Marshall, who had been a soldier most of his life, was equally opposed to breaking the blockade" (Murphy 1964, 316).

10

Brezhnev Doctrine:
Is It Yes, No, or Maybe?

As of the Malta Summit of December 1989, the answer to the question in the chapter title is no. Or, as I suggest later in this chapter, maybe.

During a state visit to Finland, President Gorbachev was quoted by his spokesman, Gennadii I. Gerasimov, as saying that the Soviet Union had "no right, moral or political right to interfere" in the affairs of its East European neighbors. Gorbachev added, "We assume others will not interfere either." Gerasimov, spokesman for the Soviet Foreign Ministry, said, "I think the Brezhnev Doctrine is dead" (*New York Times* 7 March 1989).

However, Gerasimov evaded a direct answer when asked what Moscow's response would be if its East European allies wanted to become as neutral as Finland and Austria are. Gerasimov noted that Hungary and Poland still have treaty obligations toward the Soviet Union as members of military and economic organizations. Said Gerasimov: "We may witness a change of government in Warsaw or Budapest, but international organizations do not necessarily go away with a change of government" (Ibid.).

The Brezhnev Doctrine has a great bearing on Soviet treaty diplomacy, especially because its victims are the Soviet Union's allies, willing and unwilling. Under the application of the open-ended Brezhnev Doctrine, everything is up for Soviet grabs, including countries that are not members of the Soviet bloc.

The Brezhnev Doctrine comprises the following points ("Sovereignty and the Internationalist Obligations of the Socialist Countries," *Pravda* 26 September 1968):

1. It proclaims the legitimacy of Lenin's doctrine that every law, including international law and the United Nations Charter, is subordinate to the "laws" of the class struggle.
2. Once "socialism" has been installed in any country by a Communist Party, that "socialism" can nevermore be disestablished. It is forever.
3. Any attempt at "socialist" disestablishment can, by definition, be considered an act of capitalist aggression.
4. Such an act permits any counteraction, including military, by the Soviet Union and its Warsaw Pact allies so as to preclude restoration of capitalism.
5. The sovereignty of Warsaw Pact countries, except that of the Soviet Union, is limited by the interests of the world revolutionary movement. Those interests are defined exclusively by (thanks to "proletarian internationalism," the "scientific" buzzwords for the Brezhnev Doctrine) the senior partner of the Warsaw Pact alliance, the Soviet Union. [193]

"Historical Necessity"

Promulgation of the Brezhnev Doctrine emerges out of that *omnium gatherum* Leninist phrase "historical necessity." The Brezhnev Doctrine is a direct outgrowth of Leninism, from which comes the self-justification for seventy years of Soviet imperialism.

Lenin, as I have pointed out, granted minority nationalities the right to secede from Russia. He conceded that "the right of self-determination [secession] is an exception from our general policy of centralism" (Fainsod 1963, 57-59). But then came the Leninist exception to the exception. Whether

---

193 The official Soviet definition of "proletarian internationalism" reads: "Internationalism is an inseparable component of the proletarian revolutionary outlook. Every proletarian revolutionary must be a convinced, consistent supporter of the international co-ordination of all revolutionary forces and, primarily, of the communist and workers' parties as well as of their unity in views and actions. Internationalism is incompatible with concessions to bourgeois and petty-bourgeois nationalism. Every retreat from internationalism is a betrayal of the working-class cause. Departure from internationalism by parties controlling socialist states is especially dangerous, since it undermines the bulwark of the world revolutionary forces—the world system of socialism" (*Soviet Analyst* 10[8] [15 April 1981], page 2).

or not the right of secession could legitimately be exercised in any particular case would be a decision taken by the Communist Party "from the point of view ... of the interests of the class struggle of the proletariat for socialism" (Ibid.). Comments Professor Fainsod: "In the grand strategy of Bolshevism 'self-determination,' like so many other slogans, turned out to have almost exclusively tactical significance" (Ibid.). Stalin in those early years argued that "the principle of self-determination must be an instrument in the struggle for socialism and must be subordinated to the principles of socialism" (Ibid.). From such a Leninist-Stalinist thesis, the Brezhnev Doctrine was ideologically inevitable.

While demanding absolute sovereignty for what the Kremlin defines as the "socialist world," the Brezhnev Doctrine offers little more than a temporary and limited sovereignty for the nonsocialist world. For the Soviet Politburo, the "laws" of class struggle are superior to "bourgeois law."

Soviet treaty diplomacy is no diplomacy at all. It is merely a prelude to action—diplomatic, military, or a mix of both—at times and places of the Kremlin's own choosing. Where definitions of "historical necessity" are unilaterally subsumed into the political system, as they are by the Soviet Union, negotiating positions by non-Soviet negotiators have no more than temporary meaning.

Delegitimized "Bourgeois Diplomacy"

Leninist doctrine delegitimizes what it calls "bourgeois diplomacy." For example, the *Great Soviet Encyclopedia* (1975, 278) article on "diplomacy" describes the diplomacy of "bourgeois society" as:

1. Having "much in common with that of the feudal period, insofar as both are the diplomacies of exploitative states."
2. Used by "the major capitalist states as a means for achieving their expansionist, aggressive aims...."
3. To further serve as part of the struggle against a neocolonialist policy.
4. Using as weapons and tactics (a) loans and economic "aid" or dollar diplomacy (b) military and political pressure (c) espionage.

In other words, by contrasting bourgeois diplomacy with socialist diplomacy, the Soviets have created a theory that legitimizes noncompliance, overt or covert, with treaties signed with bourgeois governments whenever it is possible to do so with impunity. And as I have shown earlier, there are no penalties to be assessed against the Soviet Union for violations. In fact, President Reagan has been criticized for making public, as required by law, such noncompliance as regards arms control agreements.

Self-Definition

On the other hand, Soviet diplomacy is, by self-definition, always legitimate because it "rests on respect for the principle of the equality and self-determination of nations, broad cooperation in matters pertaining to development and strengthening of the independence of states, implementation of the principles of peace and peaceful coexistence with states that have different socio-economic systems" (Ibid.).

As for the purpose of Soviet treaty diplomacy, or what the *Great Soviet Encyclopedia* (Ibid.) article calls "the diplomacy of the socialist states[, it] constantly exposes the aggressive designs of imperialist governments and the diplomatic maneuvers masking them." How does Soviet treaty diplomacy develop such certitude about its views? Simple:

> The theoretical basis of Soviet diplomacy is the Marxist-Leninist understanding of the international situation, the laws of social development, the laws of the class struggle and the Marxist analysis of the correlation of internal and international forces. (Ibid.)[194]

Officially, there is no "Brezhnev Doctrine"—just as, officially, there is no "Comintern" or "Cominform" (The International Department of the Soviet Central Committee is the latest version of the Third International). And in the sense that the Soviet Communist Party has not officially promulgated and named it as such (as Khrushchev "established" a doctrine when he revived the phrase "wars of national liberation" in his 6 January 1961 speech) the Brezhnev Doctrine can be perceived as a piece of Western factitiousness, a rhetorical artifact.[195]

---

194 A more objective description of Soviet treaty diplomacy was written by Gordon A. Craig (1962, 361): "It was reserved for the Soviet regime to devise new techniques of negotiation, while at the same time challenging the patience and ingenuity of the West by the way in which it adapted the traditional techniques to its own purposes."

195 The phrase "Brezhnev Doctrine" was used in a policy speech by Secretary of State George Shultz in 1985 when he described the meaning of "the infamous Brezhnev Doctrine [as] simple and chilling: "Once you're in the so-called 'socialist camp,' you're not allowed to leave. Thus the Soviets say to the rest of the world: 'What's mine is mine. What is yours is up for grabs'" (Shultz 1985, 2). However, as noted earlier in this chapter, in announcing the new Gorbachev line on regional intervention, Gennadii I. Gerasimov did use the phrase "Brezhnev Doctrine."

Soviet Imperialist History

It is not, however, a misleading term. There is, or was, a Brezhnev Doctrine in the sense that the phrase epitomizes a particular moment in Soviet imperialist history: specifically, the five-nation (the Soviet Union, Bulgaria, East Germany, Hungary, and Poland) invasion of Czechoslovakia on 20 August 1968, twenty years after Stalin's original *coup d'état* against Czech independence.[196]

Twenty-three Red Army divisions, two each from East Germany and Poland, one from Hungary, and one from Bulgaria, crossed the Czech borders. Not one of the various treaties signed since 1940 by the Soviet Union with the East European nations allowed Soviet intervention in the internal affairs of these countries nor proposed any limitation on their sovereignty (Merglen 1985, 28).

Three months after the invasion of Czechoslovakia, at the Fifth Polish Party Congress on 12 November 1968, Leonid Brezhnev spelled out almost in syllogistic form the justification not only for the invasion of Czechoslovakia but for the invasion of Afghanistan or, for that matter, any other country outside of the Soviet periphery. Said Brezhnev:

> We emphatically oppose interference in the affairs of any States, violations of their sovereignty. At the same time, the establishment and defense of the sovereignty of States which have embarked upon the road of building Socialism is of particular significance for us Communists.... When internal and external forces hostile to Socialism seek to reverse the development of any Socialist country toward a restoration of the capitalist order ... this is the concern of all Socialist states.... Experience shows that in present conditions the victory of the Socialist order in this or that country can be regarded as final and the restoration of capitalism can be regarded as excluded only if the Communist Party, as the guiding force of society, firmly carries through a Marxist-Leninist policy in the development of all spheres of public life. (U.S. Senate 1969, 83)

Four months earlier, the Warsaw Pact countries, except Romania, had addressed a letter to the Czech Communist Party Central Committee:

> We cannot agree to have hostile forces push your country from the road to Socialism and create a threat of severing Czechoslovakia from the Socialist community. This is something more than your cause. It is the common cause of all the Communist and Workers' parties and States united by alliance, cooperation and friendship. (*Pravda* 18 July 1968)

---

196 See also N. Rostow, *Yale Journal of World Public Order* 7 (1981), page 209.

Limited Sovereignty

On 26 September 1968, *Pravda* published an article under the title "Sovereignty and the International Obligations of Socialist Countries" that declared that "Each Communist party bears a responsibility not only to its own nation but to all the Socialist countries, to the entire Communist movement." Written by S. Kovalev, the article clearly spelled out what had long been obvious: the sovereignty of communist states, certainly those contiguous to the Soviet Union, was strictly limited, while in the name of "proletarian internationalism," the Soviet Union claimed absolute sovereignty for itself. *Pravda*'s writer said: "The sovereignty of individual socialist countries must not run counter to the interests of ... the world revolutionary movement" ("Sovereignty and the Internationalist Obligations of the Socialist Countries," *Pravda* 26 September 1968).

On 30 March 1971, at the Twenty-fourth Soviet Party Congress, Brezhnev (1971, 18) sanctified the doctrine with these words: "The peoples of the socialist countries have clearly demonstrated to the whole world that they will not give up their revolutionary gains, and that the borders of the socialist community are immutable and inviolable."

And the then Soviet Ideologist-in-Chief, Mikhail Suslov, wrote that "the transition to a communist system of rule is irreversible" (*National Security Record* 82 [August 1985], page 2).

Reason for the Theorizing

The extensive Soviet theorizing about the "duty" of communist countries to the "Communist Commonwealth" was not aimed at the free world that, of course, condemned the invasion of Czechoslovakia. It was directed at those powers, much more important to the Soviet Union, that had also condemned the invasion and the Brezhnev Doctrine. These included China (which called the doctrine an "out-and-out fascist 'theory'"), Yugoslavia, Albania, Romania (which did not participate in the 1968 overthrow of the Dubcek government), and the Italian Communist Party.

The assault on Afghanistan, however, gave a new twist to the Brezhnev Doctrine and its relationship to Soviet treaty diplomacy. The Soviet trespass into an independent country meant that Afghanistan's sovereignty was also limited. Alexander Bovin, the *Izvestia* correspondent, wrote in *Soviet News* (22 April 1980) four months after the Soviet invasion of Afghanistan: "There are situations when nonintervention is a disgrace and betrayal. Such a situation arose in Afghanistan" (Ibid.).[197]

Ideological Justification for Invasion

The broad ideological justification for the invasion of Afghanistan came early (31 December 1979) in a *Pravda* article that said that the Soviet Union "would not allow Afghanistan to be turned into a bridgehead for the preparation of imperialist aggression against the Soviet Union" (*Pravda* 31 December 1979). A subsidiary theme was that the invasion was necessary in order to defend "the gains of the April Revolution" (Ibid.).

Yuri V. Andropov, then chairman of the KGB and member of the Politburo, was quoted in the 12 February 1980 issue of *Pravda* as describing the invasion as "a lofty act of fidelity to the principle of proletarian internationalism, which was necessary to defend the interests of our Motherland." It little mattered to Andropov, later to become party general secretary, that the Afghan *mujaheddin* rejected his view of proletarian internationalism—if, that is, they had ever heard of proletarian internationalism.

ON 15 March 1980, the newspaper of the Soviet Defense Ministry, *Krasnaya Zvezda*, explained that the invasion of Afghanistan had been made at the request of the Government of the Afghanistan Democratic Republic "in accordance with the December 1978 Treaty of Friendship, Good Neighborliness and Cooperation between the Soviet Union and the DRA." In other words, the friendship treaty had been interpreted to legitimize the invasion of a neighboring country that was neither socialist nor within the Soviet bloc. East Germany (1953), Hungary (1956), Poland (1956), and Czechoslovakia (1968), all of which had suffered Soviet Red Army interventions after they had been incorporated into the Soviet Empire, were part of the bloc. Afghanistan was not.

---

197 Eight years later, demonstrating that flexibility of mind usually associated with Soviet propagandists, Alexander Bovin wrote in *Izvestia* (16 June 1988) that the Soviet Union had been mistaken in invading Afghanistan and that Soviet leaders had been too quick to resort to force to ensure the security of the Soviet state (*Radio Liberty* 258/88 [17 June 1988], pages 10-11). Bovin also wrote about the "new thinking," that is, the willingness of the Soviet Union to accept "deep compromises" taking into account the interests of other states.(*Soviet Analyst*. 17[13] [29 June 1988], page 4).

For ten years the Soviet Communist Party and government defended the Soviet invasion of Afghanistan. Finally, in October 1989, Foreign Minister Edward A. Shevardnadze told the Soviet legislature that the invasion "violated the norms of proper behavior" (*New York Times* 24 October 1989, page 1). He said:

> We went against general human values. I am talking, of course, about the dispatch of troops to Afghanistan. We committed the most serious violations of our own legislation, our party and civilian norms.... The decision, with such serious consequences for our country, was taken behind the backs of the party and the people. The Soviet people were presented with a fait accompli. (Ibid.)

In other words, all the Soviet propaganda to the contrary, the Afghanistan invasion was illegal, even by Soviet standards. What makes the Shevardnadze confession all the more remarkable was that, as the Soviet Foreign Minister was speaking, his government had, since the Soviet troop withdrawal in February, poured in some $2 billion of equipment to help the Soviet-installed government ("U.S. Must Reassess Afghan Policy," *Wall Street Journal* 18 October 1989, page A15). Some 900 SCUD surface-to-surface missiles had also been shipped in, according to a CIA report. This was on top of at least $1 billion worth of military equipment and installations left behind for the illegitimate Kabul regime to continue, on behalf of the Soviet Union, a war that, if the communist regime in Kabul were successful in defeating the mujaheddin, would only benefit the Soviet Union ("Moscow Aims at Journalists in Probe of Afghan Disaster," *Washington Times* 27 March.1989, page E3).

"Where Will Catherine Dine?"

The invasion of Afghanistan was reminiscent of something Burke once said of Catherine the Great: "She has breakfasted in Poland, where will she dine?" (Schapiro 1970, 48)[198]

The recent history of Afghanistan is an object lesson in the meaning of Soviet treaty diplomacy. Afghanistan has long been a target of opportunity—first for czarist Russia and, most recently, for Leninist Russia. Afghanistan, moreover, need never have been invaded. It was being subverted most efficiently by an apparatus with long experience in subversion. Its people only asked to be left alone. No anti-Soviet alliances were even contemplated

---

198 Averell Harriman, in his book *America and Russia in a Changing World*, reported that at Potsdam, in June 1945, he congratulated Stalin on the Red Army's reaching Berlin. Stalin then replied: "But Czar Alexander reached Paris" (Jaffe 1975, 223).

by Afghanistan. But the Politburo was being driven by an elemental force—Leninism—that demands hastening capitalism's inevitable day of reckoning. No matter the price in human suffering; strategic gains are required by Leninism. Perhaps an impatient Politburo and an even more impatient Red Army saw easy pickings in Afghanistan, which might cow neighboring Pakistan and, thereby, gratify India. As Cavour once noted, You can do anything with bayonets except sit on them.[199]

The result of such behavior is that even when the Soviet Union seems to be acting decently, as during the negotiated withdrawal in 1955 of its occupation troops in Austria, only those ignorant of Soviet history will believe that its leadership has adopted a new policy of live and let live.[200]

As Harold Rood has pointed out:

One difficulty in dealing with the Soviet Union where strategic warning is concerned is that the Soviet government seems capable of taking measures in one year that have no relation to anything immediate but only to some action or series of events that will occur much later. Soviet policy in Afghanistan seems to illustrate this.... The trouble is that the Soviet Union and its allies are doing things all the time which in past times one would have considered preparations for war. ("Early Warning: Part IV," *Grand Strategy: Countercurrents* 15 June 1983, pages 10-11)

Trade Agreement with Afghanistan

In 1950, the Soviet Union signed a trade agreement with Afghanistan—one of hundreds of such bilateral instruments between the countries over and beyond the treaties of friendship. For the next quarter century, the Soviet Union provided economic and technical aid. Soviet technicians and advisers assisted in the country's development, trained the military and undertook a fifty-year plan to develop the Afghanistan capital of Kabul. The Soviet Union completed a network of highways and communications and built a number of military airfields along the highway systems. In December 1979, the Soviet Union invaded Afghanistan in full force—airborne divisions used the recently

---

199 A partial listing of Soviet-Afghan treaties, agreements, contracts and other accords are to be found in Appendix A.

200 Suspicions about Soviet professions of peace and harmony recall the story told to me by Sir Isaiah Berlin in 1969 of Talleyrand's rejoinder to an unexpected obituary announcement. During one of the post-Napoleonic four-power meetings, an aide burst into the chambers of the worldly wise French foreign minister with the somber announcement that the Russian ambassador had just dropped dead. Talleyrand looked pensive for a moment and quietly asked, "I wonder what his motive was."

built airfields and Soviet ground forces used the recently laid out highways (Ibid.).

In 1989, with the negotiated withdrawal of Soviet troops from Afghanistan, the question was whether the Soviet retreat might mean the end—at least for the foreseeable future—of the Brezhnev Doctrine, especially in the light of Gorbachev's visit to Yugoslavia 14-18 March 1988.

In 1955, an event occurred that gave rise to the hope that the Soviet Union was changing for the better. In May 1955, Nikita Khrushchev and Nikolai Bulganin, the duumvirate that had taken over the ruling posts in the Soviet Union, traveled to Yugoslavia. The 1955 Belgrade Declaration, as indicated in chapter 8, promised no interference into the affairs of other countries.

There was yet another restriction on Soviet intervention into the affairs of its satellized neighbors, one described in chapter 8: the Communist Party proclamation adopted 31 October 1961, by the Twenty-second Soviet Party Congress that said that "the Communist party of the Soviet Union ... regards it as its internationalist duty to abide by the appraisals and conclusions which the fraternal parties have reached jointly concerning their common tasks in the struggle against imperialism, for peace, democracy and socialism" (*New York Times* 2 December 1968).

Clearly, the Soviet Union has violated over and over again its solemn commitments concerning the independence of its neighbors—commitments that should be of far greater moment to the Kremlin since they are undertakings with communist countries, not with untrustworthy and doomed bourgeois states.

Gorbachev's Visit to Yugoslavia

But similarly, Soviet Party Secretary Gorbachev's visit to Yugoslavia in March 1988 makes an interesting parallel to the Khrushchev journey in 1955. At the end of the 1988 visit, another Belgrade declaration was issued. It, too, called for "the autonomy and independence of parties and socialist countries in defining their own paths of development" ("Gorbachev in Yugoslavia: Burying the Brezhnev Doctrine?" *Soviet Analyst* 17[6] [23 March 1988], page 2). Compliance with such a doctrine, said the manifesto, is "of great significance ... for the development and establishment of socialism as a world process" (Ibid.). And it concluded:

Proceeding from the conviction that no one has a monopoly of truth, the sides declare their lack of any claim to impose their own ideas about social development upon anyone else whomsoever. (Ibid.)

As one can see, this is not the first time, nor the last, that a Soviet leader on a Canossa mission has promised, in such sweeping language, that there would be no Soviet interference in the internal affairs of another country, socialist or otherwise. The first paragraph of the 14 April 1988 agreement between the Soviet puppet government in Afghanistan and Pakistan guaranteed by the United States used standard Soviet parlance:

> Relations between the High Contracting Parties shall be conducted in strict compliance with the principle of noninterference and nonintervention by states in the affairs of other states.

Soviet tactics may vary from situation to situation, but Soviet strategy, whether in foreign policy or relations with other communist countries, has had a continuity that is rarely appreciated by Western policy makers. When the frustrated lover switches his offerings from a bouquet of roses to a case of Dom Perignon, it is a change of tactics, not a change of strategy.

In 1943, Josef Stalin promulgated the theory of "different roads to socialism." A few years later, when Tito tried to implement Stalin's theory of "different roads to socialism," Stalin asserted hegemonic ambitions over Yugoslavia in the name of "proletarian internationalism." Yugoslav consciousness of the talent of Soviet statesmen for overnight about-faces, treaty or no treaty, has led to a caution that has thus far successfully kept Yugoslavia out of the Soviet "camp" despite Kremlin pressure, temptations, and Belgrade declarations.

Khrushchev Retaliates Against Tito

I remember well a visit to Yugoslavia in 1958. Ten months earlier, in November 1957, Tito—unlike other communist leaders, including China's Chou En-lai—had refused to sign a Moscow declaration attesting to Soviet seniority in the communist world. One of Tito's associates, former UN Ambassador Ales Bebler, told me that Khrushchev had retaliated by canceling a multimillion-dollar economic aid program. The Yugoslav government, in anticipation of the Soviet credit, had invested large preliminary appropriations from its skimpy treasury to create an infrastructure for a hoped-for industrial development. What had been an economic agreement signed by the Soviet Union was wiped out—just like that. We should have known better, said Bebler, than to trust the Russians.

Ambassador Micunovic's diary entry for 28 May 1958, notes that "the Soviet Government has unilaterally postponed for another five years the Soviet-Yugoslav agreements on credits for the creation of a new Yugoslav aluminum industry, a fertilizer plant and some other enterprises. It was not the first time" (Micunovic 1980, 389).

Discussing the cancellation of the agreement with then Foreign Minister Gromyko, Micunovic complained that the Soviets "were again refusing to carry out intergovernmental agreements simply because there were ideological differences between us which had existed for some time" (Ibid.). He continued:

> I said we had much greater differences with other states, but that they did not refuse unilaterally to carry out agreements which they had signed with Yugoslavia. The matter assumed the character of economic reprisals on account of ideology. Under such conditions it was not possible for an independent country to maintain normal relations with another country. We had reached agreement on these matters with the Soviet government when normal governmental relations were restored three years ago. We now realized that they thought differently and had gone back on what we agreed in June 1955. (Ibid.)

Nagy's Unsafe Conduct

One of the worst examples of Soviet noncompliance with its freely given word was the Soviet-Hungarian violation of a guarantee of safe conduct to Imre Nagy. On 4 November 1956, the deposed anti-Soviet Hungarian revolutionary and a group of dissident Hungarians had been pledged political asylum in the Yugoslav embassy in Budapest to which they had fled when the Red Army smashed its way back to the city. After protracted negotiations between the new Soviet puppet premier, Janos Kadar, and the Yugoslav Embassy, Kadar pledged *in writing* on 21 November that Nagy and his companions could leave the embassy "and proceed freely to their homes" (Radvanyi 1972, passim).

The next evening, a bus arrived at the Yugoslav Embassy that Nagy and his companions boarded. They were followed into the bus by Soviet army commanders who ordered the bus to be driven to Soviet military headquarters in Budapest. Officers who had accompanied the bus to ensure that the Nagy party, as per the signed agreement, would be allowed to return to their homes, were ordered out of the bus by a Soviet officer. The bus, accompanied by Soviet armored vehicles, drove the prisoners to a local airport from which they were flown away to an unknown destination.

Nothing was heard of the captured Hungarians until 16 June 1958. After nineteen months of silence, it was announced that the People's Tribunal of the Hungarian Supreme Court had found the defendants guilty at a trial about which no details were ever given. Nagy and three others were sentenced to death, the remainder to long jail terms.

A Surprising Ally

With the emergence of Soviet-U.S. détente diplomacy under President Nixon, the Brezhnev Doctrine found a surprising ally—the United States. What disturbed some observers was that the Nixon and then the Ford administrations seemed to regard any challenge to that formula for an esurient Soviet imperialism as a danger to world peace.

In December 1975, Helmut Sonnenfeldt, counselor to the Department of State and Henry Kissinger's spear carrier, spelled out to an assembly of U.S. ambassadors in Europe the relationship between national security and détente policies vis-à-vis the Soviet Union. According to an official State Department summary (International Security Council 1985, 13ff.), Sonnenfeldt said:

> With regard to Eastern Europe, it must be in our long-term interest to influence events in this area—because of the present unnatural relationship with the Soviet Union—so that they will not sooner or later explode, causing World War III. This inorganic, unnatural relationship is a far greater danger to world peace than the conflict between East and West....

> So it must be our policy to strive for an evolution that makes the relationship between the Eastern Europeans and the Soviet Union an organic one.... [O]ur policy must be a policy of responding to the clearly visible aspirations in Eastern Europe for a more autonomous existence within the context of a strong Soviet geopolitical influence. This has worked in Poland. The Poles have been able to overcome their romantic political inclinations which led to their disasters in the past.[201]

This remarkable formulation with its patronizing air toward tragic Poland—partitioned victim of Nazi and Soviet totalitarianism and subsequently of Anglo-American self-declared impotence in the face of Soviet tenacity—was made by an American statesman who actually believed that the Soviets would become sated with their conquests. The Sonnenfeldt-Kissinger doctrine meant, of course, that the United States was accepting the

---

201 According to Senator Malcolm Wallop ("American Partnership in the Brezhnev Doctrine," *Global Affairs* [Winter 1986], page 28), there are two versions of the Sonnenfeldt "doctrine": an unofficial account published by the syndicated columnists Rowland Evans and Robert Novak, and "the considerably toned-down official version later made available by Sonnenfeldt."

Brezhnev Doctrine as a legitimizing principle of Soviet conquests and the corollary, the absolute irreversibility of those conquests. Eduard Goldstücker, the one-time Czech communist who played a leading role in what is now known as the 1968 Prague Spring, derided the Sonnenfeldt formulation—that East Europeans should seek "a natural relationship to Moscow," meaning they should submit to the leading precept of Soviet ideology: "proletarian internationalism." The Czechs, said Goldstücker, referred to the Sonnenfeldt-Kissinger doctrine as the "Brezh-feldt Doctrine" ("The Eagle & the Small Birds," *Encounter* 358 [September-October 1983], page 37).

Sonnenfeldt himself demonstrated a particular misunderstanding of Soviet foreign policy and a tasteless condescension toward his American constituency. Writing about the problems inherent in U.S.-Soviet negotiations, he said:

> What is involved is, of course, a long-term evolution which requires constant attention and effort and which will see many occasions that will defy clear characterization as to whether they represent progress, retrogression, success, failure or "irreversibility." There is no joy in ambiguity, especially for Americans. But that is precisely what will mark our relations with the Soviet Union for a long time to come. ("Russia, America and Détente," *Foreign Affairs* 56 [January 1978], pages 292-93)[202]

Deplorable Rhetoric

It is this kind of rhetoric that I find deplorable. It isn't difficult to determine success or failure in U.S. foreign policy, especially in examining the Nixon-Ford-Kissinger record. There was no ambiguity, certainly as far as Soviet perceptions are concerned, about who profited from détente. Leonid Brezhnev was reported by Ambassador Max Kampelman (in his speech 17 November 1980 at the Madrid review conference of the 1975 Conference on Security and Cooperation in Europe, or Helsinki accords) to have boasted at a meeting of Communist parties in Prague in 1973, at the height of the Nixon-Kissinger détente policy:

> We have been able to achieve more in a short time with détente than was done for years pursuing a confrontation policy with NATO.... Trust us, Comrades, for by 1985, as a consequence of what we are now achieving with détente ... we will be

---

202 This haughty tone toward the American people is a *déformation professionelle* of American diplomatists. On another occasion, Sonnenfeldt talked about the difficulties of arriving at agreements with the Soviet Union, saying: "That is a very long and tough row to hoe: it is very expensive and Americans do not like long, tough rows to hoe. We prefer solutions that come quickly and are sort of final like the Salk vaccine" (Whelan 1979, 545 n. 44).

able to extend our will wherever we need to. (*Freedom-at-Issue* 60 [May-June 1981], pages 5, 8)

The dramatic and welcome changes in Eastern Europe in fall 1989 came about because the Soviet economy had reached the end of its tether. The Soviet economy has reached that moment when it is barely ticking, when simple consumer needs like tea, soap (facial or laundry), towels, and matches have disappeared, when the ruble is virtually valueless paper, and where there is no trust among the Soviet millions in Gorbachev, his Politburo, or his party.

The Dangers of Leninism to Peace

So long as the present Soviet leadership, whether that be Gorbachev or his successor, espouses Leninism as its guiding philosophy, no country, whether within or outside the Soviet bloc, is safe from the military application of the Brezhnev Doctrine. Under the tenets of Marxism-Leninism, the Brezhnev Doctrine can be repealed and repromulgated.

It is this overriding apprehension of self-justifying Soviet aggression in the name of Leninist praxis, even at a moment when the Politburo is professing an undocumentable pacifism, that makes Soviet treaty diplomacy so risky to friends, neighbors, or Warsaw Pact allies whether in Eastern Europe, Western Europe, Africa, or Asia.

Let me recall the recent (1 July 1986) *Pravda* editorial that I quoted earlier and that said:

> To threaten the socialist system, to try to undermine it from the outside and wrench a country away from the socialist community, means to encroach not only on the will of the people but also on the entire postwar arrangement, and, in the final analysis, on peace.

One may well ask if the organ of the Communist Party of the Soviet Union in 1986 is associating the party with "the will of the people," and whether the will of the people in, say, the Baltic Republics has been considered—or the will of the people in Eastern Europe or in the Ukraine or in other subordinate territories of the Soviet Empire.

Unclear, Says the London Economist

On 7 May 1988, the *London Economist* (page 23) said that "it is not even entirely clear whether the 'Brezhnev Doctrine,' the excuse to invade Czechoslovakia in 1968, is still in force.... " The article is surprising since Gorbachev has in two speeches, one in 1986 and one in 1987, said, in effect, that the Brezhnev Doctrine is very much in force. But in November 1989, his spokesmen said it was not. And in December 1989, the Malta summit with President Bush seemed to confirm the demise of the Brezhnev Doctrine. We shall see.

At the Polish Party Congress in June 1986, General Secretary Gorbachev warned those pushing for genuine independence from the Kremlin:

> [S]ocialism now manifests itself as an international reality, as an alliance of states linked by political, economic, cultural and defense interests. To threaten the socialist system, to try to undermine it from the outside and wrench a country away from the socialist community means to encroach not only on the will of the people but also on the entire postwar arrangement and, in the final analysis, on peace. ("Gorbachev: A New Foreign Policy?" *Foreign Affairs* 65:3 [1986], page 487)

Gorbachev's speech 2 November 1987 commemorating the Bolshevik Revolution's seventieth anniversary quite clearly showed that the Brezhnev Doctrine was still operational. He said that relations between the bloc states and the Soviet Union was based on "unconditional and total equality" ("The Soviet Historical Debate," *Orbis* Summer 1988, page 13). But, he added, this "unconditional and total equality" was not *really* unconditional because that condition applied only when another condition had been fulfilled, namely, when "the ruling [communist] party was responsible for the affairs in its state" and within the framework of "the general interests of socialism" (Ibid.). Such relations represented "a combination of mutual interests and those of socialism as a whole" (Ibid.). As Jiri Hochman has written: "In other words, this was the Brezhnev Doctrine reformulated with a touch of elegance" (Ibid.).

Gorbachev's Endorsement

By 1987, Gorbachev had effectively endorsed the Brezhnev Doctrine of "limited sovereignty" for Eastern Europe (or what is called "proletarian internationalism" or "socialist internationalism"), concerning which Professor Karen Dawisha wrote:

> Lest the East Europeans feel that the Brezhnev Doctrine really is dead, it is well to remember that in two of the intra-bloc agreements reached by Gorbachev—the Soviet-Polish Declaration and the renewal of the Warsaw Treaty—the General Secretary has endorsed the doctrine. ("Socialist Internationalism in Eastern Europe," *Problems of Communism* xxxvi[2] [March-April 1987], page 14)[203]

---

203   The Soviet-Polish declaration is dated 22 April 1987 and the Warsaw Treaty renewal 26 April 1985.

In the summer of 1989, the *London Economist* was asking whether Gorbachev had renounced the Brezhnev Doctrine. The question arose because of a paragraph in the Gorbachev speech before the Council of Europe in Strasbourg on 7 July 1989:

> Social and political orders in one or another country changed in the past and may change in the future. But this change is the exclusive affair of the people of that country, it is their choice. Any interference in domestic affairs and any attempts to restrict the sovereignty of states, both friends and allies or any others, are inadmissible. ("The Gorbachev Doctrine," *London Economist* 15 July 1989, pages 40-41)

The *London Economist* interpreted this passage as perhaps foreshadowing renunciation of the Brezhnev Doctrine. However, it cited other sections of the same speech, indicating that attempts at "overcoming" socialism would provoke "confrontation." Gorbachev had spoken earlier of the need to recognize present "realities" in Europe, meaning, said the *London Economist*, "presumably the boundaries of his camp" (Ibid.). Reforms are proceeding in Poland and Hungary, presumably with Gorbachev's encouragement, "and nobody really knows how far they can go." Said the *London Economist*: "The proof of the Gorbachev doctrine, if such a thing exists, has yet to come" (Ibid.).

On the other hand, Evgenii Ambartsumov, a Soviet student of Soviet relations with other communist-ruled countries said that "the Brezhnev Doctrine is dead" and that he was persuaded that the Soviet Union will never again undertake a military intervention in a neighboring communist-ruled country ("Soviet Foreign Policy: More Glasnost," *Soviet/East European Report* 6[35] [1 September 1989]).

Until Further Notice

For the present, the Brezhnev Doctrine could just as easily be called the Lenin or Stalin Doctrine, the Khrushchev or the Andropov Doctrine—as it might still be called until further notice the Gorbachev Doctrine.[204]

The fact is that so long as Gorbachev adheres or says he adheres to Marxism-Leninism as a guiding philosophy, the Brezhnev Doctrine remains an integral part of Soviet foreign policy and its treaty diplomacy, and is no more amendable or revocable than the political power of the CPSU. As Richard Pipes ("What Divides Us," *Moscow News* no.21. [29 May-5 June 1988]), during the *glasnost* period, wrote in the *Moscow News*:

---

204 Soviet legal theorists call it "socialist self-determination." See Moore 1985, 6.

... Marxism is a global ideology which conceives the coexistence of capitalism and socialism as a temporary expedient. Such an ideology is in and of itself a major source of world tension.

Since the Brezhnev Doctrine rationalizes Soviet aggression at times and places of the Kremlin's own choosing, it is not enough to issue an occasional "Belgrade Declaration" (that the cosigner rarely takes seriously) as indicating the Soviet will to live peacefully with its neighbors. Nor is a Shevardnadze "confession" sufficient. The so-called "new thinking" of the Gorbachev era, if it is in earnest, demands the drastic alteration of the Soviet political system.

For example, for more than seventy years, a *nomenklatura* in various epiphanies but totally unrelated to the will of the Soviet peoples has run the country. And *glastroika* or not, its power, as an ideologically sanctified elitism, remains undiminished. For example, an official Soviet publication (*Argumenty i fakty* no. 35, 5-11 September) wrote in 1987:

> The personnel *nomenklatura* plays a major role in personnel policy, and is one of the effective ways of ensuring the correct selection and placement of managerial staff in keeping with their political, professional and moral qualities. This *nomenklatura* makes possible the timely creation of the necessary reserve of personnel and its training. ("The Barrier to Change," *Soviet Analyst* 16[20] [14 October 1987], page 7)

An Upper Class Dictatorship

The pretext for this elite upper-class dictatorship (what Hugh Seton-Watson called the "state-bourgeoisie") is that the Soviet Union and its satellites are permanently besieged by capitalism's *cordon sanitaire*, i.e., the industrial democracies; therefore, the Soviet Union has no alternative but to maintain its party dictatorship. Historical necessity, as the cant phrase goes, predetermines Soviet action. But when commitments made by the Soviet Union can be annulled overnight or dissolved into inconsequentiality through a sort of sulfuric acid of "interpretations" all in the name of "historical necessity," what happens to mankind's hopes for a stable international system?

The importance of this "state-bourgeoisie" in determining the course of Soviet foreign policy, even under Gorbachev, is stressed by Michael Voslensky (1984, 352):

> When I search my memory of the many years I spent living and working in the Soviet Union, I can find nothing whatever to cause me to doubt the seriousness of *nomenklatura* aspirations to world hegemony. On the contrary, the whole mentality of the nomenklaturists, their talk, their behavior and their ideas, are evidence of those intentions, which to them seem perfectly natural.

A Hungarian Ambiance

I must, however, cite two statements, both interestingly enough made in a Hungarian ambiance, dealing with the whereabouts of the Brezhnev Doctrine. On 16 March 1989 for example, the Hungarian Foreign Minister Peter Varkonyi told the Royal Institute of International Affairs in London that he regarded the Brezhnev Doctrine as "dead," adding that "there should not be any foreign troops on foreign soil" ("Brezhnev Doctrine Dead, Foreign Minister Says," *Soviet/East European Report* 6[19] [1 April 1989], page 3). He added this significant proviso one day later on Radio Budapest:

> The situation is that our policy aims at the simultaneous dissolution of the alliance systems, preferably tomorrow, *but we are not thinking of neutrality.*[my emphasis] (Ibid.)

One might ask the Hungarian Foreign Minister: If he isn't "thinking of neutrality," what is he thinking of? If NATO and the Warsaw Pact are to be simultaneously dissolved, why shouldn't Hungary think of neutrality? Ferenc Molnar, the roguishly witty Budapest playwright, would have appreciated such ambiguity.

Then there was the speech on Hungarian television by the Soviet Foreign Ministry spokesman, Gennadii Gerasimov, ten days earlier. He was asked 6 March 1988 about the Brezhnev Doctrine. He said that the fate of every East European country "is in its own hands." Every country, he said, must make its own decisions. He said "we can give advice, we can discuss issues, but the right to decide is not ours" (*Radio Liberty* 1[11] [17 March 1989], page 3). Are the nineteen Georgians who were killed in April 1989 when they demonstrated for independence a warning to East Europeans who might want to test whether the Brezhnev Doctrine has gone the way of the Cheshire cat?

Bogomolov's Ipse Dixit

In Washington, D.C., on 7 July 1988, Oleg Bogomolov, director of the Institute of Economics of the World Socialist System, told an audience that the Soviet Union had "completely changed [its] relations with the Eastern European countries.... Everyone has to follow very strictly the principles of sovereignty, noninterference and mutual respect" (*Washington Times* 8 July 1988, page A9).

Now hear this, the Bogomolov *ipse dixit*: "The Brezhnev Doctrine is completely unacceptable and unthinkable" (Ibid.).[205]

---

205 Academician Bogomolov at a televised Moscow press conference 25 June 1988

Georgii Shakhnazarov, an important Communist Party Central Committee spokesman, gave hope a few years ago that it was possible that the Brezhnev Doctrine might be laid to rest soon. Speaking on Moscow television in 1985, he said:

> It is appropriate to say that the process of building a new type of international relations [between Socialist countries] is far from being completed ... It can happen that theory and practice move in parallel directions. They may even diverge, and this does, unfortunately, occur. ("Soviet Author Repudiates 'Brezhnev Doctrine'," *Radio Liberty* 4/86 [20 December 1986], page 2; "Kremlin May Be Toning Down Brezhnev Doctrine of Intervention," *Los Angeles Times* 28 December. 1987)

Perhaps even more significantly (in reality one doesn't always know what is or isn't significant in Soviet affairs) was an article in a Soviet publication— *Argumenty i fakty*[206]—by Leonid S. Yagodovsky, deputy director of the Institute of Economics of the World Socialist System, which Oleg Bogomolov heads.

Gorbachev Doctrine

Yagodovsky concedes that the Czechoslovak reforms introduced in 1968 by the ousted leader, Alexander Dubcek, were "largely identical" with those being introduced by Gorbachev in the Soviet Union and, in fact, Czechoslovakia itself. Yagodovsky introduces what he calls the "Gorbachev Doctrine"—assertions by the party general secretary that each ruling Communist Party is autonomous and responsible to its own people. The "Gorbachev Doctrine" means, said Yagodovsky, "complete independence" (*Radio Liberty* 368/88 [15 August 1988], page 1).

On the other hand, the 19 August 1988 issue of Tass criticized the Western press and former "Prague Spring" activists who were reaping "a propaganda harvest" from this year's twentieth anniversary of the invasion of

---

said that because the Soviet Union no longer questions the independence of its Socialist neighbors, application of "what is known in the West as the Brezhnev Doctrine [is] inconceivable" (*Radio Liberty* 368/88 [15 August 1988], page 2). On the other hand, President Gorbachev has in some of his statements implied that, to quote George Schoepflin, each communist country has some share of responsibility for the development of the socialist world as a whole ("The Brezhnev Doctrine After Twenty Years," *Radio Liberty* 35/89 [11 January 1989]).

206 This weekly tabloid is said to have the largest circulation in the world—26 million. Its editor, V.A. Starkov, has recently come under attack by Gorbachev, who asked him to resign ("Why I'm Fighting Gorbachev for My Job," *New York Times* 11 November 1989, page 27).

Czechoslovakia. Tass said the invasion was necessary to prevent the country from being torn apart by hostile Czech elements allied with "centers of foreign subversion" (Ibid.).

Shakhnazarov, Bogomolov, Yagodovsky, and Gorbachev himself have said in various ways, "The Brezhnev Doctrine is dead, long live the Gorbachev Doctrine." Tass seems to disagree. Tass argues the necessity for the Brezhnev Doctrine.

Three Tests

Which is it, then? There are three tests that will prove whether the Brezhnev Doctrine is alive or dead, whether it is still part of the Soviet operational code:

1. Let one member of the Warsaw Pact announce its intention to secede from that pact and to become a neutral. The last East European country that tried to do that was Hungary in October 1956. The Soviet Red Army invasion vetoed the application.
2. Let one of the East bloc countries—Poland, say—announce its withdrawal from the Soviet-controlled World Federation of Trade Unions (WFTU) and apply for entry into the International Confederation of Free Trade Unions (ICFTU).[207] The last East European country to try that was Hungary in October 1956. The Soviet Red Army invasion vetoed that application also.
3. Let one of the East bloc countries—say Czechoslovakia—announce its withdrawal from the Soviet-controlled Council for Mutual Economic Assistance (COMECON). In fact, let one of the bloc countries announce its abandonment of all communist international fronts, from the World Peace Council to the International Organization of Journalists to the Women's International Democratic Federation—the whole lot—and then we'll know better whether the Brezhnev Doctrine is dead or alive.

---

207 "Soviet officials have denied a request by the AFL-CIO," reported the *New York Times* , "to send the first official delegation in its history to the Soviet Union to meet with striking coal miners" (30 November 1989, page A7). Had the Soviet Union permitted this visit, it would have been the first time in AFL-CIO history that an official AFL-CIO delegation had gone to the Soviet Union. For decades the Soviet Union had been seeking just such a labor visit, but when the moment came rejected it lest the breath of democratic trade unionism infect the Soviet atmosphere. However, in early 1990 the Soviet government allowed a group of coal mine strikers to tour the United States as guests of the AFL-CIO and the United Mine Workers.

Recently, William Safire wrote:

Even in Eastern Europe, where people in nations long held captive are growing restive, Mr. Gorbachev's man in charge, Aleksandr Yakovlev, has made it clear that the Brezhnev Doctrine remains in force: any sign of revolt will be met by "fraternal assistance"—which means Soviet tanks. ("A Second Yalta," *New York Times* 6 March 1989, page A19)

The Alive-and-Well Brezhnev Doctrine

I feel as confident as William Safire in predicting that the Brezhnev Doctrine merely awaits an unforeseen circumstance for its promulgation once more. It may be in a deep freeze, in a state of suspended animation. But again, *until Gorbachev and company discard their ideological engine, Marxism-Leninism, a few moments in the Kremlin microwave will surely restore it to life.*

At the Bush Administration's first East-West conference, Secretary of State James A. Baker III called upon the Soviet Union formally to annul the Brezhnev Doctrine. Said Baker:

Those in the West should be free of the fear that the massive forces under Soviet command might invade them. Those in the East should be free of the fear that armed Soviet intervention, justified by the Brezhnev Doctrine, would be used again to deny them choice.... "New thinking" and the Brezhnev Doctrine are in fundamental conflict. We call today upon General Secretary Gorbachev to renounce the Brezhnev Doctrine—beyond any shadow of a doubt. (*New York Times* 23 October 1989)

So long as Gorbachev & Co. adhere to their Marxist-Leninist convictions, there can be no renunciation of the Brezhnev Doctrine. That is, to quote Secretary Baker, "beyond any shadow of a doubt." In February 1990, there were reports from Moscow that Gorbachev was ready to jettison Leninism. We shall see.

11

"Mistrust—But Verify"

"I don't mean to deny that the evidence is in some ways very strongly in favor of
your theory, I only wish to point out that there are other theories possible."

Sherlock Holmes to Inspector Lestrade[208]

I have argued that Bolshevik history and the Soviet political system make
that country's treaty diplomacy permanently suspect. If, however, President
Mikhail Gorbachev and his "new thinking" are credible, namely that he is
engaged in one of the greatest Russian reform movements since Peter the
Great, then my thesis falls.

Obviously, if I believed in the durability, fundamentalism, and
irreversibility of the recent changes in the Soviet Union, there would be no
point in pursuing a thesis whose validity—broadly if sometimes reluctantly
accepted during the Stalinist and post-Stalinist decades—had been impeached
by events. Whatever *raison d'être* for this book, its proposition would be
shattered were it provable beyond a reasonable doubt that the Soviet Union
under President Gorbachev had embarked on a road to peace and freedom
from which there could be no turning back.

The question, then, is this: Can a case be made for the argument that a
great deal must change in the Soviet Union before we can feel safe that the
"new thinking" has produced or is producing a Soviet Union utterly different

---

208 A. Conan Doyle, *The Adventure of the Norwood Butler.*

from the monstrosity (and "monstrosity" is not too strong a word) it has been for more than seven decades?. So much that is now being published in the Soviet Union as "now it can be told" history is on a level of a massified Grand Guignol. According to Zbigniew Brzezinski: "It has been openly admitted that 60 out of its [the Soviet Union's] 70 years involved sustained criminality" ("A Proposition the Soviets Shouldn't Refuse," *New York Times* 13 March 1989, page A19).

Has Anything Fundamental Changed?

I argue, first, that nothing *fundamental* has changed in the Soviet Union, thus far, since the Gorbachev accession. Second, so long as the Soviet Union bases itself on Marxism-Leninism, nothing fundamental *can* change (I will define further on what I mean by fundamental). If there has been no fundamental change in the Soviet Union, then it brings into question the Western attitude toward treaty negotiation with that country.

In discussing Soviet treaty diplomacy, an important question to ask is whether the Soviet Union feels itself bound by international law. In fact, can it ever be bound by international law while it lives by the tenets of Marxism-Leninism? A few weeks before Gorbachev came to power 11 March 1985, Secretary of State George Shultz said:

> In contrast to the Soviets and their allies, the United States is committed to the principles of international law.... So long as communist dictatorships feel free to aid and abet insurgencies in the name of "socialist internationalism," why must the democracies, the targets of this threat, be inhibited from defending their own interests and the cause of democracy itself? (Shultz 1985, 4)

Shultz Rejects Double Standard

In rejecting the "double standard" of international behavior favored by the Soviets and their Western acolytes, Secretary Shultz was saying in that forceful, direct manner for which he was famous that "the Soviets and their allies" are not committed to international law. Of course, he was speaking seventeen days before the Politburo chose Gorbachev as general secretary of the CPSU to succeed Konstantin Chernenko. Whether Shultz would feel the same way today about the Soviet lack of commitment to international law is another matter.[209]

---

209 Jean-François Revel says: "We are faithful to an assumed—an alleged—international law whose definition goes back to Yalta or Helsinki which the Soviets simply do not respect, do not implement" (Buckley 1989, 119). Revel made this statement in 1984.

Why Endless Negotiation

Now here is a puzzlement: A U.S. secretary of state tells the world that the Soviets do not honor international law. Why, then, you may well ask, do we engage in endless treaty negotiations with the Soviet Union? The question is apposite because, during his service, Shultz didn't seem to be wedded to treatyism—the unamendable credo among State Department elites, the treaty priesthood, which maintains that a day that passes without some U.S.-Soviet treaty negotiation is a day lost.

A treaty may sometimes endanger peace, not sustain it.[210] Similarly, arms control agreements can actually "accelerate longstanding trends that make war more likely," Angelo Codevilla ("Arms Control Pacts Make War More Likely," *Campus Report* [Stanford University] 24 May 1989, page 10) told a Senate Foreign Relations Committee on 15 May 1989. For him, the principal danger in U.S.-Soviet Union arms control pacts "is not outright violation but total circumvention."

In his memoirs, Larry Speakes (1988, 155) quotes Shultz as saying during the White House meetings preparatory to the 1985 Geneva summit with Gorbachev that if the Soviets insist on abandonment of the Strategic Defense Initiative (or SDI), "We are prepared to say to the Russians, 'If you don't want an agreement, that's fine, we can go home without one.'"

Costless Reforms

Since his arrival on the scene, Gorbachev has introduced a series of costless reforms—costless in the sense that he is still the autocrat, more powerful than ever since his election as party general secretary and chief executive of the Soviet government, and costless in the sense that the party bureaucracy is thus far still intact and the *priviligentsia* still enjoys its privileges ("Restructuring the Kremlin Leadership," *Radio Liberty* 423 [4 October 1988). Most deplorable of all, these reforms do little to improve the

---

210 See Brodie (n.d., 12), where he says that not all treaties are a good idea, including the Versailles Treaty. "It could be said, for example, that it was the Washington Naval Treaty of 1922 which made the Pacific phase of World War II possible, for it assured to Japan something much closer to naval parity with the United States than would have been anywhere near her reach in any real building competition ensuing from the absence of such a treaty. The Treaty did avoid for a time a 'costly' naval building competition. But was not the war with Japan immeasurably more costly? And would Japan have dared embark upon a war against an America boasting a naval power which was—as it easily could have been, without any untoward strain upon the American economy—two or three times her own?"

quality of life for the Soviet people. For Gorbachev, the costless reforms have a particular value. They win him great goodwill among those Western cave-dweller elites who, as in Plato's *Republic*, mistake the shadows on the wall for reality.[211]

For example, a page one story in the *New York Times* of 9 March 1989 reported that the Kremlin had agreed to accept binding adjudication of the World Court in cases arising from five basic human rights agreements, such as those dealing with women, prostitution, slavery, racism, and torture. A *Times* editorial the following day (page A18) praised the Soviet Union for its action and derided the United States for not having ratified most UN human rights conventions.

No Standing

Now, as everyone knows, the World Court can only take up cases initiated by governments. Individuals have no standing before the Court to enforce compliance by their own or any other government. So, any Soviet dissident who thinks he can obtain justice from the World Court at the Hague against, say, the KGB, is in for a surprise.

The Court has no power to enforce its decisions. Over more than four decades, it has functioned about as well as any court can when it is blessed with a complement of Soviet or Soviet bloc jurists. (Presently, the International Court of Justice includes nationals from the People's Republic of China, the Soviet Union, and Poland.) So what's all the cheering about? What's so exhilarating that, to quote the *Times* editorial, "the Soviet Union has gone further than the United States in risking an adverse ruling"? True, as the editorial says, "[t]he most important gain is intangible." And what is this intangible "most important gain"? The *Times* answers: The Soviet decision has added "to the value of universal codes in how governments should treat their citizens" (Ibid.). But that would mean that the Soviet Union feels itself

---

211 Book VII, chapter 25, of Plato's *Republic* contains his famous parable of the cave: The prisoners, who have dwelt inside the cave since childhood, are chained by the leg and by the neck. They cannot turn their heads. Behind them a fire blazes, creating shadows on the wall. For the prisoners, these swooping shadows are the world of reality, the only reality they have ever known. In actual fact, the shadows thrown by the firelight are created by puppeteers (Cornford 1945, 227 ff.). Plato was discussing the human condition—mankind's inability to distinguish between truth and shadow. The Greek philosopher might find his parable particularly applicable today to the great shadow event of our time—*glasnost* and *perestroika*.

bound to the principles of international law. Does the *Times* really *believe* that?

Tangible Violations

How about the *tangible* Soviet violations of the ILO Charter that gives workers the right of freedom of association and the right to form free trade unions? How about the *tangible* aggression by the Soviet Union on Afghanistan? How about the thirteen *tangible* resolutions passed by the UN General Assembly in 1956-57 against the Soviet invasion of Hungary? Or the Soviet refusal to allow a UN emissary to enter Hungary to investigate the Soviet sack of Budapest? How about the *tangible* perversion of Soviet psychiatry for political purposes, as attested to by a team of Western psychiatrists. But what are all these *tangible* violations and many more against the fluttering of an "intangible" gain? Unconcernedly, the Soviet Union has for decades risked "adverse" rulings by the international community on the most serious violations of international law.

Or, to quote another *New York Times* editorial (8 December 1988) about President Gorbachev's UN speech:

Perhaps not since Woodrow Wilson presented his fourteen points in 1918 or since Franklin Roosevelt and Winston Churchill promulgated the Atlantic Charter in 1941 has a world figure demonstrated the vision Mikhail Gorbachev displayed yesterday at the United Nations.... Breath-taking. Risky. Bold. Naive. Diversionary. Heroic. All fit. [212]

Slobbering Schlock

Imagine writing this slobbering schlock—comparing a Gorbachev speech to the words of Wilson, Roosevelt, and Churchill!—about a man who holds office by virtue of the vote of a tiny handful of unelected Politburo members in a still party-controlled state devoid of free and honest elections for seventy years, including the one held in March 1989. Do *Times* editorial writers have a long-term lease on Plato's Cave? At a time when millions of people were trying to flee from Marxist-Leninist countries or were engaging in rebellions and illegal strikes within the Soviet Union, the *Times* editorial page on 21 May 1989 wrote:

---

212 As Bertram Wolfe has written: "In a land where secrecy and power are alike total, every smallest flutter of a leaf is likely to be magnified into the fall of forests." The *New York Times* hailed publication of Gorbachev's 1987 book, *Perestroika: New Thinking for Our Country and Our World,* as "the international publishing event of the year."

Imagine that an alien spaceship approached Earth and sent the message: "Take me to your leader." Who would that be? Without doubt, Mikhail Sergeyevich Gorbachev.

Wouldn't it be nice for the world if the *New York Times* editorial board were to take off in the alien spaceship with Mikhail Sergeyevich Gorbachev as leader of the Universe!

Soviet Quality of Life

To talk about costless reforms is not to say that the Soviet Union cannot, in the light of *glastroika*, be a less oppressive place for its people than it was during the ghastly Stalin years or during the stagnationist Brezhnev decades. I am unsure how significant a contribution to a better life it is that under *glasnost* in 1988 a change occurred allowing living émigré Russian writers to be published. Before 1988, only works by dead émigré writers could appear in the Soviet press ("The Development of *Glasnost* in 1988," *Radio Liberty* xxx/xx [3 February 1989], pages 7-10).

Nor do these reforms raise the living standards of the Soviet peoples. When the Soviet government invites Mtislav Rostroprovich and the National Symphony Orchestra to concertize in Moscow and Leningrad, how does it improve the quality of life for the people? The West greeted this announcement with page one rhapsodies. Another costless reform but excellent public relations (Associated Press 13 April 1989). On the very same day of the Rostroprovich announcement, the Soviet Union announced that rationing of sugar was to begin in May 1989 in Moscow. Sugar had been rationed in many parts of the Soviet Union for months, but now it would come to the country's capital, which had been immune to such rationing since World War II.

True, reforms and changes in the sociopolitical (if not economic) climate can make for a more stable and even a more peaceful world. As Edwin Luttwak ("The Alliance, Without an Enemy," *New York Times* 3 February 1989) has written: "Enlightened despotism à la Gorbachev is far better than repression, but it does not insure a less threatening Soviet Union.[213]

Among the free nations, various schools of thought contend about the meaning of the new Gorbachev dispensation. Some think the changes in Soviet politics and culture since March 1985 portend a gentler and kinder

---

213 Luttwak also points out that "although Soviet political liberalization is very real and progressing, it remains entirely reversible. There has been no real devolution of power" ("The Alliance, Without an Enemy," *New York Times* 3 February 1989).

Soviet Union or, to put it simply: the Cold War is over. Others remain skeptical that the present Soviet ruling class can or will ever surrender any of its power. Still others—cautious optimists like Prime Minister Margaret Thatcher—have great faith in Gorbachev. In an NBC Today Show TV interview 4 January 1989, Mrs. Thatcher told David Frost:

> You can't have liberty in a Socialist-Marxist system.... We are very fortunate in having a person like Mr. Gorbachev, who's a person of great vision and boldness and courage.... And when he gets through with his reforms, the world is a safer place. And if he gets through with his reforms then I think the Cold War is at an end.

> At the moment, the Cold War is very much less cold, because the Cold War was just two systems, very little discussion across the boundary between them. Now discussion is much more total. We do much more trade. We do much more culture. We have much more freedom of movement. We are affecting things inside the Soviet Union.

Mrs. Thatcher Errs

Mrs. Thatcher has personalized the present Soviet relationship in disregard of seventy years of Soviet history. When she was asked by David Frost if she trusts Gorbachev, she replied:

> I have talked a long time to Mr. Gorbachev on a number of occasions. Every single thing he has undertaken to do, to me, he has done. And I am satisfied that if he undertakes to do something, he will do it to the very best of his ability. (Ibid.)[214]

Obviously, Soviet treaty diplomacy, as far as the perceptions of the British government are concerned, can be regarded as having changed dramatically. Perhaps Mrs. Thatcher has left herself an out ... just in case. As she put it, if Gorbachev promises to do something, "he will do it to the very best of his ability," which may means nothing more than that he'll sure give it a good try and is therefore to be pardoned in advance if he should "fail" to deliver. She

---

214 Would that Mrs. Thatcher would heed the wise words of Robert Conquest who has written that "the error at the heart of most misapprehensions about international politics, and in particular the issue of disarmament, is misunderstanding of the attitudes and motives of the Soviet leadership ... that the Politburo are unlikeable people, addicted to misleading doctrine, but nevertheless, 'rational' and willing to draw 'sensible' conclusions from the facts of the world situation.... We must get these respectable stereotypes out of our minds" (*London Daily Telegraph* 13 November 1982, page 12).

seems to have ignored a statement she made on a visit to China in 1984 that "those who don't honor one treaty will not honor another" ("Exodus," *The New Republic* 23 May 1989, page 22).

More recently, during a phone-in interview over the BBC Russian Service, Mrs. Thatcher called the summer 1988 Communist Party conference "a milestone for freedom of discussion [because] those who came up to the platform to speak did not always speak from fixed notes, but sometimes they spoke just as they felt" ("Betrayal," *Resistance Bulletin* 7 [Summer 1989], page 8).

And there are those like former Secretary of State Kissinger who take a "centrist" position.[215]

It is unnecessary to debate whether there has been a basic conversion of the Soviet leadership or to gear one's policy entirely toward one particular Soviet leader. Domestic conditions impose a respite on Soviet foreign policy, but in the end so does the international environment....

A new American president with a generous spirit and a Soviet leader who has shown a willingness to challenge preconceptions now face a challenge essentially at odds with the missionary bent of America and the expansionist tendency of Russia: to advance peace by balancing their national interests. (Kissinger 1989, V:1)

Kennan's View

George Kennan ("After the Cold War.,"*New York Times Magazine* 5 February 1989, page 58)[216] has said that in Gorbachev there has arrived on the world stage, "a Russian leader intelligent enough to recognize that the rationale of the Cold War was largely unreal, and bold enough to declare this publicly and to act accordingly." Thus "the world was brought to realize that one epoch—the epoch of recovery from the enormous dislocation of World War II—had passed; and that a new one was beginning—an age that would ... to be sure, create new problems ... but would at the same time also present new possibilities." Gorbachev, he said, "has given every evidence ... of an intention to remove as many as possible of the factors that have hampered

---

215 Kissinger has defined himself as a centrist. Reporting on a meeting with President Gorbachev, Kissinger said he told the Soviet leader that "some Americans want agreements virtually for their own sake regardless of content ["treatyism"?]; others oppose any agreement regardless of content. I belong to a third group, I said, that wants agreements if they really make a difference" (*Washington Post* 19 January 1988, part 5, page 1).

216 For Kennan's earlier and evolving views, see his *The Cloud of Danger* (Boston, Mass.: Little, Brown, 1977), especially chapter 12, "The Soviet Union—the Reality," pages 173 ff.

Soviet-American relations in the past; and a number of bold steps he has taken in that direction do testimony to the sincerity of his effort."
Yet in the same article, Kennan writes:

> If realistic and solid agreements are made now ...; if these agreements, as is to be expected, are seen in Moscow as being in Soviet interest; *if they are, as they should be, inherently self-enforcing* [my emphasis]; if as is to be expected, they are sealed in formal undertakings—-then they are not apt to be undone simply by changes in the Soviet leadership." (Ibid.)

Self-Enforcement

Here we have a concrete idea, or what seems to be a concrete idea: self-enforcement as a basic principle of treaty diplomacy between the United States and the Soviet Union. Make agreements between the two sides self-enforcing. However, Kissinger's view expressed while he was still Secretary of State disputed this thesis:

> No agreement in history has ever enforced itself; every agreement in history that has been observed has depended either on the willingness of the parties to observe it or on the willingness of one or the other parties to enforce it or on the rewards for compliance and the risks of noncompliance. (U.S. Department of State 1973, 54)

But haven't so many of these instruments between both powers been self-enforcing and yet violations occurred without leading to their abrogation? What if the Soviet Union denies, as it did until 23 October 1989, that the deployment of the last of the six ABM radars in Krasnoyarsk is a violation of the Anti-Ballistic Missile treaty? Self-enforcing means that a treaty lapses automatically when a violation is perceived and proven. But supposing one side argues that the violation is not a violation at all? Is there an answer?

Let me recall (see chapter 3) that the United States for several years had argued that the giant Soviet radar at Krasnoyarsk violated the 1972 Antiballistic Missile Treaty that limited strategic defensive weapons. At first, the Soviet Union denied that Krasnoyarsk violated the treaty. Later, its spokesmen admitted that Krasnoyarsk was intended to track ballistic missiles and thus violated the ABM treaty. Fine. What is the Soviet Union going to do about the violation? As of June 1989, nothing—unless the United States accepts the Soviets' interpretation of the ABM treaty, which would limit the scope of the Strategic Defense Initiative. As Richard Perle wrote, "The Kremlin will tear down the illegal radar (in other words, it will comply with its treaty obligation) only if the United States makes concessions that we have no obligation to make under the terms of the ABM treaty." Finally, the Soviet Union admitted it had cheated at Krasnoyarsk.

For his part, Ambassador James Goodby, onetime deputy chairman of the U.S. delegation to the START talks in Geneva, has said that a "revolution" has occurred in Soviet attitudes toward arms control verification and that Gorbachev "has challenged us as never before over our willingness to accept verification" ("Veteran Negotiator Calls for Major Long-Term Defense Cuts," *Campus Report* 5 March 1989, page 7). On the other hand, there is the pessimism about the Soviet future from Professor Richard Pipes. He disagrees with Prime Minister Thatcher's assessment of the Cold War:

> Cold War is the Soviet way of waging political warfare. They always prefer political warfare to military warfare. They wage political warfare which is essentially a strategy they have devised under Lenin, divide and rule, threats, promises. Depending on internal needs, the Cold War is either exacerbated or attenuated. Lenin conducted Cold War until 1921 when the economy collapsed and he needed credits from the West. So he called off the Cold War, no more world revolution so give us money. A few years later, the situation changed and we were back to the Cold War.
>
> So long as the Soviet government exists and there is no complete transformation, there's going to be no end to the Cold War. It is naive to think that the Cold War is the result of misunderstanding or bad attitudes. The Cold War is the result of a certain kind of regime and a certain kind of ideology. And as long as the Soviet regime is in place, the Cold War is going to be attenuated or sharpened, as Soviet internal politics dictates. ("Reading history's tea leaves," *Washington Times* 6 February 1989, page D3)

The Era of Gorbymania

Much of what I have written in earlier chapters will in the era of Gorbymania be regarded by some as a kind of secular blasphemy, based perhaps on what Ambassador Kennan might call "outdated Cold War assumptions [that] lack serious current justification." At a time when serious and sober voices are heard proclaiming the end of the Cold War, when remarkable events occur almost daily behind what was once called the Iron Curtain, when President Reagan finds it admirable that Gorbachev was informed by Leninism rather than Stalinism,[217] when the Soviets have withdrawn the Red Army from Afghanistan[218] and are allowing Eastern

---

217 On Gorbachev and Leninism, see Reagan interview of 26 February 1988 with Lou Cannon, cited in chapter 7.

218 On the other hand, the *New York Times* predicted in a 1988 editorial that "it's hard to imagine the Soviet-backed Afghan government's surviving long after the initial Soviet pullout" (*New York Times* 11 February 1988, page 24). In April 1990, the Afghan government was still in place.

Europe to secede from the Socialist Commonwealth but not from the Warsaw Pact or COMECON—one can go on and on with examples of this kind—it seems perverse to be writing a book that rejects the sunny significance of the Gorbachevian reform wave or his *offensive de charme*. Who could have predicted that one day a Soviet leader would be hopping about the streets of Washington, D.C., pressing the flesh, as Gorbachev did during the White House summit? And if such a miracle could be displayed in the capital of the greatest capitalist country in the world, are other miracles not possible?

Mine is not a lone skepticism. For example, at the height of the East German events in November 1989 and the breaching of the Berlin Wall, the *London Economist* was warning:

> East Germans may have lost their fear of the party, but the party not yet lost its power of retaliation. For all the recent images of smiling soldiery, the army is no less capable than China's of scattering protesting crowds in a hail of bullets. And if Mr. [Egon] Krenz cannot defend creaking communism in East Germany, it remains quite possible that a Russian—presumably not Mr. Gorbachev—might be tempted to try. ("Beyond the Wall," *London Economist* 18 November 1989, page 13)

The *London Economist* was wrong, of course. Egon Krenz is gone and forgotten. East Germans were not shot as they were in June 1953. There were to be democratic elections in East Germany. There may even be the beginnings of a Germany united in freedom. Still, until there is a Soviet Union united in freedom, the risk of dealing with Gorbachev remains.

What Yakovlev Said

I claim the right to be as skeptical about Soviet promises of reform as official Soviet spokesmen like Aleksandr N. Yakovlev (reportedly one of President Gorbachev's closest collaborators) are skeptical about the possibilities of benevolence in American foreign policy. A widely traveled Politburo member and chairman of the Commission on International Policy, Yakovlev was an exchange student at Columbia University in 1959. In 1984, he published a book, *On the Edge of the Abyss*,[219] in which occurs this typical passage:

> The United States is as a nation governed more by deception and demagoguery than by conviction, more by force than the law, more by deadening habits and traditions than by respect for and interest in whatever is new, more by hatred,

---

219 Other titles in the Yakovlev *oeuvre* include: *The Call to Slaughter: American Falsifiers of the Problems of War and Peace* (1965), *The Ideology of the American Empire* (1967), *Pax Americana—the American Ideology* (1969) and *U.S.A.: From "Great" to Sick* (1969).

suspicion and intolerance than by the ability to recognize there may be another way of life and thought. ("Moscow's Other Mastermind," *New York Times* Sunday Magazine 19 February 1989, page 41)

What Yakovlev says about the United States would more accurately describe the Soviet Union even in its present epiphany.[220] That he may have offered more felicitous statements about the United States on more recent occasions should not detract from my claim to be as analytically pessimistic about the course of the Soviet party dictatorship as Yakovlev is (with far less justification) about American democracy.

Present Climate of Opinion

I doubt, however, that in the present climate of opinion my claim will receive much sympathy among optimists and realissimists. The political environment of the Western democracies today is informed not only with a will-to-believe but, even in the face of the gruesome statistics of the Soviet aggression against Afghanistan, with a will-to-forgive, as leading Western opinion has forgiven or forgotten over and over again diverse Soviet atrocities. After all, it was President Reagan who so kindly pointed out that the Afghanistan invasion had begun on Brezhnev's, not Gorbachev's, watch.

It is an old Western custom, even among conservatives, to allow the new Soviet leader to begin with a *tabula rasa*, a clean slate. Whatever terrible things happened before the new general secretary came to power are not his fault. How about the system's fault? Well, goes the cant, he's going to make changes. You'll see.

In Andropov's case, his major reform that was widely acclaimed in the West was his attempting to rid the country of slackers by ordering the police to raid the Turkish baths in the daytime and woe to anybody without a good excuse caught wielding a soapy besom in the hot room. The shooting down of an unarmed Korean air liner was accompanied by charges from respectable people that the whole business was a CIA provocation.

---

220   The post-Gorbachev Yakovlev has been speaking apprehensively about the present situation in the Soviet Union. In a speech December 1988, he said that "we probably have no more than two, three years to show ourselves and others that socialism in its Leninist version is not utopia.... If we get cold feet when faced with the difficulties of *perestroika*, then destructive tendencies in the economic and moral-political sphere may acquire irreversible characteristics. Then we may be threatened not simply with a return to the situation we had before, to stagnation thinking, but by an aggressive and vengeful conservatism reveling in its victory" ("The Resistance Movement," *Soviet Analyst* 18[4] [22 February 1922], page 1).

The same is true for President Gorbachev. Nothing bad is his fault—Chernobyl, killing Georgian protesters with poison gas, the collapse of the Soviet economy. He is only responsible for good things; bad things are the fault of so-called conservatives, dogmatists, saboteurs, and, in the West, a category known derisively as "commie-bashers." The Teflonization of President Gorbachev continues. As even the late I.F. Stone, a long-time Soviet sympathizer has written:.

> [T]he cult of personality around Gorbachev has grown so great outside the Soviet Union that it fosters a tendency to overlook whatever he says that does not fit the mythic image of this energetic and gifted but often contradictory Russian ruler who has aroused so much hope at home and abroad. ("The Rights of Gorbachev," *New York Review of Books* 16 February 1989, page 3)

Astonishing Changes

Let me concede that there have been some astonishing changes in the Soviet Union since the Gorbachev accession ("The Development of *Glasnost* in 1988," *Radio Liberty* 3 February 1989, pages 6-10). Gorbachev himself has called for "civilized relations" with the West, thereby intimating that East and West have fundamental values in common ("Soviet National Security Under Gorbachev," *Problems of Communism* xxxvii[6] [November-December 1988], page 3). Such a sentiment could mean that Gorbachev did not believe in the inevitability of war between capitalism and communism, a central tenet of Leninism.[221]

It could, for example, be argued that the withdrawal of the Red Army from Afghanistan in mid-February 1989 as per an international agreement means the end of the Brezhnev Doctrine. If hitherto the Brezhnev Doctrine meant that once a socialist country, always a socialist country, then self-liberated Afghanistan is an exception. Yet, as I have shown in chapter 7, Gorbachev has implied that he would apply the Brezhnev Doctrine to the Baltic countries. Thus far, however, the Brezhnev Doctrine has not been applied to Czechoslovakia, Romania, East Germany, Hungary, or Poland.

There have even been discrete attacks on the once untouchable Lenin, something that skeptics like myself had found difficult to predict. Yet if by savaging Lenin's memory it could mean saving Lenin's "socialist revolution," I am sure Lenin would approve. And if his embalmed remains are ever removed from the Red Square mausoleum, I am persuaded he would

---

221 On the other hand, such a kindly thought reminds me of Winston Churchill's remark during the war that it doesn't hurt to be polite to an enemy agent you're going to hang in the morning.

agree. As George Kennan once said: "The greatest law of human history is its unpredictability" (Kennan 1966, 92).[222]

It used to be said: *Ex Africa semper aliquid novi*, or, "From Africa, there is always something new." Perhaps it is time to amend Pliny to read, *Ex Russia semper aliquid novi*, for it seems that almost each day something startling and perhaps even unprecedented is reported to have happened in the Soviet Union. Recently, it was an article in a Soviet publication denouncing the Communist Party and indirectly criticizing President Gorbachev ("Another Taboo Is Broken: Paper Attacks Communist Party," *New York Times* 9 February 1989, page 1). Another day it was an article by a high Soviet foreign ministry official repudiating the Leninist concept of the "international class struggle," the very essence of Leninism ("From Moscow: Why Soviet Foreign Policy Went Awry," *Washington Post* 9 January 1989, page 10[223]). A four-part article in the Soviet journal *Nauka i Zhizn* proclaimed that Stalinism is a product of Marxist theory. The writer, Aleksandr Tsipko, however, tried to exonerate Lenin from any blame for the terror ("Soviet Scholar Sees Roots of Stalinism in Bolsheviks' Terror and Marxist Theory," *Radio Liberty* 14 February 1989, page 1). There are almost daily exposés of terrible living conditions for the Soviet masses which, had they been published in Western publications in the pre-Gorbachev era, would have been denounced as imperialist propaganda.

Even more astonishing is what seems to be the split that has developed in the communist world over Gorbachev's reforms. When the Moscow journal *Novoye Vremya* printed an article about the undesirability, under present Soviet standards, of Cuban socialism, Castro restricted entry of succeeding issues ("Life Without Marx," *The National Interest* 14 [Winter 1988], page 115). Even the Kremlin's poodle, the Communist Party USA, has criticized the Soviet publications *Moscow News* and *New Times* for being too frank about Soviet shortcomings ("American Communists Criticizing Moscow?" *Up Front* 1[1] [March 1989], pages 1-2).[224]

---

222 Or, to quote Proudhon, "The fecundity of the unexpected far exceeds the statesman's prudence" (*Time* magazine 16 October 1989, page 96).

223 The author of the article is Andrei Kozyrev, deputy chief of the International Organizations Administration in the Soviet foreign ministry. The article appeared the summer of 1989 in the ministry publication, *Mezhdunarodnaya Zhizn* (International Affairs). So powerful is the hold of Lenin's ideas on his acolytes that, after amending Lenin's basic ideas, Mr. Kozyrev contended that he was actually returning "to Leninist policy."

224 *Up Front* reports that Gus Hall, CP-USA general secretary, told a party meeting in Cleveland on 2 August 1988: "I've been battling with the *Moscow News* now for a year or two. I met with some leading comrades there [in Moscow].... I said

Perhaps the most signal development of all was the legalization after nine years of struggle of the independent, nongovernmental Polish labor union, Solidarity, in April 1989. As the *London Economist* described the meaning of this event, "Poland's communists look prepared to make a formal surrender of their monopoly of power." (*London Economist* 8 April 1989, page 51). And, indeed, one might say they have. Jean-François Revel ("Hastening the Death of Communism," *Commentary* 88[4] [October 1989]) wrote that in Poland "the underlying principle of the system—namely, the monopoly of the Communist Party—has been effectively challenged for the first time in any Communist country."[225]

A possible reason for such unprecedented surrender of power by a Communist Party, as in Poland and perhaps even in Hungary, was suggested by Maciej Kozlowski, the Polish journalist and historian who said:

Everything has its high price, and the Polish price for this democracy and freedom we have ... is total ruin of the Polish economy. That's why the Communists have given the power to us. If the economy was still in more or less good shape, they wouldn't give it to us. There is a direct connection between the economic situation and the political freedom. The Communists are not exchanging guns for butter, but are exchanging freedom for lack of butter. The less butter, the more freedom. ("Polish Journalist Applauds Reforms," *Stanford Daily* [Stanford, Calif]) 10 October 1989, page 1)

What this unprecedented step in the Soviet satellite world means for the Soviet Union we shall have to see. For example, does it mean that the Soviet Union is prepared to grant Soviet workers the right to organize free trade unions—that is, organizations free of government control? If the Soviet Union were to allow such freedom of organization, it would then be in compliance with the ILO charter, a subject I dealt with in chapter 2. The coal miners' strikes in Siberia and the Ukraine in July 1989 seemed to have been settled peacefully. Does this event herald a liberated trade union dawn in the Soviet Union? Free trade unions in the Soviet Union would necessarily mean

---

why don't you remove the editor of the *Moscow News*, 'cause he's publishing a lot of nonsense, and I said if you can't do that burn down the goddamn building. I mean get rid of it. But they laughed and they haven't done it. *Moscow News* is the worst of their publications" (*Up Front* [National Forum Foundation Newsletter, Washington, D.C.] 1988).

225 Revel makes the point that such challenges to the Communist Party in Poland and to a lesser degree in Hungary have been possible because in Eastern Europe "Communism was imposed from without and is therefore more derivative than organic" ("Hastening the Death of Communism," *Commentary* 88[4] [October 1989], page 20).

the end of Marxism-Leninism as the reigning ideology. It would mean an end to the Leninist myth that since, absent capitalists, the working class "owns" the means of production, strikes mean that the working class is striking against its own interests, which is irrational (and, therefore, counterrevolutionary) behavior.

Despite such hopeful developments—especially in Poland since the legislative elections in June 1989 and the earlier elections, and in the proceedings of the new Soviet Congress of People's Deputies—most of these self-lacerating articles have thus far avoided full-scale attacks on V. I. Lenin himself. He has always been the holy icon. Say anything you want but leave Lenin out of it. If someone is to blame, let it be Stalin, Khrushchev, or Brezhnev. Never Lenin. Criticism of Lenin is still officially taboo. The chief Soviet censor, Vladimir A. Solodin, told a Dutch journalist that, while there had been some easing of the censorship, "nonsense about Lenin and ... clear anti-Soviet fabrications" are barred. That means, said Solodin, that Solzhenitsyn's *Gulag Archipelago* cannot be published in the Soviet Union because "Solzhenitsyn slanders Lenin" ("A Soviet Censor Uncensored," *New York Times* 13 February 1989, page 11).[226] However, the *Gulag* volumes have begun to be published in the Soviet Union.

Professor Hook's Argument

Professor Sidney Hook has argued that a social system, communism included, is a historical phenomenon. Its possible development cannot be predicted by logic. The question of its future can only be based on what he calls "a whole web of probabilities" ("The Future of Marxism," *Free Inquiry* Summer 1989, page 14). What do we know about what is going on now in the Soviet Union? No hard evidence exists that Gorbachev or any other Soviet leader has either given up his faith in communism or renounced the Leninist version of Marxism.

Empirical evidence is needed to show that the Soviet Union has changed its character, much as Spain evolved from a dictatorship to a constitutional

---

226   However, a small circulation (89,000 copies) Soviet magazine broke the ban on Solzhenitsyn's work in its February 1989 issue. The magazine, *Twentieth Century and Peace*, the monthly journal of the official Soviet Peace Committee, reprinted a thousand-word essay by the exiled Russian author titled "Live Not By Lies!" Because it was regarded as a propaganda journal, the magazine was given permission to work without Glavlit supervision. Within days after publication, the magazine was ordered to submit its contents to Glavlit before going to press ("Obscure Soviet Magazine Breaks the Ban on Solzhenitsyn's Work, " *New York Times* 20 March 1989, page 1). However, in 1990 Solzhenitsyn's volumes had begun to be published in the Soviet Union.

monarchy. In other words, a *fundamental* change—one that would make it possible to trust the Soviet Union as a treaty partner.

The Indispensable Minimum

The indispensable minimum for a fundamental change would be a situation in which, says Professor Hook, "the political legitimacy of the monopoly of power of the Communist Party could be challenged in any uncoerced election in which there would be no official engineering of consent, in which there would be guaranteed freedom of the press, access to television and all other media of communication" (Ibid., 15).

If fundamental reforms were *institutionalized* so that political minorities could expect, peacefully, to become majorities, that could be regarded as empirical evidence that the Soviet Union had embarked on the road to democracy, i.e., a fundamental change (Ibid., 14-15). And if such evidence could be found, one could place some trust in the Soviet Union as a treaty partner, particularly concerning arms control.

As I write, the Red Army continues to occupy Eastern Europe—true, in diminishing numbers. The Associated Press has reported that, according to U.S. intelligence, the Soviet Union exported about $515 million worth of military equipment to Nicaragua in 1988, the second highest total since Moscow initiated weapons deliveries in 1980.[227] The 1988 delivery of some 19,000 tons of equipment took sixty-eight ship visits to Nicaraguan ports, an average of about one every six days. Although Congress suspended military aid to the Contras in 1988, the high level of Soviet shipments continued ("Soviet Arms Shipments to Nicaragua Increased Last Year," *Washington Times* 28 February. 1989, page A10).

'Active Measures' Still Flourish

Most important concerning Soviet intentions is the fact that Soviet "active measures" still flourish as a "Cold War" weapon against the United States. It is estimated that Moscow, to this end, is spending between $3 billion and $4 billion dollars a year and employing 15-30,000 people at home and abroad to weaken the United States, particularly in the Third World. An unreconstructed Stalinist, Valentin Falin, runs the active measures campaign as head of the Soviet Communist Party's International Department ("Soviet Active Measures and Disinformation Forecast," *Disinformation* 11 Winter

---

227 The peak year for Soviet arms shipments was 1986, when the Sandinistas received $550 million worth of equipment.

2244 The Long Pretense

1989], pages 1ff.). Are we to assume that Falin is operating in defiance of Gorbachev's policies? Gorbachev had assured Charles Z. Wick after the December 1988 summit that Moscow would end its anti-U.S. disinformation efforts ("Soviets Said to Renew 3rd World Disinformation Drive," *Los Angeles Times* 18 January 1988, page 18; "Have the Soviets Changed Their Disinformation Ways?" *Washington Times* 29 September 1988, page F5).

Here we have yet another violation of an agreement. It's like seeing the same old newsreel again and again. Ever since Soviet reassurances that such active measures would stop, two official Soviet publishing houses have released books about the CIA. One of these, published by Novosti, a so-called Soviet news agency, recounts alleged "crimes" by the United States. (In chapter 8 I dealt with Soviet "active measures" in greater detail.)

The "Crimes" of the CIA, KGB Version

The second book released by Moscow's Progress Publishers is called *The CIA in Asia: Covert Operations Against India and Afghanistan.* It quotes a pro-Soviet Indian newspaper that alleged that the CIA was behind the killing of U.S. Ambassador Adolph Dubbs in 1979. It further accused the United States of underwriting a genetic engineering program in Pakistan to develop a lethal strain of mosquito ("Glasnost Brings Little Change to Disinformation Activities," *Washington Times* 18 August 1987, page A3).

If one is to have faith in Gorbachev's promises and intentions, there must be an end to the kind of character assassination of the United States by KGB "active measures" specialists—the kind of Soviet-inspired rumor-mongering like the CIA assassinated Indira Gandhi and Olaf Palme or the United States is responsible for the AIDS epidemic.

What would President Gorbachev and his Western acolytes say were U.S. official agencies, the State Department, the U.S. Information Agency, or the Republican National Committee to publish books making similar allegations against the Soviet Union? Well, we know the answer to that question.

One would have greater trust in Gorbachev's promises of a better world if the CPSU Central Committee's International Department and the KGB were visibly dismantled. How can one trust the head of a state who, while negotiating all kinds of treaties with another state, has also approved not-so-secret "active measures" against the treaty partner? Or is one to believe that Gorbachev is helpless before the Central Committee's International Department and the KGB? What happened to Gorbachev's call for "civilized relations" with the West?

Perhaps the U.S. Information Agency that monitors Soviet active measures against the West, particularly those aimed at the United States, should make *daily* public reports of Soviet propaganda against the United States while its leader is talking about a truce in the Cold War. That would be one way of checking the meaning of "glastroika."

Actually there are simple tests one can pose as to the significance of Gorbachev's reforms.

When Gorbachev arrived for a visit to Britain April 5, he was greeted by a full-page ad in the *London Times* signed by 212 parliamentarians. The advertisement accused the Soviet Union of human rights abuses despite four years of talk about *glasnost* reforms. They offered a checklist for testing the Soviet commitment to improve human rights conditions. The *glasnost* checklist included:

> Freedom to emigrate, freedom of religious and political expression; freedom from discrimination; freedom of all prisoners of conscience; freedom of speech; freedom to monitor these basic human rights.

A General Weakness

Without minimizing the value of the parliamentarians' *glasnost* checklist, it suffers from a general weakness: the need for researching and investigating these rather complicated matters, all of which take time and manpower and arguments with Soviet propagandists.

There are some simpler methods for monitoring *glasnost*. My proposed *glasnost* checklist, worked out with Professor Paul Seabury of Berkeley, can tell you pretty well whether *glasnost* is for real.

Let us call it the Glasnost Compliance Register (GCR), a handy reference list of "indicator" categories with questions that can be answered yes or no. The categories would include, for openers, availability of telephone directories: Are city phone directories available in Moscow, Leningrad, Vladivostok, Kiev, Smolensk, Kaliningrad, or other cities, especially closed cities?

Another category would be availability of maps in languages other than Russian, particularly accurate city street maps of large Soviet cities that any tourist could purchase without any formalities.

Here are some others:

- Availability of foreign newspapers and magazines like the *New York Times, International Herald Tribune, Le Monde, L'Express, Der Spiegel, The Spectator, National Review,* or the *Washington Times.* Could city street maps indicate kiosks where foreign newspapers are available?
- Availability to Western scholars of archival material dealing with, say, the Katyn Forest slaughter, the Sverdlovsk anthrax accident, Alger Hiss, Leon Trotsky, and Stalin's genocidal agricultural policies in the 1930s.

- Names, addresses, phone numbers, and salaries of members of the Politburo, the Central Committee, and Supreme Soviet. Such information about U.S. officials is readily available in publicly-distributed government publications.
- Can photographs be purchased of such historic figures as Trotsky, Bukharin, Stalin, Kirov, Khrushchev, Kerensky, or Czar Nicholas II and his Czarina?
- Publication of the annual Soviet military budget—item by item, line by line—as the United States and other democracies do.
- Can hotels or any other institutions supply the location of stores in the Soviet Union that sell postage stamps for philatelists, coins for numismatists, typewriters, mimeograph and photocopying machines, computers and computer software, Bibles, the Koran, and the memoirs of Svetlana Alleluyeva (née Stalin)?
- Has the Soviet Union stopped producing such films as *Who Killed Olof Palme?* (which accuses the United States of the assassination) or stopped distributing forged documents alleging nefarious White House deeds in Latin America, Asia, and Africa?
- Has there been a reduction in the number of Soviet cities and regions barred to both tourists and Soviet citizens?
- Soviet militiamen in Moscow "guard" apartment blocks around the clock where foreigners, especially correspondents, live. Soviet citizens who visit foreigners' homes must show their identification papers to the police before they can enter a building. When, if ever, will these policemen be removed?
- Are food parcels and other packages from abroad being delivered to addressees?

A Simple Yes or No

Other categories could be selected for the GCR where a simple yes or no could easily be provided. The requisite information could come from tourists, who could be provided with the checklist as part of their tickets and other documentation. The Register itself could be published semi-annually so that comparisons could be made between one time period and another in order to discern the general direction of the Gorbachev *glasnost*.

Let me argue against myself.

Very well, Gorbachev is sincere in his will to reform. Let us even agree that he would privately admit that he became head of party and state in order to preside over the liquidation of the burdensome Soviet empire. Grant him all the good will in the world. Credit him with the best of intentions for the Soviet peoples. Will the best of intentions be enough to satisfy the remorseless material and spiritual demands that are being made by a long-frustrated populace?

Unless drastic changes are made, the Soviet system is doomed either to fall into a state of malevolent, quasi-Stalinist desuetude or move toward a prerevolutionary condition. Yes, let us concede, Gorbachev is ready to move. But can he? Can the Soviet system be changed within the system?

I was in Finland a week before the 1988 Moscow summit, talking with veteran analysts, official and unofficial, about Gorbachev's reform program. One of them, a Finnish diplomat with years of residence in the Soviet Union, summed it up best: "All that Gorbachev is doing is trying to reform the system within the system. It simply can't be done."

A Modern Soviet Economy?

It is as impossible to develop a modern economy with a central bureaucracy at the helm as it is to make fried snowballs, as Leszek Kolakowski once said in another context. To put it simply, communism/socialism may be a lot of things; the one thing it most definitely is not is an economic system. As Jacques Rupnik has written:

Can Gorbachev's reforms, designed to bring the Soviet Union into the 21st century, sustain an increasingly absurd imperial system inherited from the 19th century? ... After four years in office, Gorbachev has discovered that the reform of the Soviet system and the stability of the Soviet empire are incompatible. ("The Empire Breaks Up," *New Republic* 20 February 1989, pages 21, 24)

Not all the good will in the world, not all the Western loans will create the kind of country that Gorbachev presumably wants. For example: The Soviet newspaper *Socialist Industry* recently published an article about photocopying machines based on an interview with a leading Soviet expert in photocopying technology. The Soviet expert, Dr. Abram Borisovich Dravin, asked the reporter at the outset if his newspaper, with a circulation well in the millions, had a photocopier, and if it did, was it Soviet-made or foreign? Much embarrassed, the Soviet reporter replied that the paper did indeed have a copying machine and added, "But I've never seen it. It's locked in a room with an iron door" ("Gorbachev's Choice: Secrecy or Progress," *Soviet Analyst* 17[24] [7 December 1988], pages 5-6).

Dr. Dravin then told the reporter that in the West copying technology was commonplace and not at all unusual, even in private homes. He pointed out that just one of the five big Japanese producers, Ricoh, could make ten times more photocopiers in a month than the whole Soviet industry could in a year. The Soviet output, he said, is "unreliable and cumbersome" (Ibid.).

The moral of the story is that *glastroika* without the exploitation of modern communication technology is almost meaningless if one is trying to redeem and modernize an economy that is barely ticking over. As of January 1990, there were an estimated half-million computers in the Soviet Union, less than 1 percent of the 60 million in the United States (*London Economist* 27 January 1990, page 70).

Pravda described the effect of facsimile technology in expediting Japanese business relationships. But first the paper had to explain to an audience that had probably never seen a fax machine just what it was that fax did. Japan, said *Pravda's* Tokyo correspondent, had some 2.2 million fax machines installed in government, business, and private hands (*Pravda* 17 October 1988).

A Fax Manufacturer

The *Pravda* correspondent asked a Japanese fax manufacturer whether he wasn't worried that secrets would be lost since such equipment is capable of "transmitting the texts of any document, unimpeded and uncontrolled, not only beyond the walls of your company but even beyond the country's borders" (Ibid.). The company executive replied that they trusted their employees.

The *Soviet Analyst* writer Iain Elliot said the Soviets can't afford to ban fax, "yet once its use becomes widespread, the vast resources now devoted to preventing the importing of undesirable literature, or [preventing] distributing and exporting samizdat publications, will be wasted; just one more sad example of an outmoded political structure clinging to power to the detriment of its own citizens" ("Gorbachev's Choice: Secrecy or Progress," *Soviet Analyst* 17[24] [7 December 1988]). Imagine a fax machine in the hands of a dissident intellectual group. The Politburo trembles at the mere thought.[228]

That is why control of the media still exists, despite some Western news reports that censorship in the Soviet Union is gone. The chief Soviet censor, Dr. Vladimir Boldyrev, heads what is called the "Main Directorate for the Protection of State Secrets in Print," known by its Russian acronym, Glavlit. On 3 November 1988, Baldyrev told *Izvestia* that while "censorship was in

---

228 Machiavelli (1950, 3:443) wrote that "the ruin of states is brought about ... because they do not modify their institutions to suit the times."

part responsible for the braking mechanism in the bureaucratic command system which arose in our society" and while he bemoaned the "unnecessary and harmful 'cult of secrecy,'" nevertheless there was "also an authentic secrecy," that is, the need to prevent dissemination of anything which might "damage the interests of the state" ("A Soviet Censor Uncensored," *New York Times* 13 February 1989, page 11).

Import of Western publications is still subject to government control. The *Soviet Analyst*, a scholarly British biweekly, is barred from the Soviet Union. It is included in "the production of known anti-Soviet or anti-communist organizations," along with the Posev publishing house, various "nationalist organizations" in the West, and, naturally, *Index on Censorship* (*Soviet Analyst* 18[7] [5 April 1989], page 6; *Moskovskiye Novosti* 10 [1989], page 291).

Glavlit's role in the future, therefore, would be to censor news items of "authentic secrecy" yet still allow readers access to the "achievements of national and world culture." Baldyrev did not indicate what standards would be used in judging between inauthentic and authentic secrecy. Thane Gustafson evaluated the existing censorship system in the summer of 1989, four years into the era of *glastroika,* with the finding that "the power of the state over the media remains intact." He added: "Just what is permitted and what is forbidden cannot be predicted from day to day. But what is not in question is the state's fundamental power to intervene to suppress or to excise material it considered undesirable" ("Party Favors," *New Republic* 19 June 1989, pages 35-36[229]).

A more recent example of what could be considered the power of the state over the media was the strange silence of the Soviet media over the bloody events in China in the early days of June 1989. John Hughes wrote that "in the long list of nations critical of China there is one notable exception—the Soviet Union." Said Hughes:

Countries around the world condemn the massacre of Tiananmen Square and deplore the hard-line crackdown on students and workers who thought their ruling regime might be ready for a little freedom.... But from Moscow there is a discomforting silence. Mikhail Gorbachev may talk grandly of more democracy in

---

229 In this essay review of Walter Laqueur's *The Long Road to Freedom: Russia and Glasnost* (New York, N.Y.: Scribner's, 1989). Gustafson gives an example of what party control of publishing means: A resourceful former editor was able to set up a cooperative, obtain printer and paper and publish a handsome paperback of the writings, banned in the Soviet Union since the 1920s, of Sigmund Freud. The books were seized by *Goskomizdat*, the State Committee for Publishing. However, under *glastroika* there is hope that the books will someday be unseized.

the Soviet Union and of the rights of people abroad. But China can commit murder and terrorize student leaders who survive without fear of any disapproving glower from the Soviet leader.

Indeed, in a country whose media is supposed to be basking in the new freedom of glasnost *the Soviet press has been muted in its coverage of the China story*. [my emphasis]. ("Rethinking South Africa," *Christian Science Monitor* 21 April 1989, page 19)

What these reports demonstrate is that *glastroika* must fail as a remedy for Soviet social and economic ills so long as political power is centralized in a handful of unelected commissars responsible to no one but themselves and, in the final analysis, to the omnipotent Politburo. The American penchant for "treatyism" and summit meetings cannot substitute for the real revolution that Russia failed to achieve in 1917.

As long as the copying machine at a newspaper is kept behind an iron door; as long as there is censorship to protect an undefined "authentic" secrecy; as long as men frightened of the people they rule regard a fax machine as counterrevolutionary; as long as a fortnightly eight-page commentary edited in England and printed on pink paper called the *Soviet Analyst* is barred from circulation in the Soviet Union, Gorbachev can huff and puff but, fundamentally, nothing will change, certainly not in the economy.

It takes people with spirit and ambition to make an economy function. But in an atomized society,[230] which characterizes the Soviet Union today (although far less so than in the Stalin years), entrepreneurial ambitions will not be satisfied. As John Stuart Mill wrote in his essay *On Liberty*, "A State which dwarfs its men in order that they may be more docile instruments in its hands—even for beneficial purposes—will find that with small men no great thing can really be accomplished."

Again, let us give Gorbachev every possible benefit of the doubt. The Western press is full of articles of homage to Gorbachev, especially in the *New York Times*.[231]

---

230 An atomized society is one in which politics and decision making exist only at the level of unelected ruling elites. In such a regime, neither individuals as individuals nor individuals comprising society are autonomous. Consequently, personal relationships are subordinated to and dominated by the self-defined and unpredictable interests of the party-state.

231 On 6 February 1989, under the headline, "Let's Do All We Can for Gorbachev," Jeremy J. Stone, president of the Federation of American Scientists, wrote on the *New York Times* Op-Ed page, "The Soviet Union, known for 70 years for cynicism and pretension, today is led by a pragmatic visionary who acts with idealism and statesmanship.... Mr. Gorbachev is, from our viewpoint, the best General Secretary we could dream of seeing." On 30 January 1989, under the

A Motivated Work Force?

Yet to create the kind of working economy he presumably seeks, to create a motivated work force, to restore some faith in the state, to restore initiative—in fact, to make individual initiative a shining virtue, not a badge of dishonor—Gorbachev will have to disenfranchise Marxism-Leninism and thereby enfranchise the Soviet peoples. Gorbachev's random reforms within the system, like those of Khrushchev before him, have not done any good and cannot do any good because the Soviet political system is utterly ill-adapted to deal with the concomitant socioeconomic problems that the system itself creates.

To establish a trustworthy foreign policy, and therefore a credible treaty diplomacy, the Soviet ethos must be altered from within the Soviet power structure. Highfalutin' speeches at the United Nations may captivate the editorial page of the *New York Times,* but Soviet rhetoric will not reassure those who know Soviet history. And those who know Soviet history best are those who have lived through it—namely, the peoples of the Soviet Union.

All or Nothing

My thesis may sound like an all-or-nothing all-at-once right-now demand upon a communist superpower to stand and deliver. Yet liberal opinion, which rejects as an unbearable presumption an all-or-nothing approach to the Soviet Union, demands an all-or-nothing approach to South Africa. For the Soviet Union, patience; for South Africa, no compromise. In fact, all Soviet "reforms" are greeted ecstatically while no South Africa reform ever goes far enough. If the gradualist approach is satisfactory for the Soviet Union, why not for South Africa as well?

In the past decade, Pretoria has abolished segregated eating places, theaters, and public parks; there are now multiracial hotels; sports and universities are integrated, the Mixed Marriages and Immorality Acts have been scrapped. Job reservation for whites has been abolished so that one can now talk about upward mobility for blacks. Black unions are legal and now have a membership of 2 million members. Strikes are legal. The hated Pass Law has been abolished so blacks can move into urban areas, and there are now legally desegregated residential areas. The Dutch Reformed Church,

---

headline, "Don't Humiliate Gorbachev," former Ambassador William H. Luers wrote on the *Times* Op-Ed page that the United States "should recognize that for the first time in modern history we may have a common cause with the Soviets in Eastern Europe: peaceful change toward more efficient, more humane systems.... [I]t is important that [President Bush] understand the need to avoid humiliating the Russians at this time."

onetime pillar of apartheid, now proclaims apartheid is a sin. There are yet to be reported equivalent dramatic changes in the Soviet Union.[232]

I would agree with Robert Conquest (1987, 10) that "we mustn't judge the Soviet progress by Soviet standards." If we seek and hope for a democratic evolution in the Soviet Union, then obviously democratic criteria should apply. Is there some other way to establish trust in the Soviet Union? Let me offer as a test of credibility the words of Andrei Sakharov's 1975 Nobel lecture. He said:

> I am convinced that international trust, mutual understanding, disarmament, and international security are inconceivable without an open society with freedom of information, freedom of conscience, the right to publish and the right to travel and choose the country in which one wishes to live.

> I am also convinced that freedom of conscience, together with other civic rights, provides both the basis for scientific progress and a guarantee against its misuse to harm mankind.

Perhaps Dr. Sakharov's words ought to be the test of whether the Soviet Union is approaching a historic moment of truth. If the free market democracies or, more specifically the United States, represent a standard of civic rights by which Gorbachev's Soviet Union must be measured, then obviously we should, like Lewis Carroll's whiting to the snail, urge the Soviet Union to "walk a little faster" in its putative departure since March 1985 from seven decades of unyielding totalitarianism.

For, after all, Marxism and Lenin's strategic doctrines have together been shown to be a fraudulent nostrum once they are applied to human beings and not to political science models. Can a country that still, despite minor modifications, insists upon living by a system that has brought more evil to humanity than all the Black Plagues put together—can such a country be trusted to keep its commitments?

Agreed, that because world peace is at stake, the United States and the Soviet Union must somehow be the guarantors of that peace, to which must be added the phrase, "and freedom." But even with the best bipolar will in the world, the international system is now populated by actors who may not be amenable to international discipline. I am thinking of Muammar Qadaffi, Syria's Hafez al-Assad, the Ayatollah Khomeini's heirs,Iraq's Sadam Hussein and Yasir Arafat and the power they enjoy.[233]

---

232 In 1965, I was allowed to enter South Africa, where I wrote articles for the then *New York Herald Tribune* and the *Columbia University Forum.* When I applied for a visa in 1966 to accompany Senator Robert F. Kennedy on his tour of South Africa, my application was rejected. I have not been back since.

233 Bismarck once said: "We live in a wondrous time in which the strong is weak

A peace in freedom when such *enragés* bestride the world may not be easy to establish. But does that mean that in the interests of world peace those countries still dominated by Marxism-Leninism must remain dominated by the abomination imposed upon them? As Secretary of State Shultz said in a speech I cited earlier:

> How can we as a country say to a young Afghan, Nicaraguan, or Cambodian: "Learn to live with oppression; only those of us who already have freedom deserve to pass it on to our children." How can we say to those Salvadorans who stood so bravely in line to vote: "We may give you some economic and military aid for self-defense, but we will also give a free hand to the Sandinistas who seek to undermine your new democratic institutions.

A Hostile Congress

With a new U.S. administration in place and a Congress hostile to a U.S. foreign policy that challenges the Soviet Union, the predilection to "treatyism" among policy-making elites supported by policy-influencing elites is on a roll. As I write, we do not yet know when the drive for a START treaty will begin. But it will begin with the Soviets' pressing for negotiations. Yet many Western experts recognize that, to quote Patrick Glynn ("Nuclear Revisionism," *Commentary* 87[3] [March 1989], page D9), "the agreement will be destabilizing, probably cannot be verified, poses a major potential for Soviet breakout and will increase rather than lessen the economic costs of deterrence.... Still the arms control juggernaut rolls on."

Or to quote William F. Buckley:

> The effect of across-the-board nuclear reduction is always to the disadvantage of the superpower unlikely to initiate a first strike. And we must abide by the ABM treaty. Abiding by the ABM treaty is Soviet shorthand for denying ourselves the testing in space of technology designed to protect from random nuclear missiles from nth-power nations and to render, ultimately a first strike by the Soviet Union inconceivable. The Soviets have never for one moment strayed from their goal of dismantling our Strategic Defense Initiative, and the march together taken by Mr. Reagan and Mr. Gorbachev toward peace in our time is designed to further that effort. (*National Review* 27 January 1989, page 70)

The sorry U.S. record vis-à-vis Soviet treaty diplomacy demands a new approach by the free nations, particularly the United States, toward negotiations with the Soviet Union. The new approach should heed these wise words by Harold Nicolson:

---

because of his moral scruples and the weak grows strong because of his audacity" (*Daedalus* Summer 1968, page 906).

I have not observed as yet that this [Marxist-Leninist] dialectic has improved international relationships, or that the Soviet diplomatists and commissars have evolved any system of negotiation that might be called a diplomatic system. Their activity in foreign countries or at international conferences is formidable, disturbing, compulsive. I do not for one moment underestimate either its potency or its danger. But it is not diplomacy: it is something else." (Nicolson 1954, 90)

To get off the treatyism treadmill, U.S. negotiators should consider the following principles:

First, treaties between the two countries should be self-enforcing. If the Soviets are in serious violation of an agreement, consequences should come into play immediately. Despite the Kissinger view I cited earlier, I think treaties should still be negotiated on a self-enforcing basis. There is really no alternative.

Second, treaty diplomacy with the Soviet Union should be kept on hold until the Soviet Union stops threatening the security of the United States and other countries in the hemisphere.

Third, a ban should be placed on loans or technology transfers to countries that fail to comply with the Helsinki accords, even though they are signatories.

There could be more recommendations: for example, legislation that would ban future imprudent behavior of large American banks that have already made loans to the Soviet Union unless there are ironclad guarantees for repayment. By ironclad guarantees, I mean that the Soviet Union should place its gold reserves in a neutral Swiss bank pledged to the debt ("East/West Trade and Finance Opportunities or Losses for the West?" *Resistance Bulletin* 1[6] [Winter 1988/89], page 8).[234]

Martin Colman scoffs at those international bankers who say that the Soviet Union has an excellent credit and a good payment record. The bankers never ask how the Soviet Union repays its debts or with whose funds. And what about long-term reliability? Says Colman:

Most of the companies currently engaged in U.S.-Soviet trade are indeed being paid.... The funds, however, comes from U.S. taxpayer-guaranteed banks who actively participate in a shellgame of rolling the debt from banking consortium to

---

234 Colman's article quotes from a Senate Banking Committee report (*Congressional Record*,19 March 1987) as follows: "Hard currency is the fuel of the Soviet Empire and international terrorist network. It buys terrorist bombs and funds hostage-takers. And when the Soviet Union finds a willing seller in the West and evades our export controls, they have to use hard currency to purchase their bargains and save themselves billions in weapons development costs. U.S. banks ... make untied, no-purpose loans that put ready cash into Soviet hands" ("Hastening the Death of Communism," *Commentary* 88[4] [October 1989], page 20).

banking consortium, continuously creating new loans to pay off the old ones when due. Typically, loans to the Soviets are for eight years with no payment on principal until five or six years into the loan. It is at the time just before the principal payments begin that the Soviets will obtain a new loan to repay the old loan. This loan cycle has created an image of good credit while in fact the Soviets never reduce the total amount of principal outstanding from their own resources. (Ibid., page 8)

What is surprising is to read in the *Wall Street Journal* that "the Soviets have an excellent credit history and low levels of external debt" (5 December 1988, page A5).

Systemic Crisis

The systemic crisis that now afflicts the Soviet Union will continue through the next decade and most likely outlive President Gorbachev. So argues Zbigniew Brzezinski, who says that Communism has lost its ideological legitimacy ("A Proposition the Soviets Shouldn't Refuse," *New York Times* 13 March 1989, page A19).

With or without ideological legitimacy, there is simply no way to avoid continuing treaty diplomacy between the United States and the Soviet Union, perhaps at a more intense level because of Gorbachev's great skill than under previous Soviet leaders. In the same way we continue membership in the UN, knowing all the while that it's a fraudulent organization in that it and its subsidiary subsystems regularly violate their charters, so it is with treaty making with the Soviet Union. Knowing all the while they will violate or circumvent what they sign, the United States will continue to negotiate various joint instruments with the Soviet Union, aware that everything is subject to change with or without notice.

But at least now, let the negotiations between the two powers be far different from what has been the case for more than half a century. We must develop a policy of deterrence in our treaty diplomacy. It is well to remember the words of Thomas Jefferson, who once said that we held in our hands "those peaceable coercions which are in the power of every nation, if undertaken in concert and in time of peace" (Kennan 1966, 59).

There must be a new approach to treaty diplomacy, an approach undertaken with full Western consciousness that the past is no longer acceptable as prologue to the future. Those frustrating days when the Soviet Union violated treaty or other obligations with impunity (and we accepted with a historical fatalism) should come to an end. If those words *glasnost* and *perestroika,* now part of the Western vocabulary, have any meaning, then the free world must insist that *pacta sunt servanda.* Firmness and knowledge of the adversary's past and present should enable us to enjoy peace in freedom while those victimized for so long by Marxism-Leninism seek, peacefully, to reorder their lives as captive nations approaching their manumission. In the light of the 4 June 1989 "massacre at Beijing," it is not easy to predict a peaceful resolution to the conflict between desperate Politburos and desperate people.

A Rosier Future?

These conditions are all the more important today because of Gorbachev's promises of a rosier future for the Soviet peoples. Assuming that Gorbachev means everything he says, what happens to the treaty instruments he negotiates with the West should he die or be overthrown or, himself, return to the principles of Stalinism? George Kennan predicts Soviet compliance with treaty obligations—but what if Gorbachev is replaced by someone even tougher than the Gorbachev whom Andrei Gromyko described as having "iron teeth"?

Former President Reagan said in June 1989 that President Gorbachev represents the only hope in the Soviet Union and that "we should take the risk of believing that the Soviets are serious in their efforts to reach genuine arms reductions with the West" (Associated Press dispatch #1347 [13 June 1989]).

A year earlier, then Defense Secretary Frank Carlucci fashioned this scenario, which might be a reply to Mr. Reagan's let's-take-a-chance proposal:

> If the end result is that the Western alliance relaxes its defense effort and the Soviet Union modernizes its industrial and technological base, and if some time in the 1990s it ends up as a society that can produce enormous quantities of weapons even more effectively than it does today, then we will have made an enormous miscalculation. ("A New Era," *Wall Street Journal* 8 June 1989, page 22)

The question remains: shall we live by the promise of *glastroika* or shall we live steadfastly by the most difficult of all codes in international relations, the code of realism? If we are lured by an *ignis fatuus,* the miracles of *glastroika,* and forget the seventy years of Leninist dissembling because of the infirmity that Jean-François Revel has described as the West's "collective amnesia," then we will forfeit the breathtaking opportunity created by the Great Turnaround.

Of course, we must negotiate with the Soviet Union whenever President Gorbachev emerges with some new and dazzling proposal. Soviet Foreign Minister Maxim Litvinov startled the world with a speech at the World Disarmament Conference in Geneva as far back as 1932 calling for "total disarmament" immediately. Nothing ever came of it because Stalin would never have allowed anything to come of it. In the same way that we go right on "negotiating" with Deng as if he and his associates would ever surrender power as the result of a democratic election, we must go right on negotiating with the Soviets as if they would allow the concrete realization of their "peace-loving" rhetoric.

In Edward Gibbon's *Decline and Fall of the Roman Empire* occurs this memorable passage:

> If a man were called to fix the period in the history of the world during which the condition of the human race was most happy and prosperous, he would, without hesitation, name that which elapsed from the death of Domitian to the accession of Commodus. (Gibbon 1912, 1:78)

The democracies are entering what may be one of the most humane periods in the history of civilization—a period which I would call the era of the Great Turnaround. The world is leaving behind the era of Marxism-Leninism—that period when each day, it seemed, brought a new communist conquest, whether in Europe, Asia, Africa, or Latin America. Francis Fukuyama's essay in *The National Interest*, is titled, "Have We Reached the End of History?" His answer is: "What we may be witnessing is not just the end of the Cold War, but the universalization of Western liberal democracy as the final form of human government" ("Have We Reached the End of History?" *The National Interest* [Washington, D.C.] Summer.1989, page 4). But, as Disraeli once said, finality is not the language of politics.

Epilogue

All political movements, Marx wrote, have been slaves to the symbols of the past .... But history is a process of progressive disenchantment.

Daniel Bell (1974, 93)

Who can tell what the Gorbachev era will bring in its train? I have tried to show that if the Leninist past has any bearing on the Gorbachev future, we can expect little from Soviet treaty diplomacy except the same mixture as before. President Gorbachev might even be the second communist leader (Khrushchev was the first) able to ram the genie back in the bottle, a metaphor that implies the repression of hundreds of thousands of peoples in the Soviet Union and, improbable as it may seem at the present time, even in Eastern Europe. If it turns out indeed that Gorbachev cannot force the *perestroika* genii into the bottle and that *glasnost* is here to stay, then it is possible to hope that the world is entering what may become one of the most humane periods in the history of civilization—the era of the Great Turnaround.

The world is leaving behind the era of Marxism-Leninism, that period when it seemed that each day brought a new communist conquest in violation of solemn treaty engagements or of the United Nations Charter (See appendix B for a chronology of Soviet Russian imperialism from 1917). Soviet and Soviet surrogate armies now seem to be retreating from lands where they shouldn't have been in the first place. Nowhere in the world, it seems, is the Soviet Union, its ideology, and its system of rule welcome as the bringer of all good things. As Henry Kissinger said so presciently thirty years ago,

"Marxism is accepted where it doesn't exist, rejected where it does" (Kissinger 1969, 84).

Can It Happen Peacefully?

If the rejection can be accomplished peacefully, then the Reagan-Bush-Gorbachev era might well turn out to be Gibbon's Domitian-Commodus happy time.[235] The question is whether the global "progressive disenchantment" with Marxism-Leninism will also infect President Gorbachev and his Politburo colleagues.

One could argue that the events in Poland (that few had predicted were possible) should be regarded as exemplifying Gorbachev's *bona fides*. After all, as I write, the new Prime Minister of Poland is an anticommunist Solidarity official who but a few years ago resided in a communist jail. Lech Walesa has said, "Now those who were under the wagon are on it" ("Revolution in Poland," *Christian Science Monitor* 22 August 1989, page 20). And incredibly, Lech Walesa, without an office or a title, addressed a joint session of the U.S. Congress, as did President Vaclav Havel of Czechoslovakia, with a title. Yet, at the same time that a counterrevolution was occurring in Poland, the Soviet Central Committee was warning the Baltic peoples not to expect the legitimization of their right to secede from the Soviet Union, even though it is widely admitted even by Soviet spokesmen that Latvia, Lithuania, and Estonia were forcibly incorporated into it. And the "revolution from below" in East Germany, Hungary, Romania, Bulgaria, and Czechoslovakia has not yet run its course, even though as of January 1990 there were still Soviet Red Army occupation troops in those countries.

Despite such significant changes, I am deeply pessimistic about the possibility of a fundamental democratizing change in the Soviet Union which would render its treaty diplomacy responsible and trustworthy by democratic standards. My position is that of a British statesman who observed of Nazi Germany that it was wrong to regard a nation with unalterable suspicion. But then he asked, what if that nation gives unalterable cause?

Such unalterable cause is to be found in the continuing Soviet disinformation campaigns intended to discredit the United States (See

---

235 The 1989 annual Freedom House survey showed that the 1980s had seen a global trend against dictatorships and in favor of democratic change. Twenty-one nations in the 1980s elected civilian rulers by ousting one-party or military governments. Even South Africa can now be regarded as partly free with the release of political prisoners and some changes in apartheid restrictions ("Greed Decade Was Really the Freed Decade," *Wall Street Journal* 8 December 1989, page A10).

chapters 8 and 11 for detailed discussion on Soviet active measures). These campaigns continue despite Soviet reassurances that they are no longer necessary. I refer to Gorbachev's best-selling book in which he wrote:

> We certainly do not need an "enemy image" of America, neither for domestic nor for foreign policy interests. An imaginary or real enemy is needed only if one is bent on maintaining tension, on confrontation with far-reaching and, I might add, unpredictable consequences. Ours is a different orientation. (Gorbachev 1987, 216-17)

Forged Documents

Many of these propaganda campaigns against the United States, based on forged documents, were launched during the Gorbachev years. Some of the campaigns that have landed in the press of Asia, Africa, and Latin America have reported disgusting lies, such as American citizens are buying the organs of Latin American babies for transplants in the United States, or the United States has created an "ethnic weapon" that kills blacks but not whites. The AIDS epidemic is blamed on the Pentagon. These campaigns have continued despite the 1988 promise by Gorbachev at the December 1987 summit to then USIA Director Charles Z. Wick that they would be stopped ("Active Measures Under Gorbachev: The Campaigns Continue,"[236] *Disinformation: Soviet Active Measures and Disinformation Forecast* [Washington, D.C.: Consortium for the Study of Intelligence] 9 [Summer 1988], pages 1-3).

In addition to the continuation of Soviet "active measures" in the Era of Glastroika, there is a further test for determining the genuineness of Gorbachev's "new thinking"—Soviet arms expenditures. In its 1989 annual report on Soviet Military Power, the Defense Department disclosed that since 1985, when Gorbachev took over, Soviet military expenditures have grown at a rate of 3 percent a year in real terms. That is a faster rate than in the pre-Gorbachev years. By the most conservative estimates, the Soviet Union is spending between 15 and 17 percent of its Gross National Product on the military; in 1989, the United States was spending 6 percent.

Soviet factories turned out 2,800 tanks a year in the pre-Gorbachev era; between 1985 and 1988, Soviet factories turned out 3,400 a year. Discussing strategic nuclear weapons, Secretary of Defense Dick Cheney said that the United States "faces a more formidable Soviet offensive strategic arsenal today than we did four years ago when Mr. Gorbachev came to power." The

---

236 This article is based on a congressionally mandated report (U.S. Information Agency 1988). On this subject, also see U.S. Department of State 1987 and Romerstein and Levchenko 1989.

Soviet Union is still, as the *Wall Street Journal* put it, "the world's largest military power" ("Still an Empire," *Wall Street Journal* 3 October 1989, page A22).

I am aware that there is always the possibility that a nation's leadership can change for the better. One might even be tempted to agree with Professor Seweryn Bialer, who wrote during the pre-Gorbachev era:

> To look at the Soviet political elite today as revolutionary fanatics whose every concrete act is colored by the ultimate ends as prescribed by Marxist and Leninist holy writ is as nonsensical as it is to see them only as cynical manipulators who simply drift toward undefined goals and whose response to reality is not influenced by their intellectual and political revolutionary origins. The question is not whether their beliefs have changed, but which beliefs, how much, and in what direction; not whether they have an ideology but to what ideology they subscribe. (Bialer 1976, 45)

After Four Years, What?

Gorbachev has been in power five years. Has his "glastroika" in that time produced any meaningful and irreversible *structural* change in the politics of power within the Soviet Union? Can the Soviet Communist Party effect such change by a peaceful transition while it lives or behaves as if it lives by the tenets of Marxism-Leninism? I have my doubts, although the Soviet Communist Party is on the run. The reason for such probable failure is summed up for me in one sentence written long ago by Hilaire Belloc, the British essayist. Said Belloc: "The control of the production of wealth is the control of human life itself" (Hayek 1944, 88).

While Glasnost & Co. might bode well for the possibility of a democratized Soviet Union, Gorbachev has yet to tackle, except with hortatory rhetoric, the Soviet economy. He still stands by the Leninist design of a command economy. This finding is not my own; it belongs to Soviet observers who have been writing extensively about the failures of the Soviet system. Here is one example of economic ruin by central planning dogma, as described in a book by two Soviet economists, Nikolai Shmelev[237] and Vladimir Popov, titled *The Turning Point:*

---

237   Nikolai Shmelev, a member of the Soviet parliament, is a senior staff member of the prestigious Institute of USA and Canada. On 16 June 1987, the *Christian Science Monitor* reported on a lecture by Shmelev dealing with Stalin. According to Shmelev, at least 17 million Soviet citizens had been sent to labor camps as political prisoners between 1937 and Stalin's death in 1953. Another five million peasants were deported thousands of miles from their homes to wastelands during the forcible collectivization of farmland in the late 1920s and early 1930s. According to Radio Liberty, which quoted the *Monitor* interview, this was the first instance of a Soviet scholar providing figures on the scale of Soviet atrocities.

At a bus factory in Kurgan, workers take partially-assembled trucks from the Gorki car factory and demolish them with sledge hammers. That's what they are paid to do. They then place a bus on the truck chassis that remains after their sledge hammer handiwork.

So, here's a riddle: Why doesn't the Gorki car factory send only the chassis to the Kugan bus factory? Ah, here you have the joys of central planning. There exists a special state all-union standards board, called by its Russian initials GOST, which has decreed, as the *London Economist* described it, that "trucks have to be made with all the bells and whistles on, even if all that is required is the chassis to make a bus." The Soviet economist, Mr. Shmelev, writes that "It is much harder to change GOST than to swing a sledgehammer" ("In the Lunatic Bus Factory," *London Economist* 25 November 1989, page 101).

Economic Ruin by Dogma

Here is another example of economic ruin by central planning dogma: Of three million tractors in the Soviet Union, some 250,000 are out of commission at any one time. Collective farms must send the broken down tractors to specialist repair shops. Each of these repair shops is assigned, according to plan, an individual target: the number of tractors it is supposed to fix in a year. According to Mr. Shmelev, the number of repairs requested by collective farms covered only 56 percent of the repair shops' plan target. So the repair shops compelled the farms to ship their functioning tractors for *repairs they didn't need.* Says Mr. Shmelev, "repair becomes an end in itself: repair doesn't exist for the tractor. The tractor exists to fulfill the repairmen's plans" (Ibid.).

These are but two of many, many more examples of economic ruin by dogma which underscore the now widely admitted failure of the command economic system. Shmelev doubts that the Soviet economy could cope with a free market economy. The Soviet Union, he said, is heading for "100% rationing of everything—a labour camp economy" (Ibid.). Is it in the interest of the Western democracies to bail out the Soviet economy? General William Odom gave a good answer recently: "We should applaud perestroika but not finance it."

So long as the Soviet economy, operating on what is called central planning, is welded to a bureaucracy responsible solely to a single interest group, namely the Soviet Communist Party, so long will the Soviet Union remain what it has been for more than seventy years: an economic depression without end, the Sahel of Europe. Even more urgent for Western policy makers is to consider that whatever political changes have been brought about by Glasnost & Co., those changes are always in danger of a recidivist fate.

In February 1990, President Gorbachev promulgated a new policy platform for the Soviet Communist Party to adopt. The new program was heralded as the end of communist history, a Gorbachevian New Economic Policy. Yet it was really a mass of contradictions.

While the statement urged freedom of the press, it spoke against dissemination of ideas that could be interpreted (by whom?) as "alien to humane, democratic socialism." on the one hand, the statement warned against "ideological blinkers" and on the other the statement said that the party would under its new dispensation still be chaperoned by the "dialectical methodology of Marx, Engels and Lenin." While the new platform demonstrated, perhaps, an indebtedness to Montesquieu in urging a separation of powers doctrine among the legislative, executive, and judicial branches, it came out in favor of a new chief executive position for President Gorbachev that placed all three branches into his hands.

The platform could be read as enshrining private property rights, yet it excluded private ownership that could involve, as the platform stated, "the exploitation of man by man." Such rhetoric is Marxism redidivus. After all, who, after a century of free trade unionism and labor shortages, could be for "the exploitation of man by man"? Yet that empty metaphor has been the driving force behind Russia's seventy-year economic crisis ("Document Outlining Soviet Party Reform Is Full of Confusion and Contradictions," *Wall Street Journal* 14 February 1990, page A13).

Ivan Ribnikar, a Yugoslav economist, put the issue starkly and how well it applies to the Soviet Union: "The lesson of Yugoslavia is that there is no compromise between a market economy and a centrally planned economy. One must have a true market economy. It can be harder, like America, or softer, like Sweden or Austria. But it surely shouldn't be like Yugoslavia" (Ibid.).

Can the Party Produce Wealth?

There could be no question in Gorbachev's mind that the reason there is no above-ground functioning economy in the Soviet Union is because the production of wealth is not in the hands of people motivated to produce wealth. Rather, it is in the hands of party functionaries whose interest is *not* in producing wealth but in controlling the lives of their victims, their twentieth-century serfs.

By party definition, the task of the central planning authority is not to put commodities essential to a decent way of life on the shelves of the government stores but to ensure party control of the production of wealth. The occasional permission granted a few enterprising souls to open an ethnic restaurant in Moscow for the foreign tourist trade changes nothing. Such a minor "reform" gives visitors and journalists alike a colorful and even appetizing confirmation of their will-to-believe in Glasnost & Co. As Jane Kramer has suggested, "'free market communism' is a contradiction in terms, as is 'pluralistic parliamentary communism'" ("Letter From Europe," *New Yorker* 12 March 1990, page 82).

It is my argument that Glasnost & Co. intends to divert our attention from the fact that, as far as the Soviet system is concerned, whatever limitations on the power of the state have been imposed so far, those limitations are reversible because there is as yet no body of law to make state actions predictable. Half a century ago, Friedrich A. Hayek pointed out that a "planned society" and the rule of law are incompatible.

An exposé, which *Literaturnaya Gazeta* published, of the Moscow Sausage Trust's piling sawdust and old shoe leather into the casings may be hilarious reading in the West, but it does little to provide better and more sausage for the average consumer. Parades for Georgian independence will not feed the people of Leningrad. Nor will *lèse-majesté* toward Lenin provide the hard currency needed to import goods from the industrial West.

At such time as Gorbachev announces the dissolution of central planning and promulgates the right of the people, not just of the *nomenklatura*, to enrich themselves; when he begins to talk about privatization of the means of production in his still garrison state; in short, when Gorbachev acts to end the economics of swindle and national ruin, then will we be entitled to believe in the possibility of fundamental changes for the welfare of the Soviet peoples, and for us in the West, in the possibility of an honorable Soviet treaty diplomacy. I'm afraid though that all these hopes will only be realized, to use Nikita Khrushchev's metaphor in another context, when a shrimp learns to whistle.

An Unjustified Pessimism?

Perhaps mine is an unjustified pessimism. Yet history does not permit a sanguine disposition about Russia. I cannot forget the historic strategies of Lenin and Stalin. For, as Lenin put it, "The entire history of Bolshevism, both before and after the October Revolution is jam-packed with instances of maneuvering, temporizing and compromising with other parties (including bourgeois parties)" (Westoby 1989, 95). Milovan Djilas, the Yugoslav heretic, quotes Stalin as urging Tito at the end of World War II to accept King Peter as the monarch: "You don't have to take him back forever. Just temporarily, and then at the right moment—a knife in the back" (Ibid.).

As I write, it seems obvious that the Soviet Union has reached a dead end. Neither its social institutions nor its economic system seem capable (assuming that the Soviet *nomenklatura* would wish it) of satisfying the long-ignored needs of the Soviet peoples. We are watching in this, the last decade of the century, the decomposition of the first communist monolith, a process camouflaged by the cheery Gorbachev image. That image veils the gap between Gorbachev utterance and Gorbachev deed, in Communist Party power, certainly in arms control, in regional conflicts, imperial design (as in the Far East) and, above all, in Afghanistan.[238]

What then is the Soviet/Russian future? Is there a viable answer to a question that haunts the democracies as never before? An American foreign policy and the concomitant treaty diplomacy must base itself on a forecast of the Soviet future.

For me, the Soviet/Russian future hinges on whether or not the legitimizing ideology of Marxism-Leninism is formally and openly delegitimized by the Soviet Politburo. World peace will always be at risk so long as Marxism-Leninism reigns, even if only on paper. It must be noted that three years after the People's Republic of China announced to the world that Marxism didn't have all the "answers," the "People's Army" in June 1989 supplied a sanguinary Marxist-Leninist answer to the several thousand students and workers massed in Beijing's Tiananmen Square.

Toppled Dictatorships

The decade of the 1980s will be remembered in history when dictatorships the world over were toppled, either by forces from within or by forces from without or by both: Husak of Czechoslovakia, Honecker of East Germany, Zhivkov of Bulgaria, Ceausescu of Romania, Stroessner of Paraguay, Noriega of Panama. Ortega of Nicaragua and Pinochet of Chile lost elections. Jaruzelski's Polish Communist Party lost an election. P.W. Botha was ousted as president of South Africa. Who remained? Fidel Castro, Kim Il Sung, Qadaffi and, at this writing, Deng Ziaoping. There are others, but we can now believe that there is hope that their dictatorships are not forever.

---

238 The Soviet Union announced that, as provided under the Geneva accords, it had pulled out its soldiers from Afghanistan in February 1989. However, it left behind $1 billion of military equipment and installations for its puppet regime in Kabul. Since that withdrawal and as of October 1989, the Soviet Union has poured in $2 billion, equivalent to all U.S. aid to the Afghan resistance in nine years. Questions have even been raised about the claimed withdrawal of Soviet forces. Rep. Bill McCollum (R., Fla.) has reported that some 20,000 to 30,000 Soviet Central Asian KGB Border Guards, ethnically indistinguishable from Afghans and wearing unmarked uniforms, have been assigned to Afghanistan ("U.S. Must Reassess Afghan Policy," *Wall Street Journal* 18 October 1989, page A15).

The 1989 annual Freedom House survey showed that the 1980s had seen a global trend against dictatorships and for democratic change. Twenty-one nations in the 1980s elected civilian rulers by ousting one-party of military governments. Even South Africa can now be regarded as partly free with the release of political prisoners and some changes in apartheid restrictions ("Greed Decade Was Really the Freed Decade," *Wall Street Journal* 8 December 1989, page A10).[239]

One big question remains: What of President Gorbachev whose power has grown amazingly during these glastroika years? Will he turn out to be a democratic leader, willing to face election, or will he be a new kind of czar, a new kind of little white father, legitimized by his own personal machine within party and government? On the answer to these questions rests the important question: Can the democracies trust the Soviet Union as a treaty partner in the decades ahead? The answer: Those who have faith in President Gorbachev as a treaty partner must test that faith against the ever-present possibility that the Soviet leader could be supplanted by hard-liners of the neo-Stalin variety who would repudiate international treaty commitments with a snap of the thumb.

Mikhail Gorbachev has yet to prove to the world and to his own people that Red Square will not become Tiananmen Square tomorrow. He can only prove this when he institutionalizes freedom. Only then can we accept the Soviet Union (or whatever its new name will be) as a trustworthy practitioner of treaty diplomacy now and into the twenty-first century.

---

239 It is significant that the annual 1990 Freedom House survey of the state of freedom in the world still listed the Soviet Union among the nations that were "not free" as compared, for example, to South Africa, which the survey categorized as "partly free." And the description of South Africa as "partly free" came weeks before the release of Nelson Mandela in mid-February. It said that the Soviet Union "is clearly a country in transition, but is as yet 'not free'" ("Why the USSR is 'Not Free'," *Freedom at Issue* 112 [January-February 1990], pages 14-15 and "Case Study: Why South Africa is 'Partly Free'," pages 16-17).

Appendix A

If any one country has a right to update Virgil and say, "I fear the Russians when they come bearing treaties," it would be Afghanistan.

The number of accords between the Soviet Union and neighboring Afghanistan are in the hundreds, and the character of the instruments is most instructive, even the partial listing given below. When one ponders almost ten years (1979-89) of pitiless war visited upon Afghanistan in furtherance of the Soviet Union's quest for "absolute security" and the courage with which the Afghan people have fought the invader, there is no need to ask what the purpose was of all the made-in-Moscow treaties and aid programs since the Bolshevik revolution.

Looked at carefully, these treaties are like the silken threads a spider wraps around a future victim. They make credible the theory that the economic aid projects were intended as military preparations for a Soviet invasion.

There is little question that the Soviet Union did comply with the economic agreements. What need, after all, was there to violate the agreements when they prepared for the invasion and eventual takeover of Afghanistan? Note the 11/13/60 agreement permitting Soviet experts to explore for lapis lazuli deposits in Afghanistan, or the 1/6/66 treaty allowing Soviet "tourists" to ramble about in Afghanistan exploring ancient towns. I am sure the record of Soviet treaty compliance was 99.99 percent perfect. Except, of course, for the invasion on 27 December 1979. That was the only exception to an otherwise spotless record of compliance.

From 7 January 1958 to September 1973, well over 100 agreements, protocols, and exchange of notes were signed between the Soviet Union and Afghanistan. That's about six diplomatic instruments a year (Ginsburgs & Slusser 1981, passim). And what kind of agreements were they? Here's a sampling (Klass 1987, 148-49):

1/7/58—contract concerning Soviet aid in prospecting and surveying for oil.

1/18/58—agreement signed between the Soviet Union and Afghanistan concerning their common border; ratified by the Soviet Union 6/14/58 and by Afghanistan 8/27/58; entered into force 10/5/58 with a duration of five years, extendible every five years if not denounced six months before expiration; made possible other categories of agreements.

2/4/59—agreement regarding direct radio-telephone communications.

5/19/59—contract for reconstruction of Kabul airport.

7/18/59—agreement concerning Soviet technical aid in construction of three motor-highway bridges.

1/11/60—contract on Soviet technical aid in construction of the 750-km. Kushka-Herat-Kandahar highway.

2/18/60—exchange of letters concerning the admission of fifty Afghan workers and specialists to the Soviet Union for production-technical instruction.

5/25/60—protocol on Soviet technical aid in construction of the river port Qyzil-Qala.

11/13/60—exchange of notes constituting an agreement on assignment to Afghanistan of Soviet specialists to give technical aid in evaluating deposits of and organizing mining of deposits of lapis lazuli.

5/20/63—protocol on execution of hydrometric work on border river, Pyandzh.

10/17/63—agreement re Soviet technical aid in development of natural gas deposits in northern Afghanistan.

10/10/63—protocol granting Aeroflot transit rights through Afghanistan to Karachi and Southeast Asia.

7/19/64—Agreement on joint survey of possibility of complex utilization of hydrographic and power resources of the Pyandzh and Amu-Darya rivers.

9/24/64—exchange of notes on Soviet technical aid in construction of a city power-grid.

8/6/65—protocol on extension of duration of Treaty of Neutrality and nonaggression of 24 June 1931.

1/6/66—permission for Soviet tourists to visit any part of Afghanistan, cross the desert and explore ancient towns of Herat, Ferahrud, and Kandahar, and travel over Kushka-Herta-Kandahar road.

1/9/66—exchange of letters on questions of Soviet economic and technical assistance in construction of Mazari-Sherif-Tashguzar highway.

5/66—protocol providing for teachers from the Soviet Union to work at Kabul Polytechnical Institute and Jangalak auto-engineering school.

12/3/69—Contract on Soviet technical assistance in planning new roads.

7/21/73—Soviet recognition of the Republic of Afghanistan.

9/73—Visit to Kabul by a Soviet military delegation headed by Marshal

Semanovich followed by an increase in Soviet military aid to Afghanistan.

12/78—Treaty of Friendship and Cooperation, one of whose clauses were later cited by the Soviet Union as justifying the invasion a year later.

What the War Cost Afghanistan

The latest statistics of what the Soviet war cost Afghanistan come from a State Department official whom I interviewed in February 1989 but who asked to remain anonymous:

1. At least 9 percent of the population was killed, or 1.5 million people (in U.S. population terms, almost 20 million Americans). The total figure includes civilians and guerrilla fighters.
2. None can say for certain, but the number of Afghans wounded could be as high as 1 million, perhaps higher.
3. Fully a third of the population is in exile—3 million in Pakistan, 2 million in Iran.
4. Some 2 million Afghans were in internal exile when the Soviets retreated. For example, Kabul, which before the war had a population of less than 1 million, now has a population of 2.2 million.
5. There is no dollar figure on the destruction of Afghan towns and villages. One city, Kandahar, was destroyed by Soviet bombing.
6. Standing livestock has been destroyed for all of Afghanistan. The procommunist regime in Kabul has been importing chickens from Bulgaria.
7. There is no agriculture because for the decade of the war there was no way to grow anything. The farm land has gone untended for almost a decade.

It will take a mighty effort to restore the Afghan economy to its prewar status. The United Nations, which has undertaken an aid program, and the United States simply cannot—and should not—alone supply the resources for a country that has been a Soviet killing field for a decade.

Appendix B

The retraction of Soviet power from its present bloated and unhealthy limits is essential to the stability of world relationships.

George F. Kennan (1966, 76)

Following is a chronology of Soviet imperialism involving aggression or treaty violations by Russia since the 7 November 1917 Bolshevik Revolution. (In December 1922, Russia became the Soviet Union—i.e., the Union of Soviet Socialist Republics.)

Post World War I

Year	Victim	Status
1919	Ukraine	Annexed
1919	Byelorussia	Annexed
1920	Poland	Invaded
1920	Kazakhstan	Annexed
1920	Azerbaijan	Annexed
1920	Armenia	Annexed
1921	Georgia	Annexed
1921	Mongolia	Colonized
1924	Khiva and Bukhara	Annexed

273

World War II and Postwar

Year	Victim	Status
1939	Eastern Poland	Annexed
1940	Eastern Romania	Annexed
1940	East Prussia, north	Annexed
1944	Lithuania	Annexed
1944	Bessarabia, Bukovina	Annexed
1944	Latvia	Annexed
1944	Estonia	Annexed
1944	Poland	Occupied
1944	Bulgaria	Occupied
1944	Romania	Occupied
1944	Eastern Finland	Annexed
1944	Tannu Tuva	Annexed
1944	Hungary	Annexed
1945	Yugoslavia	Ally[240]
1945	Albania	Client State
1945	East Germany	Occupied
1945	Eastern Czechoslovakia	Annexed
1945	Eastern Austria	Occupied[241]
1945	North Korea	Soviet puppet
1945	Sakhalin Island	Annexed
1945	Kurile Islands	Annexed
1948	Czechoslovakia	Occupied
1949	China	Ally until 1960
1950	N. Korea invades S.Korea	Fails
1953	Worker uprising, 17 June	Suppressed
1954	North Vietnam	Client state
1956	Hungary uprising	Suppressed
1959	Cuba	Client state
1968	Czechoslovakia rebellion	Suppressed

240 Expelled from Soviet bloc in 1948.
241 In 1955, signed Austrian State Treaty and withdrew occupying forces from eastern Austria occupation zone.

Détente

Year	Victim	Status
1975-76	Angola	Cuba/Soviet Union Occupation[242]
1975-76	Mozambique	Cuba/Soviet Union Occupation
1975-78	Ethiopia	Cuba/Soviet Union Occupation
1977-78	South Yemen	Client State
1978	Afghanistan	Client State
1979	Cambodia	Invaded by Hanoi
1979	Grenada	Cuba/Soviet Union Occupation[243]
1979-80	Nicaragua	Client State
1979-80	Afghanistan	Invaded by Soviet Union[244]
1980	Poland	Martial rule declared

---

242 In late June 1989, a cease-fire between the Angolan government and the Savimbi UNITA forces was announced.
243 U.S. forces invaded and overthrew Soviet-directed regime.
244 Soviet troop withdrawal began in 1988, but the Soviet Union continued to provide huge military supplies to puppet regime.

Appendix C

I cherish no illusions about the Soviets ... for them, past arms control treaties were like diets. The second day was always the best, for that's when they broke them.

President Reagan (18 November 1987)

Among the many documents dealing with Soviet treaty noncompliance, I found one of the most useful to be the one prepared by the minority staff of the Senate Foreign Relations Committee (U.S. Senate 1988)[245]. What made it so helpful was that it examined "all aspects of the U.S.-Soviet relationship" rather than just the treaty alone. The memorandum raised ten questions, all of them of great significance to U.S. foreign policy.

Despite what might be assumed would be biased and partisan data, the memorandum itself is well researched. Its conclusions are obviously controversial and were intended to be so. The memorandum to Republican Senators was updated as of April 1989, almost a year after the INF Treaty went into force, and distributed by Senator Jesse Helms to his colleagues on the Senate Committee on Foreign Relations. Helms is ranking minority member.

For my purposes, the most noteworthy question that the memorandum raised was number five: "Soviet record of cheating: Does the history of

---

245 The cover of the 25 January 1988. oversize document reads:
Memorandum to: Republican Senators on the Senate Foreign Relations Committee.
From: Jesse Helms
Re: The Treaty on Intermediate-range Nuclear Weapons: Does It Decrease—or Increase—the Danger of Nuclear War?

Soviet cheating on arms control treaties make it more likely or less likely that they will cheat on the INF treaty?"

The Senate minority report found, on the basis of President Reagan's first of seven reports to Congress on Soviet SALT violations (23 January 1984), as follows:

SALT I ABM Treaty—ten confirmed violations.
SALT I Interim Agreement—five confirmed violations.
SALT II Treaty—now twenty-five confirmed violations.
Limited Test Ban Treaty—over thirty confirmed violations.
Threshold Test Ban Treaty—over twenty-four probable violations.
Biological warfare convention—multiple confirmed violations.
Geneva Protocol on Chemical Weapons—multiple confirmed violations.
Kennedy-Khrushchev Agreement—multiple confirmed violations.

Issue Number five is a summary history of confirmed Soviet violations of international security treaties since 1917 based on U.S. government documentation. Three Senate Judiciary Committee reports in 1955, 1959, and 1964 and a Defense Department report in 1962 reported more than 150 Soviet violations of international security treaties from 1917 to 1964. These violations included countries other than the United States, such as Britain, Afghanistan, and Iran.

What is striking is that from 1964 until 1984 there was, says the memorandum, "total, complete silence with regard to Soviet treaty violations" (Ibid.). That is, during the Johnson, Nixon, Ford, and Carter administrations, Soviet violations of international security treaties were kept secret from the American people and the world.

That twenty years' silence was broken 23 January 1984 with President Reagan's first report, as described above, to Congress on Soviet SALT treaty transgressions. As of the 1988 date of the memorandum, based on eleven U.S. government reports, there is now a record of more than 200 violations of international security treaties.

The updated memorandum of April 1989, referred to earlier, said that then-President Reagan reported to Congress on 2 December 1988 a whole series of violations of the INF Treaty

Intractable Problem

I have examined documents dealing with the intractable problem of Soviet treaty diplomacy published by the U.S. Arms Control and Disarmament Agency under the rubric "Soviet noncompliance." I have also examined presidential reports to Congress on Soviet noncompliance with arms control agreements as required by the 1984 Arms Control and Disarmament Act. These reports are dated 23 January 1984, 10 June 1985, 23 December 1985, 1 February 1985, 27 May 1986, 5 August 1986, 10 March 1987, and 2 December 1987. These are either White House releases by the press secretary, reports issued by the State Department's Bureau of Public Affairs or press releases by the U.S. Arms Control and Disarmament Agency. Other useful information is to be had in the ACDA series of Occasional Papers.

Richard Perle's testimony while assistant secretary of defense for international security policy before the House Foreign Affairs Committee dealt with an important ploy used by many arms control advocates who regard Soviet violations as trifling at best, as "Cold War-mongering" at worst. They accept the evidence that indicts the Soviets for cheating, but they offer as a demurrer, to quote Perle's characterization, that "while the Soviets might have violated *some* provisions of *some* agreements they had not violated *all* provisions of all agreements." He attributed this charitable view to a Stanford University faculty study that argued, again to quote Perle, that "in assessing the Soviet record on compliance we ought to consider the percentage of provisions that have been violated."

Perle acknowledged that the Soviets have violated only a few provisions of the arms control agreements, explaining that "they have only violated those provisions that they found inconvenient, those limitations that turned out to be inconsistent with their military plans."

Another series of reports on Soviet treaty compliance is to be found in the periodic reports of the International Labour Office Committee of Experts on the Application of ILO Conventions and Recommendations. These reports deal with compliance by various ILO members with the ILO Charter and ancillary engagements. Of great interest was the report to the ILO Governing Body in 1979 of the mistreatment of Soviet workers who tried to form a nongovernment trade union (International Labour Office 1979, 74ff.).

References

Acheson, Dean. 1959. *Sketches from the Life of Men I Have Known*. New York, N.Y.: Harper and Brothers.

Acheson, Dean. 1987. *Present at the Creation*. New York, N.Y.: Norton.

Adelman, Kenneth L. 1987a. *ACDA Occasional Papers*. Washington, D.C.: U.S. Arms Control and Disarmament Agency. 21 January.

Adelman, Kenneth L. 1987b. "Verification in an Age of Mobile Missiles." Address to U.S. Arms Control and Disarmament Agency, San Diego, California, 26 June. Mimeo.

Adelman, Kenneth L. 1989. *The Great Universal Embrace*. New York, N.Y.: Simon & Schuster.

Adomeit, Hannes. 1982. *Soviet Risk-Taking and Crisis Behavior: A Theoretical and Empirical Analysis*. London, England: Allen & Unwin.

Alexiev, Alexander R. 1985. "The Soviet Campaign Against INF: Strategy, Tactics, Means." (N-2280-AF, February) Santo Monica, Calif.: Rand Corporation.

Allison, Graham T. 1971. *Essence of Decision: Explaining the Cuban Missile Crisis*. Boston, Mass.: Little, Brown.

Allison, Roy. 1985. *Finland's Relations with the Soviet Union 1944-84*. London, England: Macmillan.

Aron, Raymond. 1966. *Peace and War: A Theory of International Relations*. New York, N.Y.: Doubleday.

Baring, Arnulf. 1972. *Uprisings in East Germany: June 17, 1953*. Ithaca, N.Y.: Cornell University Press.

Barron, John. 1974. *KGB*. New York, N.Y.: Reader's Digest Press.

Barron, John. 1983. *KGB Today: The Hidden Hand*. New York, N.Y.: Reader's Digest Press.

Bauer, Raymond A., Alex Inkeles, and Clyde Kluckhohn. 1956. *How The Soviet System Works*. Boston, Mass.: Harvard University Press.

Beichman, Arnold. 1987. "Soviet Active Measures and Democratic Culture." In *Soviet Strategic Deception*, edited by Brian D. Dailey and Patrick J. Parker. Lexington, Mass.: Lexington Books.

Bell, Daniel. 1966. "Marxism-Leninism: A Doctrine on the Defensive." In *The Appeals and Paradoxes of Contemporary Marxism*, edited by Milorad Drachkovitch. New York, N.Y.: Praeger.

Bell, Daniel. 1974. "The Problem of Ideological Rigidity." In *Failure of a Dream*, edited by John H.M. Laslett and Semour Martin Lipset (New York, N.Y.: Anchor Press).

Berkowitz, Bruce. 1988. *Calculated Risks: A Century of Arms Control, Why It Has Failed and How It Can Be Made to Work*. New York, N.Y.: Simon & Schuster.

Berman, Harold. 1983. *Law and Revolution: The Formation of the Western Legal Tradition*. Cambridge, Mass.: Harvard University Press.

Bernstam, Mikhail. 1988. "Economic Systems and Global Conflict: An Essay on the International Invisible Hand." Paper presented at Conference on Demographic Change and Western Security, University of London, 21 July.

Besançon, Alain. 1978. *The Soviet Syndrome*. New York, N.Y.: Harcourt, Brace.

Besançon, Alain. 1984. *Lenin and the Twentieth Century: A Bertram D. Wolfe Retrospective*, edited by Lennard D. Gerson. Stanford, Calif.: Hoover Institution Press.

Bialer, Seweryn. 1976. "The Soviet Political Elite and Internal Developments in the Soviet Union." In *The Soviet Empire: Expansion and Détente*, edited by William E. Griffith. Lexington, Mass.: Lexington Books.

Bialer, Seweryn. 1986. *The Soviet Paradox: External Expansion, Internal Decline*. New York, N.Y.: Knopf.

Blitzer, Wolf. 1989. *Territory of Lies: The Exclusive Story of Jonathan Jay Pollard: the American Who Spied on His Country for Israel and How He Was Betrayed*. New York, N.Y.: Harper & Row.

Bohlen, Charles E. 1973. *Witness to History, 1929-69*. New York, N.Y.: W.W. Norton. For a recent and highly critical review of FDR's diplomacy, see Marks 1988.

Bratov, A., trans. 1972. *The World Socialist System and anti-Communism*. Moscow, U.S.S.R.: Progress Publishers.

Brezhnev, Leonid. 1971. Report of the CPSU Central Committee to the 24th Congress of the Communist Party of the Soviet Union. Moscow, USSR: Novosti Press Agency Publishing House. 30 March.

Brezhnev, Leonid. 1972. *Following Lenin's Course*. Moscow, USSR: Progress. Publishers.

Brodie, Bernard. n.d. "The Atom Bomb as Policy Maker." In *Essays on Arms Control and National Security*. Publication #123. Washington, D.C.: U.S. Arms Control and Disarmament Agency.

Brown, Anthony Cave. 1987. *"C": The Secret Life of Sir Stewart Menzies*. New York, N.Y.: Macmillan.

Brzezinski, Zbigniew, and Samuel P. Huntington. 1965. *Political Power: USA/USSR*. New York, N.Y.: Viking Press.

Buckley, William F., Jr. 1989. *On the Firing Line*. New York, N.Y.: Random House.

Burke, Edmund. 1867. "Letters on a Regicide Peace." In *Works of Edmund Burke*, Boston, Mass.: Little, Brown.

Burke, Edmund. 1960. *Selected Works*. New York, N.Y.: Modern Library.

Byrnes, Robert F. 1976. "Can Culture Survive Cultural Agreements?" In *Détente*, edited by G. R. Urban. London, England: Universe Books.

Byrnes, Robert F. 1989. "The Soviet Ferment about Soviet History." Mimeo.

Carlucci, Frank C. 1989. *Annual Report to Congress: Fiscal Year 1990*. Washington, D.C.: Government Printing Office.

Carr, E. H. 1966. *The Bolshevik Revolution*. New York, N.Y.: Penguin.

Churchill, Winston. 1951. *Closing the Ring*. Boston, Mass.: Houghton Mifflin.

Clay, Lucius D. 1950. *Decision in Germany*. New York, N.Y.: Doubleday.

Colvin, Jan. 1971. *The Chamberlain Cabinet*. New York, N.Y.: Taplinger.

Conquest, Robert. 1967. *Soviet Nationalities Policy in Practice*. London, England: Bodley Head. For more on Georgia, see Carr 1966, 1:395-400.

Conquest, Robert. 1987. "Ideology and Deception." In *Soviet Strategic Deception*, edited by Brian D. Dailey and Patrick J. Parker. Stanford, Ca.: Hoover Press.

Cornford, Francis M., trans. 1945. *The Republic of Plato*. New York, N.Y.: Oxford University Press.

Costello, John. 1988. *Mask of Treachery*. New York, N.Y.: Morrow.

Craig, Gordon A. 1961. "Totalitarian Approaches to Diplomatic Negotiation." In *Essays on Diplomatic History in Honor of George Peabody Gooch*, edited by A. O. Sarkissian. London, England: Longmans.

Craig, Gordon A. 1962. "Techniques of Negotiation." In *Russian Foreign Policy: Essays in Historical Perspective*, edited by Ivo J. Lederer. New Haven, Conn.: Yale University Press.

Crankshaw, Edward, ed. 1970. *Khrushchev Remembers*. Boston, Mass.: Little, Brown.

Daniels, Robert V. 1988. *Is Russia Reformable? Change and Resistance from Stalin to Gorbachev*. Boulder, Colo.: Westview Press.

de Custine, Marquis. 1951. *Journey for Our Time*. Edited and translated by
   Phyllis Penn Kohler. Introduction by General Walter Bedell Smith.
   London, England: Arthur Barker.
de Sola Pool, Ithiel, Frederick W. Frey, Wilbur Schram, Nathan Maccoby,
   and Edwin B. Parker, editors. 1973. *Handbook of Communication*.
   Chicago, Il.: Rand McNally.
Degras, Jane, ed. 1951. *Soviet Documents on Foreign Policy*. Oxford,
   England: Oxford University Press.
Diplomaticheskii Slovar. 1960. Moscow, U.S.S.R.: State Publishing House
   for Political Literature
Douglass, Joseph D. Jr. 1988. *Why the Soviets Violate Arms Control Treaties*.
   McLean, Va.: Pergamon-Brassey's.
Douglass, Joseph D., Jr., and Amoretta M. Hoeber. 1979. *Soviet Strategy for
   Nuclear War*. Stanford, Calif.: Hoover Institution Press.
Dunlop, John B. 1985. "Solzhenitsyn's Reception in the the United States." In
   Solzhenitsyn in Exile, edited by Dunlop et al. Stanford, Calif.: Hoover
   Institution Press.
Dunlop, John, Richard S. Haugh, and Michael Nicholson. 1985. *Solzhenitsyn
   In Exile*. Stanford, Calif.: Hoover Institution Press.
Dziak, John. 1987. *Chekisty: A History of the KGB*. Lexington, Mass.:
   Lexington Books.
Eden, Sir Anthony. 1965. *The Memoirs of Sir Anthony Eden, Earl of Avon:
   The Reckoning*. Boston, Mass.: Houghton Mifflin.
Epstein, Edward Jay. 1989. *Deception: The Invisible War Between the KGB
   and the CIA*. New York, N.Y.: Simon and Schuster.
Fainsod, Merle. 1963. *How Russia Is Ruled*. Cambridge, Mass.: Harvard
   University Press.
Feuer, Lewis. 1986. *Imperialism and the anti-Imperialist Mind*. Buffalo,
   N.Y.: Prometheus Books.
Fitzgibbon, Louis. 1975. *Unpitied and Unknown: Katyn ... Bologoye ...
   Dergachi...* London, England: Bachman and Turner.
Friedrich, C. J. 1950. *Constitutional Government and Democracy*. Boston,
   Mass.: Ginn & Co.
Frolov, I. T., ed. 1980. *Filosofskiy slovar*, 4th ed., Moscow, U.S.S.R.
Galenson, Walter. 1982. *The International Labor Organization: Mirroring
   the U.N.'s Problems*. Washington, D.C.: Heritage Foundation.
Gates, Robert M. 1989. "Gorbachev and Critical Change in the Soviet
   Union." White House press office. Mimeo.
Gerson, Lennard D., ed. 1984. *Lenin and the Twentieth Century: A Bertram
   D. Wolfe Retrospective*. Stanford, Calif.: Hoover Institution Press.
Gerth, H. H., and C. Wright Mills, eds. 1958. *From Max Weber: Essays in
   Sociology*. Stanford, Calif.: Oxford University Press.

Gibbon, Edward. 1912. *Decline and Fall of the Roman Empire*. London, England: Methuen.

Gilmour, Ian. 1971. *The Body Politic*. London, England: Hutchinson.

Ginsburgs, G., and R. M. Slusser. 1981. *A Calendar of Soviet Treaties 1958-1973*. Dordrecht, Holland: Sijthoff & Noordhoff.

Goldwin, Robert A., ed. 1959. *Readings in Russian Foreign Policy*. New York, N.Y.: Oxford University Press.

Gorbachev, Mikhail Sergeyevich. 1988. Address to plenary meeting of the forty-third session of the UN General Assembly. 7 December. Mimeo.

Gorbachev, Mikhail. 1987. *Perestroika: New Thinking for Our Country*. New York, N.Y.: Harper & Row.

Great Soviet Encyclopedia. 1975. New York, N.Y.: Macmillan.

Harriman, W. Averell, and Elie Abel. 1975. *Special Envoy to Churchill and Stalin, 1941-46*. New York, N.Y.: Random House.

Haselkorn, Avigdor. 1978. *Evolution of Soviet Security Strategy 1965-1975*. New York, N.Y.: Crane, Russak & Co.

Hayek, Friedrich A. 1944. *The Road to Serfdom*. Chicago, Il.: University of Chicago Press.

Heller, Mikhail, and Aleksandr M. Nekrich. 1986. *Utopia in Power: The History of the Soviet Union from 1917 to the Present*. New York, N.Y.: Summit Books.

Heller, Mikhail. 1988. *Cogs in the Wheel: The Formation of Soviet Man*. New York, N.Y.: Knopf.

Henderson, Loy W. 1987. *A Question of Trust: The Origins of U.S. -Soviet Diplomatic Relations*. Stanford, Calif.: Hoover Institution Press.

Horelick, Arnold, ed. 1986. *U.S. -Soviet Relations: The Next Phase*. Ithaca, N.Y.: Cornell University Press.

Hudson, G.F. 1967. *The Hard and Bitter Peace*. New York, N.Y.: Praeger.

Iklé, Fred. 1964. *How Nations Negotiate*. New York, N.Y.: Harper & Row.

International Labour Office. 1979. Committee on Freedom of Association, 190th report, GB.209/6/6 (27 February-2 March).

International Security Council. 1985. "The Brezhnev Doctrine and the Challenge of Soviet Imperialism." Washington, D.C.: International Security Council.

Jaffe, Philip J. 1975. *The Rise and Fall of American Communism*. New York, N.Y.: Horizon Press.

James, William. 1968. "Faith and the Right to Believe." In his *Writings*. New York, N.Y.: Random House.

Jeffreys-Jones, R. 1977. *American Espionage from Secret Service to CIA*. New York, N.Y.: Free Press.

Johnson, Paul. 1983. *A History of the Modern World*. London, England: Weidenfeld and Nicolson.

Kaufman, William W. n.d. "The Requirements of Deterrence." In *Essays on Arms Control and National Security*. U.S. Arms Control and Disarmament Agency, Publication #123. Washington, D.C.: U.S. Government Printing Office.

Keep, John. 1967. "Lenin as Tactician." In *Lenin*, edited by Leonard Schapiro and Peter Reddaway. London, England: Pall Mall Press.

Kennan, George. 1960. *Russia and the West Under Lenin and Stalin*. Boston, Mass.: Little, Brown.

Kennan, George. 1966. *Realities of American Foreign Policy*. New York, N.Y.: Norton. Paperback.

Kennan, George. 1967. *Memoirs 1925-1950*. Boston, Mass.: Little Brown.

Kennan, George. 1971. *The Marquis de Custine and His Russia in 1839.* Princeton, N.J.: Princeton University Press.

Khrushchev, Nikita. 1970. *Khrushchev Remembers*. Boston, Mass.: Little Brown.

Kintner, William R. 1987. *Soviet Global Strategy*. Fairfax, Va.: Hero Books.

Kirkpatrick, Ambassador Jeane J. 1984. Speech by the former USUN ambassador to the American Society of International Law, 12 April. Mimeo.

Kissinger, Henry. 1958. *Nuclear Weapons and Foreign Policy*. New York, N.Y.: Doubleday Anchor.

Kissinger, Henry. 1969. *American Foreign Policy: Three Essays*. New York, N.Y.: Norton.

Klass, Rosanne. 1987. *Afghanistan: The Great Game Revisited*. New York, N.Y.: Freedom House.

Klose, Kevin. 1984. *Russia and the Russians*. New York, N.Y.: Norton.

Lazitch, Branko, and Milorad Drachkovitch, eds. 1972. *Biographical Dictionary of the Comintern*. Stanford, Calif.: Hoover Institution Press.

Lenin, V. I. 1902. *What Is To Be Done?* New York, N.Y.: International Publishers.

Lenin, V. I. 1917. *Collected Works*. Moscow, U.S.S.R.

Lenin, V. I. 1930. *Left Wing Communism, An Infantile Disorder*. New York, N.Y.: International Publishers.

Lenin, V. I. 1932. *Works*. 3d ed. Moscow, U.S.S.R.

Lenin, V. I. 1937. *Collected Works*. London, England: Lawrence & Wishart.

Lenin, V. I. 1943. "Speech to Moscow Party Nuclei Secretaries" (26 November 1920). In *Selected Works*. New York, N.Y.: International Publishers.

Lenin, V.I. 1924. *Collected Works*, 2d edition. Moscow, U.S.S.R.

Lenin, V.I. 1980. *Collected Works*. In *War and Peace: Soviet Russia Speaks* (Washington, D.C.: National Strategy Information Center).

Light, Margot. 1988. *The Soviet Theory of International Relations*. London, England: St. Martin's Press.

Lynch, Allen. 1987. *The Soviet Study of International Relations*. Cambridge, Mass.: Cambridge University Press.

Machiavelli, Niccolo. 1950. *The Discourses*. New York, N.Y.: Modern Library.

Machiavelli, Niccolo. 1960. *The Prince*. Milan, Italy: Feltrinelli.

Mannheim, Karl. 1936. *Ideology and Utopia*. New York, N.Y.: Harcourt, Brace, World.

Marks, Frederick W. III. 1988. *Wind Over Sand: The Diplomacy of Franklin Roosevelt*. Athens, Ga.: University of Georgia Press.

Marx, Karl, and Friedrich Engels. 1967. *The Communist Manifesto*. New York, N.Y.: Penguin. A.J.P. Taylor, who wrote the introduction, says (page 7) that the Marx-Engels tract "contains the essential doctrines of the outlook known as Marxism."

Marx, Karl. 1972. "Circular Letter to Bebel, Liebknecht, Bracke and Others." In *The Marx-Engels Reader*, edited by Robert C. Tucker. New York, N.Y.: Norton. Paperback.

McLellan, David S. 1969. "Comparative 'Operational Codes' of Recent U.S. Secretaries of State: Dean Acheson." Paper read at American Political Science Association (APSA) annual meeting.

Medvedev, Roy. 1983. *All Stalin's Men*. Oxford, England: Oxford University Press.

Menges, Constantine. 1988. *Inside the National Security Council*. New York, N.Y.: Simon & Schuster.

Merglen, Brig. Gen. Albert (ret.). 1985. "The Strategic Implications of the Brezhnev Doctrine for Western Europe." In *International Security and the Brezhnev Doctrine*. Washington, D.C.: International Security Council.

Micunovic, Veljko. 1980. *Moscow Diary*. New York, N.Y.: Doubleday.

Minogue, Kenneth. 1985. *Alien Powers: The Pure Theory of Ideology*. New York, N.Y.: St. Martin's.

Montesquieu, Charles Louis. 1977. *Spirit of Laws*, edited by David Wallace Carrithers. Berkeley, Calif.: University of California Press.

Moore, John Norton. 1985. "The Brezhnev Doctrine and the Radical Regime Assault on the Legal Order." Paper delivered at Conference on International Security and the Brezhnev Doctrine 10 June. Mimeo.

Mosely, Philip. 1951. "Some Soviet Techniques of Negotiation." In *Negotiating with the Russians*, edited by Raymond Dennett and Joseph E. Johnson (New York, N.Y.: World Peace Foundation).

Moynihan, Senator Daniel Patrick. 1980. *Count Your Blessings*. Boston, Mass.: Little Brown.

Murphy, Robert. 1964. *Diplomat Among Warriors*. New York, N.Y.: Doubleday.

National Strategy Information Center. 1981. *Intelligent Layperson's Guide to Nuclear Freeze and Peace Debate*. Washington, D.C.

Nicolson, Harold. 1954. *Evolution of Diplomatic Method*. London, England: Constable.

Nicolson, Harold. 1964. *Diplomacy* New York, N.Y.: Oxford University Press.

Nisbet, Robert. 1989. *Roosevelt and Stalin: The Failed Courtship*. Washington, D.C.: Regnery/Gateway.

Nixon, Richard. 1988. *1999: Victory Without War*. New York, N.Y.: Simon and Schuster.

Orwell, George. 1965. "Notes on Nationalism." In *Decline of the English Murder & Other Essays*. Middlesex, England: Penguin.

Payne, James L. 1989. *Why Nations Arm?* Oxford, England: Basil Blackwell.

Pipes, Richard. 1972. "Some Operational Principles of Soviet Foreign Policy." In International Negotiation, Memorandum to U.S. Senate, Subcommittee on National Security and International Operations. Washington, D.C.: U.S. Government Printing Office.

Pipes, Richard. 1984. *Survival Is Not Enough: Soviet Realities and America's Future*. New York, N.Y.: Simon and Schuster.

Pipes, Richard. 1986. "Expansionism and the Soviet System." In *Security of the Northern Flank and the Baltic Approaches*. Washington, D.C.: International Security Council.

Podhoretz, Norman. 1987. "Speech at Committee for the Free World, May 2, 1987." In *Proceedings*. New York, N.Y.: Orwell Press.

Pye, Lucian and Sidney Verba, eds. 1965. *Political Culture and Political Development*. Princeton, N.J.: Princeton University Press. Political culture is defined by the authors as consisting "of the system of empirical beliefs, expressive symbols, and values which define the situation in which political action takes place. It provides the subjective orientation to politics."

Radvanyi, Janos. 1972. *Hungary and the Superpowers*. Stanford, Ca.: Hoover Institution Press.

Reagan, Ronald. 1986. "Speech by President Reagan, November 21, 1985." In *The Summit and the Peace Process: Addresses by President Reagan 1985*. Stanford, Ca.: Hoover Institution.

Regan, Donald T. 1989. *For the Record*. New York, N.Y.: St. Martin's Press.

Romerstein, Herbert, and Stanislav Levchenko. 1989. *The KGB Against the "Main Enemy": How the Soviet Intelligence Services Operates Against the United States*. Lexington, Mass.: Lexington Books.

Ruarz, Zdzislaw M. 1988. "The Soviet Approach to Arms Control." In *Why the Soviets Violate Arms Control Treaties.*, edited by Joseph Douglass Jr. McLean, Va.: Pergamon-Brassey's.

Rusk, Dean. 1976. "Coexistence without sanctimony." In *Détente*, edited by G. R. Urban. London, England: Universe Books.

Russell, Bertrand. 1920. *Bolshevism: Practice and Theory*. New York, N.Y.: Harcourt, Brace and Howe.

Russell, Bertrand. 1950. *Unpopular Essays*. New York, N.Y.: Simon & Schuster.

Schapiro, Leonard, ed. 1950. *Soviet Treaty Series*. Washington, D.C.: Georgetown University Press.

Schapiro, Leonard. 1970. "International Negotiation." U.S. Senate. Committee on Government Operations. Subcommittee on National Security, 91st Cong., 2d session (16 April).

Senja, Jan. 1982. *We Will Bury You*. London, England: Sidgwick & Hudson.

Sherwood, Robert E. 1948. *Roosevelt and Hopkins*. New York, N.Y.: Harper.

Shevchenko, Arkady N. 1985. *Breaking With Moscow*. New York, N.Y.: Knopf.

Shirer, William L. 1961. *End of a Berlin Diary*. New York, N.Y.: Popular Library.

Shultz, George. 1985. "Address to the Commonwealth Club of San Francisco 22 February." *Current Policy* (U.S. State Department) no. 659.

Sivard, Ruth Leger. 1989. "World Military and Social Expenditures, 1987-1988." Washington, D.C.: World Priorities.

Snow, Edgar. 1958. *Journey to the Beginning*. New York, N.Y.: Random House.

Solzhenitsyn, Alexander. 1972. *Nobel Lecture*. New York, N.Y.: Farrar, Straus & Giroux.

Solzhenitsyn, Alexander. 1975. Speech to AFL-CIO. 30 June.

Sontag, R. J., and J. S. Beddie, eds. 1948. *Nazi-Soviet Relations 1939-1941. Documents from the Archives of the German Foreign Office.* Washington, D.C.: U.S. Department of State.

Sorensen, Theodore C. 1966. *Kennedy*. New York, N.Y.: Bantam.

Soviet Constitution. 1985. Moscow, U.S.S.R.: Novosti Publishing House.

Spaulding, Wallace. 1988. *1987 Yearbook on International Communist Affairs*. Edited by Richard Staar. Stanford, Calif.: Hoover Institution Press.

Speakes, Larry. 1988. *Speaking Out: the Reagan Presidency from Inside the White House*. New York, N.Y.: Avon.

Staar, Richard F., ed. 1986. *Public Diplomacy: USA Versus Soviet Union*. Stanford, Ca.: Hoover Institution Press.

Staar, Richard F., ed. 1990. *1989 Yearbook on International Communist Affairs*. Stanford, Calif.: Hoover Institution Press.

Stalin, J. V. 1954. *Works*. Moscow, U.S.S.R.: Foreign Languages Publishing House.

Stalin, J. V. n.d. *Leninism*. New York, N.Y.: International Publishers.

Stalin, J. V. 1933. *Collected Works*. Moscow, U.S.S.R.: Foreign Languages Publishing House.

Steel, Ronald. 1980. *Walter Lippmann and the American Century*. Boston, Mass.: Little Brown.

Steinberg, I. N. 1953. *In the Workshop of the Revolution*. New York, N.Y.: Rinehart.

Stephanson, Anders. 1989. *Kennan and the Art of Foreign Policy*. Cambridge, Mass.: Harvard University Press.

Tatu, Michel. 1980. *Power in the Kremlin: From Khrushchev to Kosygin*. New York, N.Y.: Viking.

Taubman, William. 1982. *Stalin's American Policy*. New York, N.Y.: W.W. Norton.

Thatcher, Prime Minister Margaret. 1985. Address to a joint meeting of the U.S. Congress February 20, 1985. New York, N.Y.: British Information Services. PR 4.

Thayer, Charles W. 1959. *Diplomat*. New York, N.Y.: Harper.

Tolstoy, Nikolai. 1977. *The Secret Betrayal 1944-1947*. New York, N.Y.: Scribners. The book's British title was Victims of Yalta.

Topitsch, Ernst. 1987. Stalin's War. New York, N.Y.: St. Martin's Press.

Trilling, Lionel. 1958. Introduction to *The Broken Mirror* edited by Pawel Mayewski. New York, N.Y.: Random House.

Trilling, Lionel. 1971. *Sincerity and Authenticity*. Cambridge, Mass.: Harvard University Press.

Triska, Jan F., and Robert M. Slusser. 1962. *The Theory, Law, and Policy of Soviet Treaties*. Stanford, Calif.: Stanford University Press.

Truman, Margaret, ed. 1989. The Personal and Private Writings of Harry S. Truman. New York, N.Y.: Warner Books.

U.S. Arms Control and Disarmament Agency. n.d. Essays on Arms Control and National Security (publication #123). Washington, D.C.

U.S. Congress. 1987. *Congressional Record*. Senate. 100th Cong., 1st sess., 133(58). Washington, D.C.: U.S. Government Printing Office.

U.S. Department of State. 1973. Publication 8733 (August). Washington, D.C.: U.S. Government Printing Office.

U.S. Department of State. 1975. "Conference on Security and Co-Operation in Europe Final Act., Helsinki, Finland." Bureau of Public Affairs, Office of Media Services. General Foreign Policy Series 298.

U.S. Department of State. 1987. "Soviet Influence Activities: A Report on Active Measures and Propaganda, 1986-87." (Publication 9627) (August). Washington, D.C.: U.S. Government Printing Office.

U.S. Government Printing Office. 1974. *Public Papers of the Presidents of the United States: Richard M. Nixon, 1972*. Washington, D.C.: U.S. Government Printing Office.

U.S. Information Agency. 1988. "Soviet Active Measures in the Era of Glasnost." Washington, D.C.: U.S. Government Printing Office. June.

U.S. Secretary of State. 1959. Treaty text TIAS 4362, section XII, part 3. In United States Treaties and Other International Agreements. Washington, D.C.: U.S. Government Printing Office.

U.S. Senate. 1961a. Hearings. Judiciary Committee, Subcommittee to investigate the administration of the Internal Security Act (87th Cong., first sess.). Washington, D.C.: Government Printing Office.

U.S. Senate. 1961b. Report. Judiciary Committee, Internal Security Subcommittee. 16 June. Washington, D.C.: U.S. Government Printing Office. The subcommittee report includes a literal translation of the speech from the Russian by a Western translator and the version, quite different and somewhat softened for Western consumption, that ran in the World Marxist Review January 1961.

U.S. Senate. 1969. "The Soviet Approach to Negotiation: Selected Writings." Compiled by Committee on Government Operations, Subcommittee on National Security and International Operations. Washington, D.C.: Government Printing Office.

U.S. Senate. 1988. "The Treaty on Intermediate-range Nuclear Weapons." Memorandum to Republican Senators on the Senate Foreign Relations Committee from Jesse Helms, 25 January.

Ulam, Adam B. 1974. *Expansion & Coexistence: The History of Soviet Foreign Policy 1917-1967*. New York, N.Y.: Praeger.

Ulam, Adam B. 1983. "The World Outside." In *After Brezhnev*, edited by Robert F. Byrnes. Bloomington, In.: Indiana University Press.

Urban, George. 1982. "From Containment to Self- Containment." In *Stalinism: Its Impact on Russia and the World*. London, England: Maurice Temple Smith.

Volten, Peter M. E. 1982. *Brezhnev's Peace Program: A Study of Soviet Domestic Political Process and Power*. Boulder, Colo.: Westview Press.

Voslensky, Michael. 1984. *Nomenklatura: The Soviet Ruling Class*. New York, N.Y.: Doubleday.

Wallop, Malcolm, and Angelo Codevilla. 1987. *The Arms Control Delusion*. San Francisco, Ca.: ICS Press.

Weeks, Albert L., ed. 1987. "Speech to the Lenin School of Political Warfare" (1931). In Brassey's *Soviet and Communist Quotations*. McLean, Va.: Pergamon-Brassey's.

Westoby, Adam. 1989. *The Evolution of Communism*. New York, N.Y.: Free Press.

Wheeler-Bennett, John. 1963. *Brest-Litovsk: The Forgotten Peace*. London, England: Macmillan.

Whelan, Joseph G. 1979. *Soviet Diplomacy and Negotiating Behavior: Emerging New Context for U.S. Diplomacy*. House Document No. 96-238 (96th Congress, 1st session).

Wight, Martin. 1966. *Diplomatic Investigations*. Cambridge, Mass.: Harvard University Press.

Wright, Peter. 1987. *Spycatcher*. New York, N.Y.: Bantam Doubleday.

Young, Harry F. 1987. *Atlas of the Soviet Union*. U.S. Department of State publication 9621 (September 1987). Washington, D.C.: U.S. Bureau of Public Affairs.

Zawodny, J. K. 1962. *Death in the Forest: The Story of the Katyn Forest Massacre*. Notre Dame, Ind.: University of Notre Dame Press. This book has been reprinted by Hippocrene Books (New York) as a paperback. On this topic, see also Fitzgibbon 1975.

Index

ABM Treaty, 5, 54, 199, 235; and
Soviet violations, 55-56,
(Buckley) 253-54.
Acheson, Dean, 143-44, 174, 175
Adelman, Kenneth, 13, 43, 174; on
Soviet cheating, 17-18, 20; on
arms control, 158-59, 182, 199
Adomeit, Hannes, 73
Afghanistan, 41, 168; and Geneva
accords, 12, 88, 152; invasion
of, 100-102, 210-14, (Carter)
138; agreement with Pakistan,
215; Russian withdrawal from,
266, (*New York Times*) 236;
treaties, agreements with
Soviet Union, 269-71; and cost
of war, 271
AFL-CIO, 196-97, 202, 225
Agee, James, 79
"Agreement...for Cooperation in
Exchanges in the Scientific,
Technical, Educational and
Cultural Fields in 1960-61,"
196
Agreement on the Control
Mechanism in Germany
(1944), 185

Ambartsumov, Evgenii, 221
Anderson, Martin, 151
Andropov, Yuri V., 70, 203, 238;
and Afghanistan, 102, 211; on
opposition of Socialism and
Imperialism, 128. *About;*
(Bush) 85
Anglo-Soviet Treaty (1942), 124
Antiballistic Missiles Treat. *See*
ABM Treaty
AP. *See* Associated Press
Arbatov, Georgi, 129
Aron, Raymond, 8-9
Associated Press, 27, 172
Austrian State Treaty (1955), 144,
188-89, 199

Baker, Howard, 15
Baker, James, 146, 155, 226
Baltic states, 166-68, 260
Barron, John, 112
Bauer, Raymond A., 41, 74
Bebler, Ales, 215
Beichman, Arnold: answers
objections, critics, 3-4, 58-60;
skeptical, pessimistic of change
in Soviet system, 67, 260, 262,

265; questions Gorbachev's future Declarations (1955 and 1988), 169-70, 214
Belloc, Hilaire, 262
Bellow, Saul, 30
Bennett, William, 119
Berkowitz, Bruce, 189
Berlin, Sir Isiah, 213
Berlin, 81; Berlin Wall, 53-54, (Gorbachev on) 184; Berlin Blockade, 143-44, 184; East Berlin, attacks on U.S. personnel in, 184-96
Berman, Harold, 109
Besançon, Alain, 7, 64, 75, 192
Bestuzhev-Lada, Igor, 182
Bevin, Ernest, 144, 192
Bialer, Seweryn, 70-71, 262
Bickel, Alexander, 108
Billington, James, 188
Bismarck, Otto Eduard Leopold von, 253
Bogomolov, Oleg T., 101, 117, 223
Bohlen, Charles, 34, 75
Boldyrev, Vladimir, 248-49
Borchgrave, Arnaud de. See De Borchgrave, Arnaud
Borovik, Genrikh A., 87
Bovin, Alexander, 32, 33, 65-66, 210-11
Brest-Litovsk Treaty, 12, 31-33
Brezhnev, Leonid Ilych, 203; and invasion of Afghanistan, 102; no law under, 114; on Soviet foreign policy, 116; on the collapse of imperialism, 124; and "nuclear freeze," 125; on triumph of the Socialist cause, 128; and invasion of Czechoslovakia, 209; and Yom Kippur War, 200-201; and detente, 218. About: (Gates)

47, (Andropov) 70
Brezhnev Doctrine, 6, 133, 168, 170, 171, 205-27 passim; and Nixon, 216-217; and Gorbachev, 219-20, 226, 239; "Alive or dead" tests for, 225; and Afghanistan, 239. About: (Ullman) 170, (Abartsumov) 219, 221, (London Economist) 219, 220-21, (Bogomolov) 223, (Gerasimov) 223, (Shakhnazarov) 224, (Tass) 224, (Baker) 226
Brock, David, 151
Brodie, Bernard, 99, 229
Brown, Harold, 177
Brzezinski, Zbigniew, 127, 228, 255
Buckley, William F., 253-54
Bukovsky, Harold, 133
Burke, Edmund, 95
Bush, George, 46, 48, 85, 118
Buzychkin, Vadim, 158

Caldicott, Helen, 125-27
Cannon, Lou, 146
Carter, Jimmie, 77, 137-38, 152
Central Intelligence Agency. See CIA
Chamberlain, Neville, 30, 72-73, 77
Chayes, Abram, 6, 92
Chernobyl, 127
Chicherin, Georgi V., 31, 131, 170
Churchill, Winston, 82-83, 89, 118, 239; and Katyn massacre, 84-85
CIA, 201, 244
CIA. See AFL-CIO
Clausewitz, Karl von, 93, 131
Codevilla, Angelo, 30-31, 138, 229
Colman, Martin, 254-55
Colville, John, 81

Cominform, 123, 130
Comintern, 36, 37, 123, 178
Communist Information Bureau.
    See Cominform
Communist International. See
    Comintern
Communist Party of the Soviet
    Union. See Soviet Communist
    Party
Commynes, Philippe de, 8
Conference of the Communist and
    Workers' Parties of Europe
    (1976), 85
Conference on Security and
    Cooperation in Europe
    (CSCE), 19, 154; Helsinki
    Final Act, 151-54; Helsinki
    process, 18, 154, 156; Helsinki
    Accords, 170-71
Congress of the United States. See
    U.S. Congress
Conquest, Robert, 167, 233, 252
Constitution of the Soviet Union.
    See under Soviet Union
CPSU. See Soviet Communist Party
Craig, Gordon A., 125, 208
Cuban missile crisis, 7, 53, 175,
    176
Custine, Marquis de, 194
Czechoslovakia, 209, 224

Daily Worker, 36
Danilov, Nicholas, 154
Davies, Joseph E., 78-79
Davis, Angela, 66
Dawisha, Karen, 220
De Borchgrave, Arnaud, 142-43
De Commynes, Philippe de. See
    Commynes, Philippe de
De Custine, Marquis de. See
    Custine, Marquis de
Diplomatischeskii Slovar, 103

Disraeli,l Benjamin, 5-6, 257
Djilas, Milovan, 3, 116, 117, 265
Dobrynin, Anatolii, 123-24
Donaldson, Robert, 64
Dravin, Abram Borisovich, 247-48
Dubinin, Yuri, 42-43, 44, 173
Dukakis, Michael, 125-126
Dulles, John Foster, 79
Duranty, Walter, 102
Dziak, John, 117, 122

East Berlin. See under Berlin
East Germany. See under U.S. State
    Department
Economist. See London Economist
Eden, Anthony, 84, 86
Egorov, Boris, 157
Eisenhower, Dwight D., 81-82
Elliot, Iain, 248
Estonia, See Baltic states

Fainsod, Merle, 116-17, 207
Falin, Valentin M., 167-68, 243-44
Feith, Douglas J., 22
Finland, 168, 169
FMDs (Free Market Democracies),
    14, 22, 23, 94
Force Ratios, 49
Fossedal, Greg, 142
Freedom House, 154; its 1989
    survey, 260, 266-67; its 1990
    survey, 267
Friedrich, C.J., 20
Fukuyama, Francis, 256

Galvin, John, 48
Gankovsky, Yuri V., 101
Gates, Robert, 45-48, 146; his
    U.S.-Soviet meeting agenda,
    46-47
GATT (General Agreement on
    Tariffs and Trade), 105

Geneva Accords. *See under*
　　Afghanistan
George, Lloyd, 104
Georgia (USSR), 164-66
Gerasimov, Gennadi, 149, 205, 223
Germany: East Germany, 184, 237;
　　Nazi Germany, 107, 117-18,
　　260. *See also* Berlin
Ghanaian Times, 173-74
Gibbon, Edward, 83, 157
Gillespie, J. David, 59
Glasnost Compliance Register
　　(GCR), 245-46
Glasnost (Soviet journal), 109
Glynn, Patrick, 22, 253
Goebbels, Josef, 98
Goldstücker, Eduard, 217
Goodby, James, 236
Gorbachev, Mikhail, 7, 17, 19, 56,
　　72, 245, 256, 257, 259-67
　　passim; and Article 6, 2; and
　　Western opinion, credence, 4,
　　5, 12, (newspaper polls) 199-
　　20; and arms cut, 44; and
　　Marxism-Leninism, 64, 68,
　　226; and censorship, 111; his
　　changes, reforms, 229-30, 239-
　　40, 246-47, 251, (questioned)
　　246-47; and the Brezhnev
　　Doctrine, 219-21; the
　　"Gorbachev Doctrine," 224;
　　Gorbachevian New Economic
　　Policy, 263-64. *Quoted:* his
　　speech to UN (1988), 11-12;
　　on peace, 33; on one-party
　　system, 40; on proletarian
　　internationalism, 63; from his
　　book, *Perestroika,* 96, 131,
　　(Hungarian edition) 132; on
　　class antagonism, 69; on Soviet
　　unreadiness for private
　　property, competing parties,

89; his speech at Bolshevik
　　70th anniversary (1987), 130,
　　150; on peaceful competition,
　　131; and Soviet libel of U.S.,
　　174; on Stalin, 181, 182; on the
　　Berlin Wall, 184; on threat to
　　the socialist system, 219.
　　About: (Revel) 1, (Simes) 33,
　　(Thatcher), 41, 233, (Gates)
　　47-48, 146, (Besançon) 64,
　　(Caldicott) 125, (Carter) 138,
　　(Reagan) 146, (Ullman) 170,
　　(Schoepflin) 223, (*New York
　　Times*) 231-32, (Kennan) 234-
　　35, (Kissinger) 234, (Goodby)
　　236, (I.F. Stone) 239, (J.J.
　　Stone) 250-51, (Beichman) 267
Gorizia (Italian cruiser), 72
Great Soviet Encyclopedia, 17, 59,
　　207, 208
Gromyko, Andrei, 7-8, 144; and
　　Afghanistan, 102; on American
　　and Soviet foreign policy, 85-
　　86; on the commonwealth of
　　socialist states, 121; on
　　peaceful coexistence, 129
Gustafson, Thane, 249

Hail, Gus, 140-41
Harriman, Averell, 76, 212
Harries, Owen, 94
Hartley, Anthony, 139
Hartman, Arthur, A., 172
Hecht, Chic, 186, 187
Heller, Mikhail, 50, 178
Helms, Jesse, 277-78
Helsinki Accords, Final Act,
　　process. *See under* Conference
　　on Security and Cooperation in
　　Europe (CSCE)
Henderson, Loy W., 34-35
Hoeber, Amoretta M., 22

Hochman, Jiri, 220
Hoffer, Eric, 75
Hong Kong, 107
Hook, Sidney, 18, 76, 242, 243
Hopkins, Harry, 76
House of Representatives. See
    under U.S. Congress
Hughes, John, 249-50
Hungary, uprising of 1956, 52, 105-
    106, 107
Huntington, Samuel, 95
Huskey, Eugene, 113-14

Iklé, Fred, 51-52, 193-94
ILO, 27-30, 279
INF Treaty, 54-55, 56, 140; and
    Symms' amendment; 141-42;
    and Helms' memorandum,
    277-78
Inkeles, Alex, 74
Intermediate Range Nuclear Forces
    Treaty. See INF Treaty
International Labor Organization.
    See ILO
International Monetary Fund, 105
Iran, 188; Iran-Contra affair, 106-
    107
Iraq, 21
Israel, 95
Izvestia, 64-65; on the legal code
    and dissidence, 110-11; on the
    KGB, 112; on journeying in
    the Soviet Union, 157; and
    Guyana suicides, 173
Izvestia Tsk KPSS, 148

James, William, 23
Jefferson, Thomas, 109, 256
Johnson, Lyndon B., 13
Johnson, Paul, 81
Johnson, Samuel, 20, 25

Kador, Janos, 216
Kamenka, Eugene, 114
Kampelman, Max M., 110, 134-35,
    156, 218
Kapitsa, Petr, 144
Katyn massacre, 83-85
Kellogg-Briand Pact (1928), 26
Kecskemeti, Paul, 124
Kennan, George F., 26, 34, 67, 131,
    236, 240; on Roosevelt and
    Stalin, 82; on world law and
    U.S. dilemma, 103-104; on
    Russian ignorance of friendly
    relations, 135-36; on the
    Belgrade Declaration, 169; his
    warnings on negotiating with
    the Soviet Union, 191; on
    Gorbachev, 234-35; on self-
    enforcing agreements, 235
Kennedy, John F., 53, 175-76
Kennedy, Joseph P., 77
Kethly, Anna, 105-106
KGB, 111-13, 244
Krushchev, Nikita, 53, 179, 203,
    208; and Cuban crisis, 53, 176;
    his "bury" metaphor, 96-97;
    remarks to Stevenson, 98; on
    teachings of Marx, Engels,
    Lenin, 128
Kirilenko, Andrei, 100
Kierkegaard, Sören, 10, 38
Kissinger, Henry: as critic of the
    State Department, 15-16; on
    the ILO, 28; on deterrence, 38;
    on communist ideology, 65;
    and Solzhenitsyn (Kissinger-
    Scowcroft memo), 79-81; on
    diplomatic good faith, 104; on
    U.S. viewed as obstacle, 120;
    Kissinger-Sonnenfeldt
    Doctrine, 217; as "centrist,"
    234; on enforcement of

agreements, 235. *About:*
(Besançon) 104, (*London
Economist*) 104, (Solzhenitsyn)
118, (Rostow) 201
Kloss, Kevin, 112
Kluckhohn, Clyde, 74
Kobysh, Vitaly, 102
Kolakowski, Leszek, 108, 138, 190,
247
Kommunist, 12, 65
Koppel, Ted, 5
Kortunov, V., 103
Kovalev, S., 210
Kozlowski, Maciej, 241
Kozyrev, Andrei, 240
Kramer, Jane, 264
Krasnaya Zveszda, 185, 211
Krasnoyarsk radar, 55-56, 235
Krauthammer, Charles, 126
Kristol, Irving, 122
Kudrin, Leonid, 114
Kudryavtsev, Gennadii, 19

Latvia. *See* Baltic states
Lazitch, Branko, 135
Lenczowski, John, 56
Lenin, V.I., 2, 16, 131, 239-40; and
Brest-Litovsk Treaty, 31, 32,
33; and system of law
(Kolakowski) 108. *Quoted:* 17,
97, 135, 196; on control over
capitalism, 73; on ideology,
92-93; on temporizing, 93; on
violence, 93; on defeating
capitalism, 95-96; on
communist morality, 99; on
exploiting opposition, 116; on
conflict being unavoidable,
129; on a single, worldwide
Soviet, 130; on diplomacy,
133-34; his "first" and
"second" principles, 159; his

forgotten statements, 164; on
secession, 206-207; on
Bolshevism and compromising,
265. *About:* (Stalin) 58, (Pipes)
147-48, (Gorky) 148, (Russell)
148
Leninism. *See* Marxism-Leninism
Leonhard, Wolfgang, 113
Liberman, Adam, 142
Libya, 140-41
Ligachev, Yegor K., 27-28
Lippmann, Walter, 79, 139
Literaturnaya Gazeta, 265; its
roundtable on law, 109-10
Lithuania. *See* Baltic states
Litvinoff, Maxim, 82, 257;
"Litvinov Pact," 3;6
Loewenheim, Francis L., 77
London Economist, 29, 39, 41-42,
45, 104, 263; on Soviet POWs,
195; on the Brezhnev Doctrine,
219, 220-21; on East Germany,
237
Los Angeles Times, 173
Luers, William H., 251
Luttwak, Edwin, 48, 232
Lynch, Allen, 59

Machiavelli, Niccolo, 160, 248
MAD Doctrine, 62
Mannheim, Karl, 71, 197-98
Manuilsky, Dmitri Z., 129
Marx, Karl, 17, 74
Marxism-Leninism, 6, 32, 59, 64;
Marxist-Leninist states,
changes needed in, 1;
Roosevelt's misunderstanding
of, 7, 35-37; and Gorbachev,
68, 226; in educational
institutions, 68, 89; on war, 69;
and treaty diplomacy,
questions on, 70; and Soviet

leaders, 70-71, 121-22; ignored
by Western leaders, 83; Soviet
retreat from, 89; grants
legitimacy, 95; its five
components, 95; regards
agreements as temporary, 116;
and the "enemy," 117; its aims
uncompromisable, 127; its
ultimate aim, 130; Leninism
and self-determination of
minorities, 206-207; Leninism
delegitimizes "bourgeois
diplomacy," 207; Leninism and
Brezhnev Doctrine, 207, 219;
and no fundamental change,
228; and international law,
228; era being left behind, 257,
259; needs to be delegitimized,
266. *About:* (Gates) 47-48,1
(Nogee and Donaldson) 64,
(*Kommunist*) 65; (Odom) 69,
(Fainsod) 117, (Stalin) 127
Massacre at Beijing (June 1989).
See under Tiananmen Square
McCollum, Bill, 266
Meany, George, 80, 196-97
Medvedev, Roy, 68, 182
Meyer, Alfred, 93
Micunovic, Veljko, 215-16
Mill, John Stuart, 4, 250
Minogue, Kenneth, 61
Molotov, V.M., 131, 167
Molotov-Ribbentrop Pact (1939),
167-68; Hitler's treaty, 117-18;
Nazi-Soviet Pact, 179
Montesquieu, Baron Charles Louis
de Secondat, 13
Montreux Convention (1936), 141
Moscow News, 240-41
Mosely, Philip, 134, 192-93
Moynihan, Daniel Patrick, 177-78
Mutually Assured Destruction

Doctrine, *See* MAD Doctrine

Nagy, Imre, 105, 216
Nazi Germany. *See under* Germany
Nazi-Soviet Pact. *See under*
Molotov-Ribbentrop Pact
(1939)
NBC/*Wall Street Journal* Poll. *See
under* Polls
Nekrich, Alexander, 50, 178
Neue Zuercher Zeitung, 86-87, 123
New Times, 173, 240
New York Times, 87, 186, 225; on
Soviet treaty violations, 55-56;
on human rights agreements,
230; on Gorbachev, 231-32; on
Afghanistan, 236
News Polls. *See Polls*
Nicholson, Arthur D., 184-85
Nicolson, Sir Harold, 8, 254
Niebuhr, Reinhold, 77
Nisbet, Robert, 81
Nixon, Richard, 39, 191, 192, 203;
on Eisenhower and Suez, 82;
on detente, 85, 202; on summit
meetings, 175; on Stalin and
Gorbachev, 182; on negotiating
with the Russians, 199-200; on
Soviet foreign policy, 201; and
the Brezhnev Doctrine, 216-17
Nogee, Joseph L., 64
Novak, Michael, 151, 52
Novoe Vremya, 33, 240
Nunn, Sam, 54

Oakley, Phyllis, 174
Odom, William E., 69, 263
O'Malley, Owen, 84
Orwell, George, 71-72

Pakistan, 88
Pashukanis, E.B., 114

Patton, George, 81
Payne, James L., 48-49
Pentagon, 186-87, 203; its Defense
    Planning Guidance, 4-5
Perle, Richard, 126, 140, 235, 279
Philosophical Dictionary, 102
Pipes, Richard, 7, 62, 75, 147-48;
    on Soviet regime, 201-03; on
    mutual deterrence, 190-91; on
    the Cold War, 236
Plato, 230
PLO, 21
Plutnik, Albert, 44-45
Podhoretz, Norman, 139
Poland, 217, 241, 260
Politburo, 113
Polls, 119-20; *Wall Street
    Journal*/NBC News Poll, 118
Popov, Vladimir, 262-63
Potsdam Agreement (1945), 184
Powell ,Colin, 151
Pravda, 111, 171, 219; on
    responsibility to Communist
    community, 210; on
    Afghanistan, 211; on fax
    machines, 248
Prokhanov, Alexandr, 101

Reagan, Ronald, 54, 56, 80, 85, 86;
    on Soviet treaty violations, 57,
    278; compared to Gorbachev in
    polls, 119; on the House of
    Representatives, 142-43; as
    realissimist, 144; his
    transformation, 145-47, 150;
    on Gorbachev, 146; his
    misunderstanding of Lenin,
    149, 151; his hardheaded
    judgments, 150. *About:*
    (Regan) 7, 21, 154, (Brock)
    151
Reddaway, Peter, 113

Regan, Donald, 7, 20-21, 154
Revel, Jean-François, 1-2, 86, 228-
    29, 241; on economic detente,
    105; on Soviet treaty
    diplomacy, 135
Ribnikar, Ivan, 264
Richardson, Lewis F., 94
Rocca, Raymond, 161
Rodino, Peter, 80
Rood, Harold, 213
Roosevelt, Franklin D., 30, 35-37,
    79; his misunderstanding of
    Stalin, 75-77, 81, 82; and the
    League for American writers,
    76; and Chamberlain, 77
Rostow, Eugene, 201
Rowney, Edward, 139-40
Ruarz, Zdzislaw M., 63
Rupnik, Jacques, 247
Rusk, Dean, 53-54, 193
Russell, Bertrand, 10, 17, 148
Russian Liberation Army. *See*
    Vlasov Army

Safire, William, 15, 155-56, 225
Sakharov, Andrei, 252
SALT, 278
Schapiro, Leonard, 72
Schifter, Richard, 153
Schoepflin, George, 223
Schopenhauer, Arthur, 23
Scowcroft, Brent, 79-81, 146
SDI, 46, 54, 86, 229, 254
Seabury, Paul, 245
Serebryannikov, Vladimir, 127-28
Shakhnazarov, Georgii, 224
Shalayev, Stepan A., 27
Sharlet, Robert, 113
Shatrov, Mikhail, 33
Shcharansky, Natan, 108
Shchukin, Alexandr, 8
Shchuykin, Alexandr, 199

Shevardnadze, Eduard, 5, 56, 140-41, 211-12
Shevchenko, Arkady N., 85, 140
Shipler, David K., 114-15
Shmelev, Nikolai, 262-63
Shulman, Marshall, 104-105, 155
Shultz, George, 228-29, 253
Simes, Dmitri, 32, 33
Slusser, Robert, 13, 26, 34, 57
Sobran, Joseph, 142
Socialist Industry, 247
Solidarity, 28
Solodin, Vladimir, 242
Solzhenitsyn, Alexander, 17, 86, 978, 108, 242; on Soviet ideology, 63; on the Vlasov Army, 78; and the White House, 79-81; on the "Kissinger Syndrome," 118; on communism, 187
Sombart, Werner, 10
Sonnenfeldt, Helmut, and Sonnenfeldt Doctrine, 166, 217-18
Sorenson, Theodore, 176
South Africa, 23, 30, 251-52
Soviet Analyst, 249, 250
Soviet Communist Party, 63, 156, 214; its Central Committee, 67; and its "theses," 108-109, 110, 115
Soviet-Japanese Neutrality Pact (1941), 169
Soviet-Jugoslav Treaty of Friendship, Mutual Assistance and Postwar Collaboration, 169
Soviet Union: its constitution (Article 6) 2, (Article 28) 133; and "treatyism," treaty diplomacy, 14-15, 70; and radio jamming, 19-20; its lies, libels, 29, 172-74; its military

budget, 43-46; law and rule of law in, 108-16; and arms control, 139-40; travel restrictions in, 156-58; its foreign policy precepts, 179; on negotiating with, (Senate compendium) 190-91, (Kennan) 191, (Mosely) 192, (Adelman) 192-94, (Iklé) 193-94, (Nixon) 199-200
Stalin, Josef, 16, 70, 117-18, 167; on Lenin, Leninism, 58; defines revolutionary, 63; his failures, 77; and Roosevelt, 82; and Katyn massacre, 83-85; on international agreements, 99; on world revolutionary movement, 100; and Hitler, 117-18; characterizes a diplomat, 179-80; his repression, 182; and the Stockholm "Peace" Campaign, 202-203; on self-determination, 207; and Tito, 215, 265. *About:* (Hopkins) 76, (Roosevelt) 76-77, (Truman) 78, (Eden) 86, (Brzezinski) 127, (Volkognov) 147, (Gorbachev), 181, 182
Staar, Richard, 123
START Treaty, 22, 253
Stimson, Henry L., 83
Stone, I.F., 239
Stone, Jeremy J., 250-51
Strategic Arms Limitations Treaty. *See* SALT
Strategic Defense Initiative. *See* SDI
Suez, 106
Surguladze, Akaki, 166
Symms, Steve, 141-42

Talbott, Strobe, 22

Talensky, Nikolai, 96
Talleyrand-Périgord, Charles
    Maurice de, 151, 213
Tass, 19, 109, 173-74, 224
Terebilov, Vladimir, 109
Thatcher, Margaret, 41, 128, 144,
    233, 234
Thom, Françoise, 4
Tiananmen Square, 3, 9, 266;
    massacre at Beijing, 23, 29;
    and silence from Moscow, 249-
    50
Tito, 215, 265
Tolz, Vera, 89
Treaty Concerning the
    Establishment of the Union of
    Soviet Republics (1922), 164
Treaty of Friendship, Good
    Neighborliness and
    Cooperation between the
    Soviet Union and the DRA
    (1978), 211
Trilateral Commission, 105
Triska, Jan, 68
Tronin, Igor, 102
Trotsky, Leon, 31-32, 148, 198
Truman, Harry, 78
"The Trust," 160
Tsipko, Aleksandr, 240
Turner, Ted, 125-26
Twentieth Century and Peace, 242

Ulam, Adam, 43-44, 77
Ullman, Richard H., 170
United Nations, 8-9, 12, 22-23, 155,
    255; its voting, 9; violates own
    rules (Vassilev), 9-10; and
    Gorbachev's address (1988),
    11-12; and Anna Kethly, 105-
    106; and the Hungarian
    uprising, 106; and the Suez
    assault, 106

Urban, George, 135
U.S. Congress. House, 142-43;
    Senate, 54, 141-42, 190-91;
    Senate Foreign Relations
    Committee, 277-78
U.S. State Department, 15-16, 153;
    Eastern European Division, 35-
    36
U.S.-Canada Trade Pact (1988), 94

Vaksberg, Arkadii, 110
Varkonyi, Peter, 222-23
Vishinsky, Andrei, 144
Vlasvow Army, 78
Volkognov, Dmitri, 147
Von Clausewitz, Karl. See
    Clausewitz, Karl von
Vorontsov, Yuli M., 62
Voslensky, Michael, 113, 183, 222

Walesa, Lech, 260
Wall Street Journal, 21, 132; its
    poll with NBC, 118
Waller, J. Michael, 142
Wallop, Malcolm, 30-31, 51, 186,
    217; on arms control, 138-39;'
    on Helsinki agreement, 152
Washington Naval Treaty (1922),
    229
Washington Post, 12-13
Weber, Max, 102
Wheeler-Bennett, John, 32, 192
Whelan, Joseph, 31, 32
Wick, Charles, 18, 173, 174
Will, George, 18, 80-81
WIN, 161
Wolfe, Bertram, 231
Womack, John, 66
World Court, 230
World Peace Council, 67

Yagodovsky, Leonid S., 224

Yakovlev, Alexander N., 78, 116,
    182, 225; on the U.S., 237-38
Yalta (1945), 75-77, 79
Yashchenko, V., 157
Yazov, Dmitri, 42
Yeltsin, Boris, 71
Yom Kippur War, 200-201

Young, Harry F., 156
Yugoslavia, 169, 215-16

Zagladin, Vadim V., 62, 191
Zemribo, Gvido, 115-16
Zhdanov, Andrei, 130